THE ANTHROPOLOGY OF EXPERIENCE

THE
ANTHROPOLOGY
OF EXPERIENCE

EDITED BY VICTOR W. TURNER
AND EDWARD M. BRUNER

WITH AN EPILOGUE
BY CLIFFORD GEERTZ

UNIVERSITY OF ILLINOIS PRESS

URBANA AND CHICAGO

This book is printed on acid-free paper.

Library of Congress Cataloging in Publication Data

Main entry under title:

The anthropology of experience.

  Includes index.
  1. Ethnology—Philosophy—Addresses, essays, lectures.
  2. Ethnology—Methodology—Addresses, essays, lectures.
  3. Symbolism—Addresses, essays, lectures. 4. Humanities
  —Methodology—Addresses, essays, lectures. 5. Experience
  —Addresses, essays, lectures. I. Turner, Victor Witter.
  II. Bruner, Edward M.
  GN345.A58   1986   306′.01   85-1200
  ISBN 0-252-01236-4 (cloth; alk. paper)
  ISBN 0-252-01249-6 (paper; alk. paper)

To Vic and Barbara

Contents

Introduction

1

Experience
and
Its Expressions

EDWARD M. BRUNER

Victor Turner passed away in December 1983, while this volume was still in process of preparation. The idea for this collection of essays arose at a symposium on the anthropology of experience, organized by Victor, Barbara Myerhoff, and me, for the American Anthropological Association annual meeting in 1980. All of the participants in the symposium contributed papers, and additional contributions were solicited from James Fernandez, Frederick Turner, and Phyllis Gorfain to round out the volume by adding a humanistic perspective and a touch of humanistic elegance. Subsequently, Victor and I used the manuscript as the basis for graduate seminars at the University of Virginia and the University of Illinois, affording us additional opportunities to think through key issues. Clifford Geertz, who had been a discussant at the AAA symposium, agreed to incorporate his comments and reflections on the project in an epilogue.

The formulation of an anthropology of experience belonged to Victor Turner. He wrote independently on the topic in 1982 and most of us view it as a continuation of his lifelong "rebellion against structural-functional orthodoxy, with its closed static model of social systems" (Babcock 1984:462). We also note his recognition in the late 1970s that anthropology was "withering on the structuralist vine," although he acknowledged then that the "neo-Kantian storm [had] almost abated." For Turner, however, the immediate inspiration for an anthropology of experience derived from the German thinker Wilhelm Dilthey (1833–1911) and his concept of an experience, *Erlebnis*, or what has been "lived through." Indeed, the revitalizing message that Dilthey offered

presents us with a new anthropological ancestor, in the tradition
of the human sciences and hermeneutics, as opposed to the more
familiar ancestral line of Emile Durkheim, A. R. Radcliffe-Brown,
and the many later varieties of French and British structuralism.

This introduction includes a brief discussion of Dilthey and
his work, so that the reader may better appreciate the inspiration
that Victor Turner found there, and elaborates on Dilthey's key
concepts of experience and expressions to highlight their anthropological relevance, before turning to the essays themselves.
Let me say at the outset that the reader will find no final answers
or definitive paradigms here, no totally "new" anthropology, but
rather a further articulation of a growing trend to which many of
the authors in this volume have contributed. In deciding on the
title of the volume, Victor and I chose "the anthropology of experience" for good reason—namely, it best captures what it is we have
to say—but we did consider alternative titles that were indicative
of the embeddedness of this work within anthropology. Among the
alternatives were "processual anthropology," which seemed too
vague; "poststructural anthropology," which implied that we were
once structuralists or that structuralism is over, neither of which
is the case; "hermeneutic, or interpretive anthropology," although
the interpretive perspective has already become widely known and
accepted; and "symbolic anthropology," although the papers do
not deal with the analysis of symbols as such, except in the general sense that everything cultural is symbolic. In his epilogue
Geertz uses the phrase "behavioral hermeneutics," which is appealing; however, our focus is more on experience, pragmatics,
practice, and performance. So, we decided to go with the anthropology of experience.

DILTHEY'S HERMENEUTICS

Dilthey (1976:161) wrote that "reality only exists for us in the facts
of consciousness given by inner experience." What comes first is
experience. The anthropology of experience deals with how individuals actually experience their culture, that is, how events are
received by consciousness. By experience we mean not just sense
data, cognition, or, in Dilthey's phrase, "the diluted juice of
reason," but also feelings and expectations. As Fernandez points

out, experience comes to us not just verbally but also in images and impressions. As social scientists we have long given too much weight to verbalizations at the expense of visualizations, to language at the expense of images. Lived experience, then, as thought and desire, as word and image, is the primary reality.

Experience, in our perspective, is not equivalent to the more familiar concept of behavior. The latter implies an outside observer describing someone else's actions, as if one were an audience to an event; it also implies a standardized routine that one simply goes through. An experience is more personal, as it refers to an active self, to a human being who not only engages in but shapes an action. We can have an experience but we cannot have a behavior; we describe the behavior of others but we characterize our own experience. It is not customary to say, "Let me tell you about my behavior"; rather, we tell about experiences, which include not only actions and feelings but also reflections about those actions and feelings. The distinguishing criterion is that the communication of experience tends to be self-referential.

The difficulty with experience, however, is that we can only experience our own life, what is received by our own consciousness. We can never know completely another's experiences, even though we have many clues and make inferences all the time. Others may be willing to share their experiences, but everyone censors or represses, or may not be fully aware of or able to articulate, certain aspects of what has been experienced. How, then, do we overcome the limitations of individual experience? Dilthey's (1976:230) answer was that we "transcend the narrow sphere of experience by interpreting expressions." By "interpreting" Dilthey meant understanding, interpretation, and the methodology of hermeneutics; by "expressions" he meant representations, performances, objectifications, or texts. For example, the expressions analyzed by the contributors to this volume include theater, narratives, hunting stories, revitalization movements, curing rites, murals, parades, carnival, Thoreau's *Walden*, Shakespeare's *Hamlet*, and Helen Cordero's pottery. Certainly a broad array, but nonetheless expressions that are presented to us by the cultures we study; they are what is given in social life. Expressions are encapsulations of the experience of others, or as Turner (1982:17) wrote, they are "the crystallized secretions of once living human experience." For Dilthey (1976:175), we deal with the subject matter of human studies, including anthropology, "when we experience human states, give expressions to them, and understand these expressions." Turner, in this volume, refers to Dilthey's distinction between mere "experience" and "an experience": the former is received by consciousness, it is individual experience, the temporal flow; the latter is the intersubjective articulation of experience, which has a beginning and an ending and thus becomes transformed into an expression.

The relationship between experience and its expressions is always problematic and is one of the important research areas in the anthropology of experience. The relationship is clearly dialogic and dialectical, for experience structures expressions, in that we understand other people and their expressions on the basis of our own experience and self-understanding. But expressions also structure experience, in that dominant narratives of a historical era, important rituals and festivals, and classic works of art define and illuminate inner experience. As we well know, some texts (e.g., *Hamlet*), are more intense, complex, and revealing than everyday experience and thereby enrich and clarify that experience. More simply put, experience is culturally constructed while understanding presupposes experience. To Dilthey, these dialogic relationships of mutual dependence were not an impossible dilemma but rather were basic to the nature of data in the human sciences. That experience structures expressions and expressions structure experience was for Dilthey a hermeneutic circle, something to be worked through: "Our knowledge of what is given in experience is extended through the interpretation of the objectifications of life and their interpretation, in turn, is only made possible by plumbing the depths of subjective experience" (1976:195).

The critical distinction here is between reality (what is really out there, whatever that may be), experience (how that reality presents itself to consciousness), and expressions (how individual experience is framed and articulated). In a life history, as I have indicated elsewhere (Bruner 1984:7), the distinction is between life as lived (reality), life as experienced (experience), and life as told (expression). Only a naive positivist would believe that expressions are equivalent to reality; and we recognize in everyday life the gap between experience and its symbolic manifestation in expression. Some experiences are inchoate, in that we simply do not understand what we are experiencing, either because the experiences are not storyable, or because we lack the performative and narrative resources, or because the vocabulary is lacking. As we ourselves are telling others about an experience, we sometimes realize, even as we speak, that our account does not fully encompass all that we thought and felt during that experience. Every anthropological fieldworker would readily acknowledge that the accepted genres of anthropological expression—our fieldnotes, diaries, lectures, and professional publications—do not capture the richness or the complexity of our lived experience in the field. There are inevitable gaps between reality, experience, and expressions, and the tension among them constitutes a key problematic in the anthropology of experience.

In this perspective an expression is never an isolated, static text. Instead, it always involves a processual activity, a verb form, an action rooted in a social situation with real persons in a particular culture in a given historical era. A ritual must be enacted, a myth recited, a narrative told, a novel read, a drama performed, for these enactments, recitals, tellings, readings, and performances are what make the text transformative and enable us to reexperience our culture's heritage. Expressions are constitutive and shaping, not as abstract texts but in the activity that actualizes the text. It is in this sense that texts must be performed to be experienced, and what is constitutive is in the production. We deal here with performed texts, recognizing that the anthropology of performance is part of the anthropology of experience.

As expressions or performed texts, structured units of experience, such as stories or dramas, are socially constructed units of meaning. If we write or tell about the French Revolution, for example, we must decide where to begin and where to end, which is not easy, so that by our arbitrary construction of beginnings and endings we establish limits, frame the experience, and thereby construct it. In real life every beginning has its antecedents, and an ending does not imply that time has stopped or that the event is over. We create the units of experience and meaning from the continuity of life. Every telling is an arbitrary imposition of meaning on the flow of memory, in that we highlight some causes and discount others; that is, every telling is interpretive. The concept of an experience, then, has an explicit temporal dimension in that we go through or live through an experience, which then becomes self-referential in the telling.

For Dilthey, life was a temporal flow, a "restless progression," and all events occupied a position in a time sequence. Experience and meaning were in the present; the past was a memory, a reproduction; and the future was always open, linked by expectation and potentiality. However, present experience always takes account of the past and anticipates the future. What holds the present and the past together is a unitary meaning, yet that "meaning does not lie in some focal point outside our experience but is contained in them [in experience] and constitutes the connections between them" (Dilthey 1976:239). Dilthey's processual perspective emerged clearly when he wrote that "the moment the future becomes the present it is already sinking into the past" (1976:209). Although life is a flow, we can never experience that flow directly because every observed moment is a remembered moment. Temporal succession cannot be experienced as such because the very observation of time fixes our attention and interrupts the flow of experience, leading to periods of reflexivity when the mind becomes "conscious of itself."

Much of what Dilthey had to say is familiar to us because it resonates strongly with the interpretive-performative perspective in contemporary anthropology and contrasts sharply with alternative theoretical perspectives. For example, as Rosaldo points out, our ethnographies focus on generalized routines, clusters of customs, norms, habits, and prevalent patterns of social relations. Monographic descriptions tend to be synthetic in that they are composites based on abstractions from a series of particular instances. They seek the general so as not to be misled by the unique. But in striving for a balanced, representative account, much of the meaning and the drama in the event itself is lost. "Lived experience is robbed of its vitality," in Rosaldo's terms. A similar critique applies to structuralism, which also seeks a generalized pattern, a model, but on a deeper level, somehow underneath or behind the behavior, conceived of as a surface manifestation. Experience is thus dissolved into a set of transformational rules. Culture and personality, especially in the early years of Edward Sapir and Ruth Benedict, shared much with the anthropology of experience. The focus, however, was on the individual and society. Yet the individual as a total human being, with biological and cultural dimensions, is not conceptually the equivalent of subjective experience, nor is the concept of society the same as cultural expression.

Further, culture and personality turned to issues far removed from the anthropology of experience in the development of cross-cultural personality assessment, methods of child rearing, and national character studies.

The anthropological enterprise has always been concerned with how people experience themselves, their lives, and their culture. Traditionally, anthropologists have tried to understand the world as seen by the "experiencing subject," striving for an inner perspective. Indeed, this is still the rationale for long-term field research, and the field tradition, in fact, is what sets anthropology apart from such related disciplines as sociology and history. The difficulty, however, is not in the fieldwork experience but in our conceptual apparatus for interpreting the field data, which tend to filter out experience. Most good ethnographers, interestingly enough, reintroduce vitality in their descriptive accounts by including illustrative snatches of personal narrative, bits of biography, or vivid passages from their fieldnotes (Peacock 1984). In effect, the experiential component returns to the account as a by-product rather than as an explicit object of research. We systematically remove the personal and the experiential in accordance with our anthropological paradigms; then we reintroduce them so as to make our ethnographies more real, more alive.

The anthropology of experience turns our attention to experience and its expressions as indigenous meaning. The advantage of beginning the study of culture through expressions is that the basic units of analysis are established by the people we study rather than by the anthropologist as alien observer. By focusing on narratives or dramas or carnival or any other expressions, we leave the definition of the unit of investigation up to the people, rather than imposing categories derived from our own ever-shifting theoretical frames. Expressions are the peoples' articulations, formulations, and representations of their own experience. Although expressions are not necessarily easy places to start, because of their existential complexity, they usually are accessible and isolable, in part because they have a beginning and an ending. As Milton Singer, Dell Hymes, Richard Bauman, Victor Turner, and others who have written about performance have taught us, expressions are not only naturally occurring units of meaning but are also periods of heightened activity when a society's presuppositions are most exposed, when core values are expressed, and when the symbolism is most apparent. Even if the events in an expression are not contiguous in time and space, they do have a coherence based on a common meaning. The interpretive process, however, always opeates on two distinct levels: the people we study interpret their own experiences in expressive forms, and we, in turn, through our fieldwork, interpret these expressions for a home audience of other anthropologists. Our anthropological productions are our stories about their stories; we are interpreting the people as they are interpreting themselves. Some of the papers in this volume (e.g., Rosaldo and Kapferer) focus more on the first level, on how people move between experience and expressions—for example, between the experience of hunting and stories about the hunt, or between the experience of illness and curing rituals—whereas other papers (e.g., F. Turner and Gorfain) tell us more about the experience of anthropologically coming to know. My own paper on narratives about American Indians claims that the two levels merge and that the Indian stories about themselves and the anthropological stories about Indians are essentially similar.

I noted earlier that the relationships between experience and expressions are always problematic. Now I turn to a different point, that neither experiences nor expressions are monolithic entities, for each breaks down into smaller processual units, and the interplay between these units frequently constructs its own dynamic. Schechner, for example, writes that in going from script to performance in the theater there are at least two intermediary stages: the workshop, a time of breaking down, play, and experimentation; and the rehearsal, a time of building up and polishing preparatory to the actual performance. I refer to a workshop-like stage in anthropological field research when we transform direct observations and interactions in the field situation into our fieldnotes. In our notebooks we can play with ideas and express our fears and feelings, without concern for the performative conventions of the discipline. Then, in the rehearsal-like stage we transform our fieldnotes and impressions into first drafts, preliminary lectures, and papers presented at meetings. At this stage we may receive feedback from our colleagues that enables us to change and polish before the final product is submitted for publication, thereafter to be forever fixed in print—except insofar as each reader interprets our message differently.

There are additional ways of opening the gap between experience and expressions, and of expanding each term. Fernandez reminds us that experience consists of words and images, that the two are not necessarily concordant, and that rituals are not based on one metaphor but rather on mixed metaphors; hence the play of tropes. Myerhoff's paper on elderly Jews in California analyzes a parade and a mural, which are not equivalent. Kapferer breaks down Sinhalese curing rituals into words, music, and action, showing us how each of these activities plays off against the others within the context of the whole performance. Gorfain writes about the play within the play in *Hamlet*, and about the various mechanisms of reflexivity when the play comments on itself. Lévi-Strauss has dealt with different sensory codes, and Bateson has shown that we can enrich our information by combining different sources, with the difference between the sources becoming new information. From Derrida we have learned that writing is not a copy of speech and that representations never simply re-present. In this volume Boon demonstrates that expressions in different domains of culture are decentered and radically plural. Some varieties of structuralism would reduce house plans, village organization, ritual, and mythology to the same structural model, but Boon makes the point that the different domains do not stack up and that various expressive modes do not replicate each other or tell the same story. We know that participants in a performance do not necessarily share a common experience or meaning; what they share is only their common participation.

All of these points then, highlight different dimensions of the problematic between experience and expression. And although this volume deals with large-scale expressions, the same problematic would apply to the little performances of everyday life as well as to those that are not "art" but are more political or work-oriented, such as demonstrations or meetings.

It is in the performance of an expression that we re-experience, re-live, re-create, re-tell, re-construct, and re-fashion our culture. The performance does not release a preexisting meaning that lies dormant in the text (Derrida 1974; Barthes 1974). Rather, the performance itself is constitutive. Meaning is always in the present, in the here-and-now, not in such past manifestations as historical origins or the author's intentions. Nor are there silent texts, because once we attend to the text, giving voice or expression to it, it becomes a performed text, active and alive. It is what Victor Turner called "putting experience into circulation."

The anthropology of experience rejects all such binaries as static-dynamics, system-process, continuity-change, ethnography-history, and synchrony-diachrony, because these oppositions postulate a fixed and timeless world of essences, an imaginary world; and having done so, they can only account for change by having it originate from outside that timeless entity, as if change were always exterior to the system. So the source of change becomes the introduction of the steel ax, the proverbial raiders from the north, or the penetration of a money economy. The main problem is that there is no conceptualization of the system from the inside, so that all creativity is relegated to a separate outside domain, beyond the boundaries of ordinary life. By contrast, the anthropology of experience sees people as active agents in the historical process who construct their own world. Using Myerhoff's phrase, we are "the authors of ourselves." Selves, social organizations, and cultures are not given but are problematic and always in production. Cultural change, cultural continuity, and cultural transmission all occur simultaneously in the experiences and expressions of social life. All are interpretive processes and indeed are the experiences "in which the subject discovers himself" (Dilthey 1976:203).

What was considered "traditional" for Dilthey is a process of scanning the past until we identify a perceived similarity with the present. It is a triumph of reexperiencing when we believe ourselves to be confronted by a continuity. Cultural transmission is not simply a replication of an old original, a mechanical transfer of the cultural heritage from generation to generation, as if we were passing along the class banner to each new cohort. The "little people" of Cordero's pottery reflect not only her grandfather's pottery but also her own life experiences. Culture is alive, context sensitive, and emergent.

There are no raw encounters or naive experiences since persons, including ethnographers, always enter society in the middle. At any given time there are prior texts and expressive conventions, and they are always in flux. We can only begin with the last picture show, the last performance. Once the performance is completed, however, the most recent expression sinks into the past and becomes prior to the performance that follows. This is straight Dilthey. Life consists of retellings.

THE ANTHROPOLOGICAL EXPRESSIONS

To orient the reader, I turn now to an overview of the papers themselves, each an anthropological expression in its own right. We will see how they develop and elaborate themes in Dilthey's hermeneutics and how they go off in their own directions. Just as the various domains of culture do not stack up, neither do the contributors to this volume. As independent scholars, they refuse to be concordant or to say the same things. They have their own perspectives, and they even use the term "experience" differently. Clearly, what is presented here is a living argument. However, it is an editor's responsibility to isolate common themes and to suggest how the papers collectively say more than any one paper individually. There is a convergence of theory that is not fully contained in any one contribution but is implied by all.

Victor Turner noted in a 1981 personal communication that anthropologists usually studied cultures in their duller, more habitual aspects. "Experience," he wrote "always seeks it 'best', i.e. most aesthetic expression in performance—the vital communication of its present essence, though always in a dialectical dance with what it conceives to be its semiogenetic, meaning-begetting past. Cultures, I hold, are better compared through their rituals, theaters, tales, ballads, epics, operas than through their *habits*. For the former are the ways in which they try to articulate their *meanings*—and each culture has a special pan-human contribution for all of our thinking, remembering species." Turner's paper in this volume supports that perspective by referring to John Dewey and Wilhelm Dilthey, who both saw life as pulsating and rhythmical, as a combination of breaks and re-unions. Dewey wrote that "moments of fulfillment punctuate experience" and that the passage "from disturbance into harmony is that of intensest life." Dilthey viewed experience as an eruption from routine and saw in it an urging toward expression. Turner stresses the disruptions that are cut out from the everyday and sees experience as an isolable sequence marked by beginnings, middles, and endings, as ways in which people tell what is most meaningful about their lives. "The flow of experience is constantly arrested by reflexivity," he wrote.

Turner's paper, as did his lifework, stresses process, sequences through time, the drama and aesthetics of social life, and those moments when life is lived most intensely. The people in his writings see themselves and their cultures as part of the historical process, in a time sequence, with meaning emergent from perform-ance, but emergent with reference to the semiogenetic, meaning-begetting past. That past, for Turner, was always problematic, never monolithic, and frequently contradictory.

Abrahams's paper is about the connections between the routine and the extraordinary, between the everyday and the more intense, framed and stylized expressions in cultural performance. His phrasing of the overall question is not the same as my formu-lation of the problematic between subjective experience and its expressions, but he does explore the concept of experience and stresses throughout the Americanness of the term. He tells us that Americans, are preoccupied with experience, that we hunger for it and have an obsession with novelty. Not by accident does Ab-rahams return to those uniquely American philosophers, the prag-matists William James and John Dewey. He quotes James, "Life is in the transitions," and individuals live "prospectively as well as retrospectively"; and Dewey, "Life is no uniform uninterrupted march or flow. It is a thing of histories. . . . "These pragmatists focused on the processual; they did not take tradition or custom as a given, and they saw meaning as emergent rather than prior to events. If only our anthropological forebears had sought their theoretical inspiration in Dilthey, James, and Dewey!

Abrahams raises profound questions: Is this volume on the anthropology of experience a reflection of the American preoccu-pation with experiencing? How do our American (or Western) no-tions of experience affect our theories about experience? Is the American proclivity for experience more in our discourse about experience than in our real-life seeking after experience? In other words, is it talk or action?

Another theme in Abrahams's paper is the double conscious-ness of experience: we participate in the action but also report about it; we are part of the experience but also detached witnesses to that experience. This double consciousness is an essential condi-tion of the ethnographer who participates as he or she observes. In ethnography, there are always at least two double experiences to be dealt with: on the one hand, our experiences of ourselves in the field, as well as our understanding of our objects; and on the other hand, our objects' experiences of themselves and their ex-perience of us.

This double consciousness is universal, for with every experience in the present we have one eye on the past and the other on the future. As we are experiencing, we model our actions after prior texts and previous accounts of similar experiences, and we also change our actions with reference to the future. Rosaldo provides an ethnographic confirmation. The Ilongot begin a hunt based on their direct experience of prior hunts as well as on their understanding of the Ilongot repertoire of hunting stories. During the actual hunt, however, the Ilongot may modify their action, may actually change their behavior in the forest, and hence the nature of their hunting experience, so as to return to home camp with a good story to tell. Viewed differently, products of the Ilongot hunt are both game and stories, and the Ilongot double consciousness is apparent when we realize that they are simultaneously hunters and storytellers. Stories, as culturally constructed expressions, are among the most universal means of organizing and articulating experience. As Gorfain writes, during *Hamlet*, itself the retelling of an old story, the last act of the dying prince is to beseech his friend Horatio "to tell my story"; the revenger, Hamlet, begs his orator, Horatio, to become his surrogate, a storyteller. The Ilongot and Horatio certainly do belong in the same volume!

Frederick Turner's paper should be seen in its historical perspective as a contribution to intellectual history as well as to the anthropology of experience. He notes that Henry David Thoreau was a contemporary of both Lewis Henry Morgan and Charles Sanders Peirce, and that the writing of *Walden* coincided with the writing of *League of the Iroquois* and with Peirce's semiotics—all were products of nineteenth-century America, an era with a special capacity for reflexivity. Thoreau went to Walden Pond to seek the foundations of his own experience; Turner went to Thoreau to seek the foundations of the anthropological experience. The point here is that the analysis of personal experience lies at the core of not only *Walden* but anthropology. Put another way, Thoreau practiced a kind of minimalist anthropology, for he was both subject and object, but in a sense this is true of all of us, because in the field we are in a dialogue with ourselves as much as we are in a dialogue with others. Field experience is indeed a "personal voyage of self-discovery."

Thoreau wrote that he had become "sensible of a certain doubleness by which I can stand as remote from myself as from another. However intense my experience, I am conscious of the presence and criticism of a part of me which, as it were, is not a part of me, but spectator, sharing no experience, but taking note of it. . . ." Anthropologists go to foreign lands so as to become better observers of the other; Thoreau went to a familiar land to become a better observer of himself. The distance traveled is secondary to the processes involved, which in the cases of Thoreau and anthropology are essentially similar.

What emerges so strongly from Thoreau's writing is the sense that self and society, like nature, is "continually undergoing a process of evolutionary development," is always in process. Experience itself is not just passive acceptance but rather an active, volatile, creative force. For Turner, experience structures expressions and expressions structure experience, but it is less a static circle than a historical evolutionary spiral, a progressive construction and reconstruction. Thoreau, like Dilthey and the American pragmatists, is yet another ancestor of the anthropology of experience.

The first three papers, then, constitute an introductory section of the volume in that they explore the concept of experience and define, each in a different way, an anthropology of experience. They are the general, more theoretical contributions. The remaining papers are equally theoretical but are narrower in scope, more data-based, and deal with expressions more than with subjective experience. These papers are organized into four somewhat arbitrary sections: "Narrative," with papers by Rosaldo and Bruner; "Images," with papers by Fernandez and Kapferer; "Reflexivity," with papers by Gorfain, Boon, and Myerhoff; and "Enactments," with papers by Stewart, Babcock, and Schechner.

Both Rosaldo and I employ a narrative framework, although Rosaldo writes about Ilongot stories and I about anthropological ones. Rosaldo chooses the narrative perspective to "privilege actors' interpretations of their own conduct," thereby providing a route to indigenous meaning. The difficulty with ethnoscience and monographic realism, he says, is that we never learn from these approaches what people consider to be significant and vital in their lives.

Ilongot hunting stories are especially revealing because they highlight the discrepancy between experience and its expression.

There are stories about a python ambushing a man and about long-tailed people-eating monsters using dogs to hunt down human beings. The stories celebrate mishaps and accidents rather than virtuoso success, Rosaldo tells us. They portray human vulnerability, taut alertness, and quick improvisation. Some of these qualities, such as the ability to respond to an immediate challenge, are important in everyday hunts. Others enable the storytelling to become self-referential, for the man who was attacked by a python can tell his own story, what happened to him, rather than relate a general Ilongot story. Yet the stories are clearly reflexive, for they invert the normal order by placing humans in the position of being hunted by pythons and dogs. The everyday is transformed into the extraordinary through narration. Rather than emphasizing the routine, these stories stress breaks from daily life. Hunting becomes more dangerous, intense, and dramatic, as the stories deal with the inverted world of the peak experience rather than the world of survival. By commemorating the unexpected and depicting the hunter as the hunted, hunting becomes HUNTING. The Ilongot stand back and examine the hunt as they examine themselves.

These stories, as forms of expression, do not mirror the experience of the hunt. But if one measure of the success of a hunt is the story that is subsequently told about it, then what happens on a hunt is partly determined by cultural notions of what makes a good story as well as by the ecosystem of the forest. The key, again, is the problematic between reality, experience, and expression. As Rosaldo says, a hunting story is true not only in reference to the reality of the hunt but also in reference to its fidelity to the cultural conventions of narration and to already established stories. There is a continuity from one story to the next; after the Ilongot have told a story and say "It's yours to keep now"—just as Hamlet says "Tell my story"—they are giving others the opportunity for a retelling, for retellings are what culture is about. The next telling reactivates prior experience, which is then rediscovered and relived as the story is re-related in a new situation. Stories may have endings, but stories are never over.

Although stories may be universal, they are not necessarily linear, because narrative structures are culturally specific. Ilongot stories may consist of a series of place names or incidents, like beads on a string, to use Rosaldo's phrase; they do not necessarily state a problem, develop a plot, or provide a resolution. My stories, by contrast, are linear; they are anthropological narratives and hence an essentially Western genre.

We do not usually think of ethnographic stories about American Indian culture change and Ilongot narratives within the same framework because we usually make a sharp separation between the anthropologist and the native, between subject and object. But ethnography is not the privileged authoritative voice about native peoples; it is, rather, one mode of representation. If life is a temporal flow, and if Victor Turner was correct in that what connects past, present, and future is a common meaning, then Rosaldo and I can claim that stories are units of meaning that provide the connection. As we can only enter the world in the middle, in the present, then stories serve as meaning-generating interpretive devices which frame the present within a hypothetical past and an anticipated future.

My essay refers to the 1930s story that anthropologists told about American Indians in which the present was disorganization, the past was glorious, and the future assimilation. I compare it with the 1970s story in which the present was resistance, the past was exploitation, and the future was ethnic resurgence. My point is that these are the dominant narratives of particular historical eras, in the sense that during these periods they were most frequently told, served as guiding paradigms or metaphors, were the accepted wisdom of the time, and tended to be taken for granted. They are what Abrahams would call large-scale stories. Between the 1930 and the 1970 tellings there was a sharp epistemological break, not a smooth transition from one story to another. Of course, there were multiple conflicting, competing stories all along, in both eras, but they were generally discounted and were not given equal weight in the discourse of the period. The importance of dominant narratives is that they become the major interpretive devices to organize and communicate experience, but they remain largely unexamined. Only in a later time period, in a different social place, or in a new phase of history can we adopt the perspective that enables us to see these narratives for what they are—social constructions. As such, dominant narratives are forms of expression which do not necessarily reflect or mirror actual experience, either anthropological field experience or Indian life experience.

I argue that both American anthropologists and American Indians share the same narratives as they are both part of the same larger society during the same time frame. If this is so, then the subject-object distinction is dissolved and it becomes difficult to differentiate between the outside view and the inside view. Anthropologists and Indians are co-conspirators who construct their ethnography together, in part because they share the same plot structures. In Foucault's sense they are part of the same episteme. The retellings of dominant narratives, however, are not just mindless repetitions but change as the context changes. Each anthropological retelling points out the uniqueness of the given situation and compares the case under study with previously reported instances, that is, with prior texts.

Because ethnography is embedded in the political process, dominant narratives are units of power as well as of meaning. The ability to tell one's story has a political component; indeed, one measure of the dominance of a narrative is the space allocated to it in the discourse. Alternative, competing stories are generally not allocated space in establishment channels and must seek expression in underground media and dissident groupings (Bruner and Gorfain 1984). Power, as we know, is not simply a question of manipulation of the media. It has a much broader base, for it depends on what most people are predisposed to accept and what they consider legitimate and appropriate. Myerhoff's characterization of the predicament of aging Jews in Venice, California, may be seen in this framework. The general condition of old people in this country has been one of invisibility. In the case Myerhoff cites, no one would listen to the elderly Jews of Venice, who were denied the means of communicating their story. So they devised their own ways of calling attention to themselves through a mural and a parade, the latter being clearly political. Similarly, Stewart's description of carnival in Trinidad over various historical periods highlights the political aspects of the festival. Clearly, no expressions are ideologically or politically neutral.

Fernandez's paper deals with the mechanisms that lead to the conviction of wholeness, that is, to the experience of "overarching conviviality," coherence, and relatedness. The experience of the whole emerges in social movements, particularly in revitalization movements, which are designed precisely to overcome feelings of fragmentation, alienation, and disorganization. The aim of a revitalization movement is to re-vitalize, to return to the whole, as Fernandez notes. His paper takes the revitalization of social groups and the experience of wholeness as problematic and asks, How is the experience generated?

Fernandez begins by stating that the elementary and primordial organizing structures do not consist of such verbalizations as the basic premises, postulates, or axioms of a culture, because these articulations provide "an ideational explicitness and clarity" that they do not in fact possess. Ideas do not have the primacy we attribute to them. Rather than looking to categories and labels to capture experience, Fernandez turns to organizing images as pictorializations of domains of experience. His African examples are the "Christian soldiers" or "the tribes of Israel" which serve as tropes, as metaphors or metonyms, and are made the basis of ritual. The key here is an enacted image or the performance of a visualization. Fernandez does not find in each ritual performance a single metaphor, for his data show that religious movements always mix metaphors, so that there is a play of tropes, a dynamic interaction among tropes that gives people the impression of coherence and wholeness.

Among the issues dealt with by Fernandez that are central to the anthropology of experience are: how persons experience their culture, the factors which give rise to the experience of the whole, the acknowledgment that we must go beyond language to images, the emphasis on performance and the enactment of images, the rejection of the notion of one underlying metaphor, and the recognition of the openness and interplay between tropes. Ultimately, the argument is that tropes fashion experience. But we could also ask if experience fashions tropes. Fernandez's view is that the "nether regions of the mind . . . are a repository of images of former sociohistorical experiences," and that these prior images are brought forward and predicated on the subjects of a religious movement, subsequently becoming the basis of a performance. But that performance then refashions the image, which in turn becomes the basis of future enactments. The argument of images fits so well with the arguments of Dilthey and Victor Turner, particularly in the discussion of mechanisms: that the acting out of images restores vitality to a domain of experience; that the performance in one domain resonates with another to produce a sense of coherence between domains; and that the use of metaphors creates more-inclusive classifications which yield a sense of the integrity of things.

Kapferer, like Fernandez, starts with the problematic of phenomenology: how individuals transcend their aloneness in the world and come to share lived experience. "I do not experience your experience," he tells us, "... I experience my experience of you." We act as if we do share experiential worlds; the question is what are the mechanisms we use to accomplish the sharing. Kapferer's answer is the same as Dilthey's and Turner's: we transcend individual experience through participation in cultural expressions. But we no longer assume that there is a spontaneous sharing which emerges automatically whenever people find themselves in aggregations and participate together in performance. Kapferer's contribution is to take ritual, in this case Sinhalese exorcism, and to analyze it in ways that give us insight into the processes of sharing and the establishment of meaning.

Kapferer notes that what is usually glossed as ritual is actually a complex compositional form, like an opera, consisting of music, dance, drama, song, story, and liturgy, all of which are, in effect, different modes or languages of ritual expression and communication. Each mode has its own structural properties, and one is not reducible to the other; nor does one mode replicate any other. There is a dynamic interplay between the modes—each objectifies experience in its own way, each has different reflexive properties, and in a complex ritual, each mode may become more prominent at a particular time in the progression of the performance.

In exorcism, at dusk, at the beginning of the ritual, there is a spatial and experiential separation of patient and audience. The patient is alone and terrified in one space, and the audience is engaged in everyday activities—drinking, playing cards, gossiping—in another space. Around midnight, through the modes of intense music and dance, the audience is recontextualized and moved from the outside, everyday world to identification with the patient and to sharing the patient's experience. Through music and dance the audience approaches the experiential world of the patient. At dawn, the ritual ends in comic drama, which through juxtaposition, inconsistency, and contradiction plays with order. Drama is "quintessentially reflexive," since persons are enjoined to adopt perspectives different than their own subjective standpoints and to reflect on these new perspectives. Music and dance appeal more directly to the senses than does drama, although they, too, are reflexive in their own way. The object of the entire ceremony, as a ritual through time, is to get rid of the demons, which it does.

Kapferer sees performance as critical in the analysis of meaning and experience, although he goes beyond performance as the mere enactment of a text. For him, the text consists of the structural principles ordering the rite and the rules governing the syntagmatic progression of ritual events, but it does not exist independently of the audience to the enactment of that text. We cannot, in Kapferer's view, deal with the enactment to the neglect of the structural properties in the text. Thus, "'performance' constitutes a unity of text and enactment, neither being reducible to the other." Performance, then, is the "structuring of structure," in the sense that the performance does the structuring of the structure in the text. To generalize thus far from Kapferer and the other papers, we are not dealing with culture as text but rather with culture as the performance of text—and, I would add, with their re-performance and retellings.

Like *Walden*, the story of *Hamlet* is a mirror of our own enterprise from which we, as anthropologists, can learn about the interpretation of texts. *Hamlet* is indeed a "master text" and, as Gorfain tells us, is about "the unclosable distance between behavior and its meanings, between the immediacy of experience and the shaping of experience into transmittable forms. . . . " Anthropologists analyze society and probe human behavior to find pattern, truth, and meaning, but they discover only "other images of text making." The anthropology of experience analyzes such representations as stories, revitalization movements, curing rites, parades, and carnivals; Gorfain analyzes such representations as reports, narratives, pretenses, games, dramas, rituals, and punning in *Hamlet*. The aim for both anthropologists and Hamlet is to "secure the truth and authority of experience," but instead each search "yields only another shadowy text, a resemblance." Anthropologists, like Hamlet, find that their own "knowledge" of society is a kind of text, a story about stories, and that such knowledge is never final but always in process.

Reflexivity is critical in this enterprise, for we take expressions as objects of study and we become "conscious of our self-consciousness" of these objects. We become aware of our awareness; we reflect on our reflections. Anthropologists of experience take others' experiences, as well as their own, as an object. Our inquiry is inherently reflexive, just as *Hamlet* is a reflexive text.

Clifford Geetz, Victor Turner, and other theorists have repeatedly informed us that cultural expressions and performances are not mere reflections of society but are metacommentaries on society. Under Gorfain's sure hand we see that the multiple expressions within *Hamlet* are not simply reflections but subtle commentaries about Hamlet's predicament, about the situation depicted in the play, about other characters, about the play itself, and about the world beyond, all of which folds back on itself. Gorfain analyzes Hamlet's indeterminate madness, the appearance of the ghost, the arrival of a group of professional players, the killing of Polonius, and the final fencing match. In Shakespeare's work, as in our ethnographic work, we see how "humans re-present reality to themselves in one imaginative substitution of experience after another." Gorfain's paper, then, is about the relevance of fictions, play, and reflexivity, but so, in a sense, is ethnography. In social life, in ethnographies, and in plays, we "create a genealogy of audiences by making meaning through re-visions," through retellings. It is not mere repetition, however, for in the end all of us must accept responsibility for "committed interpretations." Just as Fernandez tells us how revitalization movements work, and Kapferer tells us how curing rituals work, Gorfain tells us how a play works by revealing the mechanisms of artifice.

Boon makes a number of points essential to the argument of an anthropology of experience. One is that culture is symbolic in all domains, not just in such selected domains as art and ritual, where we find the most conspicuous symbolic expressions, at least in Bali. Some varieties of functionalism, structuralism, and Marxism make a distinction between domains, like religion, that are more expressive and symbolic, and other domains, like nature or labor or economics, that are considered more utilitarian. The result is that culture is reduced to a materialist basis. In Boon's view, as in Roland Barthes's and Marshall Sahlins's, the symbolics never run out. We must take culture as a text, rather than focusing on the texts produced by culture. Politics and the everyday are as symbolic as Balinese shadow theater.

For Boon, culture is radically plural. It is not that we have a limited number of alternative perspectives, a kind of comfortable liberal pluralism that acknowledges diversity and difference. Rather, we have in culture an uncontrollable plurality, such that the production of meaning can never be contained and we can never know in advance the constructions that will be placed on a text. Texts are radically open and plural, and there are no limits on meaning.

In Boon's view, the various domains, or the "Machineries," of culture do not stack up; that is, they do not simply reinforce or replicate one another. The Balinese, for example, have a number of systems or Machineries for status ranking, such as ritual purity, political power, prestige, titles, noble houses, Indian caste categories, wealth, court hierarchies, and temple rights. But Boon's point is that these Machineries are not congruent, nor do they say the same thing. Rather than being mere replications of one another, they "seem made for contradiction." The Machineries of status are "variable constructions to satisfy different parties, each interpreting to its own advantage. What the rivals share is a set of hierarchical principles that form the ground rules for an ongoing cultural argument." It has sometimes been assumed in previous literature that the status mechanisms add up to a fixed stratificational scheme. Boon argues, however, that the status Machineries are decentered, that one is not reducible to the other, that no Machinery is redundant, and that one scheme does not simply re-present another. One Machinery can be translated into the terms of another, but each one is unique. It is, of course, the play between the status Machineries that provides the openness and dynamics of culture. The status Machinery does not, however, simply index something external to it, such as power or exploitation. There is no singular quality, no unified synthesis, no deep structure, no underlying binaries, no master symbol, no essence of culture, and nothing that is "quintessentially Balinese." If there is one key to Balinese status Machinery, it is the perpetuation of an ongoing cultural argument; and if there is one key to Boon's position, it is that "a text is in a state of continual production; it is not a fixed re-production of something outside itself that it merely refers to."

Myerhoff shows the creativeness and productivity of culture in her paper on how a community constructs a series of imaginative performances, not only to characterize their own view of their experience, but to consciously project a desired truth to the larger society. The members of the community, elderly Jews in California, refused to accept the "establishment" telling of their experience and decided, in the retelling, to characterize it in such a way that it would be accepted, or at least acknowledged, by outsiders. Her paper breathes with the aliveness of culture and shows how persons make sense of themselves and construct their culture in the process. To paraphrase both Stephen Lansing and Myerhoff, people not only construct their worlds but watch themselves doing the construction and then enter and believe in their constructed worlds.

The community described by Myerhoff is exceptionally self-conscious for a variety of reasons. The people are double migrants, as most were born in Eastern Europe, lived in northeast America, and then moved to California in retirement. They are old, many in their eighties and nineties, and they share the knowledge that the Holocaust eliminated their natal homes and culture. Their children have moved away and assimilated, so there are no natural witnesses to their past lives. They are neglected by the mainstream to the point that, until recently, there was no one to whom they could transmit their culture or explain who they are— which is not merely East Europeans, modern Americans, or religious Jews, but all of these.

When they assigned themselves the task of painting a mural of their culture, they depicted scenes from the Old World, the Mayflower, the Statue of Liberty, the sweatshops of New York City, and their community center in California with Hebrew, Yiddish, and English signs. The mural is a bricolage, an amalgam that incorporates all layers of history—past, present, and future; the real and the imagined; their dreams and desires. They "constructed" their culture, more obviously than most, but the processes involved were universal. All cultures are constructions that take historical elements from different eras and sources; all combine images and words and are based on lived and imagined experience. All constructed cultures require belief; that is, the participants must have confidence in their own authenticity, which is one reason cultures are performed. It is not enough to assert claims; they have to be enacted. Stories become transformative only in their performance.

Stewart provides a striking synthesis of history and sociological insight in showing how participants located in different social segments and in different historical periods have experienced the Trinidad carnival. Brought to the island in the 1780s by French settlers, carnival was initially "an urban festival of the salon," from which Africans and Creoles were excluded. After the emancipation of the slaves in 1838, African and Creole elements were incorporated into the festival and it took on a more licentious and rebellious quality, featuring competitive performances, mock combat, and caricatures of colonial officials. In the 1840s "the police were empowered to prohibit revelers from wearing face masks, blowing horns, playing noisy instruments, carrying torches, stick-fighting, drumming, and singing obscene songs." By the latter half of the nineteenth century, carnival had become a time of rioting and fighting in the streets. In the early twentieth century, however, it segmented into two separate festivals; one a locally based, rowdy, potentially violent carnival of the masses, and the second an extension of European culture, characterized by the "glitter and stiff-back decorum" of the British governor's ball. Stewart describes the agony of the Creole middle class of this period, who had little taste for the "fighting, bloodletting, and public eroticism" of the mass carnival, which they considered vulgar, but who longed for invitations to the elite festival, which they rarely received.

After the independence of Trinidad, carnival came under the control of a central government committee whose aim was to promote indigenous culture for nationalistic purposes and to attract international tourism. It had moved from a spontaneous, ribald expression of desire to a staged and regulated enactment that received national television coverage. From a participatory street event it became a spectator event; the steel band and calypso were relegated to the status of folk art. Although heavily patronized by locals, carnival was designed mainly for tourists. The performance was controlled by the central government and had, for some, lost its capacity for fantasy and passion. Local critics complained of bureaucracy and commercial exploitation. In effect, the politicians had "framed" carnival to enhance national income and image, but in the process they also "framed" the locals, robbing them of their major festival.

Obviously, how one experiences carnival depends very much on one's ideology and position in the system. Stewart observes that the most enthusiastic audiences now are the visitors, both

Trinidadian returnees and tourists, who have no commitment to the politics of the event. In carnival, all layers of history are represented, as well as all sociopolitical contradictions in contemporary Trinidad. If everyday tensions are too fully expressed in the carnival, it is reduced to disorder; but if harmonious integration or performance for outsiders is overemphasized, then carnival loses its ritual vitality. The reaction has already set in, however. Carnival has changed radically in the past; the present carnival is reconstituted in every production; and there is hope for the future of carnival.

At the age of forty-five, Helen Cordero, a Cochiti potter, reactivated a previously moribund Pueblo tradition and shaped her first Storyteller, a ceramic form depicting her grandfather, as a storyteller, surrounded by many children. Babcock's paper about Cordero stresses themes recurrent throughout this volume. One theme is that tradition is a construction and we cannot assume continuity either for Cochiti pottery or the Pueblo Tricentennial described in my paper. Even though figurative pottery is one of the oldest forms of Native American representation, dating back to A.D. 300, Cordero reinvented the form in 1964. Another theme is that Storytellers, like Ilongot hunters, Horatio, and American ethnographers, shape and reshape their own lives and their culture as they tell and retell stories. Cordero's grandfather, Santiago Quintana, was a storyteller in another domain; as Babcock writes, he was "the valued informant for several generations of anthropologists," including Adolph Bandelier, Edward Curtis, and Ruth Benedict. A third theme of the paper is that material objects, too, are representations of cultural and personal experience and that "all textualization is not verbal." Pottery is symbolic action. Both Fernandez and Babcock stress the nonverbal, but they employ different emphasis. Fernandez's point is that we experience in the form of images; Babcock argues that we give nonverbal expression to experience in the form of material objects. Clearly, objects do speak, or in Geertz's words, "materialize a way of experiencing."

The last three papers in the volume direct our attention to how culture is represented for outsiders. We have a good understanding of how people represent themselves to themselves, in Balinese cockfights and other expressions for a home audience, but Cochiti pottery and the Trinidad carnival are shaped for tourists, and members of the Jewish center in Venice, California, designed their parade to influence the outside community. Despite the fact that Cordero's ceramics are rooted in Pueblo tradition and reflect her deepest personal experiences, her art is influenced by what sells in the Anglo market. Certainly Cochiti pottery, the Trinidad carnival, and a parade in California are authentic cultural expressions—after all, the issue is not one of authenticity— but we must nevertheless pay more attention to the fact that tourists and the mass media are the ultimate consumers of many cultural expressions. Previously, anthropologists have had a tendency to deprecate "tourist" objects and performances, but I suggest that an anthropology of experience may well have to take these forms more seriously. Babcock writes, correctly I think, that destination does not determine meaning, but we must ask what the differences are between cultural expressions and performances designed for outsiders, as opposed to those designed for the people themselves.

Schechner's paper is an exploration of "aspects of the magnitudes of performance from the standpoint of individual experience," or in my terms, it returns to some of our original questions about the relationship between reality, experience, and expression. He asks, What is ordinary everyday behavior in relation to acting as performed by professional actors? Two acting strategies are used by theater people. The first is Stanislavski's classic exercise of "emotional recall," which is similar to the "method" acting of Lee Strasberg at the Actors' Studio. The actor relives a past emotional experience by recalling a previous incident in all its detail, with the objective of aligning feelings to produce a more authentic and convincing performance. The second strategy is more mechanical. The actor learns which muscles to contract while practicing in front of a mirror. The aim is to obtain physical control of such indicators of emotion as facial displays, vocal cues, and body postures. Schechner notes that mechanical acting is the strategy employed by the Balinese and by Hindu Indians in their classical dance-dramas. It is a rigorous system of training the muscles of the face and the body.

Based on Paul Eckman's studies of the autonomic nervous system, as measured by heart rate and skin temperature, Schechner concludes that professional actors feel exactly the same when following either strategy. In other words, mechanical acting yields the same results in the physiological register and in the actor's subjective experience as the emotional recall approach. This raises for us the issue of the emotional concomitants of performance. Victor Turner notes in his paper that we go back to previous expressions as a guide to the present, but do we recall just cognitions or associated affect from the past? And how much of the affect is from the past or generated anew? Do people follow the Stanislavski-Strasberg method in everyday life? Schechner suggests that if we behave appropriately, then we will feel appropriately, that actions generate emotions (and the reverse as well), irrespective of whether those actions are "really happening" or "skillfully pretended." Further, emotions are brought out in both performers and audience because there is a "universal language" of emotions, neurologically based, encoded in our nerve and brain processes. What Schechner really suggests is that there is not that much difference between ordinary behavior and professional acting, and here he returns to basic Goffman. In dealing with the biological basis of ritual behavior, Schechner comes back to some of the most recent interests of Victor Turner on the relationship between brainwork and performance.

Such questions on biology and behavior make one dizzy, yet Schechner's paper is evocative and raises basic issues for the anthropology of experience. Acting appears to be very much like doing ethnography, in that actors cannot just "become" characters, for if they were to forget themselves completely they could no longer act. The actor, then, must be half in and half out, a predicament characterized so well by Thoreau. Ethnographers, too, must be deeply enough involved in the culture to understand it, but uninvolved to the point where they can communicate effectively to their colleagues. Both acting and ethnography are reflexive in the attention given to the self in the en-act-ment.

To conclude this introductory essay, let me quote from Schechner's piece. "Each society," he writes, "has its own often shifting definitions of [the actual and the feigned]. I would say that everything imaginable has been, or can be, experienced as actual by means of performance. And that, as Turner said, it is by imagining—by playing and performing—that new actualities are brought into existence. Which is to say, there is no fiction, only unrealized actuality." Yet it is realized actuality that turns experience into expression, and it is cultural expression that we live by.

REFERENCES

Babcock, Barbara A. 1984. Victor W. Turner, Obituary. *Journal of American Folklore* 97 (386): 461–64.

Barthes, Roland. 1974. *S/Z*. New York: Hill and Wang.

Bruner, Edward M. 1984. "The Opening Up of Anthropology." In: Edward M. Bruner (ed.), *Text, Play, and Story: The Construction and Reconstruction of Self and Society*, pp. 1–16. Proceedings of the 1983 annual meeting. Washington, D.C.: American Ethnological Society.

Bruner, Edward M., and Phyllis Gorfain. 1984. "Dialogic Narration and the Paradoxes of Masada." In: Edward M. Bruner (ed.), *Text, Play, and Story: The Construction and Reconstruction of Self and Society*, pp. 56–79. Proceedings of the 1983 annual meeting. Washington, D.C.: American Ethnological Society.

Derrida, Jacques. 1974. *Of Grammatology*. Baltimore, Md.: Johns Hopkins University Press.

Dilthey, Wilhelm. 1976. *Dilthey: Selected Writings*. ed. H. P. Rickman. Cambridge: Cambridge University Press.

Peacock, James L. 1984. "Religion and Life History: An Exploration in Cultural Psychology." In: Edward M. Bruner (ed.), *Text, Play, and Story: The Construction and Reconstruction of Self and Society*, pp. 94–116. Proceedings of the 1983 annual meeting. Washington, D.C.: American Ethnological Society.

Turner, Victor. 1982. *From Ritual to Theatre*. New York: Performing Arts Journal Press.

PART ONE

The Concept Of Experience

2

Dewey, Dilthey, and Drama:
An Essay in the
Anthropology of Experience

VICTOR W. TURNER

Of all the human sciences and studies anthropology is most deeply rooted in the social and subjective experience of the inquirer. Everything is brought to the test of self, everything observed is learned ultimately "on his [or her] pulses." Obviously, there is much that can be counted, measured, and submitted to statistical analysis. But all human act is impregnated with meaning, and meaning is hard to measure, though it can often be grasped, even if only fleetingly and ambiguously. Meaning arises when we try to put what culture and language have crystallized from the past together with what we feel, wish, and think about our present point in life. In other words, we reach back to the conclusions our forebears laid down in the cultural modes that we in the Western tradition now classify as "religious," "moral," "political," "aesthetic," "proverbial," "aphoristic," "commonsensical," etc., to see whether and, if so, how tellingly they relate to or illuminate our present individual problems, issues, troubles, or uneasily inordinate joys. Each such rubbing together of the hardwood and softwood of tradition and presence is potentially dramatic, for if we venerate ancestral dicta, we may have to, so we dolefully conclude, jettison present joy or abandon the sensitive exploration of what we perceive to be unprecedented developments in human mutual understanding and relational forms.

Thus, we have self-sacrifice for an ideal, if we have faith in an authoritative cultural past. But if tragedy approves of this stance, new ways of orienting to modernity may reject the self-sacrificial outcome and pose alternatives which must seem problematic, to say the least, to a general public not weaned from the nipple of tradition. Experience of this sort is the very stuff of drama—both social drama, where conflicts are worked out in social action, and stage drama, where they are mirrored in a host of aesthetic experimental frames, symbols, and hypothetical plottings. However, there may be no stark confrontation of then and now, collective then and existential personal now. Any anthropologist can tell you that any coherent sociocultural field contains many contradictory principles, each hallowed by tradition. In Japanese theater, for example, the Bunraku and Kabuki versions of *Chushingura*, the famous tale of the forty-nine Rōnin, show the tension between two equally axiomatic but conflicting loyalties—to feudal lord and to imperial edict. Obedience to both would mean death for the avenging retainers. Subordination of feudal loyalty to state law would have been an ignominious loss of social identity formed under *samurai* principles of honor and shame. Yet there is a covert subversiveness in the stage drama. The Tokugawa bureaucracy, with its spreading depersonalization of relationships, is being mutely answered by striking, complex gestures of theater that reassert passions against legalizations— those great passions that Samuel Coleridge declared, with reference to Shakespearean tragic heroes, are "atheists believing in no future." Yet the passions are under control and work their way through to honorable consummation by a tangle of devious means—and in ways that might have shocked Aldous Huxley, with his "bad means cannot produce good ends," were he not a man capable of irony and aware of ethical ambiguities.

Let me turn now to John Dewey's view of experience, which I partly share but which I must at least partly conclude needs surpassing in one important respect. Dewey (1934) held that works of art, including theatrical works, are "celebrations, recognized as such, of ordinary experience." He was, of course, rejecting the tendency in capitalist societies to set art on a pedestal, detached from human life, but commercially valuable in terms that were decided by esoteric experts. Dewey said: "Even a crude experience, if authentically an experience, is more fit to give a clue to the intrinsic nature of aesthetic experience than is an object already set apart from any other mode of experience" (quoted in McDermott 1981:526). All this and more in his great book *Art As Experience*, published when he was seventy-five years old.

In my book *From Ritual to Theatre* (1982:17–18), I attempted

an etymology of the English word for "experience," deriving it
from the Indo-European base *per-, "to attempt, venture, risk"—
you can see already how its double, "drama," from the Greek *dran*,
"to do," mirrors culturally the "peril" etymologically implicated
in "experience." The Germanic cognates of *per* relate experience
to "fare," "fear," and "ferry," since *p* becomes *f* by Grimm's Law.
The Greek *perao* relates experience to "I pass through," with implications of rites of passage. In Greek and Latin, experience is
linked with peril, pirate, and ex-per-iment.

There is a dichotomy here which Wilhelm Dilthey (1976
[1914]:210) immediately seized upon in his distinction between
mere "experience" and "an experience." Mere experience is simply the passive endurance and acceptance of events. *An* experience, like a rock in a Zen sand garden, stands out from the
evenness of passing hours and years and forms what Dilthey
called a "structure of experience." In other words, it does not have
an *arbitrary* beginning and ending, cut out of the stream of
chronological temporality, but has what Dewey called "an initiation and a consummation." Each of us has had certain "experiences" which have been formative and transformative, that is,
distinguishable, isolable sequences of external events and internal
responses to them such as initiations into new lifeways (going to
school, first job, joining the army, entering the marital status),
love affairs, being caught up in some mode of what Emile
Durkheim called "social effervescence" (a political campaign, a
declaration of war, a cause célèbre such as the Dreyfus Affair,
Watergate, the Iranian hostage crisis, or the Russian Revolution).
Some of these formative experiences are highly personal, others
are shared with groups to which we belong by birth or choice.
Dilthey saw such experiences as having a temporal or processual
structure—they "processed" through distinguishable stages.
Moreover, they involved in their structuring at every moment and
phase not simply *thought* structuring but the whole human vital
repertoire of thinking, willing, desiring, and feeling, subtly and
varyingly interpenetrating on many levels. A cognitive Occam's
razor, reducing all to bloodless abstractions (if one can visualize a
bloodless razor), would simply make no human sense here.

These experiences that erupt from or disrupt routinized, repetitive behavior begin with shocks of pain or pleasure. Such
shocks are evocative: they summon up precedents and likenesses

from the conscious or unconscious past—for the unusual has its traditions as well as the usual. Then the emotions of past experiences color the images and outlines revived by present shock. What happens next is an anxious need to find meaning in what has disconcerted us, whether by pain or pleasure, and converted mere experience into *an* experience. All this when we try to put past and present together.

It is structurally unimportant whether the past is "real" or "mythical," "moral" or "amoral." The point is whether meaningful guidelines emerge from the existential encounter within a subjectivity of what we have derived from previous structures or units of experience in living relation with the new experience. This is a matter of meaning, not merely of value, as Dilthey understood these terms. For him, value belonged essentially to an experience in a conscious present, in its affective enjoyment or failure to enjoy. But values are not meaningfully connected, they bombard us like a random motley of discords and harmonies. Each value occupies us totally while it prevails. Yet values, Dilthey claimed, have "no musical relation to one another." It is only when we bring into relation with the preoccupying present experience the cumulative results of similar or at least relevant, if not dissimilar, past experiences of similar potency, that the kind of relational structure we call "meaning" emerges.

Here the cognitive heroically asserts itself, for most experiences begin with the preeminence of emotion and desire, drives that repudiate all pasts. When war is declared, when we meet a most desirable potential lover, or when we run away from physical danger or refuse to undertake a necessary but unpleasant task, we are under the power of *value*. It is the heroic combination of will and thought that opposes value by the integrating power of relation-establishing meaning. Perhaps value will become meaning, but it must be responsibly sifted first. In most preindustrial societies this strain after meaning was reinforced powerfully by corporate cultural values which offered our cognitive faculties some ancestral support, the weight of an ethical, or at any rate consensually legitimate, past. Today, unfortunately, culture insists that we must assume the post-Renaissance burden of working each meaning out for ourselves, one by one, unassisted, unless we choose the system woven by another individual no more corporately legitimate than we, as individuals are. This is possibly a major difference between theater today and earlier kinds of theater, insofar as theater is a cultural mirroring of the meaning-seeking process at the public, generalizing level. Earlier theater removed the burden of meaning assignment from the individual to the group, though the tragic painfulness resulted then from the individual's physical terror, or at least extreme reluctance in the face of social duty whose fulfillment might mean physical or mental torment or death.

In Dilthey's view, experience urges toward expression, or communication with others. We are social beings, and we want to tell what we have learned from experience. The arts depend on this urge to confession or declamation. The hard-won meanings should be said, painted, danced, dramatized, put into circulation. Here the peacock's urge to display is indistinguishable from the ritualized need to communicate. Self and not self, ego and egolessness, assertion and altruism, meet and merge in signifying communication.

Underlying all the arts, Dewey saw an intrinsic connection between experience, whether natural or social, and aesthetic form. He wrote: "there is in nature, even below the level of life, something more than mere flux and change. Form is arrived at whenever a stable, even though moving equilibrium, is reached" (quoted in McDermott 1981:536). He argued that even at the prehuman biological level, the life of any organism is enriched by the state of disparity and resistance through which it has successfully passed. Opposition and conflict are overcome, indeed transformed "into differentiated aspects of a higher powered and more significant life." With humans, the

rhythm of loss of integration with environment and recovery of union, not only persists but becomes conscious with him; its conditions are material out of which he forms purposes. Emotion is the conscious sign of a break, actual or impending. Desire for restoration of the union converts mere emotion into interest in objects as conditions of realization of harmony. With the realization, material of reflection is incorporated into objects as their meaning. Since the artist cares in a peculiar way for the phase of experience in which union is achieved, he does not shun moments of resistance and tension. He rather cultivates them, not for their own sake but because of their potentialities, bringing to living consciousness an experience that is unified and total. In contrast with the person whose purpose is aesthetic, the scientific man is interested in problems, in situations wherein the tension between the matter of observation and of thought are marked. Of course, he cares for their resolution. But he does not rest in it; he passes on to another problem using an attained solution only as a stepping stone from which to set on foot further inquiries. . . .

The difference between the aesthetic and the intellectual is thus one of the places where the emphasis falls in the constant rhythm that marks the interaction of the live creature with his surroundings. The ultimate matter of both emphases in experience is the same, as is also their general form. The odd notion that an artist does not think and a scientific inquirer does nothing but think is the result of converting a difference of tempo and emphasis into a difference in kind. The thinker has his aesthetic moment when his ideas cease to be mere ideas and become corporate meanings of objects. The artist has his problems and thinks as he works. But his thought is more immediately embodied in the object. Because of the comparative remoteness of his end the scientific worker operates with symbols, words, and mathematical signs. The artist does his thinking in the very qualitative media he works in, and the terms lie so close to the object he is producing that they merge directly into it. . . .

Because the actual world, that in which we live, is a combination of movement and culmination, of breaks and reunions, the *experience of a living creature is capable of aesthetic quality.* The live being recurrently loses and re-establishes equilibrium with his surroundings. *The moment of passage from disturbance into harmony is that of intensest life.* In a finished world, sleep and waking could not be distinguished. In one wholly perturbed, conditions could not even be struggled with. In a world made after the pattern of ours, moments of fulfillment punctuate experience with rhythmically enjoyed intervals. (quoted in McDermott 1981:536-37, my emphasis)

Aesthetics, then, are those phases in a given structure or processual unit of experience which either constitute a fulfillment that reaches the depths of the experiencer's being (as Dewey put it) or constitute the necessary obstacles and flaws that provoke the joyous struggle to achieve the consummation surpassing pleasure and equilibrium, which is indeed the joy and happiness of fulfillment. There is also present in Dewey's work the sense that the "time of consummation is also one of beginning anew"—any attempt to prolong the enjoyment of consummation beyond its natural term is a kind of withdrawal from the world and hence a lowering and loss of vitality.

Dilthey's unit of experience stressed culture and psychology, since he saw the search after meaning and its expression in performance as the struggle and consummation phases. Dewey's process of experiencing cleaved closer to the biological. Yet both emphasized that the aesthetic has its genesis in sensible human experience and does not proceed from an ideal domain, a Platonic realm of archetypes superior to the vulgar human activities it is supposed to evaluate and organize. For both philosophers the arts, including all genres of theater, germinated in the scenes and objects of human experience and could not be considered in separation from them. The beautiful is the consummate flower of the muddled search for meaning by men and women alive in the full complexity of their mutual attraction and repulsion in war, worship, sex, economic production, and the marketplace.

As some of you know, I have been much concerned in my work with a specific kind of unit of experience, what I call "social drama." This has a protoaesthetic form in its unfolding. In many field situations in markedly different cultures, in my experience of Western social life, and in numerous historical documents, we can clearly discern a community's movement through time as taking a shape to which we can hardly deny the epithet "dramatic." A person or subgroup breaks a rule, deliberately or by inward compulsion, in a public setting. Conflicts between individuals, sections, and factions follow the original breach, revealing hidden clashes of character, interest, and ambition. These mount toward a crisis of the group's unity and continuity unless rapidly sealed off by redressive public action, consensually undertaken by the group's leaders, elders, or guardians. Redressive action is often ritualized and may be undertaken in the name of law or religion. Judicial processes stress reason and evidence; religious processes emphasize ethical problems, hidden malice operating through witchcraft, or ancestral wrath against breaches of taboo or the impiety of the living toward the dead. If a social drama runs its full course, the outcome (or "consummation," as Dewey might have called it) may be either the restoration of peace and "normalcy" among the participants or social recognition of irremediable breach or schism.

Of course this model, like all models, is subject to manifold manipulations. For example, redressive action may fail, in which case there is reversion to the phase of crisis. If law and/or religious values have lost their efficacy, endemic continuous factionalism may infect public life for long periods. Or redressive failure in a local community may lead to appeal to a higher court at a more inclusive level of social organization—village to district to province to nation. Or the ancien régime may be rejected in toto and revolution ensues. In that case the group may be radically restructured, including its redressive machinery.

Culture obviously affects such aspects as the style and tempo of the social drama. Some cultures seek to retard the outbreak of open crisis by elaborate rules of etiquette. Others admit the use of organized violence in crisis or redress, in such forms as the *holmgang* (island single-combat) of the Icelanders, the stickfights of the Nuba of the Sudan, and the reciprocal headhunting expeditions of the Ilongot hill peoples of Luzon. Georg Simmel, Lewis Coser, Max Gluckman, and others have pointed out how conflict, if brought under gradual control, stopping short of massacre and war, may actually enhance a group's "consciousness of kind." Conflict forces the antagonists to diagnose its source, and in so doing to become fully aware of the principles that bond them beyond and above the issues that have temporarily divided them. As Durkheim has insisted, law needs crime and religion needs sin to be fully dynamic systems, since without "doing," without the social friction that fires consciousness and self-consciousness, social life would be passive, even inert.

These considerations, I think, led Barbara Myerhoff (1979) to distinguish "definitional ceremonies" from "social dramas," which she conceived as a kind of collective "autobiography," a means by which a group creates its identity by telling itself a story about itself, in the course of which it brings to life "its Definite and Determinate Identity" (to cite William Blake). Here, in the Diltheyan sense, meaning is engendered by marrying present problems to a rich ethnic past, which is then infused into the "doings and undergoings" (Dewey's phrase) of the local community. Some social dramas may be more "definitional" than others, it is true, but most social dramas contain, if only implicitly, means of public reflexivity in their redressive processes. By their activation groups take stock of their current situation: the nature and strength of their social ties, the power of their symbols, the effectiveness of their legal and moral controls, the sacredness of their religious traditions, and so forth.

The point I would make here is that the world of theater, as

we know it in both Asia and the West, and the immense vari
theatrical subgenres, derive not from imitation, whether consciou
or unconscious, of the processual form of the complete or satiated
social drama—breach, crisis, redress, reintegration, or schism (although Aristotle's model for tragedy somewhat resembles this
phased movement), but specifically from the third phase, redress,
and especially from redress as ritual process. Redressive rituals
include divination into the hidden causes of misfortune, conflict,
and illness (all of which in tribal societies are intimately intercon-
nected and thought to be caused by the invisible action of spirits,
deities, witches, or sorcerers), curative rituals (which may often
involve episodes of spirit possession, shamanic trance, medium-
ship, and trance states among the patients who are the subjects of
a ritual), and initiatory rites connected with these "rituals of affliction." Moreover, many of those rites we call "life-crisis ceremonies," particularly those of puberty, marriage, and death, themselves indicate a sort of breach in the customary order of group
life, after which many relationships among group members must
change drastically, involving much potential and even actual conflict and competition (for rights of inheritance and succession to
office, for women, over the amount of bridewealth, over clan or
lineage allegiance, and so on). Life-crisis rituals (and seasonal
rituals, too, for that matter) may be called "prophylactic," while
rituals of affliction are "therapeutic."

All these "third-phase" or "first-phase" (in the life-crisis instance) ritual processes contain within themselves a liminal phase,
which provides a stage (and I use this tem advisedly) for unique
structures of experience (Dilthey's *Erlebnis*) in milieus detached
from mundane life and characterized by the presence of ambiguous ideas, monstrous images, sacred symbols, ordeals, humilia-
tions, esoteric and paradoxical instructions, the emergence of
symbolic types represented by maskers and clowns, gender reversals, anonymity, and many other phenomena and processes
which I have elsewhere described as "liminal." The *limen*, or
threshold, a term I borrowed from van Gennep's second of three
stages in rites of passage, is a no-man's-land betwixt and between
the structural past and the structural future as anticipated by the
society's normative control of biological development. It is
ritualized in many ways, but very often symbols expressive of ambiguous identity are found cross culturally: androgynes, the-

riomorphic figures, monstrous combinations of elements drawn from nature and culture, with some symbols such as caverns, representing both birth and death, womb and tomb. I sometimes talk about the liminal phase being dominantly in the subjunctive mood of culture, the mood of maybe, might be, as if, hypothesis, fantasy, conjecture, desire—depending on which of the trinity of cognition, affect, and conation is situationally dominant. Ordinary life is in the indicative mood, where we expect the invariant operation of cause and effect, of rationality and commonsense. Liminality can perhaps be described as a fructile chaos, a storehouse of possibilities, not a random assemblage but a striving after new forms and structures, a gestation process, a fetation of modes appropriate to postliminal existence.

Theater is one of the many inheritors of the great multifaceted system we call "tribal ritual," which embraces ideas and images of cosmos and chaos, interdigitates clowns and their foolery with gods and their solemnity, and uses all the sensory codes to produce symphonies in more than music: the intertwining of dance, body languages of many kinds, song, chant, architectural forms (temples, amphitheaters), incense, burnt offerings, ritualized feasting and drinking, painting, body painting, body marking of many kinds including circumcision and scarification, the application of lotions and the drinking of potions, the enacting of mythic and heroic plots drawn from oral traditions—and so much more. Rapid advances in the scale and complexity of society, particularly after industrialization, have passed this unified liminal configuration through the prism of division of labor, with its specialization and professionalization, reducing each of these sensory domains to a set of entertainment genres flourishing in the leisure time of society, no longer in a central driving place. While it is true that the pronounced supernatural character of archaic ritual has been greatly reduced, there are signs today that the amputated specialized genres are seeking to rejoin and to recover something of the numinosity lost in their *sparagmos*, in their dismemberment.

Clearly, as Dewey argued, the aesthetic form of theater is inherent in sociocultural life itself, but the reflexive and therapeutic character of theater as a child of the redressive phase of social drama has to draw on power sources often inhibited in the life of society's indicative mood. The creation of a detached, still almost-sacred liminal space allows a search for such sources. One well-spring of this excessive *meta-* power is clearly the liberated and disciplined body itself, with its many untapped resources for plea-sure, pain, and expression. Another is our unconscious processes, such as may be released in trance. This is akin to what I have often seen in Africa, where thin, ill-nourished old ladies, with only occasional naps, dance, sing, and perform ritual activities for two or three days and nights on end. I believe that an increase in the level of social arousal, however produced, is capable of unlocking energy sources in individual participants. The recent work on the neurobiology of the brain (see d'Aquili, Laughlin, and McManus 1979), shows, among other things, how the "driving techniques of ritual (including sonic driving by, for example, percussion instru-ments) facilitate right hemisphere dominance, resulting in gestalt, timeless, nonverbal experiences, differentiated and unique when compared with left hemisphere functioning or hemisphere alterna-tion" (Lex 1979:146).

My argument has been that an anthropology of experience finds in certain recurrent forms of social experience—social dramas among them—sources of aesthetic form, including stage drama. But ritual and its progeny, notably the performance arts, derive from the subjunctive, liminal, reflexive, exploratory heart of social drama, where the structures of group experience (*Erleb-nis*) are replicated, dismembered, re-membered, refashioned, and mutely or vocally made meaningful—even when, as is so often the case in declining cultures, "the meaning is that there is no mean-ing." True theater is the experience of "heightened vitality," to quote Dewey again. "At its height it signifies complete interpene-tration of self and the world of objects and events" (quoted in McDermott 1981:540). When this happens in a performance, what may be produced is what d'Aquili and Laughlin (d'Aquili et al. 1979:177) call a "brief ecstatic state and sense of union (often last-ing only a few seconds) [which] may often be described as no more than a shiver running down the back at a certain point." A sense of harmony with the universe is made evident and the whole planet is felt to be communitas. This shiver has to be won, though, to be a "consummation," after working through a tangle of con-flicts and disharmonies. Theater best of all exemplifies Thomas

Hardy's dictum: "If a way to the better there be, it exacts a full look at the worst." Ritual or theatrical transformation can scarcely occur otherwise.

REFERENCES

d'Aquili, E. G., Charles D. Laughlin, Jr., and John McManus. (eds.). 1979. *The Spectrum of Ritual*. New York: Columbia University Press.

Dewey, John. 1934. *Art as Experience*. New York: Minton, Balch & Co.

Dilthey, Wilhelm. 1976. *Selected Writings*. ed. H. P. Rickman. Cambridge: Cambridge University Press. (First published in 1914.)

Lex, Barbara. 1979. "The Neurobiology of Ritual Trance." In: E. G. d'Aquili, Charles D. Laughlin, Jr., and John McManus (eds.), *The Spectrum of Ritual*, pp. 117–51. New York: Columbia University Press.

McDermott, J. J. (ed.). 1981. *The Philosophy of John Dewey*. New York: Putnam's.

Myerhoff, Barbara. 1979. *Number Our Days*. New York: Dutton.

Turner, Victor. 1982. *From Ritual to Theatre*. New York: Performing Arts Journal Press.

3

Ordinary
and Extraordinary
Experience

ROGER D. ABRAHAMS

With the explicit opening up of the discussion on the anthropology of experience, we acknowledge that we are moving out of the discourse on social institutions and into the realm of cultural performance and display. I take this to mean that we are no longer looking for the chartering legislation that puts a social group into business and keeps it there through the exercise of authority; rather, we seek the techniques by which the individuals in some sort of collectivity develop ways of acting that will authenticate both the actors and the group simultaneously.

As teachers and scribes we share in the crisis of legitimation. When words become only the basis of establishing *meaningful relationships* and other such egalitarian fictions, then the voices of authority are no longer given value or trust, and all of those who wear robes and speak from the pulpit or the dais can no longer expect to be listened to simply because of the authority given us by our filling such roles. When holy offices no longer automatically carry the power to irreversibly transform peoples' status through simply performing acts vested in the roles, then who will listen to teachers who simply seek to inform and reveal the ways of the world?

As true modernists we respond by seeking to find new and more powerful ways of describing the ways such things work, so that our abilities to examine and perceive more deeply will be accorded some respect and admiration. Modishly, we replace the vocabulary and the practices of vested authority with terms and procedures proclaiming equality of humankind and the need to make a place in our systematic analyses for the achievement of authenticity by the individual, as each person becomes part of a community and a society.

Surely that is what is going on here, is it not? We gather to mark the demotion of the key terms of authoritative rhetoric—"tradition," "custom," even "institution"—as we make one further effort at finding in everyday speech a vocabulary that will assist us in celebrating the project of self-possession, self-fashioning, self-expression; a project that sees all life as a constant achievement and all agreed-upon practices as techniques for simultaneously amplifying and questioning what it is we have agreed to in our own little groups. Thus "experience" and its associated vocabulary is elevated to the realm of the new holy word. In this social dispensation, individuals may find a new redemption—or at least a validation—in the world of the here and now, even if it is no longer attached to a divinely sanctioned plan.

By building on this word, which embodies that segment of life carved out by each of us, we follow in the great line of secular theologians, the clerisy, who make holy words of those which are otherwise most mundane and who seek in the process to raise the place of the examining self to one of such dignity that the older and more wrathful gods, if not appeased, can at least be ignored. This has been the holy practice of secular humanism: the ritualizing of the construction of one's self. Going one further step in this reflexive development, we now acknowledge that all life involves the construction of agreed-upon fictions and that the least harmful, the least hegemonic, are those that assert self-worth. All terms connected with institutional practice become a little suspect because of the power distribution and systems of control they have carried with them—at least in past ethnographic analyses. Culture now achieves a new meaning, the achieved agreements of social practices, an agreement given reinforced value and meaning in each act of sociability. And such practices, when they are writ large in cultural displays and performances, have added power because they achieve their force through the coordination of the energies of the group involved in the celebration.

Erving Goffman, who spent many years in service to this humane discipline, left us with this litany: "Many gods have been done away with, but the individual himself stubbornly remains a deity of great importance. He walks with some dignity and is the recipient of many little offerings. He is jealous of the worship due him, yet, approached in the right spirit, he is ready to forgive those who may have offended him" (1967:95). As a human, and therefore a social animal, the individual operates on the principle of goodwill, assuming until proven otherwise that unmannerly actions and breaches in the ritual of common courtesy arise from ignorance or ineptness, this too a part of the human condition. And so let this essay, even this book, be one of those offerings to the individual.

Under such radically secular conditions, the problem facing the humanist is not so much one of replacing the gods but finding a language to effectively replace the Word with new sacred words that will allow us to celebrate the survival of the human spirit. For many years "civilization," "progress," and "culture" bore this burden, gracefully submitting themselves to elevation. Of these, only the last has retained its haloed effect, through the efforts of those who recognize in the word's capacities the possibility of linking together the way the peoples live, throughout the world.

But can any such "god term," to use Donoghue's (1976:123) designation, remain holy in the relentlessly self-examining environment in which we live? Words in this world are hallowed only so long as they retain their novelty as a sign of their vitality. And so the members of the clerisy continue to search through our everyday speech for these god terms knowing that they are not going to come from on high. As was done by Arnold, and more recently by Lionel Trilling, Erving Goffman, Raymond Williams, and Victor Turner,[1] can new ones be recovered from the passing talk of the streets and parlors and reconstituted, like frozen orange juice, simply by adding water when needed? Such key words, or root metaphors (to use some names by which such god terms have been discussed in the past), must contain such integrity and value that they can be employed, defended in their use, redeemed and re-redeemed for the spirit that resides within them. If we have such a term, "experience" is surely it. But let Donoghue's (1976:123) warning be one that we keep in mind: "There is always a temptation to assume that because a god term is holy to its celebrant[s] it must be holy to everyone; a writer may make the mistake of thinking that he does not need to establish the sanctity of the word, that he has only to invoke it."

Such a caution is especially appropriate in the present cir-

cumstances, where, as ethnographers of the behavior, performance, display, and celebration of diverse peoples, we must
worry ourselves over the two kinds of errors into which enthusiasts fall. The first and most dreadful is that we so love our
new holy words that we turn them into cliches and com-
monplaces, forgetting for the moment that we must maintain
their spirit as well as their meaning. The second is that in our
pursuit of insight we forget that the moral lesson of the new creed
is that communication of deep meanings is difficult under any circumstance, and we find correspondences between cultures especially filled with obstacles to understanding.

This second area for potential error is especially perilous for
the ethnographers who quite naturally pride themselves on being
sensitive to cultural differences. It is therefore important to remind ourselves in our pursuit of an anthropology of experience
that "experience" itself is a deeply coded word in our own culture; that is, the very conditions of modernity, especially as pursued in the United States, value experience for its own sake. Not
only do we hunger and thirst for significant doings, but when we
find them, simply by recognizing them as significant, by thinking
and writing about them, we may elevate such occurrences to a
status that makes considered examination difficult. Trilling
(1979:82) points to just such a tendency in the works of those
critically examining cultural texts: "When we yield to our contemporary impulse to enlarge all experience . . . we are in danger
of making experience merely typical, formal and *representative* and
thus losing one term in the dialectic that goes on between spirit
and the conditioned." This enlargement occurs simply in reporting the experience, isolating it from the course of everyday happenings, providing it with significant form after the fact. Lost in
such a translation, Trilling continues, is "the actuality of the conditioned, the literality of matter, the peculiar authenticity and
authority of the merely denotative." By elevating our actions
to stories and even more dramatic replayings, we lose some of
the spirit that resides in actions simply because they are hum-
drum. Such a loss is hardly inconsequential, for we cannot allow
ourselves to enter into an unexamined agreement with the thrill
seekers and the hedonists that we will be interested in the manifestations of the human spirit only in aroused states; we must

manifest our interest in the quotidian experiences as well, and perhaps even in the depressed states of boredom, lassitude, even dispiritedness.

The problem arising for the observer of the regularities of human behavior and conduct is that the simple process of observation and reporting does, indeed, alter the significance and perhaps even the meaning of the activities themselves. This problem becomes all the more intense when reports are committed to paper or some other medium of record. With the increasing distance between the act and the apprehension of it by the reader, the hearer, the viewer, a loss of the spirit is more likely. This kind of recording may make the event itself seem more significant, for now it has been elevated almost to the status of performance, while at the same time making it seem merely typical, inasmuch as it becomes a "representative anecdote."

Do not mistake me: I am not arguing that we should back away from the enterprise of discussing culture directly and openly in terms of personally registered actions. The word "experience" has such flexibility and can serve us so well in tying together the ordinary and the extraordinary; so much of life is already there, enshrined in its circle of meaning as it is used in the vernacular. Experiences happen to individuals and are therefore sometimes to be regarded as idiosyncratic; but these very same occurrences might, under other circumstances, be usefully regarded as typical. Morris (1970:115) argues in such a direction by distinguishing between "private experiences" and "common experiences." Experience is, at one and the same time, illustrative of what individuals do and of the conventional patterns of culturally learned and interpreted behavior that makes them understandable to others.

Moreover, as a concept, experience underscores the ongoingness of life and the open character of ongoing actions, yet it also encourages us to see actions as units of behavior that can be separated from the rest of the action and talked about later. It is a term of connections because it encourages us to discuss life in terms of how present activities of even the most threatening sort may be drawn on and replayed in some form in the future: "Experience is the best teacher," "Live and learn," and all that. Experience contains ordinary acts, from the casual to the most eventful occurrences. It embodies both *meanings* and *feelings*, the flowering of individual response that continually gravitates toward typicality, so that afterward we can find words to talk about what happened.

Because our individual experiences are so central to the ways in which we put together a sense of our own identity, to underscore the typicality is to confront one of our dearest held beliefs: that having been made individuals, we should do everything we can to hold on to our sense of uniqueness. Yet experience tells us that what happens to us is never so original, especially as we must discuss it. This discussion makes us all the more sensitive to the ways we ourselves are not so original, especially as we recognize ourselves as members of a generation, a network, a community. Without the deep investigation on our own part of how our experiences reflect our deepest cultural concerns, and the patterns we unwittingly impose on developing peoples, we have just another Western ethnocentric model of analysis. Further, it seems especially important to develop this self-consciousness of our own cultural patterns and limitations, because those involved in developing experience as a term of art do so in extension of the idea of the performance of culture—that is, by looking at the ways in which cultural displays, like shows and ceremonies, festivals and rituals, make explicit what is regarded by the membership of the culture itself as the significant moments of life. However, culture lies not only in such singular activities but in the connections between the everyday and these more intense, framed and stylized practices.

My worry begins, I suppose, in recognizing that as a nation of individualists, Americans have placed ever greater importance on experience, relating it to our notions of the person in constant development, always heading toward some kind of self-realization. We have been searchers after experience, always preparing ourselves for significant actions that may enhance our lives if we remain open to the new. Our "native theory" of significant action reflects this: newness, novelty, and a desire to be in on the news has been at the front of the American agenda since the beginnings of our history. Apparently the encounter with the new has been tied up in our imaginations with the prospect of social, cultural, and personal renewal. Indeed, one of the important meanings of the word refers, in shorthand, to conversion, to being saved. This obsession with novelty, accompanied by a fear of boredom, is deeply implicated in the almost compulsive need to move on. From the figure of the pilgrim-stranger to the romanticized hobo, our most admired protagonists are the ones who were able to move on . . . and sometimes move up. Traveling on has been almost institutionalized through its connection with the missionary, the peddler, or the member of the Peace Corps—all processes of Yankee ingenuity that are not too distantly related to "doing anthropology" (especially of the "applied" sort).

All of us have a double consciousness and a sometimes self-contradictory value system about the meaning of these new experiences in the creation of ourselves and the needs and rights of others. Daniel Schorr, the former newscaster who was caught up in the Pentagon Papers controversy, nicely discusses this double consciousness. To him, "reporting" and "reality" are deeply connected; he notes (Schorr 1977:vii) that as a reporter he was constantly confronted with the need "to discover the 'real story' or to extract it from the mists of vagueness and pretenses." A mighty calling, and one that demanded a certain amount of distance from the frantic events to which he and the people he interviewed were witness. This man, who could truthfully claim to be engaged directly in "the action," nevertheless responded to the experience as more the observer than the participant:

It made me feel more real not to be involved. Participants took positions, got excited, shaped events for woe or zeal, but what a strange paradox that seems—to feel more *real* not be involved—to be where it is happening but not to be engaged. To keep the action sufficiently distanced to be able, still, to call it an event, yet because that very distance provides the objectivity necessary to sort out important details of "the story." In fact, just being there, seeing the picture without being in it, qualifies the activity as an experience precisely because one is able to report, first-hand, what really happened. I remained the untouched observer, seeing the whole picture because I was not [actually] in the picture. (Schorr 1977:vii)

Schorr might be describing our work as ethnographers. Does not the field experience call for us to become professional naïfs, demanding that we self-consciously retrack ourselves? A creative regression, if you wish, but a regression nonetheless. Placing ourselves in this position, we may observe and ask and even imitate, without taking the social risks such acts might produce were we taken to be adults. This is carried out, moreover, with the knowledge that while we seem to our informants to act like children, in some ways because we are outsiders who come with devices of a powerful technology (like cars and tape recorders), we can hardly be treated as less than adults.

Doing controlled observation reflects an approach to events as experiences that provides a kind of spiritual hedge against interpreting experience-at-a-remove as simple thrill seeking or voyeurism. With our immense hunger for experience, having achieved this psychological distance while we make our professional observations, the feeling of noninvolvement—indeed, of the inability to involve ourselves fully—begins to affect the quality of our observations. Somehow we find a substitute with sufficient sustaining power to be able to say we were not actively involved. Being on the sidelines merely watching the big plays permits us to replay them later to those who were not there, on the spot; there is sufficient energy in such happenings for all those present to be recharged by the action. But even so, those who are only looking on and reporting develop a double consciousness about the activity that always threatens to undercut any claims for uniqueness.

The problem of this double consciousness is great, far greater than I am able to get a handle on here, for it has so much to do with our notions of what constitutes learning and to what extent and purpose we really do live and learn. Moreover, with the growing emphasis on the individual's control over his or her own identity, the institutional ways of engineering personal transformations have lost much of their power. For such socially sanctioned transformation to occur, we must believe in the power of those invested with authority to mark these changes for us. But in many ways such authority has been undercut because of our belief that we should do such changing on our own. This is authentication substituted for authority. If success in life were a given, there would be little question, I suppose, that experience could be a useful teacher, if not always the best one. But a corollary of our American Dream is what might be called an American Dread, of finding out that growing means eliminating some of our options. Failing in a task will do this, or course, but so will succeeding too well and being promoted in some way because of the success. Our dread is always that we can't go back.

In fact, many of the formative thinkers on the subject of the relationship between narrated experience and life and art have worked their profundities in witnessing failure. Donoghue (1976:104) takes note of just this dynamic in discussing how American writers draw on the experience of personal failure, making it into "aesthetic forms and ceremonies . . . to take away some of its 'stress', thus entering into the all-too-human process of assimilating it." His response is that of the literary critic still adhering in some degree to the "wound and bow" approach by which great art is forged out of deep personal hurt. Donoghue discerns in American letters a pattern by which the genre "achieves its vitality by a labour to transform the mere state of failure into the artistic success of forms and pageants; it learns a style not from a despair but from an apparent failure—some, like Henry Adams, by making the worst of it"; others, like Henry James, "by making the best of it, and the best of it is the same thing as the most of it" (1976:104).

The perception is important because it recognizes in such a dynamic and often self-contradictory form our attraction to experience for its own sake and our ambivalence about why we are so drawn to it. Both success and failure are useful outcomes, especially as the experience is talked about and written about later. While there is little problem for the anthropologist to recognize this complex motive in modern life, just how much does enter into the decision to become an ethnographer, to go into the field, thus testing oneself and one's own cultural moorings by a people living and identifying with the writings about the systematics of those who live according to different cultural ways? We know of this problem because doing fieldwork is regarded as a *rite de passage* for the social and cultural anthropologist.

Just how American this double consciousness of experience is emerges when looking at the number of our lasting works of literature that draw on the contrast between the doer and the watcher: the Henry James who so glories in the achievement of the occasional moment of felicity in the midst of decorous, if frivolous, doings; the Henry Adams who can only scorn the present because of its deep duplicities and its failure of nerve. There are, of course, many American works of fiction built around a pair of characters who dramatize the problem: one deeply involved in the action, whether successfully or not, the other a witness to it all and only sometimes a judge as well. While one reading of *The Adventure of*

Huckleberry Finn would make Huck and Jim into such a pair, the great example of this type of narrative is, of course, *Moby Dick,* with Ishmael being drawn unwittingly to the sea and to the cruise—drawn, as we find out, by a force of life confrontation epitomized in Ahab's obsession. More recent outstanding examples of such onlookers and reporters are Nick Carraway in Fitzgerald's *Great Gatsby;* Nick Adams in Hemingway's short stories; the more world-weary Jake Barnes and his attitudes toward bullfighting and war in Hemingway's *The Sun Also Rises;* and Stingo in Styron's *Sophie's Choice.*

We identify all of these characters with the storyteller-author and his growing up through having experienced the energy and the frenzy of these more charismatic presences, these larger-than-life figures, the Ahabs and Gatsbys who represent a mysterious power resource that guarantees that wherever these figures are, significant things will occur. These quintessential American novels are constructed around the interplay between the characters who instigate the action and those who are there to observe and record, who are caught up in the swirl of transforming events but emerge much wiser, perhaps bruised by events but relatively unscathed, "so the story can be told."

We are now informed of the ongoing American concern with experience, but what of its potential in developing ethnographic strategies. With few exceptions, most formal ethnographies tell us little about the experience of the fieldworker and almost as little about the experiences of the people being observed. Rather, we have records of the system and institutions that order the lives of people in groups, enlivened every once in awhile with a representative anecdote. On the whole, however, the reflexive dimension of the ethnographic literature has not been well developed. While we have a number of fascinating autobiographical reports from the field, there is very little address on the part of the fieldworker as to how cultural norms and professional expectations entered into the collection and reporting of materials, much less what was happening to the collector that might have made a difference (cf. Rose 1982). Even behavior on the experiential level is not often in our monographs. To be sure, there have been a series of revealing field reports that focus on the phenomenological dimensions of the discovery of self and others, through developing relationships in the field situation (Rabinow 1977 and Crapanzano 1980 are two that come to mind), in addition to the classic anthropological novels that elaborate on the representative anecdote technique. However, as ethnographic reports get even closer to the details of recurrent expressive behaviors, there has arisen a felt need to discover how individuals within a community learn cultural performances, how to prepare for them and judge them, and how to feel about them before, during, and after the actual occurrence. With this switch, more ethnographic attention is being paid to native theories of emotions and feelings, as well as to the more objective utilitarian and symbolic orders provided for participants in a culture simply by having grown up within a specific milieu (cf. Lutz 1982; Feld 1982; Myers 1979; in the area of folklore, cf. Glassie 1982).

As I see it, this drawing on experience in anthropology is a part of the process of internal monitoring of basic terms and concepts that must take place in every professional discipline. In the social sciences—especially sociology and anthropology—we have unique problems in taking stock of special terminology as key words are derived from everyday talk (see Williams 1979:180 for an indication of the importance of experience in his ongoing concern with key words). As native interpretation becomes more and more important in our ethnographic reports, experience gives promise of tying together our everyday feelings with those encountered during Big Times. Experience addresses the ongoingness of life as it is registered through the filter of culture—that is, through acts we have already learned to interpret as experiences or, in the case of shock, surprise, embarrassment, or trauma, through acts we reprocess as experiences after the fact, by talking about them and thus making them seem less personal, more typical.

At this point it is probably most useful to point out our commonsensical distinction between events—things that happen—and experiences—things that happen to us or others. The distinction is important for a number of reasons, not least of all because notions of who we are as individuals are often tied up with those unique-if-typical things that have happened, especially when those happenings have become stories we tell ourselves. In this dimension individual experiences enter into the putting together of our "identity kit," to use Erving Goffman's term. Rose (1982:220) is one of the few social scientists who has addressed the notion of experience and has consistently made distinctions between what "experiences we ... recognize as meaningful as they are occurring"; the semiotic systems by which we are able to order experiences as we are having them; and an economy of experiences in which those we have are to be regarded as personal resources that may be used in interpersonal exchanges as a way of authenticating ourselves.

This last, our using experiences as part of our personal economy, is perhaps the dimension least easily and readily dealt with by ethnographers. Stories about one's own experiences provide an important resource for not only establishing one's place in the community (because of one's special knowledge) but also for establishing one's identity, should that be an important feature of the culture. Such stories are commonly told to those who will respond in kind, or at least with some other kernel of information regarded as equally valuable. Should we bear such notions in mind, we would not be so surprised when many of the questions we ask of our informants are regarded as strange precisely because the answers call for a giving away of scarce resources.

The experience of being asked to "give yourself away," however, is far from unusual in our own most personal interactions: examine how you feel when someone tells one of your stories, one that is about something you have experienced and told about in the past. Your response is likely to be one of feeling mimicked; or worse, your ability to speak for yourself is put into question. I am not arguing that this is the feeling inspired in all cultures when personal stories are expropriated, only that a truly reflexive anthropology would make one aware of the possibility.

This domain of radical individuality, of the need to feel unique, is not held by the rest of the world. As Geertz (1976:225) has cannily put it: "The Western conception of the person as a bounded, unique cognitive universe, a dynamic center of awareness, emotion, judgment and action organized into a distinctive whole is, however incorrigible it may seem to us, a rather peculiar idea within the concept of the world's cultures." Nonetheless, he recognizes the draw that such a conception of personhood might have on ethnographic studies that attempt to get at the everyday experiences of those under observation. His caveat is a commonsensical one, even if difficult to abide by: "Rather than attempt to place the experience of others within the framework [of "person" or "self"] we must ... view their experiences within the framework of their own idea of what selfhood is" (1976:225). This calls for the collection of "native exegeses" of the experiences regarded as meaningful; that is, discussion not only of the experience itself but its value from the perspective of the one to whom it happened and others within the same interpretive community—the *emic* way of describing culture. But more commonly, in developing perspectives to effectively convey the idea of experience in any culture, we will draw on our own metaphors—that is, we will use an *etic* perspective and the anthropological terms of art that go along with it—for getting at the ways in which repeated actions within a culture are systematized and anticipated.

For some decades, for instance, following the fashion of couching matters in evolutionary terms, we discussed not only cultural history but everyday practices in specific groups in terms of the "flow" of life. This draws on the power of hydraulic metaphor that depicts "what happens" in a culture in terms of the pull of gravity on a growing stream or the pushing along of that water by some pumping mechanism. More recently, we have changed our metaphoric sources somewhat, depicting life in one or another kind of performance (those calling for "scores" or "scripts" or "scenarios"), or we have resorted to the closely related image of life as a game whose rules and plays and moves may be usefully described. The present appeal of the terms "experience" and "event" seems to respond, at least in part, to a sense that these analogical strategies have begun to lose their descriptive power, precisely because the models from which the analogies arise are ones that are privileged within our own culture and may, ethnocentrically, place the units of experience-in-common in the culture under observation in a misleading universe of discourse.

The notion of describing cultural activities in our own vernacular terms for goings-on—terms like "action," "practice," "occasion," "event," "experience"—seems, then, to be an attempt to sidestep the limitations of the tropes derived from these play activities. We are pulled toward a vocabulary drawn from the "real" exchange of energies for serious purposes with such terms: a vocabulary deeply implicated in our own very American and modern discourse on individuality and selfhood, our native notions of personhood, as discussed by Geertz.

The American pragmatic tradition of philosophy has brought this weighting of the everyday and transitional character of life as lived into the open (cf. Turner 1982 for another genealogical view). As anthropologists we are drawn to the idea for many of the same reasons our philosopher forebears were: to escape the imprisonment of using a priori ideal categories of the significant, such as the metaphysical philosophical tradition provided us in such notions as "sublimity," "virtuosity," "genius." The pragmatists sought instead to encourage a pluralistic cast of mind that would deprivilege the extraordinary moment of vision in favor of the more spontaneous chance occasion available to anyone, not just those who had refined their sensibilities and pursued their genius.

The philosopher who most fully and poetically developed this point of view was William James. "Life is in the transitions as much as in the terms connected," he insisted. "Often, indeed, it seems to be there more emphatically, as if our spurts and sallies forward were the real living line of the battle, were like the thin line of flame advancing across the dry autumnal field which the farmer proceeds to burn" (in McDermott 1967:212–13). The tradition was set in motion by Ralph Waldo Emerson, especially in his later essays when he was extending his thought to the importance of the momentary. Emerson's (1903–4, III:64) personal battle was with the moral life that could overwhelm the possibility of happiness in quotidian life: "We must set up the strong present tense against all rumors of wrath, past or to come." The only way to get out of this hold of the past, and of its inherited moral precepts, was "to fill the hour and leave no crevice for a repentance or an approval. We live amid surfaces, and the true art of life is to skate well on them" (1903–4, III:59).

James went one further step, giving moral weight to everyday experience as a way of putting such rumors to flight. He asserted that we must find means for a "reinstatement of the vague and the inarticulated in its proper place" (in McDermott 1967:212), and pursued this line to underscore the importance of "openness" in achieving meaning and purpose in our interpretive scheme. Repeatedly he asked us to contemplate the power of achieved relationships between things as well as people. However, what this perspective loses in the translation from Emerson and other transcendentalists to the pragmatic point of view is the importance of risk in the recognition of the moral weightedness taken on by our personal actions. Bloom (1984:20) evokes the problem as a gloss

on Emerson's argument in "Self-Reliance": "American restless-
ness . . . puts all stable relationships at a relatively [low] estimate,
because they lack the element of risk." Neither those who employ
the various play analogies, such as Goffman or even Victor
Turner, nor James and Dewey, who drew on tropes from fire and
other natural (and sometimes unpredictable) processes, have
reinstated this Emersonian concern with the risk involved in val-
orizing the transitional, the vague and inarticulated.

In the translation from the Emersonian to the Jamesian perspective, personal moral probation is neglected in favor of emphasizing everyday life as the baseline against which other kinds
of experiences are recognized and interpreted. We become more
concerned with the human condition than we do with the questions posed by the morally tentative person in everyday dealings
with others. Perhaps this is because James's vision encourages the
equation of time and space in the experienced moments of transition. It is at such moments in which past time and present life
most vibrantly come together, those moments when connections
may be perceived and relationships established, that "enable us
to live prospectively as well as retrospectively. [Experience] is 'of'
the past, inasmuch as it comes expressly as the past's continuation; it is 'of' the future insofar as the future, when it comes, will
have continued it" (James, in McDermott 1967:213).[2]

While James opened this subject up to philosophical speculation from the pragmatic perspective—that is, without tying it to
metaphysical concerns—Dewey placed "experience" in everyday
life at the center of his philosophical concerns. He noted, for instance, that "like its congeners, life and history, experience includes what men do and suffer, what they strive for, love, believe
and endure, and also how men act and are acted upon, the ways
in which they do and suffer, desire and enjoy, see, believe, imagine" (Dewey 1929:10). He encouraged us to link two notions of
clear importance for anthropology: life is best conceived as being
carried on by individuals who have a capacity to remember and
thus to build a future patterned on the doings of the present; and
existence is thus describable on a commonsense level, as an active
and unfolding process. By understanding the individual's role in
the process, we secure a place in the description of culture patterns for both invention and idiosyncrasy. Thus, experience as

both a personal and a social construct looks on life as being made up of rules of thumb rather than of formal and regulated patterns of behavior.

It is this very notion of personal negotiation and play that undergirds a pluralistic approach to the contrapuntal operations of the individual mind, on the one hand, and to the many interwoven voices and styles of society and culture, on the other. In the situation involving the coming together of peoples of different cultures and historical conditions, this multiplicity of voices becomes the problematic facing any attempt to adequately describe experiences. Putting forth a theory of adequate description based on experiences under conditions of high mobility, especially in frontier situations, asks not for a full-out rejection of such notions as "tradition," "custom," even "rituals." Rather, it asks for a transvaluation out of the realm of authoritative practices and into the domain of socially devised units of activity, which are valued because they are agreed on by all of those participating and because they embody patterns of expectation that can be learned and rehearsed and practiced together. Emphasizing the common features of experience calls for a redefinition of culture itself, away from the officiated practices, the regulated and obligatory behaviors of our shared lives, and toward something more like the relative "typicality" of what happens again and again to individuals finding themselves in similar situations.

When an experience can be designated as typical, then the doings of the individual and the community become shared, not only with regard to what actually happens under those circumstances, but also how one feels about the happenings. Simply stated, it is not just experiences that are shared but the sentiments arising from them as well: the doings and the feelings reinforce each other. Moreover, this system of typicality of event and sentiment provides us with a linkage between past and future, for the very recognition of typicality rests on others having gone through that experience (or something like it) before.

Then there enters the existence of the experience of experience, that is, the recognition even while something is taking place in one's own life that it is a replaying, in some dimension, of things that have happened to others. This self-perception is especially important when the experience is not only typical but intense and potentially disruptive. At that point, being able to recognize typicality becomes a means of recognizing how to feel and interpret what is going on. Through such reflexive activity we can recognize the difference between the more and the less ordinary, the everyday and the special event, as it is becoming *an* experience. This is a distinction Dewey (1934:35) pointed out: "Experience occurs continuously, because the interaction of live creatures and environing conditions is involved in the very process of living.... Oftentimes [this means that] the experience had is inchoate. Things are experienced but not in any way that they are composed into *an* experience."

The distinction between levels of self-conscious apprehension achieved a place of such importance in Dewey's scheme because he wished to reveal the continuities between art and life. Therefore, he underscored those happenings in everyday life that are most like our ways of encountering works of art within the Western tradition: by the disjunction that occurs in the flow of experience that calls for a consideration of the event as a "thing apart." "Life," Dewey (1934:36–37) argued, "is no uniform uninterrupted march or flow. It is a thing of histories, each with its own plot, its own inception and movement toward its close, each having its own particular movement." His interests were in excerpted actions that have a sense of beginning, development, and end, like a well-crafted piece of the storytelling art. Perhaps he was guided by his own underlying feeling that *an* experience not only involves an intensity of feeling that takes it out of the flow of the everyday but also a framing operation by which the ongoing activity is translated into a reportable story. Histories, in this sense, must be sufficiently interesting as well as unusual for others to agree to classify them as *an* experience. But who will thereby listen to the recounting of the happening?

Even at the level of typicality by which experience becomes *an* experience, the term's semantic field is far from fully described. Indeed, there is an even higher and more general level of typicality that enters into our discussions of how individuals enter into happenings and feelings that are so characteristic of the larger developmental patterns we call Experience—the American Experience, the Jewish Experience, the Sixties Experience, even the Growing-Up and Growing-Old Experience. In a similar acknowledgment of differences of intensity and significance, we make a distinction between events and something that become the Event, even the Big Event, referring usually to being involved in a rite of passage or something close to it.

Although it is difficult, of course, to hold this range of meanings in mind while constructing an anthropology of experience, it is necessary to do so. For while "experience" is usefully employed to discuss meaningful actions from the most ordinary to the extraordinary, we expect the more intense occasions to have a point, even to carry a message. This is true of rites of passage themselves; inasmuch as other big experiences share in this sense of the momentous, our native theory of action carries the expectation that we will be transformed in some way, simply because of the intensity of the experience itself. To regard all activities making up *an* experience or part of a significant event as necessarily having such potential would severely undercut the usefulness of the idea of experience as a way of connecting the everyday with the special, and the ordinary person with the representative human.

Yet just as surely there is a difference between the way we interpret everyday experiences and those that jump out at us as being significant. This difference is carried, in part, by the interpretive apparatus we use to discuss any experience. Somehow and somewhere between experience and the Big Experience we impose a frame on the activity by calling attention to its extraordinary character. This attention commonly is elicited by the self-conscious stylization of the activity and through developing some kind of preparation for it, through rehearsal, warming up, or simply through special kinds of anticipatory behavior.

The kind of framework I am referring to is as simply accomplished as saying "Not it!" to instigate a game of tag. But it may also be as complicated as the various ways a family anticipates Christmas or a community prepares for a pageant, picnic, or parade. Such are those times out of time when an agreement goes into effect that everything that takes place within the confines of that set-aside time and space will be judged by its own criteria of the permissible. This is such a commonsense kind of cultural device that it can be evoked by the reminders of the subjunctive character of the practice, as Victor Turner named it, the hedging that occurs whenever we say, "We're just playing," or "It's only make-believe." Any time we can agree among ourselves to enter these realms, we achieve a particular relief from responsibility for our actions. We are able to say that we are not ourselves in one way or another when we are in such a state.

This suspension of the rules may be brought into play precisely because when we are within such frames we are involved not so much in experiencing things directly but in replaying them. The elements of preparation and rehearsal and recapitulation introduce a kind of distance from the actions as they might be enacted in the "real" world. Once having said this, however, we must also recognize that any kind of replay involves the risk that the original will be so adequately represented that the frame itself may dissolve. Will any subjunctive activity operate effectively if the "as if" quality does not threaten to dissolve at any time, the players jumping squarely into the spectators to slash at them with their bats, or the firewalker pulling someone from the audience onto the coals with him?

To cast experience in the terms I have been employing, there seems to be two kinds of *an* experience: those arising directly out of the flow of life, with little or no explicit preparation; and those for which we plan and to which we look forward, where the parts are precast and each role has its set of lines. The two share a scenic wholeness and a heightening of awareness, as well as the possibility of being repeated in form or reported on in substance. The greater the degree of self-conscious preparation and stylization, the more the experience may be shared, but also the higher the risk that the prepared quality of the event will be regarded as restricting rather than liberating. This becomes problematic more in those areas left to us in which the experience is ceremonial, for here the frame placed around the event calls for us not to take on alternative selves, as in play, but to be our best selves, to present ourselves in the best possible light . . . only more so, to be on our best behavior. On such formal occasions there is no relief from being judged for what we do and how we act; on the contrary, such experiences are ones in which individual status enhancement is the raison d'être for the activity.

Having thus pointed out the disjunction between everyday experience and these larger and more openly fictive displays, it seems equally important to remind ourselves once again of the various ways in which we have guaranteed the sense of continuity between these various realms. The point is that in spite of the differences of feeling and apprehension between everyday experiences and those arising from the Big Times of our lives, American culture wishes to optimize the ease of passage between the two states. In nearly all things we value openness and apparent spontaneity, even while we depreciate most expressions for following form and convention. In our desire to optimize authenticating acts at the expense of authoritative ones, we seem to appreciate most those moments we can say afterward were big but which stole up on us and took us unawares. To encourage such moments, however, we must expend a good part of our energies secretly preparing for these breakthroughs, for these spontaneous times in which we are overcome by the fulfillment of the expectations we hardly could admit to having—like those "first-time experiences" which, when successful, are so surprising because we hear about them and even talk about them but they seem to sneak up on us anyhow. We are surprised only by the fulfillment of expectations.

Perhaps only the demystifyers in our midst, the poets and the sociologists, discuss such secret subjects openly. Such are the moments Paul Valery refers to as "the active presence of absent things," when the accumulation of the already discussed and the anticipated come together with those experiences that occurred so early and were repeated so often that they became an unacknowledged part of our repertoire. This active forgetting, then, becomes an exercise in what we used to call "custom," or even "habit": "The social world seems to us as natural as Nature, although it is only held together by magic. Is it not, in truth, an enchanted structure, a system found . . . obedience to words, the keeping of promises, the power of images, the observance of customs and conventions—all of them pure fictions?" (Valery 1962:508–9). Because of their fictional character, perhaps, we have allowed ourselves to actively forget that they are part of our cultural character-in-common.

Yet we have a number of ways of reminding ourselves of these cherished fictions: by explicitly talking about what they mean and how they have come to mean what they do. I refer here, of course, to events of celebration. Either the discussion can be waged formally, when a ceremony is built into the event, or informally, when the occasion seems to successfully come off with some degree of spontaneity. In the case of the latter, discussion occurs after the fact and usually turns on the intensity of the "good time" and what it takes to have such satisfying experiences. In spite of our distrust of the formal practices of the past because of their being attached to a power system that seems to many to eliminate mobility and choice—and by extension, self-determination—we still enter, smiling and gracious, into such times when we ornament life by planning ahead, by getting dressed up and bringing out the best china and silverware. But also consider how much we value those times when a casual "drop-in" becomes a "get-to-gether," and soon gravitates into a "party," a "blast," a "really great time."

There are many such events that heighten our sense of life without our having to go through extensive formalities. As I noted above, we make our preparations for these in secret, for so much of our sense of self is predicated on maintaining the ability to appear spontaneous that we seem to cling to the idea that parties are best when they happen on the spur of the moment—about as true as the idea that lovemaking is best when unplanned. Somehow, the appearance of spontaneity has been identified by us with our notions of the authentic self. But the value we place so strongly on authenticity in turn places a very heavy burden on us: in our heart of hearts, for how many of our acts can we really claim true spontaneity? Moreover, such questions of authenticity affect our perceptions of others, both as participants in a culture that privileges self and originality and as ethnographers constantly testing the behavior of our informants so as to judge whether or not we are being fooled. We must understand our own predisposition with regard to judging the acts of others if we are to more effectively stitch together an anthropology of experience.

To some degree, all observers of human behavior seek a corner on the market of reality, for that is *our* profession, *our* way of managing our own identities. The project of all of the humanistic disciplines has been to discriminate between the real and the unreal, the genuine and the fake, the realistic and the sentimental or fantastic, the verifiable truth (all those things we call "the facts") and illusions, the misleading, the mystified, and the mythical. Humanists seek insight into life as a means of living more fully themselves, of experiencing more knowledgeably and more deeply, and thus being able to impart these techniques and this accrued knowledge and wisdom to others.

This is, of course, precisely how Goethe presents the Faustian dilemma to the reader. But the problem and the search is hardly reserved for professional seekers of truth. The drive to distinguish the real from the ersatz is part of Western common culture, used, among other things, as a source of the criteria by which we judge the behavior of others and ourselves, and also as a way in which the relative success of our encounters and our relationships may be assessed. Repeatedly, we find ourselves reacting to the behavior of others by how "real" they seem and, in response, how much we can "be ourselves" with them—how unguarded we can be in interactions with them and still be comfortable.

Obviously, regarding someone as sincere or a fake, as an original or a show-off, far from exhausts the repertoire of ways by which we judge others. In fact, using the relative "naturalness" of someone as the basic criterion of what is real and what isn't would almost guarantee that we would be bored by all encounters and relationships. Indeed, there are many circumstances in which the ability to pull off a role with spirit, and in a manner to which we may respond in kind, appears more important than whether the other is being sincere or even authentic. Our continuing fascination with those who openly perform, especially if they are willing to take on the role of the eccentric or the vagrant spirit—from Hell's Angels and punkers to hoboes and spielers at carnivals—reminds us that those who appear to speak and act on the basis of extreme experience often seem more real to us than those involved in more mundane pursuits. In fact, in many situations we seem to judge what "the real thing" is by how fully such others are able to make us recognize the range of experiential possibilities, whether or not we go through such experiences ourselves. Again, our double consciousness is brought into play: the value we place on centered action, and those who seem to engage in life to its fullest, calls forth our admiration and even adulation as well as our fears of involving ourselves in risks.

Under such circumstances, reality is only understandable when we are able to contrast it with other kinds of experience, perception, and judgment. To William James's classic formulation of the problem ("Under what circumstances do we think things are real?") must be added, "What do we contrast with what in developing our notions of the 'real'?" In some situations we distinguish between fanciful (or poetic) and real without judging one better than the other; in another range of situations we distinguish between "real" life and "just playing," again not valuing the former more highly unless the occasion calls for high seriousness or a focus on work. Indeed, play may not only be appropriate to the occasion but may actually heighten reality by quickening our senses. To be sure, ludic activities call for a self-conscious attention to stylistic expression, and therefore depart from "real" life with regard to both preparation (as in practice or rehearsal) and actual play. But any activity that calls for us to act and react together at a high pitch can become a Big Time for us, valued for itself and used in some cases as a baseline against which everyday activity is judged—in which case the verdict is that life is boring for the most part.

Whether in the form of planned play activities or spontaneous celebrations (or even riots), some among us place increasing value on "the action," on experience for its own sake. In so doing, the breaks in the routine order of the everyday world come to provide the measure of whether life is being lived to the fullest. Ever greater importance is placed, then, on those experiential departures into the higher and deeper registers of feeling that emerge in rehearsed events and that break our routines by encouraging us to get "deep." The latter is not only part of the experience of getting serious at the performance of a work of "high art" but also in having Big Times.

These two varieties of serious experience underscore the problems as well as the strengths of the pragmatist's approach to activity, a limitation shared by the sociological phenomenologists, such as Alfred Schutz and Peter Berger. Both schools use the quotidian as a representation of the "real" world from which all other states of experience depart. Schutz (1970:225), for instance, set up the world of experience in terms of a contrast between "the world of paramount reality" and all others: "the world of dreams and phantasms, especially the world of art, the world of religious experience, the world of scientific contemplation, the play world of the child, and the world of the insane," all of which he regarded as "finite provinces" of significance. Yet, while noting the ease with which we may travel between these discrete worlds, he argued: "Within a single day, even within a single hour our consciousness may run through most different tensions and adopt most different intensional attitudes to life.... Furthermore [there are] regions belonging to one province of meaning [that are] enclosed by another" (Schutz 1970:256).

We operate both within and between these various worlds and their realities. Clearly, one is no more real than another; rather, they differ in what is brought into them in common by the participants, how focused and intense and stylized the activities become, and how important such factors are in affecting the experience itself and the understanding of it. No concept of "a world of paramount reality," whether it comes from the pragmatists' idea of experiential flow or the phenomenologists' characterization of the quotidian, allows us to understand fully enough the role of play, of having fun and making fun; nor can we comprehend the process of celebration with sufficient fullness and clarity.

On the one hand, there is a flow of activity, and on the other, distinctive marked-out acts and events, all going under the name of experience. Moreover, the very flow of the everyday assures the continuity between routine activities and the more extraordinary ones. We have become aware of the continuities between the ordinary and the "deeper" or "higher" events through performed mimetic experiences, which openly imitate (and stylize) everyday acts and interactions. Far from exhausting the relationship between the ordinary and the otherwise, such imitational play only begins the discussion. Indeed, *how* the disruption of the patterns of expectation in ordinary interactions are remedied, even transformed and used in play events, may prove to be the most important point of connection between the different states of apprehension and understanding.

Each subjunctive event is more than simply a rendering, direct or inverted, of a social practice, it is an experience itself. Each draws on a community's concern with disruption, clumsiness, embarrassment, confusion, and conflict in the everyday. But in forming and stylizing the reported events, each develops a life of its own. Each performance, for instance, draws on energies and patterns of expectation brought to the occasion not only because it embodies some life situation but because it departs from the everyday to the degree that it is self-consciously and artfully imitated, replayed, performed.

Consider, then, the complexity of the relationship between activity as it is practiced and the rendering of it as it is reported, reenacted, and intensified. Must life precede art for art to be understood? Can we not comprehend a feast without knowing everyday eating habits? Too often the line of actual experience goes the other way—someone goes through some hard times, yet to the extent that they are able to see the situation as typical, they maintain a sense of control over the individual upset. Is it not useful, then, to avoid drawing a hard-and-fast line between the finite representations of repeated events and any conception of paramount reality? In different kinds of scenes and interactions there are various relational features that past practice enables us to understand and appreciate: levels of formality, of scenic wholeness, of intensity of frame, of calls on our attention, of reaction and judgment.

My argument may seem somewhat self-contradictory. On the one hand, we have a sense of disjuncture between the flow of everyday experience; *an* experience; a typical experience that is reportable about ourselves as a means of playing out our having entered, individually, into life's recurrent problem situations; and a large-scale experience in which we recognize that over a period of time the progress and pattern of our activities are part of a much larger story, one that began long before we were born and will continue after our death. On the other hand, the placement of the openness of experience within the American ideology of self-determination makes us conscious that the distinctions between the ordinary and the extraordinary commonly do not arise from either formal demands emerging from the ceremonializing of life nor from any hard-and-fast distinction between the serious and the playful. Rather, we see life as organized around times, places, and occasions to encourage the participation of a greater or lesser number of people in a common activity. This approach sees both the larger and the smaller experiences as creative achievements; each experience, whether planned for in some manner (practiced, run through, rehearsed) or not, is interesting only insofar as it is able to enlist participation; that is, if the planning produces some sense of discovery, some appearance of spontaneous exchange of energies (as well as information) with others. For Erving Goffman the experience of even the smallest understandings (much less our larger mutual celebrations) seemed like a new rendering of an archaic holy act, one that acknowledges the existence of others and signifies a willingness to be involved in the flow of vital cultural information and, on occasion, to be exuberant in passing on this knowledge as a way of tying together self, others, and the larger worlds.

By turning to one of our new holy terms, "experience," and developing it into a moving "term of art," what might we reasonably expect from anthropologists propelled by the desire to get down on paper what has been experienced in the field? First and foremost, such ethnographers will carry into participant observation a recognition of their own culture's notions of significant actions and their related emotions and sentiments. From this will arise a willing suspension of disbelief in the "poetics" of the new culture—the things that are regarded as being in the same category, the things that may be compared and those that suggest other things in spite of not being in the same category. An anthropology of experience might well begin by noting the range of expressive means and affects, techniques and sentiments—that is, the most common and ordinary activities in the flow of life of the group under observation. And it might then provide a calendar for the events that are already set aside as extraordinary. Finally, an anthropology of experience might look for the ways in which the ordinary and the extraordinary coexist; how convention permits the framing and stylizing of activities, calls to attention the participants, and encourages a spelling out of the meanings and feelings carried within these activities. Because any anthropology of experience is going to be initially attracted to the display events of the group, the preparations for these activities will be as significant as the means and messages carried within the event itself.

As anthropologists, then, our objectives remain what they have been for some time: to demonstrate the diversity of human behavior in groups and to reveal the patterns of action and feeling that underlie this heterogeneity. Now that we have begun to move the idea of experience to the center of our concerns, however, we make it possible to elevate the representative anecdote to the same place of importance as the rite of passage. Our great discovery is not that everyone has experiences that are both unique and typical, but that everyone does seem to have a way of organizing these doings so they may be shared.

NOTES

Thanks are due to a number of people who assisted in thinking through and writing this argument: Anthony Hilfer, early on, and Ralph Ross, most recently, helped me read the pragmatists; Fred Myers and Donald Brenneis were helpful in many ways, especially in considering the relationship between feelings and reports of feelings as they have been considered by ethnographers dealing with the other cultures; David Stanley discussed the double consciousness argument with me on a number of occasions; Vic and Edie Turner first brought me into the engagement on the subject; Ed Bruner sustained my enthusiasm and interest throughout the writing; and Janet Anderson was, as always, the best and most commonsensical commentator on my prose and my argument.

1. The most important dimension of this literature for the social sciences has to do with the words "culture," "society," and "community." I include James and Dewey on my list of the high priests of this literature because they not only brought to their writings a strong interest in the relationship between key words and social theory but they also infused their discussions of key words with a concern for dignity and the human spirit.

2. Just how deeply this concept is an invention of James's generation becomes clear in the writings of the commentators on the American language. Mencken (1919:168), the most trenchant among them, noted that the verb form of "experience" was a recent American abomination, attributing the neologism to Henry James's friend William Dean Howells.

REFERENCES

Bloom, Harold. 1984. "Mr. America," *New York Review of Books*, Nov. 22, pp. 19–24.

Crapanzano, Vincent. 1980. *Tuhami: Portrait of a Moroccan.* Chicago: University of Chicago Press.

Dewey, John. 1929. *Experience and Nature.* Chicago: Open Court Publishing Co.

———. 1934. *Art as Experience.* New York: Capricorn Books.

Donoghue, Dennis. 1976. *The Sovereign Ghost.* Berkeley: University of California Press.

Emerson, Ralph Waldo. 1903–4. *The Complete Works of Ralph Waldo Emerson.* ed. Edward W. Emerson. Boston: Houghton, Mifflin.

Feld, Steven. 1982. *Sound and Sentiment: Birds Weeping, Poetics, and Song in Kaluli Expression.* Philadelphia: University of Pennsylvania Press.

Geertz, Clifford. 1976. "From the Natives' Point of View: On the Nature of Anthropological Understanding." In: K. Basso and H. Selby (eds.), *Meaning in Anthropology*, pp. 221–38. Albuquerque: University of New Mexico Press.

Glassie, Henry. 1982. *Passing the Time in Ballymenone.* Philadelphia: University of Pennsylvania Press.

Goffman, Erving. 1967. *Interaction Ritual.* Garden City, N.Y.: Doubleday Anchor.

Lutz, Catherine. 1982. "The Domain of Emotion Words on Ifaluk," *American Ethnologist* 9:113–28.

McDermott, John (ed.). 1967. *The Writings of William James—A Comprehensive Edition.* New York: Random House.

Mencken, H. L. 1919. *The American Language.* New York: Knopf.

Morris, Charles. 1970. *The Pragmatic Movement in American Philosophy.* New York: George Braziller.

Myers, Fred. 1979. "Emotions and the Self," *Ethos* 7:343–70.

Rabinow, Paul. 1977. *Reflections on Fieldwork in Morocco.* Berkeley: University of California Press.

Rose, Dan. 1982. "Occasions and Forms of Anthropological Experience." In: Jay Ruby (ed.), *A Crack in the Mirror: Reflexive Perspectives in Anthropology*, pp. 218–30. Philadelphia: University of Pennsylvania Press.

Schutz, Alfred. 1970. *On Phenomenology and Social Relations*. ed. Herbert R. Wagner. Chicago: University of Chicago Press.

Shorr, Daniel. 1977. *Clearing the Air*. Boston: Houghton Mifflin.

Trilling, Lionel. 1979. *The Opposing Self*. New York: Harcourt Brace Jovanovich.

Turner, Victor W. 1982. *From Ritual to Theater*. New York: Performing Arts Journal Press.

Valery, Paul. 1962. *Oeuvres*. I, Paris. In: Albert William Levi. 1977. "Culture: A Guess at a Riddle," *Cultural Inquiry* 4:308–9.

Williams, Raymond. 1979. *Politics and Letters*. London: New Left Books.

4

Reflexivity
as Evolution in
Thoreau's *Walden*

FREDERICK TURNER

> I would fain say something, not so much concerning
> the Chinese or Sandwich Islanders as you who read
> these pages, who are said to live in New England.
>
> Thoreau, *Walden*

THOREAU, THE ANTHROPOLOGIST OF EXPERIENCE

As Victor Turner pointed out, "experience" is a volatile word, as
hard to contain within a single definition as an incandescent
plasma, yet perhaps as productive if it can be controlled. Its an-
tonyms indicate its range of meanings: text (as in, "Did you read
that in a book or was it a real experience?"); the sociocultural
norm (as in, "My upbringing tells me one thing but all my experience tells me another"); knowledge (as in the French opposition
of *savoir*, to know, and *connaître*, to be acquainted by experience);
naïveté; ignorance; untestedness; innocence; innate ideas. In this
essay I propose to examine what Henry David Thoreau meant by
"experience." It was one of his favorite words, and his thoughts
on it are, I believe, of interest to anthropologists.

In one sense the phrase "anthropology of experience" is a
contradiction in terms. If anthropology is the study of human society and culture, and if experience is first-hand knowledge, untainted by sociocultural givens, then the anthropology of experience is equivalent to "the social life of the solitary," or to "naming
the unnameable." These latter two phrases do have a sort of poetic meaning, despite their paradoxical appearance. It is no coinci-
dence that Thoreau was fond of such ideas: "I have a great deal

of company in my house, especially in the morning, when nobody calls" (*Walden*, p. 148). And: "It is a ridiculous demand which England and America make, that you shall speak so that they shall understand you. Neither man nor toadstools grow so. . . . I fear chiefly lest my expression may not be extra-vagant enough, may not wander far beyond the narrow limits of my daily experience. . . . The volatile truth of our words should continually betray the inadequacy of the residual statement" (pp. 346–47).[1]

It does not stretch the facts, I believe, to describe Thoreau as an early anthropologist of experience, setting out to study the inner being just as his contemporary Lewis Henry Morgan set out to study the outer being. Perhaps we can find a viable conception of the anthropology of experience in the work of a man whose greatest achievement, *Walden*, coincided with the birth of American anthropology. And in so doing we can justify the inclusion of a piece of literary criticism in a volume on anthropology.

For Thoreau, social reality was rooted in, sprang from, and fed on a presocial ground. It was his ambition to discover that ground; or to put it more radically, he wished to speak of how the speakable was grounded in the unspeakable. His great metaphor for the process by which the unspeakable and the presocial give birth to the speakable and social was *cultivation,* whose three senses, the agricultural, the social, and the psychological, he explicitly related. Typically, he was not content to allow the metaphor to remain in the linguistic sphere; besides, he had to dig up two and a half acres of ground (wherein he found several Indian arrowheads, testifying to the past presence of "some extinct nation" [p. 169]) and plant beans. He said that he did it to provide himself with "tropes and expressions" (p. 176), describing himself, like Jesus, as a "parable-maker." He made "the earth say beans rather than grass" (p. 170); he "was determined to know beans" (p. 175). Note the extraordinary reflexiveness of his experience—he was an animal nourished by a crop he was cultivating, which was both an example and a symbol (a use and a mention) of the process of cultivation by which the human race became human; he was a writer whose metaphorical language cultivated his physical activities and rendered matter into meaning; and he was a critic of language who enjoyed pointing out how his own tropes both expressed and exemplified the process of self-cultivation he had embarked on. He was, so to speak, the anthropologist, the object of anthropological study, and the fieldwork all rolled into one. His autobiography, *Walden*, became simultaneously a work of self-description and of self-construction.

If social reality is rooted in a presocial ground, and if that ground is experience, then the most literally fundamental anthropology would be the anthropology of experience, although like Kurt Gödel's critique of axiomatization in mathematics, it would approach the boundaries of its own discipline and be forced to distinguish between truth and legitimate provability within the rules of the system. This is exactly what Thoreau was trying to do:

> I went to the woods because I wished to live deliberately, to front only the essential facts of life, and see if I could not learn what it had to teach, and not, when I came to die, discover that I had not lived. I did not wish to live what was not life, living is so dear; nor did I wish to practice resignation, unless it was quite necessary. I wanted to live deep and suck out all the marrow of life, to live so sturdily and spartan-like as to put to rout all that was not life, to cut a broad swath and shave close, to drive life into a corner, and reduce it to its lowest terms, and, if it proved to be mean, why then to get the whole and genuine meanness of it, and publish its meanness to the world; or if it were sublime, to know it by experience, and be able to give a true account of it in my next excursion. (p. 98)

Significantly, and paradoxically, it was only by envisioning a point of view *outside* life ("when I came to die"; "in my next excursion") that Thoreau was able to conduct his investigation of life itself. Gödel was only able to resolve the famous paradox of his statement, which claimed to be unprovable, by distinguishing from the provably true a kind of truthfulness that was not based on the logic of the system within which the statement was made.

If these paradoxes seem familiar to the anthropological reader, it is probably because they are an isotropic transformation of what is known as the hermeneutic circle, encountered whenever a field researcher settles down to study an alien society (or, for that matter, whenever a newborn baby does the same thing in its own). A society is, among other things, a system of signs, each of which gets its value from its context among the others. If that system were unchanging and incapable of reflexive description and criticism of itself, anthropology (and the education of children within the society) would be impossible, because before any given sign could be understood, other signs, which constitute its only adequate translation, would have to be understood first. It is only because the signs are variable, because the society itself has not "made up its mind" what its signs mean, and is still, through its reflexive genres of ritual, carnival, play, art, and so on, deciding on their meaning, that a chink in the armor of contextual significance is afforded through which an anthropologist (or baby) may crawl. The initiate's mistakes fall within the acceptable range of error for the system, and in the process of successive correction both the initiate and his or her society are reciprocally changed. Education cannot avoid being a test of the very ideology it indoctrinates.

Even the most uninventive and noninnovative "neutral" description of a custom by a native informant—even when that description is not heard by an outsider at all, but is expressed in the context of a secret ritual and heard only by initiates—assumes a point of view that is necessarily, by a Gödelian logic, outside the system it describes and therefore potentially subversive. The mere *statement* of dogma is itself slightly heretical—and is perhaps the very reason why initiation rites are so often secret.

The fact that there is a kind of truth about a system of signs[2] which is distinguishable from correctness within the system, and that the formulation of that truth within the language of the system changes the system, carries exciting implications for anthropology, which Thoreau explored. I shall suggest that the comfortable relativism whereby anthropologists often avoid the clash of different value systems by asserting their incommensurability becomes untenable, and that the old theory of cultural and social evolution receives unexpected support.

I suggested earlier that Thoreau believed experience to be the ground from which social reality springs. Of course, this formulation is not entirely accurate, because for Thoreau experience itself was conditioned by social reality. To press the metaphor, the "ground" itself—as Thoreau, a surveyor by trade, well knew—is provided with cardinal directions, use, beauty, significance, economic value, and even ruins, fertilizers, and buried arrowheads, by the society that inhabits it. So the initial mistaken or partial formulation must be corrected as we pursue our hermeneutic spiral toward mutual intelligibility.

Social reality and experience are not simply in a circular chicken-and-egg relationship, however; or at least the chicken-egg relationship is not what it used to be. The priority of one over the other is no longer a nonsensical concept: wherever we draw the line between the chicken and its ancestral species, at whatever crucial genetic mutation or recombination, we find something that we have legitimately, if nominalistically, defined as not a chicken, laying something that we have legitimately defined as a chicken egg, which will hatch out as an Ur-chicken. So the egg did come first. But we have been forced to resolve an Aristotelian puzzle by means of a Darwinian solution, to invoke transspecific change as an answer to a problem of intraspecific change. The question has been answered at the expense of the system that spawned it.

Thoreau used an almost identical method to resolve the problem of the relationship of experience to social reality.[3] For him, as for his contemporary Morgan, society was continually undergoing a process of evolutionary development—"The civilized man is a more experienced and wiser savage" (p. 45)—and individual experience was the leading edge of that development. Experience was where social institutions were tested (if necessary, to the point of destruction) and where new institutions took their root: "No way of thinking or doing, however ancient, can be trusted without proof. . . . I have yet to hear the first syllable of valuable or even earnest advice from my seniors. . . . Here is life, an experiment to a great extent untried by me; but it does not avail me that they have tried it. If I have any experience which I think valuable, I am sure to reflect that this my mentors said nothing about" (p. 12).

This emphasis on the primacy of experience should not be taken as a belief in "raw sense data" or Lockean "impressions" impinging on the mind's *tabula rasa*. Like Ralph Waldo Emerson and Samuel Taylor Coleridge before him, Thoreau had rejected the positivism of David Hume. He believed that experience was an *activity*, the mind's own active questioning of the world, the inner equivalent of scientific experimentation. His limnological survey of Walden Pond was the objective correlative of his inner quest for understanding. But for him experience was even more than an active quest—it was a creative act of novel synthesis: "I know of no more encouraging fact than the unquestionable ability of man to elevate his life by a conscious endeavor. It is something to be able to paint a particular picture, or to carve a statue, and so to make a few objects beautiful; but it is far more glorious to carve and paint the very atmosphere and medium through which we look, which morally we can do. To affect the quality of the day, that is the highest of arts" (p. 98). Instead of invoking sensory perception as a corrective against social custom, Thoreau asserted that both were dead and passive, and corroborated each other's deadness and passivity, in the absence of the active and volatile force of creative experience. The vicious circle of expectations governing perceptions which in turn confirm expectations, reproducing each other without novelty, was broken by the idea of evolution. The hermeneutic circle became an evolutionary spiral. And experience, in Thoreau's sense, was the locus of both mutation and selective testing.

I propose to explore the anthropological implications of Thoreau's view of experience; first, by discussing Thoreau as an object of anthropological research, as an early anthropologist, and as an explorer of the fundamental myths of anthropology; second, by setting Thoreau's ideas within their historical context and by analyzing his philosophy of experience in the light of its location near the source of pragmatist epistemology; and third, by a close reading of the "melting sandbank" episode in *Walden*.

WALDEN AS ANTHROPOLOGY

If we were anthropologists doing a field study in nineteenth-century New England, we might well have used Thoreau as a gifted native informant. He is a mine of information (usually salted with irony) on Concord customs, crafts, economics, politics, rituals, ideology, fashions, language and dialect, psychology, history, country-city relationships, land-use and architecture, though there are intriguing and significant omissions, such as kinship and sexuality. The latter are significant because we should, as anthropologists, be astonished at a certain remarkable characteristic of the society under consideration, which achieved its intensest form in our native informant; namely, the emphasis placed on the individual person as the fundamental active force in society: not the family, clan, sexual partnership, village, lineage, society, cult, caste, religious organization, guild, union, corporation, lodge, or age cohort. Thoreau avoided family and sex because, we might begin to suspect, family and sex presented to him the greatest immediate threat to personal independence. For him the final moral authority, more so than in any other society we might study, was the individual; and therefore, the central social actions, decisions, and changes must not only be confirmed at the individual level in order to be properly ratified, but preferably must be initiated there as well. "To march to a different drummer" (p. 348) was how Thoreau put it. "Wherever a man goes, men will pursue and paw him with their dirty institutions, and if they can, constrain him to belong to their desperate odd-fellow society. It is true, I might have resisted forcibly with more or less effect, might have run 'amok' against society; but I preferred that society should run 'amok' against me, it being the desperate party" (p. 186).

Of course, further study of the natives would reveal the vestiges and embryos of powerful institutions of collective moral decision. But we also would note that many of the most respectable spokespeople of the social norm (not just hermits like Thoreau) were praising self-reliance and the primacy of individual conscience—Emerson, for instance—and that the prestige of individual conscience outweighed other sources of norms, even when its power was at a disadvantage. Thoreau took positive delight in puncturing such sacred cows as progress, social responsibility, and philanthropy ("the only virtue," he says dryly, "which is sufficiently appreciated by mankind" [p. 82]). Significantly, he was sure of his moral ground; his opponents were on the defensive, not he.

As anthropologists have shown, it is around the most powerful sources of moral authority in a society that the greatest density of ritual, myth, and ideological-orectic symbolism clusters. If ritual, myth, and symbolism have the double function of transmitting and transforming the values of a society, then it is natural that they should adhere to the institutions that are most active and powerful. As anthropologists we are familiar with the rituals and myths of caste, kinship, cult, age or sex cohorts, and so on. Still, when it is in none of these units, but in the individual, that the driving force of society is found, what are the myths, rituals, and symbolisms of that peculiar social institution, the individual person? Can an individual even *have* myths, rituals, and symbolisms? Are they not collective by their very nature? It seems that we have returned to Thoreau's own paradox, of having company when nobody calls.

At this point we must abandon our pose as objective scien-

tists, for whom Thoreau would be at best a gifted native informant, because we are as much in the dark as he was; or rather,
more in the dark because he had trained himself and was a specialist in the anthropology of the individual. We must go back in
time and become his apprentices as he sets out into the wilderness, much as we remember doing ourselves in Borneo or Central
Africa, the Sahara or the tundra; as he builds his house, helped
by the natives; as he lays the economic and caloric groundwork of
his study; and as he settles down to observe his little community
in the woods. The difference is that his is a community of one,
and the researcher and the object of research are identical—
though, after we have followed him awhile, we might ask if they
really are.

With thinking we may be beside ourselves in a sane sense. By a conscious effort of the mind we can stand aloof from actions and consequences; and all things, good and bad, go by us like a torrent. We are
not wholly involved in nature. I may be either the driftwood in the
stream, or Indra in the sky looking down on it. I *may* be affected by a
theatrical exhibition; on the other hand, I may not be affected by an
actual event which appears to concern me much more. I only know myself as a human entity; the scene, so to speak, of thoughts and affections;
and am sensible of a certain doubleness by which I can stand as remote
from myself as from another. However intense my experience, I am conscious of the presence and criticism of a part of me which, as it were, is
not a part of me, but spectator, sharing no experience, but taking note of
it: and that is no more I than it is you. When the play, it may be the
tragedy, of life is over, the spectator goes his way. It was a kind of fiction,
a work of the imagination only, so far as he was concerned. This doubleness may easily make us poor neighbors and friends sometimes. (p. 146)

This extraordinary passage is not only inherently interesting
but it also contains a powerful corrective to many of our most
apparently useful assumptions about human social behavior. If
one can have commerce with oneself, then whenever we describe
social interaction we are leaving out a crucial participant in the
scene if we neglect the other in the self. If we are persuaded of the
truth of Thoreau's analysis, we can no longer assume that people
will follow their own interests, for they may themselves be a
battleground between different perceived interests, or even a little
society of their own, *creating* values and interests where they had
not existed before. The economic model breaks down, for everyone
contains a critic of his or her own values. One of Thoreau's first

acts in *Walden* was to undermine the value and reality claims of the discipline of economics, an act as subversive to the Marxist position as it was to the capitalist position that dominated nineteenth-century Massachusetts. He revealed materialism itself to be the most flimsy of metaphysical constructions.

Of course, Thoreau may have been deceiving himself when he claimed to be able to stand apart from himself and view himself objectively. But if we accept the hypothesis of self-deception, we place ourselves in the embarrassing logical position of having escaped the complications of one explanation by resort to another, still more complicated one. Thoreau supposed only a dynamic doubleness in the self; but self-deception is so problematic a notion that it requires at least three independent actors in the psychological drama: a deceiver, a deceived, and an inner authority that makes the deception necessary. Further, self-deception requires an outside source of absolute truth in order that we can assert that the "deception," by contrast with the truth, is indeed a deception. Not that Thoreau would have denied the possibility of self-deception; rather, self-deception begs even more metaphysical questions than genuine self-knowledge. If we wish to deny the possibility of two actors within the self, it will not do to assert that there are three *pretending* to be two!

Two fascinating questions open up if we accept that the "anthropologist of the self" can constitute a little society, composed of the self as known and the self as knower: What are the relations between knower and known *over time*? What are the rituals, myths, and symbols of this little society? Thoreau explored both questions.

The question of time takes us to the heart of Thoreau's discoveries. He saw at once that no study of experience can avoid being simultaneously a study of the present moment and of universal time in general. The instant the self-as-knower becomes part of the past and of the contents of memory, it becomes accessible to being known. A new self-as-knower, whose objects of knowledge now include the old self-as-knower, thus springs into being. The present moment is constituted by the completion of this cycle. Self-knowledge is a constant process of transformation of container into contents and of generation of a new container; it is a continually expanding mandala whose leading edge is the self-as-knower and whose contents is the self-as-known.

The paradox of the Laplace calculator, which contains a record of all the information in the world and can therefore accurately predict future events, is that it must be able to predict what will occur as a result of the predictions it has made. Or to put the same thing in different terms, it must include as part of the information it contains a complete account of its own construction, records, and process of calculation. The paradox is resolved only by the reflection that the universe itself is such a calculator, performing its calculations at a rate that constitutes the rate of time—that is, as fast as possible—announcing its predictions in the form of the enactment as real events, and expanding just fast enough to accommodate the new "wiring" it requires for the increased volume of calculation.

This mechanistic account gives a fair idea, I believe, of what Thoreau and Emerson meant by "nature," if we may add that the human self was for them part of the "new wiring" that the universe must add to itself in order to keep up with its own self-comprehension, and that the accumulation of self-comprehension in general was what was meant by God. A few quotations will give the flavor:

... at any moment of the day or night, I have been anxious to improve the nick of time, and notch it on my stick too; to stand on the meeting of two eternities, the past and future, which is precisely the present moment; to toe that line. You will pardon some obscurities, for there are more secrets in my trade than in most men's, and yet not voluntarily kept, but inseparable from its very nature. (p. 20)

For many years I was self-appointed inspector of snow storms and rain storms, and did my duty faithfully. . . . (p. 21)

It is true, I never assisted the sun materially in his rising, but doubt not, it was of the last importance only to be present at it. (p. 20)

There were times when I could not afford to sacrifice the bloom of the present moment to do any work, whether of the head or hands. I love a broad margin to my life. Sometimes . . . I was reminded of the lapse of time. I grew in those seasons like the corn in the night. . . . They were not time subtracted from my life, but so much over and above my usual allowance. I realized what the orientals mean by contemplation and the forsaking of works. For the most part, I minded not how the hours went. The day advanced as if to light some work of mine. . . . My days were not days of the week, bearing the stamp of any heathen diety, nor were they minced into hours and fretted by the ticking of a clock: for I lived like the Puri Indians, of whom it is said that "for yesterday, today, and tomorrow they have only one word, and they express the variety of meaning by pointing backward for yesterday, forward for today, and overhead for the passing day." (pp. 121–22)

God himself culminates in the present moment, and will never be more divine in the lapse of all the ages. (p. 105)

"So soul," continues the Hindoo philosopher, "from the circumstances in which it is placed, makes its own character, until the truth is revealed to it by some holy teacher, and then it knows itself to be Brahma." (p. 104)

Thus Thoreau discovered in the relations between knower and known, when the same person is both, a mystical conception of the human experience of time that intimately connects it with the evolutionary process of nature as a whole. "Frame," or "reflexivity," and "flow" are here identical. The distance between the knower and the known is the distance the universe expands during the present moment.

The second question, of the rituals, symbols, and myths of *Walden*, is easy to answer. The very activity of contemplation was Thoreau's central ritual. Its participants were the two sides of the self. To embody and objectify that activity he borrowed or adapted rituals from societies whose active unit was larger than the self: the "first-fruits" ritual of the Mucclasse Indians, in which they burned their domestic implements at a certain time each year, fasted, and then kindled new fire (p. 74); the fifty-two-year purification of the Mexican Indians (p. 75); the ritual bath of "King Tching-thang" (p. 96); and so on. Like his contemporary Herman Melville, he rifled the new ethnographic riches of an expanding cultural world for materials to build a vital American syncretism.

Thoreau drew his major symbols from the Concord Woods and from his own way of life: the cycle of the seasons, the sacramental bean field, the cabin he built over his head, the melting sandbank (to which I shall return), and above all the pond itself, which he called "earth's eye" (p. 202) and which became a complex symbol of his individual self. His long discussion of the color of the pond's water (pp. 191–93) is at once a piece of careful scientific observation and a lofty, mystical allegory of the nature of the soul. The doubleness of its color, which he attributed to the dialectical relation of earth and sky, is the objective correlative of the doubleness of the soul.

Walden itself is the great mythic text of Thoreau's cult of the individual soul. The genre most fitted to such a cult is autobiography, and Thoreau was not the only American to achieve a masterpiece in that genre.[4] The composition of *Walden*, which took place over a period of seven or eight years, was the central activity of the life that the book describes. *Walden* is not a retrospective memoir but a celebration of a life as lived, a life that included the composition of the book. Again, in the very circumstances of its creation, the Walden myth remains profoundly reflexive while at the same time immersed in the flow of being. Thoreau's description of night fishing on the pond, where his meditations were suddenly brought back to reality by the jerk of a fish on the line, beautifully catches this reconciliation: "It was very queer, especially in dark nights, when your thoughts had wandered to vast and cosmogonal themes in other spheres, to feel this faint jerk, which came to interrupt your dreams and link you to nature again. It seemed as if I might next cast my line upward into the air, as well as downward into this element which was scarcely more dense. Thus I caught two fishes as it were with one hook" (p. 190).

THOREAU AND THE BIRTH OF AMERICAN ANTHROPOLOGY

As a systematic field of study, the discipline of anthropology arose in Europe and America during the nineteenth century. Of course, there were already Ancient Greek, Moslem, European, Indian, Chinese, and Japanese travelers' tales and accounts of "barbarian" customs; but it took a peculiar kind of civilization to produce anthropology proper. Oddly enough, that fact is rather embarrassing to anthropologists, for it suggests a uniqueness in Western civilization that appears to contradict the institutional ideology of the field—that all societies are comparable and that values are culturally relative. However noble that prejudice—and it is noble, for it supports a generous and open-minded humanism—if it is in conflict with the truth it ought to be corrected. European and American civilization is uniquely privileged in having produced, paradoxically, the discipline which asserts that no society is uniquely privileged. The problem can only be escaped by denying the raison d'être of anthropology, which is that anthropology actually gives a better account of a society to the rest of the world than that society can, unaided, give of itself; or by denying the plain fact that the discipline of anthropology is an institution of Western society. Until other societies learned from the West the principles and techniques of the field, Western civilization possessed, in addition to the ethnocentric point of view it shared with other cultures, a unique, if however imperfect and partial, point of view that could see itself as one of a number of cultures whose values made sense in their own terms but not necessarily in others'. Of course, every society is unique in its own way. But the realization of that fact by the West gave it an asymmetrical position of epistemological superiority, a reflexive capacity not shared by other societies.

To offer an absurd analogy, it's as if all languages except English were in the beginning mutually untranslatable and only became accessible to each other via the universal skeleton key of the English language. The great dangers of such thinking are obvious, but they should not discourage us from facing its logic. What I am suggesting is that the dangers may be exorcised by a study of the cultural origins of those modes of thought that made anthropology possible. In such a study Thoreau would figure as an interesting litmus test, in one sense, and as a pioneer, in another.

The anthropology of experience may be a new topic in current circles, but I contend that it may also be at the very root of the discipline: that only when we learned how to be harmoniously and creatively alienated from ourselves were we able to understand the ideas of cultural aliens. The individualistic artistic and scientific genres of Western society[5] are to ritual what ritual is to the ordinary social life of a culture, and they sometimes achieve a separation from that ordinary life that is sufficient to permit us to step over imaginatively into the margins of an entirely different culture. Once the step has been taken, a bridge can be built. That bridge is anthropology.

Thoreau stood at that point in American intellectual history when the prerequisites for the birth of anthropology had begun to fall into place. Through immigration, economic expansion, the influence of Europe, and forces inherent in its own constitution, the narrow puritanism of New England had given way among the intellectuals to a variety of lofty theisms, Swedenborgianism, pantheism, Fourierism, scientific rationalism, and to the romantic religion of Nature. These forces cohered into the movement known as transcendentalism, whose leading light was Emerson. At the same time, an extraordinary cultural renaissance was underway: in literature alone, Thoreau's contemporaries included Emily Dickinson, Herman Melville, Henry Adams, and Edgar Allan Poe; Richard Henry Dana was his classmate at Harvard; he knew Walt Whitman, Nathaniel Hawthorne, and Henry James the elder, the Swedenborgian theologian and father of William and Henry; and one of his closest friends was Emerson.

Certain common qualities mark the work of these very different writers: a robust individualism, an ebullient and optimistic relativism, a sturdy confidence in the possibility of successful syncretism, introspection, a lively interest in and friendship for the sciences, a fascination with religion, and a mystical bent. It was in this fertile soil that American anthropology put down its roots: far enough away from the narrow ethnocentrism of the Pilgrim Fathers, yet still new enough to the wide world to encourage intense curiosity about other cultures; in touch, through the whalers and traders of New England, with the exotic lands of the Orient and the "primitives" that Melville celebrated in *Typee* and *Omoo*, but still nourished by the great classical tradition of Greek and Latin learning preserved and transmitted at Harvard and the old liberal arts colleges. The young Lewis Henry Morgan, who was educated at Union College, transformed his alumni fraternity from the neoclassical "Gordian Knot," which followed the ancient Greeks, into "The Grand Order of the Iroquois," which interpreted Lakes Indian customs in terms of the classical virtues. Thus began Morgan's lifelong interest in the Indians (see Resek 1960:23).

For the first time since the Renaissance, when the societies of pagan antiquity had come to serve as models in the initiation of the elite, the West had grasped alien cultures as being possibly exemplary or superior to its own. The profound Orientalizing of our poetry, architecture, religion, and cuisine, and our attempt to imitate imagined Amerindian virtues in our personal relations, dress, and recreation, is a consequence of this remarkable nineteenth-century movement. Castaneda's Don Juan has a New England ancestry.

Thoreau cited Gookin, who was the superintendent of the Indians subject to the Massachusetts Colony in 1674, on the comfort, convenience, and economy of Indian architecture, and contrasted their domestic economy favorably with that of his compatriots: "In the savage state every family owns a shelter as good as the best, and sufficient for its coarser and simpler wants; but I think that I speak within bounds when I say that, though the birds of the air have their nests, and the foxes their holes, and the savages their wigwams, in modern civilized society not more than one half the families own a shelter" (p. 34). As we can see from this passage Thoreau, like Morgan, implicitly assumed that contemporary savages lived as did our own ancestors, and that through an evolutionary process the "savages" arose from the brutes and civilized humans from the savage. Thus, to go "back," as Thoreau claimed to do, to the economic condition of the savage, in search of the place where we took our false turning, is the phylogenetic equivalent of his ontogenetic attempt to discover the roots of his personal experience. Thoreau was being historically as well as personally reflexive; just as he sought the foundations of his own experience, he was also seeking the foundations of the experience of his culture. What I am arguing here is that however faulty Thoreau's theory of cultural evolution may have been, he was right in assuming that the cultural journey cannot properly take place without the personal one. Except ye become as a little child, ye shall not enter the kingdom of another culture.

If it is true that some form of personal voyage of self-discovery must accompany any genuine understanding of another culture, then we may have the beginnings of an explanation for the uniqueness of the West in having generated an anthropological tradition. Perhaps it was precisely the contraction of the unit of social initiative to the individual that was essential to the early development of anthropology; and perhaps it was only in the West that this contraction took place. One might even speculate about the roles of democracy and Protestantism in encouraging this contraction: democracy, because ideally the fundamental act of political decision is the individual vote; and Protestantism—especially Puritanism—because of its emphasis on the personal encounter with God and the crucial role of individual conversion in the salvation of the soul.

In this light the central agon of the anthropological myth becomes much more intelligible. More than in other sciences whose myth often involves teamwork, anthropologists are alone, almost marooned or shipwrecked in the culture they study. They undergo, in the myth, an experience of personal conversion that involves culture shock, self-confrontation, a profound alienation from their own culture, a sense of being only a child in their newly adopted culture, an initiation into its mysteries, and an acceptance by it. Eventually, the anthropologist becomes that culture's spokesperson, interpreter, and protector against the culture from which he or she originally came. (Actually, the myth works better for female anthropologists, who by virtue of their sex are already somewhat marginal in their own society.) The personal memoirs of such anthropologists as Malinowski do, I believe, bear out this analysis.

Essential to this myth is the aloneness of the researcher. The individual person is the largest social unit within which the experience of conversion can take place, and it is only that conversion which enables a student of another culture to interpret between it and his or her own. This myth, I believe, is in process of changing, partly through the work of Victor Turner and Richard Schechner, among others, who have attempted to enlarge the unit of conversion to the size of a small group of persons by reproducing alien rituals through dramatic means (see Turner 1979). If successful, the results should surpass the achievements of the individual researcher by the power of the number in the group, although individual self-confrontation becomes even more crucial for the success of the project. Schechner's almost psychoanalytic rehearsal process is perhaps designed to bring about the necessary personal crisis. Although autobiographical, dramatic, and anthropological genres seem far apart, they possess deep affinities.

The birth of American anthropology required not only an appropriate psychosocial preparation but also an appropriate philosophical one. Here, again, we find Thoreau in attendance at the birth, wittingly or not.

American pragmatism took its origins in the encounter between British empiricism, native Yankee technical know-how, transcendentalism, and Kantian epistemology. Less passive in its notion of truth than empiricism, pragmatism had benefited from America's experience of having recently transformed its own physical environment; that is, what is the case is not only what one perceives but also what one does. From transcendentalism came a dynamic notion of Nature and a confidence in the match between the natural order and human understanding. As Thoreau put it, "The universe constantly and obediently answers to our conceptions; whether we travel fast or slow, the track is laid for us. Let us spend our lives in conceiving then" (p. 105). From Kant came the idea that the categories of our perception cooperate in the generation of the concrete world and that certain a prioris must be synthetic.

Thoreau was already, I believe, a pragmatist in many senses. Like them he believed the truth to be provisional and volatile in its essence, dependent on practice for its validation. For him experience was the inner form of *experiment,* the active "frisking" of Nature for answers, by which alone truth is discovered. Like Peirce, Thoreau saw the world as a system of mutually validating signs: "But while we are confined to books, though the most select and classic, and read only particular written languages, which are themselves but dialects and provincial, we are in danger of forgetting the language which all things and events speak without metaphor, and which alone is copious and standard. Much is published, but little printed" (p. 121). From here we might trace the development of semiological theory through Peirce and European phenomenology and into European anthropology, where it crops up, for instance, in Claude Lévi-Strauss's understanding of the world as text.

More important still was the contribution of pragmatist ideas to anthropological *method.* The participant-observer, who alters the system studied and is reciprocally altered by it, whose truths are what works best, and who penetrates the hermeneutic circle by a process of successive approximation and correction, is most comfortably and consistently accommodated within a philosophically pragmatist framework. Other philosophical systems allow for anthropological method, but only with difficulty, and they do not encourage it as pragmatism does. Thoreau impressionistically described the method: "The intellect is a cleaver; it discerns and rifts its way into the secrets of things. . . . My head is hands and feet. I feel all my best faculties concentrated in it. My instinct tells me that my head is an organ for burrowing, as some creatures use their snout and fore-paws, and with it I would mine and burrow my way through these hills. I think that the richest vein is somewhere hereabouts; so by the divining rod and thin rising vapors I judge; and here I will begin to mine" (p. 106). Experience, for Thoreau and the pragmatists, is truth. If they are right, then the anthropology of experience is the anthropology of truth.

THE SAND BANK

In the penultimate chapter of *Walden*, entitled "Spring," Thoreau wrote an extraordinary description of a bank of sand in a railroad cutting as it thawed out in the spring sunshine—a description that is also an extended metaphor of the evolution of the universe, of the creative evolution of human experience, and of linguistic expression as a continuation of that evolution.

The chapter begins with a detailed, scientifically precise description of the thawing sand and clay as they formed their complex patterns of deposition. Even the fact that the phenomenon occurred in a railroad cutting is significant. Human invention (of which the railroad was, for Thoreau, the obvious example) is an extension of the creative process of nature. Not only must we pay attention to the content of the passage, but to its form as well:

Innumerable little streams overlap and interlace one with another, exhibiting a sort of hybrid product, which obeys half way the law of currents, and half way that of vegetation. As it flows it takes the form of sappy leaves or vines, making heaps of pulpy sprays a foot or more in depth, and resembling, as you look down on them, the laciniated lobed and imbricated thalluses of some lichens; or you are reminded of coral, of leopards' paws or birds' feet, of brains or lungs or bowels, and excrements of all kinds. It is a truly *grotesque* vegetation, whose forms and color we see imitated in bronze, a sort of architectural foliage more ancient and typical than acanthus, chiccory, ivy, vine, or any vegetable leaves. . . . (p. 326)

The intensity of perception is almost hypnotic; Thoreau has reminded us of our own perceiving selves ("as you look down on them," "you are reminded"). The sequence of images follows the course of evolution, from the physical laws of currents, through the vegetable kingdom and into the animal kingdom of birds' feet and leopards' paws, concluding with the products of human art. And there is a subtle playing with the evolution of language itself, with the etymological relations of "overlap" with "lobed," "interlace" with "laciniated," with the origin of the artistic word "grotesque" in the natural "grotto" or cave, and with the phonological relations of the labial consonants *p, b, f, v.*

As the passage continues, these implicit meanings, through the process of feedback between experience and contemplation, become explicit and put out leaves of exegesis as rich and various as the leaves of multicolored mud and sand which burst out of the frozen inanimate mass of the bank. The suggestion of natural evolution implicit in the sequence of images becomes explicit:

What makes this sand foliage remarkable is its springing into existence thus suddenly. When I see on the one side the inert bank,—for the sun acts on one side first,—and on the other this luxuriant foliage, the creation of an hour, I am affected as if in a peculiar sense I stood in the laboratory of the Artist who made the world and me,—had come to where he was still at work, sporting on this bank, and with excess of energy strewing his fresh designs about.... You find thus in the very sands an anticipation of the vegetable leaf. No wonder that the earth expresses itself outwardly in leaves, it so labors with the idea inwardly. The atoms have learned this law, and are pregnant by it. (p. 327)

Next, the etymological relations themselves become explicit. Thoreau took up the phonological connection of *leaves, labor,* and *law,* and developed it in his own exfoliating language:

Internally, whether in the globe or animal body, it is a moist thick *lobe,* a word especially applicable to the liver and lungs and the *leaves* of fat, (λειβω, *labor, lapsus,* to flow or slip downward, a lapsing; λοβος, globus, lobe, globe; also lap, flap, and many other words,) *externally* a dry thin *leaf,* even as the *f* and *v* are a pressed and dried *b*. The radicals of *lobe* are *lb,* the soft mass of the *b* (single lobed, or *B,* double lobed) with a liquid *l* behind it pressing it forward. In globe, *glb,* the guttural *g* adds to the meaning the capacity of the throat. The feathers and wings of birds are still drier and thinner leaves. Thus, also, you pass from the lumpish grub in the earth to the airy and fluttering butterfly. The very globe continually transcends and translates itself, and becomes winged in its orbit. (p. 328)

Here, as in the Bean Field passage, analysis reveals a remarkable layering of reflexivity. In a language which, through his own metaphorical usage, evolved as he employed it and *because* he employed it, Thoreau described the evolution of language using as a metaphor the evolutionary process of the natural world—of which linguistic evolution is both a part and a reflection—here evoked through the description, in this very language, of an experience of natural productiveness on a spring morning. The process of thought in the passage, turning back on itself repeatedly, in a helical fashion, adds another depth to the triple pun on "spring."

The chapter continues with a minute description of the rivulets of liquid clay and sand:

If you look closely you observe that first there pushes forward from the thawing mass a stream of softened sand with a drop-like point, like the ball of a finger, feeling its way slowly and blindly downwards, until at last with more heat and moisture, as the sun gets higher, the most fluid portion, in its effort to obey the law to which the most inert also yields, separates from the latter and forms for itself a meandering channel or artery within that, in which is seen a little silvery stream glancing like lightning from one stage of pulpy leaves or branches to another, and ever and anon swallowed up in the sand. It is wonderful how rapidly yet perfectly the sand organizes itself as it flows, using the best material its mass affords to form the sharp edges of its channel. (p. 328)

This careful observation—again with its reminder of the process of observation itself, "if you look closely"—is not merely an enumeration of particulars but a graphic account of a universal creative process. These particulars are the "minute particulars" in which William Blake discovered the universal. There is, in fact, an uncanny resemblance between Thoreau's conception of the creative process and Blake's. In *The Marriage of Heaven and Hell*, one of the "Memorable Fancies" describes creation as the work of demons who melt the interior of their cave, extracting precious metals, and then cast the molten fluids out into the abyss, where they take what wonderful shapes they will. Thoreau, like Blake, insisted that no mold is needed, for the solidifying liquid contains in its own nature a perfectly adequate set of formal principles: "You may melt your metals and cast them into the most beautiful moulds you can; they will never excite me like the forms which this molten earth flows out into" (*Walden*, p. 330). The silvery icicles that Coleridge described at the end of "Frost at Midnight" constitute a similar image of the nature of creativity.

What principles can be derived from Thoreau's account of the thawing sand? The first is that the past of a given flow of events, combined with its texture, are the only constraints needed to produce more and more elaborate forms of existence. No Aristotelian Final Cause is required to draw out these shapes: they are *expressed*, pressed out, not drawn forth or externally molded. The creative process needs no metaphysical grounding except itself. Like the twigs of a tree, historical sequences propagate themselves outward into the future, drawing this sustenance from their past. One of the most striking images in Darwin's *Origin of Species* is the tree of reproductive descent. Here, that tree, the tree of life, is identical to the tree of knowledge.

The second principle is that the creative process is dialectical,

being composed of an active energy, what Blake calls "the Pro-
lific"—in Thoreau's image, the glittering lightning-like stream
of water—and an inert material deposit, Blake's "Devourer"—
here imaged as the clotted sand which both retards and records
the flow of energy, and by periodically damming it up provides it
with variation and rhythm. The third principle is that creation
always involves a sort of paradox of self-transcendence—the sand
continually overwhelms itself, the globe "transcends and translates" itself—like the mysterious paradoxes of self-awareness discussed earlier.

The fourth principle is that our human experience is not a
passive process but an active and creative one. Our very bodies,
our sense organs, are an elaboration of the same playful creative
force, as Thoreau suggested: "What is man but a mass of thawing
clay? The ball of the human finger is but a drop congealed. . . . Is
not the hand a spreading *palm* leaf with its lobes and veins? The
ear may be regarded, fancifully, as a lichen, *umbilicaria,* on the
side of the head, with its lobe or drop. The lip—labium, from
labor—laps or lapses from the sides of the cavernous mouth. The
nose is a manifest congealed drop or stalactie" (p.329). Thoreau's
century was too dedicated to allow him to extend his metaphor to
its obvious genital conclusion, but he had it in mind: ". . . more
heat or other *genial* influences would have caused it to flow yet
farther" (p. 329; italics added); "Who knows what the human
body would expand and flow out into under a more genial
heaven" (p. 329).

"Thus it seemed that this one hillside illustrated the principle
of all the operations of Nature. The Maker of this earth but
patented a leaf. What Champollion [the decoder of the Rosetta
Stone] will decipher this hieroglyphic for us, that we may turn
over a new leaf at last?" (p. 329). For Thoreau, moral and practical action ("turning over a new leaf") could not be detached from
the active discovery and probing of Nature ("turning over a new
leaf") and the reading and interpretation of the book of Nature
("turning over a new leaf"). He not only associated these ideas,
he gave them the same words. Here we find an interpretation for
"experience" that perhaps adequately contains the many meanings listed at the beginning of this paper. When we are truly experiencing we are growing by a reflexive process in which we are
only separated by our consciousness from nature in order to share
in nature's own creative process of self-transcendence.

NOTES

1. Thoreau wrote these words sometime between 1846 and 1854, which makes them almost exactly contemporaneous with the composition between 1843 and 1851 of Lewis Henry Morgan's *League of the Ho-de-no-sau-nee or Iroquois.*

2. Charles Sanders Peirce described the world as a system of signs and defined the sense of a symbol as its translation into another symbol. The father of anthropological hermeneutics, Peirce was a member of the same circle of Harvard intellectuals that had included Thoreau. Clearly, Thoreau is of historical, as well as theoretical, interest to anthropology.

3. Again, a historical note dramatizes the progress of the dialectic: *The Origin of Species* (1859) was published five years after *Walden.* Darwin could not have read *Walden;* but both Darwin and Thoreau were naturalists and both were responding to the same logical questions and the same evidence from early ethnography and biology. Thoreau knew Darwin's work and quoted him on the Indians of Tierra del Fuego (*Walden,* p. 15).

4. Benjamin Franklin, Henry Adams, and Thoreau were the originators of a great tradition, in which we also find modern poets like John Berryman, Robert Lowell, and Sylvia Plath, and novelists like Robert Pirsig, Saul Bellow, and Norman Mailer.

5. It may seem odd to speak of contemporary Western scientific genres as "individualistic," but a comparison between the institutionalized irreverence and originality of modern research and the authoritarian conformism of ancient science, which Francis Bacon took to task, would make the point clear. Galileo was less the victim of the church than of his old-science colleagues.

REFERENCES

Emerson, Ralph Waldo. 1921. *Essays.* Boston and New York: Houghton Mifflin.

Gunn, Giles (ed.). 1974. *Henry James, Senior.* Chicago: American Library.

Harding, W., and C. Bode. 1958. *The Correspondence of Henry David Thoreau.* New York: New York University Press.

McIntosh, James. 1974. *Thoreau as Romantic Naturalist.* Ithaca, N.Y.: Cornell University Press.

Miller, Perry. 1958. *Consciousness in Concord.* Boston: Riverside, Houghton Mifflin.

Morgan, Lewis Henry. 1904. *League of the Ho-de-no-sau-nee or Iroquois.* New York: Dodd, Mead. (First published in 1851.)

Paul, Sherman. 1958. *The Shores of America: Thoreau's Inward Exploration.* Urbana: University of Illinois Press.

Resek, Carl. 1960. *Lewis Henry Morgan, American Scholar.* Chicago: University of Chicago Press.

Sayre, Robert F. 1977. *Thoreau and the American Indians.* Princeton, N.J.: Princeton University Press.

Thoreau, Henry David. 1969. *Walden.* Columbus, Ohio: Merrill. (First published in 1854.)

Turner, Victor W. 1979. "Dramatic Ritual/Ritual Drama," *Kenyon Review* (n.s.) 2 (Summer): 3.

PART TWO

Narrative

5

Ilongot Hunting
as Story
and Experience

RENATO ROSALDO

Although limited in knowledge and capable of distorting our motives, we usually offer accounts of why we do what we do. These
accounts of intentions, plans, or the meaning of experience usually
shape our conduct. Notions about witchcraft, for example, can
profoundly influence human lives, leading one person to be
burned at the stake and another to endure an ordeal of exorcism.
Other cultural conceptions, ranging from ideas about mothering
to the lethal myths toted by cold warriors can prove similarly consequential. In more mundane ways we can reasonably suppose
that cattle herders know a good deal about bovine lifeways. This
point, of course, has not been lost on gifted ethnographers who,
among other things, privilege actors' interpretations of their own
conduct. Think of E. E. Evans-Prichard nuancing Nuer *kwoth* or
cieng, Victor Turner explicating Ndembu reflections on ritual, or
Clifford Geertz thickly describing Balinese deep play. In apprais-
ing unfamiliar forms of life, we need to know how cultural conceptions inform and thereby describe, in that peculiar circularity of
the social construction of reality, people's commonsense worlds.

Sketching reasons for studying the ways people interpret their
lives provides a prelude for my theme of extending anthropological
wisdom about native categories and cultural patterns. By considering two current notions of ethnographic description, ethnoscientific models of emic analysis and detailed monographs as versions
of realism, we can ask how anthropologists should represent other
people's lives. Despite their proven strengths, I shall argue in
what follows that ethnoscience and ethnographic realism share a
specific limitation. Neither approach makes central the stories

people tell themselves about themselves, and this crucial omission robs a certain human significance from anthropological accounts. Ethnographers can learn much about meaningful action by listening to storytellers as they depict their own lives.

After sketching two approaches to ethnography, my discussion will turn from ethnographic to novelistic realism, with a view to indicating certain insights its narrative forms can offer for ethnographic analysis. Rather than seeing human activities unfold through such programmed sequences as the daily round, the annual cycle, or the life cycle, novelists' narratives often play on temporal duraton to create a suspense-laden sense of meaningful action in the world. In moving from one version of realism to another, from viewing human action guided by culturally appropriate expectations to telling spellbinding tales about encountering the unexpected, I will attempt to show how narrative can provide a particularly rich source of knowledge about the significance people find in their workaday lives. Such narratives often reveal more about what can make life worth living than about how it is routinely lived. Indigenous storytellers have both deep affinities with and striking differences from realist novelists.

Therefore, I go on to peruse three Ilongot hunting stories. Unelaborated yet well formed, the first shows why such texts (for outsiders, seemingly cryptic and elliptical) must be read in the context of everyday life. These minimalist narratives assume, indeed are embedded within, the depth and range of knowledge that people whose biographies significantly overlap can share. More elaborated than the first, both remaining tales create suspense through the artful manipulation of time. Elicited by an ethnographer and told by a gifted storyteller, the second tale celebrates the way that hunters can glory in their improvised responses to unexpected life-threatening encounters. When a huntsman survives such dangers, he can tell his companions a moving story about himself as the main protagonist. The third tale displays the way that narrative time can create suspense by holding in tension the finite duration of human tasks and the ever-present human vulnerability to fatal interruption. This spontaneously told myth suggests that the significance Ilongot men seek in hunting derives more from cultural notions about what makes a story (and lived experience) compelling than from the routine subsistence techniques usually portrayed in ethnographic realism.

Ethnoscience provides the initial frame. If you happen to find yourself among the Ilongots, some 3,500 hunters and swidden horticulturalists in the hills of northern Luzon, Philippines, begin by asking (in the native language, to be sure) about the kinds of *'adiwar*, "seeking, looking for, or foraging." The answer should include at least *la'ub*, a collective hunt in which dogs flush game toward a group of huntsmen waiting in semicircular ambush, and *'auduk*, a stalking procedure in which a single man moves slowly, now starting, now stopping, hoping either to encounter or be encountered by a wild pig or deer. Further refinements require asking whether people hunt at night (*'integ*), by waiting near an acorn tree (*'alisang*), or in a collective hunt without dogs (*tuyuk*). More subtle distinctions further reward the person who asks about how the meat will be prepared and distributed.[1]

Taxonomic in design, this analysis reveals certain distinctions natives make in referring to their workaday world. Finding meaning here involves disambiguation through a process of sorting out levels of contrast, discovering the components that discriminate among terms, and pinning the right noun to the right thing in the world. Although easy to parody, the ethnoscientific enterprise should not be dismissed because huntsmen, after all, do distinguish among their various modes of catching game. Such exercises teach us to be more systematic in attending to how people classify (and perhaps act differentially toward) the world around them.

Consider another option, one less taxonomic and more monographic. Imagine yourself as the camera's eye, or perhaps more prosaically as the video tape machine, straddled on the native's shoulders alongside shades of Malinowski in his Trobriand canoe. Now, simply describe the hunt as it actually happens. Like the documentary or the grandchild of Balzac's realism, the task posed by ethnographic realism requires that we report the unadorned detailed truth about the hunt. Rather than fully reproducing such a realistic description here, let me sketch what a more fine-grained account could include.

Two men sit by the hearth talking in low tones. One of them says, "Tawad saw deer tracks yesterday by the Ma'ni." Eventually one of the men calls across the river, inviting his neighbors to join a collective hunt with dogs. The huntsmen plan where to position themselves, often describing the same locations in different terms (one says down from a rock and the other says up from the source of a stream), in part to be accurate and in part to show off their knowledge of the landscape. Then the hunters quietly walk to the ambush, usually, as Ilongot drawings indicate and my observations confirm, positioning themselves in a semicircle on a hilltop.

The omniscient narrator (i.e., the self-effacing ethnographer who has pieced together repeated observations and reports of similar events) now shifts to the man with the dogs. Shouting aloud, "uh, ah, ah, ah," he drives the dogs toward the waiting hunters, hoping to flush out the game.

In the meantime, back at the ambush, the huntsmen sit still and silent. They already have cut the underbrush, making a blind and spreading their scent on either side of themselves. The rest is hope: Will a wild pig or deer be driven toward the waiting hunter? Will the hunter have a clear shot at the game? And will the shot hit its target? With luck, then, the huntsmen return home with game to butcher and redistribute.

This documentary account derives from meticulous observation in which the ethnographic gaze exercises exhaustive surveillance over its human subjects. The ethnographer has repeatedly asked Ilongots, "What are you doing now?" This procedure, let us call it "doing good ethnography," purportedly produces a true representation of Ilongot hunting. Moreover, in the final written version the (usually unacknowledged) conventions of realism convey a convincing sense of accuracy by using telling details and careful depictions of settings.

Although ethnographic realism portrays particular local environmental niches, its account of the hunt, usually a composite amalgam of repeated observations and interviews, attempts to depict an event at once specific to and general within a single form of life. Such accounts weave together disparate materials, trusting that the design they reveal represents the universal form of Ilongot hunting rather than the idiosyncratic vicissitudes of any hunt in particular. Concerned with the Ilongot hunt as a cultural pattern, this genre captures neither the huntsman's elation in particular chases nor his fear of dangerous encounters. Thus, for example, the time Tawad accidently gashed his favorite hunting dog and abandoned the chase in utter dejection becomes conspicuous only by its absence in ethnographic realism. A more novelistic version of realism, however, better enables us to speak about the characteristic suspense of hunting.

Above all, novelists' fictions attempt to portray the fascination of particular (possible rather than actual) hunts. If ethnographers use hunts to illustrate cultural patterns and social relations, realistic novelists—at least those of James Fenimore Cooper's stripe, as we shall see in a moment—care more about revealing character and conveying why huntsmen find the chase so compelling. In other words, such novels seek out movement and drama, risk and suspense, rather than the workaday routines involved in making a living.

These considerations can be developed more fully by perusing an extended passage from Cooper's *The Pioneers* (1879), with a view to showing how he orients the reader and conveys the excitement of the chase. The following passage begins with Natty, the Leather-Stocking, as he sits in his canoe in full view of his hounds as they try to chase down a buck:

> "I knowed it—I knowed it!" cried Natty, when both deer and hounds were in full view; "the buck has gone by them with the wind, and it has been too much for the poor rogues; but I must break them of these tricks, or they'll give me a deal of trouble. He-ere, he-ere—shore with you, rascals—shore with you—with ye? O! off with you, old Hector, or I'll hatchel your hide with my ramrod when I get ye."
>
> The dogs knew their master's voice, and after swimming in a circle, as if reluctant to give over the chase, and yet afraid to persevere, they finally obeyed, and returned to the land, where they filled the air with their cries.
>
> In the meantime the deer, urged by his fears, had swum over half the distance between the shore and the boats, before his terror permitted him to see the new danger. But at the sounds of Natty's voice, he turned short in his course, and for a few moments seemed about to rush back again, and brave the dogs. His retreat in this direction was, however, effectively cut off, and turning a second time, he urged his course obliquely for the centre of the lake, with an intention of landing on the western shore. As the buck swam by the fishermen, raising his nose high into the air, curling the water before his slim neck like the beak of a galley, the Leather-Stocking began to sit very uneasy in his canoe. (p. 305)

The passage opens with the ultimate mimetic technique.[2] Presumably—at least in this possible world—the text repeats Natty's words precisely as they were said. The reader's conviction that these words have been transcribed verbatim only deepens through noticing the ungrammatical "I knowed it," the spontaneous exclamation "O!" and the shout directly addressed to the dog "old Hector." When Cooper's passage shifts to description, the narrator initially attends to the dogs as they finally follow their master's command and regroup on the shore. Using the "meanwhile" clause, the narrator then draws our attention to the deer. In the telling's peculiar geometry the dogs circle and make a straight line to shore while the deer swims straight from the shore toward the fishermen's boats; then the deer attempts to return directly to shore, only to be cut off by the barking dogs, and finally turns obliquely, following a westerly course to the other side of the lake. The description, of course, orients the reader by locating the relative positions of the main protagonists (men, dogs, and deer) and by charting the course of their movements. In this story the writer assumes that his audience (like that of the ethnographer) knows little of the landscape and lifeways being depicted; hence the need for evocative characterizations of people and places.

The excitement of the chase involves tactics and trajectories, moves and countermoves, much in the manner of competitive sports. Initially, the buck escapes the hounds, leaving them "swimming in a circle," until "their master's voice" sends them back to shore where they can close off possible retreat. On hearing Natty's shouts, however, the buck sets off on another trajectory that demands fresh tactics from the huntsman and his hounds. Much in this chase, of course, seems highly specific to American culture. Consider only the chase as competitive game, the elaborated subjectivities of both the huntsman and the animals, and the deer as a noble beast with "his slim neck" and "his nose high in the air." For my present purposes it suffices to say that Cooper succeeded in conveying a sense of the chase as an exciting and noble sport.

If we ethnographers could ask Cooper how representative his hunt was, he might retort by asking why the hunters portrayed in most ethnographies bother to get up in the morning and face nothing but routine drudgery. Indeed, we wonder how many monographs could speak to the human significance of social activities—which are these and why do people find them so?

The contrast between novelistic and ethnographic realism, between the dramatic potential of particular events and the programmed routines of generalized accounts, suggests that the parsimonious ethnoscientific account does not grossly distort the

monograph's epistemology when it reduces richly textured accounts to governing rules or, at any rate, to culturally appropriate
expectations. Whether thickly describing the language of experience or elegantly designing a formal model, much ethnography
tells more about forms of activity in general than about how any
particular instance was carried out. All too often in this process,
lived experience is robbed of its vital significance. Perhaps this
point can be made more clearly by considering the common analogy between cultural activities and games.

In talking about a game, do we want to know the rules or
how it was played? Obviously both matter. It makes no sense to
throw out the baby with the bath water. But suppose, for a moment, that we try to learn only the rules of the game. Imagine, for
example, the ethnographer returning from the last game of the
World Series and reporting these remarkable discoveries: three
strikes make an out, three outs retire the side, and so on. Eager to
learn about every move in the game's key plays, the avid fan could
only (correctly) say that the ethnographer said nothing untrue but
managed to miss the whole point of the game. This example, at
the very least, should make us pause and consider constructing
other kinds of ethnographic accounts that reveal the native point
of view.

In moving beyond the rules of the game, I propose to explore
the stories that other people tell themselves about themselves.
This foray into how people commemorate real events in story form
will involve three exemplary tales. The first, a minimal yet well-
formed story, tells about the context of storytelling. The second,
told by a gifted narrator, shows how people commemorate unexpected encounters rather than usual routines. The third, a spontaneously narrated myth, develops more through dialogue than
monologue, creating suspense by playing on the tensions between
the chores of life and human morality. In none of these cases does
the story appear as a direct enactment or after-the-fact extension
of the social activity of hunting. Instead, the key thing to understand is what makes Ilongots find a story compelling and how,
from the hunt, they can at times recover a tale that makes their
companions listen with rapt attention.

Now, as Ilongot storytellers say, be quiet and listen. Here is the
first tale:

Let's go to a far place. Let's go sleep over at the fork of the Kakidugen. We'll pass the fork of the Rawa. We'll go and stop at the fork of the
Natungan. And we'll hunt there. And after we've eaten game we'll go to
the fork of the Mabu since it's there that we can really hunt. And when
we've dried lots of meat there we'll change and go downstream to the
fork at Aluy. We'll hunt there for three nights. And we'll change and go
down the Bēmbēm. We'll try the bass fishing in the Tubu. When we
finish fishing we'll hunt for five days. When our rice supplies are finished
we'll return and go hunt at the fork of the Aluy.

"Now, you women, think about fixing our food supply since we've
all not had enough to eat." They'll get mad at us if there's no meat.
We're going to hunt the highest mountains. We're going to walk through
a pass I've seen. Let's go along the ridge there since it's there that you'll
see the game walking.

We went over lots of high mountains, and the rain almost destroyed
us in the peaks of the Kabikab. The moss dripped all over us and the
wind make us shiver. When we finished the dogs came and we caught
four wild pigs as well as five deer. We tied them to our backs to carry to
our camp. It was night. We went ahead and seared and butchered them,
since there were many of us. When we finished we cooked. We cooked all
the heads and dried the flesh to carry home.

Talikaw dictated this story to Michelle Rosaldo, who transcribed it verbatim. The orthography and simplicity of language
indicate that Talikaw told the story in August 1968, or about ten
months after we began research among the Ilongots. This story's
peculiarity, perhaps reflecting the narrator's uncertainty about our
linguistic comprehension, is that it is told three times over (as
indicated by the divisions into paragraphs). The first episode concerns plans; the second, a command for preparing supplies; and
the third, the actual hunt.

The first episode begins by projecting the hunt into the future, imitating the plans hunters make before setting out. Like a
novelist, Talikaw starts by orienting the listener in space. But in
this case the narrator invokes a litany of place-names—the ridges,
rocks, streams, and peaks that the huntsmen traversed in their
pursuit of game—rather than the more geometric directionality
traversing an undifferentiated lake surface (the line between fishermen in boats and dogs on shore; the oblique angle heading in a
westerly direction; circling; returning). The Ilongot huntsmen pass
three river forks and then hunt and eat; they pass another river
fork and then hunt and dry meat; they shift downstream and hunt

for three nights; they go down one river and reach another, where they fish and hunt for five days; and finally, their rice supplies depleted, they return homeward, stopping at a river they crossed before and hunting again.

The second episode returns to the point of departure, considering it this time, not through the huntsmen's plans, but (using a common opener for stories of long-distance visits, hunts, and raids) by having a man "command" (*tuydek*; see M. Rosaldo 1980:70–76) a woman to pound the rice for the trail. As is usual in such stories, the narrator states the command in direct address. He then comments that women become angry when men fail to provide meat. The initiative for this hunt thus came as much from women as from men, and so the story reminds us of the mutual dependence between the sexes. Then Talikaw repeats a list of geographical markers orienting the huntsmen on their trek, but this time he stresses mountains, a pass, a ridge—features of the landscape more rugged than river forks—without using any specific place-names. Perhaps he imagines himself speaking to women and intends to highlight the difficulties in the foraging quest without naming particular places (as true stories should), because relatively homebound women do not know the lay of the land in distant hunting territories.

The third episode continues and deepens the theme of the second by traversing high mountains (generalized features of the landscape) and then naming one in particular (Kabikab) where the elements (rain, dripping moss, wind) challenge the huntsmen's endurance, making them "shiver" while they await the game driven toward them by dogs. They catch four wild pigs and five deer, which they carry to camp, butcher, cook, and dry for their return walk home.

Modular in form, this tale resembles other Ilongot stories in that its episodes are like beads on a string, with each one capable of greater and lesser elaboration (see R. Rosaldo 1980:173–75). The story lines meander (not unlike the rivers they often follow) rather than rising to a climax and resolution; they order themselves more through a series of digressions than by developing nuanced understandings of a unified subject matter. Thus, tales of hunting can, as we have just seen, stop off for a little bass fishing, some unfortunate accident, or any number of other occurrences connected with hunting only because they happened along the way and not because they elaborate the story's beginning, complicate its middle, or foreshadow its ending. Indeed, for Ilongots a series of place-names can by itself be called a story. Thus, for example, the first episode above, with its series of river forks, could stand alone as a well-formed story.

Perhaps the maddeningly elliptical character of minimal Ilongot stories emerges more clearly by representing the first episode in this manner:

> Go far.
> Go sleep Kakidugen.
> Pass Rawa.
> Go and stop Nutungan where hunt and eat.
> Go Mabu and hunt and dry meat.
> Go downstream Aluy and hunt three nights.
> Go Bēmbēm.
> Fish Tubu and hunt five days.
> When rice finished go return Aluy.

Representing the text in this manner highlights the sense of movement (go, pass, return) punctuated by river names and the activities of hunting, eating, drying meat, and fishing. But what are we to make of this minimalist version of the hunt?

When we consider the richness of a novelist's account, the detail of ethnography, or the elegance of ethnoscience, we wonder why a sequence of names and activities, ordered only by their succession in time and space within a particular hunting episode, could be considered a good story. This, if there ever was one, is a story untainted by flashbacks or "meanwhile" clauses. Instead, it is governed solely by brute chronology, the one-damned-thing-after-another kind of narrative that historians never boast of writing and always deprecatingly attribute to somebody else. What can we make of listing place-names ordered only by a principle of relentless linear (call it "zero-degree") temporal succession?[3] Can we speak of narrative coherence when place-names are strung together as they are only because somebody happened to traverse them in that particular order on a specific occasion?

Although they find certain tales to be better told than others, Ilongots claim that listing the place-names where somebody walked is just as much a story (and indeed cannot be omitted from any true story) as a more fully elaborated narrative. Perhaps, this indigenous viewpoint can be placed in sharper relief by juxtaposing minimal Ilongot narratives and history's conventional threefold division into the annals, the chronicle, and history proper. Ordered only by chronological sequence rather than by narrative logic, Ilongot hunting stories resemble the supposedly lowest order of historical texts; that is, they resemble annals, not chronicles, and certainly not history proper. Yet precisely where historical studies see differences of kind, Ilongots perceive only differences of degree. Indeed, I shall argue that this ethnographic evidence suggests that history's threefold division, particularly insofar as it is hierarchical and evolutionary, derives more from parochial modern canons of narrative excellence than from the realities of other times and places. In this respect, we can lump together the errors of presentism and ethnocentrism.

Even the most astute historical thinkers could learn from what Ilongots tell in their minimal story form. Hayden White, (1980:12), for example, claims that in the annals, "social events are apparently as incomprehensible as natural events. They seem to have the same order of importance or unimportance. They seem merely to have *occurred*, and their importance seems to be indistinguishable from the fact that they were recorded. In fact, it seems that their importance consists of nothing other than the fact that they were recorded." In other words, the events recorded read like a random list that neither elaborates linkages between events nor tells readers about the greater and lesser significance of specific recorded items. Thus, according to White, events matter only because they are written down, and once recorded they assume equal import. White ignores the fact that people whose biographies significantly overlap can communicate rich understandings in telegraphic form. People who share a complex knowledge about their worlds can assume a common background and speak through allusion, whereas writers in the modern world of print must spell things out for their relatively unknown readers.

Let us call the problem with White's analysis "text positivism." Doubtless, this vice pervades (perhaps inevitably so) medieval studies, where social contexts have vanished leaving as their only trace written words to peruse. But surely ethnographers who transcribe texts need not think that the similar length of place-names they have recorded means that each item has uniform significance. To think in this way is to confuse the length of

graphic representation with the significance each item has for the
intended audience.

In nonliterate small-scale societies, storytellers speak to
people who share enormous knowledge about their cultural practices, their landscape, and their past experiences. Indeed, Talikaw
told his story (probably both over- and underestimating the
ethnographer's knowledge) to a person who had overheard the
planning, witnessed the huntsmen departing and returning, listened to huntsmen talking afterwards, and eaten some of the
catch. Thus, hunting stories, and probably annals, can communicate in a telegraphic shorthand because speakers can safely assume their listeners' depth of knowledge about the landscape,
hunting practices, the huntsmen's abilities, previous hunts in the
area and elsewhere, and so on. Realistic novels and monographs,
by contrast, must continually create their own context as they go
along by setting the scene, introducing characters, and describing
the techniques of hunting. They cannot assume that their readers
know the lay of the land, relevant biographies, and the rules of
the game. Perhaps minimal Ilongot tales resemble not novels or
monographs but the joke about the prison inmates who tell jokes
by reciting numbers representing jokes (which, as all inmates
know, vary significantly in topic, character, length, and wit).
Surely nobody would confuse the uniformity of numbers with the
heterogeneity of the jokes they represent. Or perhaps we could
compare battle tales told among surviving troops who need not
be told matters of duration, details of terrain, or lists of casualties;
after all, they shared that world and need only the briefest reminder to evoke a rich context within which to place the storyteller's dramatic or comic incident.

The notion that the text recorded by the ethnographer, here
a list of place-names, can be understood from within, on its own
terms in the manner of new criticism, simply makes no sense in
this case because the text speaks not for itself but only in the context of the shared understandings informing Ilongot everyday life.
In this society, people's lives overlap significantly from birth to
death, so that storytellers can invoke by allusion a wealth of background knowledge held in common by their listeners. Thus, for
Ilongot, place-names in and of themselves contain myriad associations. By simply saying Kabikab, Talikaw tells how long the hunters walked, characterizes the environment they traversed, and

reminds astute listeners of who hunted there recently and how they fared. Unfamiliar place-names say precious little to outsiders but speak worlds to the Ilongots for whom they are intended.

Consider now another hunting story, one verging at moments on the comic, where the narrator clearly found himself caught up in the telling. Taped rather than dictated, this story was recorded after about twenty months of field research in late May 1969. Dirup, the narrator, lived in Tamsi, and on our visit there he came forth eager to tell his good story. We knew him to be a lively storyteller and quickly took up his offer. Michelle Rosaldo transcribed the recorded text with his help and then retranscribed it with a better ear on our return among the Ilongots in 1974. Here is what he told, transcribed this time to convey the rhythms of oral speech by parsing lines where the narrator paused[4]:

> Well, the time I got carried it was like this.
> So, we called one another.
> I called to Kemmi.
> "Kemmi, let's hunt the Asimun.
> They [the game] have been eating the [fruits of the] uh, Tarang,
> and the, uh, Radēng,
> both of them.
> I happened, um,
> went, um,
> I saw them when I was hunting."
> And so they said,
> "Yes,
> let's go hunt, eh, the Asimun."
> I said,
> "Yes,
> prepare [do hunt magic].
> Would you prepare?
> And I'll prepare also,
> and Tagem will also prepare."
>
> And so we set off there.
> On that morning
> we went into Tinung's house.
> They said,
> "Hey, let's go ahead and drink this brew."
> And to that I said,

"No.
Don't do that. You won't see the game coming toward you.
Listen,
I'll stay back then.
I'll keep my dogs leashed.
They won't flush out the game anymore.
The game can just go on eating up the thicket,
because here you go just scarfing down this brew."
And they said,
"Yes,
Take it easy now.
We'll just drink a few small cups."
They just drank their few small cups,
very quickly so they could get going.

After a while,
well, they set off toward the Nalungtutan.
And I said to myself,
"I'll go toward the fork of the Nagetruwan."
And we with dogs spread out.

Thus far the story seems to follow, albeit in a better developed way, the pattern of the previous one. After announcing its subject ("the time I got carried"), the text begins, like Talikaw's dictated tale and my ethnographic sketch as well, in a mimetic mode by presenting (presumably) verbatim shouted plans for the hunt. When Dirup says he saw game eating three fruits, he orients his listener by telling her that the hunt occurred well into the rainy season, that is, between late August and early December 1968. This season, during which tree fruits ripen and fall, is culturally marked both because of the distinctive form of hunting it makes possible (lying in wait for game to come and feed) and because game at this time of year becomes especially prized as it grows fat from its enriched diet.

The next episode tells of stopping off to have a few drinks. Drinking, of course, does not occur along the pathway of every hunt, and this stopover neither elaborates the story's beginning nor anticipates its subsequent events. It is, as episodes in these tales often can be, rather more modular and self-contained. At the same time it enables Dirup to display his knowledge by not drinking before the hunt begins. Only unknowing boys would pretend to hunt while drunk; but Dirup, by threatening to withdraw his dogs, displays his culturally valued ability to temper unthinking passions with adult knowledge.

Like all stories Ilongots regard as veridical, the third episode involves traversing a significant landscape. The movement of seeking, marked by intense concentration, follows known contours uphill, downstream, along ridges, through grasslands and thickets. In the actual telling, studied gestures, repetition, and voice quality conveyed the sense of protracted searching, ever alert to spring into action. Now listen again, because the chase is about to begin:

> And that's when I had the dogs begin the chase.
> I heard my dog Woolly on the scent.
> Surely, he was after game.
> Here you were,
> Python, behind the Tarang tree,
> waiting in ambush.
> That's when I hurried up going.
> The game trampled the runo grass as it fled
> the barking dogs along the wide open slopes of the, uh, Asimun,
> where I was going upstream.
>
> And here you coiled
> snout of a
> loser of a python hiding by this Tarang tree.
> Saying nothing I stepped over that.
> I said, "I'll just look at my foot.
> HEY WHAT IS THIS
> THAT'S RISING UP
> PAST MY THIGH."
> And that's when I just said to Pudnga,
> "Oh no, Pudnga, I'm bitten, I won't live.
> Hurry."
> I called out to the boy.
>
> I said to myself then,
> "No,
> I'll slip my hand into it
> and stretch open the jaws of this snake."
> That's when I put my hand in then.
> The python clamped my hand and foot in its jaws.
> That hold made me like a
> cripple,
> like somebody in handcuffs.

That's when I stared at the snake,
staring while it twisted around.
Stretched out upstream was its big companion.
Here then it was pulling me.
"Oh, that's why it's squirming around.
So, it's pulling me along."
That's when there was this rattan
that was there
along the shore.
That's when I was pulled along by my feet.
I said,
"He's pulling my ass along the ground
as he twists around
and pulls me there."

That's when I struggled with him there
and I was reaching for the [knife] handle when
he slipped around behind my back.
Still reaching I pulled my hand free from the
teeth of that loser
by baiting him with my thigh
which he was biting.
That's when I then pulled out
the bolo and let him have it.
The snake's mouth then let go.
"Oh no,
it's coming after me again and biting."
I slashed away at it then.
It reached its mouth,
the bolo did. It [the python] then bit and held the bolo.
The two of us tugged back and forth then.
It then took off with the bolo.

Oops.
That's when it pulled me away.
Let me back up and finish that.
That's when it pulled me away.
That's when
the young shoots of the
rattan. . . .
Well, there's nobody who doesn't know about its thorns.
That's what I was scraped along as it pulled me.
That's when this, uh,
ass of mine

skidded along.
I skidded along then.
I was dragged along then.
I was burning then with
thorn after thorn in this
ass of mine.
As for you, land that I cleared,
nothing but thorns
were peeled from you by this thing that pulled me along.

That's when I really had at him
then
it let go [of my leg] when
I slashed away at it with the bolo.
We cut at each other then.
It took off with the bolo because I stuck it in [the snake].
It took off with it, going uphill and upstream with it.
It went winding upstream with it.

That's when I could only then say,
"Pudnga,
come here.
I won't live."
Here my blood was spurting all over there.
That was the last thing I said then.
I went and passed out.
Would you believe they came there
and carried me.
That's when they came to carry me then.
We went down toward the Asimun.

As the story reaches its resolution, Dirup addresses Pudnga much as he did on initially encountering the python. Then the protagonist reaches the Asimun River, the last place named before the narrator mentioned the snake's presence. Matters return to the routine hunting scene. Then the authoritative voice of the man who medicates Dirup reiterates the point of the story, thus concluding it.

That's when he splayed over his back,
to carry,
the wild pig I had caught.
As for Tanganen's hunt
it had mushrooms

and he went for them.
When I arrived also
they arrived.

Pukpuk came to me
to medicate me there.
He said,
"What if it had been a person?
What if he had gotten at you like that?
Now a person that big could beat, drag, and smash you.
What if he had attacked you?
You'd be dead now."
No, that really would have been the last time I ever spoke.
Ya'maw carried me all the way home.
My wife took care of the game,
the three animals caught.
That's the end.

This story not only conveys information, as did the first, but it also concentrates on displaying the drama of high risk and near disaster. Michelle Rosaldo (1980:113) aptly characterized these tales in this way: "Concerned less with triumph than landscape, less with the hero than matters of accident, movement, and surprise, the frame for all stories is provided by actual travels." Framed by a landscape rich in significant associations, the story meanders until the python appears, and then it tells with breathtaking flair about a close brush with death. For Ilongots, good hunting stories usually celebrate mishaps that occur along the way rather than virtuoso success. Insan, for example, tells about how his dog became trapped in a crevice, forcing him to slosh in the mud through repeated efforts to liberate the valuable animal. And Tukbaw tells, with an even better eye for comedy, about how his weapon broke, making him improvise with a knife tied to a stick and allowing a long antlered buck to chase him up a tree. More dramatic than ethnographic and more comic than romantic, elaborated stories select what is memorable from what happened during the hunt rather than directly enacting or attempting to recapture the unfolding experience of hunting.

Dirup's tale departs markedly from the usual ethnographic accounts of hunting as a workaday activity. In its portrayal of high adventure, it rather more nearly approximates a novelistic narration of a hunting episode. Unlike a novelist, however, Dirup assumes rather than portrays a rich context of hunting techniques and local habitat. Thus, the analogy between Ilongot hunting stories and modern novels, suggestive as it is in certain respects, begins to break down.

At first glance a more apt comparison would juxtapose Dirup's tale and the oral narratives of personal experience which the linguist William Labov has studied in a variety of English vernacular settings.[5] Indeed, Dirup's story, as it turns out, could well have been (though it was not) a response to the eliciting technique Labov (1972:354) describes as follows:

> The most effective of these techniques produce *narratives of personal experience*, in which the speaker becomes deeply involved in rehearsing or even reliving events of his past. The "Danger of Death" question is the prototype and still the most generally used: at a certain point in the conversation, the interviewer asks, "Were you ever in a situation where you were in serious danger of being killed, where you said to *yourself—'This is it'?*" In the section of our interview schedule that deals with fights, we ask, "Were you ever in a fight with a guy bigger than you?" When the subject says "Yes" we pause and then ask simply, "What happened?"

Dirup, of course, could have been killed while fighting that "big guy" who lay in wait for him. For Labov, the point of eliciting such stories is that the narrator becomes so caught up in the telling that the monitoring of style and content common in other interview situations drops away. I would argue against Labov, however, by noting that American narratives told to outsiders differ in form and content from Ilongot stories told to insiders, as well become especially clear below, in the third story.

Let us now review Dirup's story using Labov's key analytical terms and noting their limitations. The first sentence, containing the *abstract*, summarizes the story as follows: "The time I got carried it was like this." Then the *orientation* informs the listener about what was happening (men were planning and beginning a hunt with dogs), when (during the tree fruit season), and where (between the huntsmen's homes and the Asimun, by way of the Nalungtutan and Nagetruwan). Unlike Labov's storytellers, Dirup can provide his listener (by then an informed outsider) with necessary background for the story by selectively using condensed allusions to a complex array of hunting practices, botanical lore, and detailed knowledge of the local landscape. Ilongot stories, as I have said, can reasonably presuppose shared understandings about human events and the natural environment in their relatively shared worlds. This shared background knowledge enables the listener to understand that Dirup as narrator uses the drinking episode for further orientation by portraying Dirup and the main protagonist as a man whose knowledge can dominate his passion. Told by himself about himself, Dirup's autobiographical vignette provides him with an occasion for favorable self-characterization.

Ilongot narratives, particularly those told to outsiders, follow a chronological sequence from beginning to end (except, in this case, for the first sentence). Thus, the listener's orientation unfolds artfully through a temporally ordered sequence of actions (the shouted dialogue between Dirup and Kemmi, the dialogue between Dirup and the drinkers, and the dogs starting the chase), rather than in the spatial ordering of a realistic novel or in the detachable atemporal scene-setting introductions that Labov has found. In other words, contrary to Labov, Dirup's hunting story does not separate the orientation from the sequentially ordered narrative through either stylistic devices or timeless descriptive techniques. Instead, the orientation emerges rather unobtrusively through the early phases of the narrative.

The story's central action, culminating in his being carried off, involves Dirup's near fatal struggle with a python. No sooner does the chase begin than Dirup walks right into the snake's coiling ambush. Thus, the *complicating action* revolves around the python's persistent attacks and the protagonist's repeated efforts to free himself. The story reaches its *resolution* only when the snake slithers upstream, leaving Dirup battered, bleeding, and unconscious, yet somehow still alive.

Suspended between the complicating action and its resolution, the *evaluation* shows what makes the story tellable. Rather than saying that events were terrifying, dangerous, and extraordinary, storytellers often embed their evaluations in the narrative itself. Ideally, this embedding should be so effective that Dirup's listener can only say, "You really did?" and not, "So what?" Labov's analysis so forcefully argues for the intertwining of narrative and evaluation that the separation he proposes seems artificial. Hence, rather than listing evaluative devices, I shall instead follow evaluations as they emerge along the story line.

From the beginning Dirup places his listener fully in the action by presenting the directly quoted speech of dialogue. First Dirup and his companions shout their plans to one another. Then they resume their dialogue when they stop off for a few drinks before starting the chase. Finally, some hunters set off for the Nalungtutan River while Dirup (as he tells himself out loud in the story's initial monologue) heads with his dogs for the fork of the Nagetruwan. Once the chase begins, the narrator follows the sequence of who is chasing whom and by turns identifies himself ("I"), the dogs (specifying further "Woolly on the scent"), and the as-yet-unseen game, followed (no longer in chasing order) by the as-yet-unforeseen python "waiting in ambush." Reporting on the python resembles in its effect a "meanwhile" clause, pointing to roughly simultaneous events in two different places. Dirup further heightens suspense by hastening his reported action ("as I hurried up going"), at the same time that he thereby protracts in narrative time his coming encounter with the snake (which he, the narrator, knows will happen and which his listener by now expects, but which he, as protagonist, did not foresee). In speech increasingly rhythmic and marked by intensifying gestures, the narrator further increases tension through Ilongot storytelling devices I shall call *repetition, inversion,* and *delayed information*.

In repetition he locates himself, the dogs, the game, and the snake, but this time the sequence includes a partial inversion of who is chasing whom. The order now runs game – dogs – I + snake, rather than I – dogs + snake, as before. This partially inverted order seems consistent with the emerging fact that the snake is hunting the huntsman, who is urging the dogs to chase the game. By now Dirup has sighted either the game or, more likely, its tracks ("The game trampled the runo grass as it fled"), although the "hiding" snake remains invisible. In the partially inverted repeated sequence, Dirup also uses delayed information to draw out his listener's suspense about the coming encounter with the python.

The significant device of delayed information requires brief explication. Each line raises a question answered only in the next or a later line. This device can be illustrated by placing within parentheses the questions a hypothetical interlocutor might ask as follows:

And here you coiled

(Is this the python?)
snout of a
(Is this the python?)
loser of a (Is this the python?) python hiding by this Tarang tree.

This delayed information device works especially well in oral presentations because, unlike readers, listeners must hear the story's words in linear sequence; they cannot scan a passage with a single glance. At the same time, the device of repetition allows the narrator to create suspense through delayed information without sacrificing intelligibility.

Speaking loudly to his listener to imitate his own past words to himself, Dirup at last encounters the python rising up past his thigh. And then he closes his announcement of the complicating action by calling to his companion Pudnga for help: "Oh, no, Pudnga, I'm bitten. I won't live. Hurry." This shift from addressing himself to addressing somebody else constitutes a deeper embedding of the evaluation in the story. Dirup tells himself that the python is rising up past his thigh and reports the significance of his brute observation only when speaking to somebody else. In effect, he is saying "This is it," the encounter with death.

The struggle between huntsman and python begins when Dirup tries to pry open the snake's jaws and instead is clamped hand and foot by them. Using the only two (hence, especially powerful) similes in the story,[6] he describes his terrifying predicament through paired images of mutilation and arrest, both of which relate to headhunting practices. For Ilongots, mutilation ("like a cripple") and arrest ("like somebody in handcuffs") invoke strong feelings of disgust with one's body and terror at one's fate. Dirup ends the episode by portraying himself as staring, stunned, and immobilized in finding himself locked hand and foot in the python's jaws.

Allowing Dirup little time for dazed staring, the python then begins to pull him along the ground. In stepwise fashion the verb phrases, through the device of iterative specification, gradually reveal that the snake (a) is pulling him (b) by the feet and (c) draggling his ass along the ground:

. . . it was pulling me
. . . it's pulling me along
. . . I was pulled along by my feet
. . . pulling my ass along the ground

Dirup succeeds in wresting his knife hand free while the python bites his thigh. There follows a struggle between the snake and the man with the bolo (a long knife or machete), until eventually the snake bites the bolo and takes off with it.

Exclaiming "oops," the narrator backtracks to repeat the pulling episode and the struggle over the bolo, this time the former in more and the latter in less elaborated fashion. In this manner Ilongot hunting stories can both follow a temporally linear sequence and meander, folding back on themselves in a manner resembling a flashback. In the repetition the listener learns the significance of the rattan mentioned in the previous sequence: the snake is (c) dragging Dirup's ass over ground covered (d) with rattan thorns. Dirup makes his point about the rattan directly, stepping outside the story line and simply telling his listener, "Well, there's nobody who doesn't know about its thorns." In a sequence of lines enclosed by the term "ass," Dirup achieves intensification through repetition (his ass skidded, skidded, and was dragged). Playing humorously on invocations from magical spells, he then directly addresses "You, land that I cleared," and half-seriously, half-mockingly laments the thorns he peeled from it as the snake pulled him along.

In the next episode of the repeated sequence Dirup condenses the struggle over the bolo from sixteen lines to five, and he concludes by elaborating and intensifying through repetition the python's escape with the bolo:

> It took off
> It took off
> Going uphill and upstream
> Winding upstream

Dirup uses his last words before passing out to end the complicating action and begin the story's resolution. Telling the significance of what happened by addressing another person—" . . . Pudnga, . . . I won't live"—encloses the beginning and the ending of the complicating action. The resolution then continues over seven more lines in which Dirup spurts blood and passes out before, as he says in the following repeated phrase,

> . . . they came there and carried me
> . . . they came to carry me then

The phrase itself, of course, repeats the story's opening line and summarizing abstract. The resolution concludes by returning spatially to the point of departure, the Asimun River, where the men initially planned to hunt and where Dirup's dogs began the chase. In bringing the narrator and the listener back to where it all started, and thereby conveying a sense of closure, the resolution shades off into the *coda*, Labov's final analytical term.

The coda proper opens by returning to the mundane activities of carrying game and collecting mushrooms. Thus the narrator brings his listener to the everyday routines of life before reflecting again on what happened. Here Dirup uses his story's most deeply embedded (more so than the protagonist speaking to himself or even to somebody else) and therefore most authoritative voice, that of the man come to medicate (further enhancing his authority through his healing role), to state once again how narrow was his escape from death. The man come to medicate takes five nicely elaborated lines to say, "If it [the python] had been a person . . . you'd be dead now," echoing the gist of Dirup's call to Pudnga for help. The narrator returns again to hunting routines— "the three animals caught"—until he reaches his conventional concluding line: "That's the end."

Surely Dirup's tale could never have been deduced from even the thickest of ethnographic descriptions of the hunt itself. Yet the story is true, by Ilongot standards and mine, in that it holds for, though it does not simply derive from, the experience it purports to represent. If the protagonist, for instance, had not been pulled over the rattan thorns or had never lost consciousness, we could legitimately accuse Dirup of bad faith, trying to pass off a tall tale as if it were a true story. But this issue, after all, arises in any field of history or science where data do not produce, yet can falsify, theories and concepts. Full knowledge of the hunt, in other words, does not predict the form and content of stories told after the fact. Thus, purportedly true stories can select, even exaggerate for comic effect, or resynthesize, yet they cannot violate what actually happened.

Dirup's tale reveals the human significance of hunting rather than the richness of its ethnoscientific lore. From this perspective the chase most meaningfully involves movement away from home, unexpected encounters, putting oneself at risk, surviving through culturally valued improvisation, and returning from the quest having recovered a fine story to tell. Less substantial in brute survival terms than a wild pig or deer, the value of a good story nonetheless should not be minimized. In fact we might say that a motive for hunting (or, at any rate, one of its happy consequences) is that on occasion it enables a man to return with a story of high adventure. If matters of value derive in part from scarcity, I should add that Ilongot huntsmen return from the forest with game in their hands far more often than they do with a fine story in their hearts. Of course, telling such a terrifying story about oneself compels other people's rapt attention on oneself. It is little wonder that Dirup's eyes gleamed, as Ilongots say, with excitement while he told his story about the time he was carried.

Let me now turn to a third story. Like the preceding one, this tale involves hunting with dogs and inverts workaday modes of making a living by transforming human beings into the hunted rather than the hunters. But this time, instead of featuring the actual mishap of a python ambushing a man, the story portrays the imagined catastrophe of long-tailed people-eating monsters using dogs to hunt down human beings. Clearly mythic and not at all historic, this tale involves traversing a disorienting sea of floodwaters, not a significant named landscape. Indeed, the female narrator laces the myth with the phrase "they say" (*kunu*), indicating that her knowledge of the events reported is only hearsay. Although clearly not a true story in the sense of an eyewitness report like the previous two, the storyteller here says that she has accurately rendered a story she heard from her father. The truth of the story resides not in its reference to known events but in its fidelity to earlier tellings.

Despite their points of contact, the gulf separating hunting stories from myths could appear so vast as to invalidate any comparisons between the two. But the aim is to see how the stories are both the same and different. Their differences, for example, make clear the impact of the listeners' knowledge that when Dirup stands before us as self-referential storyteller he surely lived to tell the tale and can therefore narrate, as he does, by blending intensity and comedy. Suspense in Dirup's tale thus concerns how the protagonist will escape his predicament, rather than the mythic question of whether or not the heroes will survive. Yet these stories are the same in that, like the myth's lost headhunters, huntsmen risk sudden fatal misfortune, and in both cases good storytellers portray human vulnerability with a fine ear for suspense. This final comparison should teach us that we can understand more about good hunting stories by studying the art of storytelling than by studying the subsistence techniques.

The tale of the long-tailed people-eaters, like Dirup's story, was taped rather than dictated. This time, however, the story was being told to a fellow Ilongot and was caught in its actual cultural performance. Thus, it reveals certain characteristics that make stories (both myths and hunting tales) compelling as well as a number of significant differences between spontaneous and elicited narratives. Spontaneous narratives, of course, emerge from socially situated conversations that elicit them by making their telling appropriate. Indeed, even if the narrative text were invariant, the social context occasioning it could significantly alter its meaning.[7] This observation only underscores the point made earlier that texts must be read in context.

In this case the storytelling context involved the customary practice of bringing infants to be introduced to the parents' close relatives. A young man, his wife, and their infant son arrived from Abēka, faraway to the south, and spent the night in the Kakidugen household of Tukbaw and Wagat. Tukbaw was the young man's maternal uncle, and the two men clearly enjoyed a fond avuncular relationship.

The visitors arrived on the afternoon of March 24, 1974, early in our second period and our twenty-second month of fieldwork among the Ilongots. A supper with especially good greens, served shortly after dark, enhanced the welcome visit. After we chewed betel and chatted briefly, Tukbaw served several rounds of fermented sugarcane brew (only Wagat and the young man's wife turned down the drink, as women often do), and the drink added to the uncle and nephew's delight in each other's company. The meandering conversation took several turns around past and present local politics. The young man discussed the possible motives of those people involved in the Abēka incident of 1960, when a Philippine constabulary officer murdered an Ilongot father and son, triggering a rash of retaliatory beheadings (R. Rosaldo 1978:250–52). The conversation then shifted to recent increasing intrusions of landgrabbers and the problems Ilongots faced in gaining titles to land their ancestors had inhabited since time immemorial and in paying taxes when they had no cash income.

The mood turned lighter as people laughed about the man who had just run off with his sister-in-law, and how the abandoned woman's kin had demanded payments not only from the runaway man (as expected) but also from the runaway woman (an extraordinary demand).

After the comic interlude the young man reported on how Pantabangan, a lowland town just south of Abĕka, had been flooded by a hydroelectric project. (I learned later that this project of the Philippine government and the U.S. Agency for International Development was partially funded by the World Bank and had been approved some five years earlier during our previous field stay [Floro 1981].) The flooding displaced over 9,000 people. As the young man described the floodwaters and rumored plans to inundate his homeland, Wagat interrupted him, saying, "La, now we'll be like the long-tailed ones." When Michelle Rosaldo asked what her remark meant, Wagat proceeded to tell two stories, one about a character named Taman who drowned the long-tailed ones, and another (which I shall relate in a moment) about how headhunters tricked the long-tailed ones and killed their dogs on sharpened bamboo stakes. Both stories related to flooding as the topic of conversation. Wagat the narrator (N) and the young man's wife, her interlocutor (I), were the most sober and distantly related people, anthropologists aside, around the flickering nighttime hearth where most Ilongots tell their tales. The only person to break the silence surrounding the storytelling was the young man, the interlocutor's husband, who mainly listened (L), like the others, in rapt attention.

Briefly, the story's protagonists are three: a group of men who went on a headhunting raid and got lost after the flood; the raiders' wives who stayed behind; and the long-tailed monsters who customarily hunt people with dogs and then eat them. The story begins *in medias res*, not by design but because we did not turn on the tape recorder until after Wagat had begun. As we enter this tale without a beginning, the lost headhunters have by now found their way home and lurk in the background, hoping to trick the long-tailed monsters and avoid becoming their next victims. The monsters have just instructed the women (i.e., the headhunters' wives) on how to prepare and cook the human victims they have brought with them to eat. They tell the women not to chop up and cook their victims' vaginas and penises because eating them makes even monsters drunk to the point of passing out. The taped text begins as Wagat speaks in the voice of a monster addressing the headhunters' wives.

    N: "Don't go and get their vaginas."
    I: Ugh.
    N: "And their penises.
        Uh, they'll make us drunk."
        That's when, they say, friend,
        they chopped away,
        these Ilongots did,
        the ones who raided, got lost, and came upon them.
        Now by stealth there they chopped them up.
        Now, you, they sneaked in and chopped up their vaginas
        and their penises.
    L: No, it can't be.
    N: That was to make them drunk
        When they ate.
        They finished then
        with their chopping.

After the headhunters finished chopping the vaginas and penises, they turned to their next task and began to cook them. All the while they feared that the monsters would catch, kill, and eat them.

    N: They cooked.
        They went faster and faster then, they say.
        Alas, there was
        all that cooking
        for they were afraid and saying,
        "For pity, if we now finish this
        they move on to us next."

The interlocutor interrupts, however, and attempts to clarify whether or not the headhunters ate with the monsters and whether or not the former or the latter chopped the penises and vaginas.

    I: Did they eat with them then?
    N: Yes,
        they ate with them.
        No,
        they didn't eat together
        so they wouldn't get drunk.

> They didn't eat with them.
> I: Were the ones who got lost the ones who chopped?
> N: Yes,
>   the ones who got lost were the ones who chopped.
> I: Hum.
>   I thought maybe the people-eaters had chopped?
> N: No, no.

Matters of who did what thus clarified, the narrator picks up the story line and describes how the long-tailed people-eating monsters went ahead and ate their victims' vaginas and penises. Then, just as they had said, the monsters became drunk and passed out.

> N: Now comes when they ate them, they say, then, friend.
>   They got drunk, they say,
>   indeed.
>   They toppled down, they say, really drunk it seems,
>   uh, spread all through the house.
> I: Hum.

The opportune moment thus at hand, the headhunters commenced setting a trap to kill the monsters' hunting dogs. After going for bamboo they began the process of shaving and sharpening.

> N: The others, they say, sneaked off to set the trap.
> I: Set the trap.
> N: They went, they say, for bamboo.
> I: Hum.
> N: Shaving
>   shaving
>   sharpening through that night.
> I: Hum.
> N: They sharpened and sharpened and sharpened.
>   They, uh,
>   went and whisked (magically), they say,
>   by stealth,
>   everyone in the house.
>   The others went to whisk
> I: Hum.
> N: when they had finished sharpening, friend.
> I: Were the ones who sharpened the ones who chopped?
> N: Yes.

Once finished sharpening, the headhunters began setting up
the sharpened bamboo stakes until they were spread out "like a
blanket."

> N: They left, they say.
>   They left, they say.
>   Now, they set up sharpened [bamboo] stakes as they came.
>   It was the dogs they were setting up for
> I: Hum.
> N: because they were about to hunt with dogs.
>   They went on setting up the sharpened stakes.
>   They, uh, spread them out like a blanket, they say.
>   The sharpened stakes
>   they went on setting up and went on setting up.
> I: Hum. Hum.

But, in a terrible moment, the monsters were awakened before the
headhunters had finished setting up the sharpened stakes. The
monsters, saying that people were there but finding none, prepared their dogs to hunt down the humans.

> N: They had not, they say, finished, friend,
>   every last one, they say, that,
>   uh, was to be set up.
>   They began to stir, they say.
> I: Lord.
> N: They called one another.
>   They said, they say,
>   "There are people there.
>   There are none."
>   Over and over, they say,
>   "They are there.
>   They aren't."
>   They said, they say . . . oops.
>   They left then.
>   They leashed together then, they say,
> I: Hum.
> N: their dogs in order to hunt them with dogs.

At last the dogs fell on the sharpened stakes and were killed, leaving the monsters to make a hasty retreat.

> N: Uh, along come the dogs to that bamboo
>   they set up and sharpened for them.

I: So, they didn't go on.

N: They didn't go on because the sharpened stakes finished off
the dogs. How could they hunt with dogs, uh,

I: Without . . .

N: without the dogs
to catch
and bite us?

I: Hum.

N: Now,
truly, they say, they left then.
And they hurried away fast, they say, poor things.

I: Hum.

Although the story apparently has ended, the narrator returns to the beginning by describing where the monsters made
their mistake. When the women asked about the source of the
water, the monsters told them to drop a leaf in the water so they
could tell upstream from downstream and regain their bearings.

N: Uh, they slipped up, they did friend, by telling
the women they came upon the beginning

I: Hum.

N: at the house. [The women asked,]
"Where is the source of this water?"

I: Hum.

N: "We're lost."
That's, they say, when, uh, they went, friend, uh,
and told the women.

I: Hum.

N: Let a leaf float along."

I: [inaudible]

N: "Now the, uh, direction the leaf comes from
that's where you're from."
That's how they learned about it.
That's what they followed.

I: Did they really let the leaf float along?

N: Yes.
So then they followed, uh,
the direction the leaf came from.

I: Hum.

N: They didn't follow it floating downstream.

I: Oh, I see.

N: They didn't follow that.

And now, the matter of the leaf reviewed, the story can end.

> N: That's the end of the story, uh,
>   I heard them tell.
> I: It's yours to keep now.
> N: Yes.
>   That's the end there.

The narrator concludes the story by saying that she has told it as it was told to her; the interlocutor sighs that the tale is now hers to keep. But the conversation continues, further clarifying what happened to the floating leaf. Thus the story gradually returns to and merges with the interrupted conversation about floodwaters.

> L: Where, uh. . . .
>   The leaf didn't float along anymore?
> N: It floated along.
>   They believed them when they saw the leaf floating along
>   because you couldn't see, they say, the current in the
>   water.
> L: Water. . . .
> N: Yes.
>   It was just like, uh,
>   oozing,
>   I'd say.
> I: Seeping. . . .
> N: Seeping. . . .
>   I'd say like the ocean
>   except for the ocean's rocking.
> I: Moving. . . .
> N: Yes.
>   It was just moving, they say, uh, going along a bit.

Unlike the previous two stories, this one of the long-tailed monsters emerges more as a dialogue than a monologue. Dialogue, as it happens, confounds most current views, including Labov's, on narrative form.[8] Narratologists argue that the self-contained text comprises the only empirical evidence for interpretation; their opponents, by contrast, invoke the necessity to understand the author's intentions or the reader's expectations. In either case the narrator speaks while the audience or reader (politely) remains silent. Here, however, the young woman freely and at times insistently interrupts Wagat. The back-and-forth verbal

play they engage in requires a skilled narrator and an adept interlocutor, both of them cultural insiders. Although usually able to
follow a story, I never became sufficiently quick on the uptake to
play the role of interlocutor. Yet far from being mere ornament,
the property of dialogue deeply shapes a story's unfolding.

Narrative form both reflects and occasions the interaction between the storyteller and the interlocutor. Storytellers typically
identify actors through verbs rather than nouns, through their actions (chopping, cooking, eating, getting drunk, sharpening, setting up) rather than their individuating labels (lost raiders,
people-eaters, women). Thus, the interlocutor's questioning of the
narrator throughout the story provides basic orientation by disam-
biguating pronouns and forcing clarification of just who did what,
not as in Labov's detachable introduction. Evaluations become
apparent through the narrator and through the interlocutor's reactions ("ugh"; "No, it can't be"; "Lord"; "Did they really let the
leaf float along?"; "It's yours to keep now"), reflecting and creating moods of shock, fright, anxiety, puzzlement, and pleasure.
However, actual performance does more than provide an additional voice for clarifying who is doing what and how we should
feel about it during the telling; it also infuses narrative time with
an extra dimension of suspense that can best be explicated by
following the story line.

The taped story begins with the monster uttering the interdiction against chopping up and cooking their victims' intoxicating
vaginas and penises. Wagat uses the device of delayed information
to intensify her saying that the lurking headhunters have risked
violating the interdiction:

> That's when, they say, friend,
> (What happened?)
> they chopped away,
> (Who did?)
> these Ilongots did,
> (Which ones?)
> the ones who raided, got lost, and came upon them.

The narrator then repeats the verb phrase and gradually reveals
the who, how, what, and why of the "choppings":

> (Who?)
> these Ilongots did,

the ones who raided, got lost, and came upon them.
(How?)
... by stealth. ...
(What?)
... their vaginas
and their penises. ...
(Why?)
... to make them drunk
when they ate.

The action of chopping is thus protracted in narrative time through repetition and iterative specification of the verb phrase. But time grows short for the headhunters who have violated the monsters' interdiction when "they sneaked in" and "by stealth" began their chopping. They could at any moment get caught and be eaten by the long-tailed ones. The interlocutor and other listeners cannot wait to hear what happens next. At last, the chopping was done.

Once finished with their chopping, the humans began to cook "faster and faster." Raising her pitch and slowing her tempo, Wagat depicts their plight, their fear, and their haste through interjections ("alas," "for pity") and by speaking directly in their voice ("If we now finish this they move on to us next"). Human mortality, in other words, consists in working while being subject to fatal interruption.

Heightening suspense by delaying the story's flow, the interlocutor interrupts with questions designed to clarify just who did what. She asks whether or not the monsters and the humans ate together and whether or not the headhunters or the long-tailed people-eaters did the chopping. After thirteen lines of clarification, the narrator resumes where she left off. In quick narrative succession the monsters ate, got drunk, and toppled down, "spread all through the house." This moment provided the humans their opportunity.

The suspense resumes as Wagat echoes the adverbial phrases used to describe the chopping and says that the headhunters "sneaked off" to work "by stealth" in laying their trap. First they went for bamboo. Protracting and intensifying the narrative through repetition, Wagat says they began

Shaving
shaving

sharpening through the night.
They sharpened and sharpened and sharpened.

Afterward, the headhunters magically whisked over the monsters to prevent their awakening too soon.

Once again the interlocutor interrupts to ask whether or not both the chopping and the sharpening were done by the headhunters. Indeed, they did both. Now the headhunters began setting up the sharpened stakes so that the monsters' dogs would be killed as they began the chase and pierced themselves. This setting-up process becomes intensified and protracted through repetition, and a simile makes vivid the image of the stakes spreading "like a blanket." Although more sharpened stakes remained to be set up, the monsters "began to stir." Probably thinking that the fatal interruption had arrived, the interlocutor gasps, "Lord" (*apu*). But Wagat leaves her interlocutor and listeners in suspense awhile longer as she twice imitates the monsters shouting that there were people there, only to shout again that there were none. The monsters then began the chase, using dogs to hunt down the headhunters.

Rather matter-of-factly at first, Wagat says that the monsters abandoned the hunt and left because "the sharpened stakes finished off the dogs." But then she uses rhythmic pauses and a rhetorical question to underscore that the monsters were left impotent and that their dogs posed a grave threat. She also shifts perspective by employing the inclusive first-person plural pronoun (*kisi*, "we," including the addressee) to identify her own vulnerability (to the monsters' dogs, who can "catch and bite us") with that of her fellow human beings in the story and in the audience. The monsters, thus disarmed, leave in haste.

Let us take a moment to reflect on how the narrative protracts time and creates a sense of suspense. In its telling, this tale conveys a sense of time much deeper than the brute succession of discrete events that most theorists use both to identify a narrative segment of speech and to dismiss the significance of temporality in storytelling (see, e.g., Barthes 1977; cf. Ricoeur 1980). Wagat, for example, uses a number of key terms that embody what I call "finite irreversible duration".[9] These verbs include chopping, cooking, shaving, sharpening, and setting up, and all of them refer to human acts repeated in an identical manner over a period of time (not unlike sowing or harvesting rice in a garden). But in contrast with indefinitely repeated habitual actions—designated, for example, in the English imperfective "I used to visit"—these acts are repeated in an identical manner only until a finite task is completed (e.g., vaginas and penises chopped, the meat cooked, the bamboo stakes shaved and sharpened, and the sharpened stakes set up). This particular sense of finite duration emerges from the specific kinds of human activities to which these verbs refer, rather than the grammatical properties of verbal tense markers. These processes are as irreversible as our proverbial image of scrambling eggs. Neither the chopped nor the cooked vaginas and penises can reconstitute themselves as living humans, and bamboo, once shaved, sharpened, and set up, does not regenerate itself as a living being. Chopping, cooking, shaving, sharpening, and setting up take time, but they reach an end point and cannot be undone to restore the former state of the objects of human labor.[10] Note that the formal organization of Ilongot narratives into self-contained modular units fits nicely with a sense of time that has duration but is finite and irreversible.

It is precisely the capacity of narrators and their interlocutors to enclose the tension between the duration of such tasks and the protagonists' vulnerability to fatal interruption that creates a story's intensification and suspense. The storyteller's repetition (chopping, cooking, shaving, sharpening, setting up) and interjections ("alas," "for pity"), plus the interlocutor's sometimes insistent questions and exclamations ("ugh"; "no, it can't be"; "Lord"), protract the narrative and intensify the listener's sense that these actions are taking too long. The headhunters, after all, could be caught, cooked, and eaten at any moment; the risk is great. Not unlike Dirup's tale, the myth comments on hunting by inverting the normal order and placing humans in the position of animals who are hunted down by dogs. In the end, only stealth and wile enable the humans to survive.

Returning to the text, we find Wagat telling where the monsters went wrong: they never should have told the women (the headhunters' wives) how to find their bearings in the disorienting, undifferentiated floodwaters. The interlocutor's questions make it clear that by dropping a leaf in the water and watching it float, the women could distinguish upstream from downstream. Indeed, aside from named places, Ilongots orient themselves along two axes: upstream/downstream and uphill/downhill.

Finally, the story returns to its unrecorded beginning and to the conversational topic to which it was a response. Wagat's closing lines

That's the end of the story, uh,
I heard them tell.

at once say "the end" and remind listeners that in remembering and retelling the story, Wagat has made it hers, part of her patrimony extending through her father into her ancestral past. Her interlocutor emphasizes the latter by replying, "It's yours to keep now." Wagat agrees and repeats, "That's the end there."

In their actual performance, stories no sooner end than they become the topic for further conversation; they seldom conclude with the abrupt finality of a closed book. Hence, conversation about the leaf and the floodwater continues, and when the listener puzzles further over the leaf, Wagat turns from the leaf to the water that is seemingly without current, "oozing," "seeping," "just moving," and "going along a bit." Like Ilongots confronting the Pantabangan hydroelectric project, the headhunters faced dissolution into a world made threatening by virtually motionless water that completely covered all familiar landmarks and all orienting, directional indicators. Like Dirup's story, this one portrays the human struggle to resist fatal interruption, dissolving into the environment, and utterly ceasing to exist. Yet it is through such near escapes that Ilongots can recover a story that in the telling leaves their traces above the unendingly still and uniform waters.

To recapitulate, this paper began by asking how ethnographers should represent other people's lives. To lend substance to this conceptual concern I have explored possible ways to apprehend the human significance of hunting among the Ilongots of northern Luzon, Philippines. Sketches in two ethnographic modes stood for the discipline's conventional wisdom. Stressing indigenous systems of classification, ethnoscience has identified the cover term for hunting, 'adiwar, "seeking, looking for, or foraging," and has gone on to discover such culturally relevant discriminations as hunts with dogs versus those without dogs. Ethnographic realism, by contrast, has provided a detailed composite account that describes step-by-step how the Ilongot hunting process generally unfolds.

In both approaches to ethnography hunting emerges as a form of life at once specific to and general within Ilongot culture.

Next I turned to novelistic realism and found that it differed from the ethnographic variety by displaying a particular hunt in its unfolding, rather than by piecing together a composite account. When James Fenimore Cooper depicted a specific chase, each moment contained surprises and quick shifts in strategy. His portrayal was the opposite of the monograph in which one thing leads to another in ways that, if not predictable, are at least culturally expectable. By contrast with the novelist's account, the ethnographic sketch robs the hunt of its unexpected encounters. The point, of course, is that Ilongot hunting stories, like novels, stress precisely the qualities of suspense and improvisation that the monograph suppresses.

What, then, have we learned from reading of the telling of hunt stories? This question involves both the subjects that can be told as stories and the qualities depicted in their telling. Hunting becomes historiable (unlike gardening, which never does) through the measured search over significant terrain, the alert capacity to pounce on game that presents itself, and the ability to cope with misfortunes—pythons, trapped dogs, broken weapons. Story forms that recollect experience and create new experiences in the telling embody the culturally valued activity of 'adiwar. They both describe and play out the central qualities of hunting: taut alertness and quick improvisation.

The stories these Ilongot men tell about themselves both reflect what actually happened and define the kinds of experiences they seek out on future hunts. Indeed, their very postures while hunting resemble those used in storytelling, and in this respect the story informs the experience of hunting at least as much as the reverse. Huntsmen measure their prowess not only in numbers of animals killed but also against their capacity to improvise in the face of adversity. In fact, the qualities that make a man admirable by Ilongot standards stem more from the latter capacity than the former record of achievement. When responding to a challenge with speed and imagination, Ilongot huntsmen experience themselves as the main characters in their own stories. Through these stories, as ethnographers we can, in turn, gain access to the culturally shaped experiences that Ilongot men find most significant as they go about making their living by hunting.

NOTES

Field research among the Ilongots, during 1967–69 and 1974, was financed by a National Science Foundation predoctoral fellowship, by National Science Foundation Research Grants GS–1509 and GS–40788, and by a Mellon award for junior faculty from Stanford University. This paper was written while I was a Fellow at the Center for Advanced Study in the Behavioral Sciences, Stanford, California. I am grateful for financial support provided by the National Science Foundation (#BNS 76 22943) and by a Postdoctoral Fellowship for Minorities, Funded by the Ford Foundation and the National Endowment for the Humanities and administered by the National Research Council. I have benefited from the comments of Charles Altieri, Bruce Kapferer, Mary Pratt, Paul Riesman, Michelle Rosaldo, and Sylvia Yanagisako.

1. Further material on Ilongots and their subsistence can be found in M. Rosaldo (1975, 1980), Rosaldo and Atkinson (1975), and R. Rosaldo (1980a, 1981).

2. The notion that direct speech (quoted verbatim) is the ultimate mimetic device in written narrative abounds in the writings of literary critics. Genette (1976:3), for example, argues that such direct imitation literally repeats words that were really uttered and literally constitutes fictional discourse. Booth (1961:8–20), however, reminds us, by invoking Henry James's famous terms, that even if current fashion prefers "showing" over "telling," authors always intervene in their stories even if only by choosing to show one thing rather than another.

3. The method of Genette (1980) assumes that even in fictional narrative there is an underlying story (events in the world ordered temporally by sequence, duration, and frequency). If narrative and story match in their temporal ordering, Genette can speak (playing on Roland Barthes's term) of "zero-degree" temporality. But this method should be used with caution because, among other reasons, it surely is bizarre to regard, as Genette does, all differences between human and calendrical time as if the former were deviations from the latter as norm.

4. This technique of parsing lines has been most fully outlined in a paper by Tedlock (1971) and in a recent book by Seitel (1980). Although this mode of presenting oral narrative can bring out its force and meaning, it risks making stories about specific events appear timeless in their poetic beauty (see, e.g., Peynetsa 1971). My project here attempts to hold poetry and history in tension by making both present without reducing either one to the other.

5. The key paper here is Labov's (1972). For a lucid explication of his concepts and methods, as well as the implications of his work for literary theory, see Pratt (1977:38–78). Pratt uses the term "natural narrative" to oppose "ordinary" versus "literary" language and then to indicate the continuity between the two. But, of course, culture-specific forms rather than universal or natural ones constitute oral narratives. When such eminent literary critics as Barthes (1977:79; cited approvingly in White 1980:5) speak about the universality of narrative, one hopes that they intend their remarks in the family resemblance sense that anthropologists use in speaking of the universality of kinship systems—every society

has something of this kind, yet they vary widely in form, content, scope, depth, and consequences.

6. Such similes occur frequently in Ilongot magical spells (see M. Rosaldo 1975), hence the appropriateness of remarking on their relative absence and particular force in this oral narrative.

7. The notion that the same text can convey different meanings in different contexts has been stated most forcefully in relation to proverbs. Smith (1978:70), for example, says that "by a sort of natural selection, those proverbs that survive are literally the *fittest*; that is, they fit the widest variety of circumstances or adapt most readily to emergent environments. And this is because their meanings are indeterminate enough to cover almost all human, natural, and historical exigencies." Data closer to the anthropologist's usual terrain also have been used to make the same point (e.g., Ngal 1977; Paredes 1970). These examples seem to be especially clear cases against text positivism or seeing meaning emerging only from within the self-contained text.

8. Although people have long considered story forms as emergent from the context of social interaction (see, e.g., Georges 1969), as I do here, most theories of narrative tacitly assume that the form involves monologue rather than dialogue. Present camps in literary theory have been oppositionally displayed in Valdes and Miller (1978). One can learn the current state of the art, to a reasonable extent, from *Critical Inquiry* (vol. 7, no. 1, 1980) and *New Literary History* (vol. 11, no. 3, 1980). Seminal sources for current work include Booth (1961) and Scholes and Kellog (1966). The discussion on narrative in the philosophy of history has a rather different cast and can be surveyed initially in various issues of *History and Theory* (see also R. Rosaldo 1980b).

9. Current fashion in literary theory tends to downplay the notion of narrative time. But Hans Meyerhoff's (1960) classic work stimulated my formulations here. Most discussions of temporality make sequence and duration particularly central; and Genette (1980) has also considered frequency or repetition. The notion of simultaneity (events happening at the same time in different places) has been given much less thought than it deserves.

10. Note that the myth is framed by a natural event (the flood) that transforms the culturally marked landscape into a disorienting natural void. Conversely, the human tasks involve labor processes that irreversibly transform natural living beings (human bodies, bamboo plants) into lethal cultural objects (intoxicating chopped and cooked vaginas and penises, shaved and sharpened stakes set up all around). These observations, of course, suggest a point of departure for a Lévi-Straussian analysis which, given my present concerns, I have not pursued here.

REFERENCES

Barthes, Roland. 1977. Introduction to the Structural Analysis of Narratives. In: *Image, Music, Text*, pp. 79–124. New York: Hill and Wang.

Booth, Wayne. 1961. *The Rhetoric of Fiction*. Chicago: University of Chicago Press.

Cooper, James Fenimore. 1879. *The Pioneers: Or the Sources of the Susquehanna*. Boston: Houghton, Osgood and Co.

Floro, Maria Sagrario. 1981. "Pantabangan: From Self-Sufficiency to Rural Poverty," *Anthropology Resource Center Newsletter* 5(1):6.

Genette, Gerard. 1976. "Boundaries of Narrative," *New Literary History* 8:1–13.

––––––. 1980. *Narrative Discourse: An Essay in Method*. Ithaca, N.Y.: Cornell University Press.

Georges, Robert A. 1969. "Toward an Understanding of Storytelling Events," *Journal of American Folklore* 82:313–28.

Labov, William. 1972. "The Transformation of Experience in Narrative Syntax." In: *Language in the Inner City: Studies in the Black English Vernacular*, pp. 354–96. Philadelphia: University of Pennsylvania Press.

Meyerhoff, Hans. 1960. *Time in Literature*. Berkeley: University of California Press.

Ngal, M. A. M. 1977. "Literary Creation in Oral Civilizations," *New Literary History* 8:335–44.

Paredes, Americo. 1970. "Proverbs and Ethnic Stereotypes," *Proverbium* 15:95–97.

Peynetsa, Andrew. 1971. "When the Old Timers Went Hunting," *Alcheringa* 3:76–81.

Pratt, Mary Louise. 1977. *Toward a Speech Act Theory of Literary Discourse*. Bloomington: Indiana University Press.

Ricouer, Paul. 1980. "Narrative Time," *Critical Inquiry* 71:169–90.

Rosaldo, Michelle. 1975. "It's All Uphill": The Creative Metaphors of Ilongot Magical Spells." In: M. Sanches and B. Blount (eds.), *Sociocultural Dimensions of Language Use*, pp. 177–203. New York: Seminar Press.

––––––. 1980. *Knowledge and Passion: Ilongot Notions of Self and Social Life*. New York: Cambridge University Press.

Rosaldo, Michelle, and Jane Monnig Atkins. 1975. "Man the Hunter and Woman." In: Roy Willis (ed.), *The Interpretation of Symbolism*, pp. 177–203. London: Malaby Press.

Rosaldo, Renato. 1978. "The Rhetoric of Control: Ilongots Viewed as Natural Bandits and Wild Indians." In: Barbara Babcock (ed.), *The Reversible World: Symbolic Inversion in Art and Society*, pp. 240–57. Ithaca, N.Y.: Cornell University Press.

––––––. 1980a. *Ilongot Headhunting, 1883–1974: A Study in Society and History*. Stanford: Stanford University Press.

––––––. 1980b. "Doing Oral History," *Social Analysis* 4:89–99.

––––––. 1981. "The Social Relations of Ilongot Subsistence." In: Harold Olofson(ed.), *Adaptive Strategies and Change in Philippine Swidden Societies*, pp. 29–41. Laguna, Philippines: Forest Research Institute, College.

Scholes, Robert, and Robert Kellog. 1966. *The Nature of Narrative*. New York: Oxford University Press.

Seitel, Peter. 1980. *See So That We May See: Performances and Interpretations of Traditional Tales from Tanzania*. Bloomington: University of Indiana Press

Smith, Barbara Herrnstein. 1978. *On the Margins of Discourse*. Chicago: University of Chicago Press.

Tedlock, Dennis. 1971. "On the Translation of Style in Oral Narrative," *Journal of American Folklore* 84:114–33.

Valdes, Mario, and Owen J. Miller. 1978. *Interpretation of Narrative*. Toronto: University of Toronto Press.

White, Hayden. 1980. "The Value of Narrativity in the Representation of Reality," *Critical Inquiry* 7(1):5–27.

6

Ethnography
as
Narrative

EDWARD M. BRUNER

> ...of all learned discourse, the ethnological seems to
> come closest to a Fiction.
>
> Roland Barthes

My aim here is to take a reflexive view of the production of
ethnography; my thesis is that ethnographies are guided by an
implicit narrative structure, by a story we tell about the peoples
we study. We are familiar with the stories people tell about themselves in life history and psychiatric interviews, in myth and ritual,
in history books and Balinese cockfights. I wish to extend this
notion to ethnography as discourse, as a genre of storytelling.[1] To
develop this position I take as an example ethnological studies of
Native American culture change. It is an area in which I have
had direct field experience and for which the facts are widely
known; also, the subject has occupied a prominent place in the
history of American anthropology.

In the 1930s and 1940s the dominant story constructed about
Native American culture change saw the present as disorganization, the past as glorious, and the future as assimilation. Now,
however, we have a new narrative: the present is viewed as a resistance movement, the past as exploitation, and the future as ethnic
resurgence. What is so striking is that the transition from one narrative structure to another occurred rapidly, within a decade after
World War II. Equally striking is that there is so little historical
continuity between the two dominant stories: one story simply
became discredited and the new narrative took over. The theoreti-

139

cal concepts associated with the outmoded story, such as acculturation and assimilation, are used less frequently and another set
of terms has become prominent: exploitation, oppression, colonialism, resistance, liberation, independence, nationalism, tribalism,
identity, tradition, and ethnicity—the code words of the 1970s.

The transition from a story of acculturation to one of ethnic
resurgence is not merely characterized by a change in theoretical
concepts on the level of vocabulary—there has also been a shift in
the way the ethnography is constructed, on the level of syntax. In
the old story the golden age was in the past and the descriptive
problem was to reconstruct the old Indian culture, to create a
beginning (Said 1975). The end of the narrative, the disappearance of Indian culture, was not problematic—it was assumed—
and the middle, the present-day scene, was interpreted in terms
of this sense of an ending (Kermode 1967) as progressive breakdown, pathology, and disintegration. In the 1970s story, however,
the golden age is in the future, as the indigenous people struggle
against exploitation and oppression to preserve their ethnic identity. The ethnographic problematic is now one of documenting resistance and telling how tradition and ethnicity are maintained;
or if they are seriously threatened, the anthropologist may even
make a political decision to intervene on behalf of the people, or
possibly to take steps to help prevent cultural extinction or
genocide. In the early development of American anthropology
there was definite concern with cultural extinction, but as it was
assumed to be inevitable, the aim was to describe Indian cultures
before they disappeared, not to facilitate their continuity. In this
sense narrative structures provide social roles for the anthropologist as well as for the Indian people. Regarding the latter,
from my own experience in 1948 among the Navajo, and starting
in 1951 among the Mandan-Hidatsa of the Fort Berthold Reservation, I can testify that we met many Indian informants, particularly older men, who were eager to provide information about the
glorious past, whereas now we meet many Indian activists fighting
for a better future. In the 1930s narrative it was the past that
pervaded the present; in the 1970s narrative it is the future.

Stories make meaning. They operate at the level of semantics
in addition to vocabulary and syntax (White 1980; Turner 1980).
Just as a story has a beginning, a middle, and an end, culture
change, too, almost by definition, takes the form of a sequence

with a past, a present, and a future. Our predicament in ethnographic studies of change is that all we have before us is the present, the contemporary scene, and by one means or another we must situate that present in a time sequence. It would be naive to believe that we anthropologists simply describe the present but reconstruct the past and construct the future, even though we use language that suggests this—for example, when we talk of gathering or collecting the data as if it were like ripe fruit waiting to be picked, or when we talk of our special anthropological methodologies for reconstructing the past, as if the present were not equally constructed. The past, present, and future are not only constructed but connected in a lineal sequence that is defined by systematic if not casual relations. How we depict any one segment of the sequence is related to our conception of the whole, which I choose to think of as a story.

My position may become clearer when contrasted with that of Lévi-Strauss. He writes that "all myths tell a story" (1966:26), but "instead of reducing the story or myth to a mere narrative [he urges us] to try to discover the scheme of discontinuous oppositions governing its organization" (1966:136). The power of his method of analyzing paradigmatic structures has been amply documented, but we may do equally well to try to discover the syntagmatic structure beyond the surface narrative. Such structures cannot be reduced to metonymy precisely because they are more than relations of contiguity—they are systematically ordered, and therein lies their meaning. If classificatory schemes provide a science of the concrete, narrative schemes may provide a science of the imagination. At the very least, a reemphasis on temporality may enable us to deal more directly with change, and thereby to make structural and symbolic studies more dynamic.[2]

Let me illustrate the semantic dimension with the 1930s narrative. Given the master story of a once proud people whose spirit had been broken and who would soon become assimilated into what was then called the "mainstream of American life," all tribes could be located—the acculturated Sioux in one chapter, the more traditional Hopi in an earlier chapter, and the Indians of the East Coast, who were thought to be virtually extinct, in the last chapter. Ethnographers were able to interpret their field experience in terms of how their particular reservation situation fitted into the lineal sequence of the dominant story of the era.

As editor of a volume of seven case studies prepared in the late 1930s, Linton (1940:462) wrote of the San Ildefonso: "Although the old ceremonies are still going on with full apparent vigor . . . it seems probable that the next few years will see a collapse of the esoteric aspects of the culture and a rapid acculturation of the society." And " . . . Ute culture steadily approaches its final resolution in complete assimilation" (1940:201). Of the White Knife Shoshoni he wrote: "There seem to be no internal factors which would prevent their complete Europeanization" (1940:118). "Lastly, everything indicates that the ultimate end of situations of close and continuous first hand contact is the amalgamation of the societies and cultures involved, although this conclusion may be postponed almost indefinitely . . . " (1940:519). We are told that amalgamation is inevitable but that it may be postponed indefinitely—a neat trick. What is so remarkable is that in not one of the seven cases discussed had complete assimilation occurred, but such a distinguished anthropologist as Ralph Linton assumed that it would, despite evidence to the contrary in the very case studies he was analyzing. Such is the power of a story once it has captured the imagination.

Given this 1930s vision of the future and the convention of reconstructing the "aboriginal" past as an integrated culture, the present could only be interpreted as disintegration, framed as it was by both glorious integrity and eventual disappearance. My aim here is not to review a literature with which we are all familiar, but rather to emphasize that the present is given meaning in terms of that anticipated present we call the future and that former present we call the past (Culler 1979:162). Stories are interpretive devices which give meaning to the present in terms of location in an ordered syntagmatic sequence—the exact opposite of anthropological common sense. As anthropologists, we usually think that we first investigate the present, more or less scientifically, and thereafter reconstruct the past and anticipate the future. In my view, we begin with a narrative that already contains a beginning and an ending, which frame and hence enable us to interpret the present. It is not that we initially have a body of data, the facts, and we then must construct a story or a theory to account for them. Instead, to paraphrase Schafer (1980:30), the narrative structures we construct are not secondary narratives about data but primary narratives that establish what is to count as data. New narratives yield new vocabulary, syntax, and meaning in our ethnographic accounts; they define what constitute the data of those accounts.

My claim is that one story—past glory, present disorganization, future assimilation—was dominant in the 1930s and a second story—past oppression, present resistance, future resurgence—in the 1970s, but in both cases I refer to dominance in the anthropological literature, in ethnographic discourse, not necessarily in Indian experience. My focus is on our talk about Indians, not on Indian life itself. Our anthropological stories about Indians are representations, not be confused with concrete existence or "real" facts. In other words, life experience is richer than discourse.

Narrative structures organize and give meaning to experience, but there are always feelings and lived experience not fully encompassed by the dominant story. Only after the new narrative becomes dominant is there a reexamination of the past, a rediscovery of old texts, and a recreation of the new heroes of liberation and resistance. The new story articulates what had been only dimly perceived, authenticates previous feelings, legitimizes new actions, and aligns individual consciousness with a larger social movement. What had previously been personal becomes historical; a "model of" is transformed into a "model for" (Geertz 1973). From the perspective of the present we construct a continuous story, stressing the continuity of resistance, whereas actually there was a marked discontinuity from the diminution of one narrative to the rise of another. Foucault's (1973) notion of strata is relevant here, but more as an archaeology of discourse than an archaeology of epistemological fields. Certainly, there was active Indian resistance in the past, probably more so in expressive culture than in direct political action, in the form of jokes (Basso 1979), and in such religious movements as the Ghost Dance, the Sun Dance, and the Native American Church. Retrospectively, we see that there always were expressions of resistance in Indian experience, and there were early formulations of the story of resistance. Nevertheless, we can pinpoint the time when the new narrative became dominant in discourse—with the formation in 1961 of the National Indian Youth Council and the American Indian Chicago Conference (Lurie 1961), with the publication of the *Indian Historian* in 1964, with the establishment of AIM in 1968, with the publication of Vine Deloria's *Custer Died for Your Sins* in 1969, and with the anthropological writings of Clemmer (1970), Jorgensen (1972), and others.

I am reasonably confident in my identification of the two narrative structures and in the prominence of one in the discourse of the 1930s and of the other in the 1970s. A possible explanation of the two narratives is that the Indian story *is* resistance and the white story *is* assimilation—that the two are just the different points of view of the oppressed and the oppressor. I reject this explanation because it is, in effect, only another telling of the resistance story and because I do not believe it is historically accurate. The resistance story was not dominant in Indian discourse until after World War II, and by the early 1950s American anthropologists (e.g., Vogt 1957; Province 1954) were questioning Indian assimilation, the myth of the melting pot. Further, both Indian and anthropologist share the same narrative—not that one narrative is Indian and the other white—a fact that subsequently will be made evident.

Another view is offered by Jorgensen (1972:ix) who wrote that the acculturation story is "nonsense" and the resistance story is "truth," so that in effect the movement from one story to the other is seen as an advance in scientific understanding. Jorgensen was simply privileging one of the two stories, but I understand the reasons for his conviction. I have published on the side of ethnicity and against the acculturation-urbanization framework in a series of papers dating back to 1953 (e.g., Bruner 1953, 1961, 1974). I also realize that stories are not ideologically neutral.

Narratives are not only structures of meaning but structures of power as well. The assimilation story has been a mask for oppression; the resistance story is a justification for claims of redress for past exploitation. Both carry policy and political implications. The reasoning in the assimilation narrative is that if Indians are going to disappear anyway, then their land can be leased or sold to whites; in the ethnic resurgence narrative we are told that if Indians are here to stay, tribal resources must be built up. Assimilation is a program for redemption; resistance, for self- and ethnic fulfillment. The terms themselves—acculturation, resistance, neocolonialism—are pregnant with meaning. Each narrative uses different images, language, and style. The Indian in the acculturation narrative is romantic, the exotic Other; the resistance Indian is victimized. Stories construct an Indian self; narrative structures are constitutive as well as interpretive.

The two narratives, in my view, are dual aspects of the same phenomenon; one is a counterpoint to the other. There may even be cycles of narratives, for each contains a basic contradiction. The assimilation story leads to outside pressures for change, which thereby generate resistance. The resistance story, in time, will lead to greater security in the people's own culture and identity, making it easier to change more rapidly and thereby facilitate assimilation. In any case, there also was resistance in the 1930s and acculturation in the 1970s, for the dual processes of change and persistence, of acculturation and nationalism, have occurred simultaneously throughout Indian history. My only claim is that different narratives are foregrounded in the discourse of different historical eras.

The key elements in narrative are story, discourse, and telling. The *story* is the abstract sequence of events, systematically related, the syntagmatic structure. *Discourse* is the text in which the story is manifested, the statement in a particular medium such as a novel, myth, lecture, film, conversation, or whatever. *Telling* is the action, the act of narrating, the communicative process that produces the story in discourse. No distinction is made here between telling and showing, as the same story may be recounted or enacted or both.[3]

We may ask whether the "same" story is told in different versions, as Chatman (1978) assumes. If a story is conceived of as an "invariant core" (Culler 1980:28), independent of its presentation, then it becomes a kind of "Platonic ideal form ... that occupies a highly privileged ontological realm of pure Being within which it unfolds immutably and eternally" (Herrnstein-Smith 1980:216). The issue is a familiar one to anthropologists. In explaining the distinction between model and behavior, for example, Leach (1976:5) uses a musical analogy: although we may hear an incompetent performance of a Beethoven symphony, we must remember that the real symphony exists as a musical score, as a model, and not in any particular manifestation. My friends in musicology tell me that Leach might well have selected Mahler instead of Beethoven, as Mahler's scores are exceedingly detailed and precise whereas Beethoven's scripts are loosely written and hence subject to more varied interpretation. In any case, Leach's perspective is theoretically paralyzing, as he has no way to take account of experience and no way to discriminate between a flawed performance and structural change. For Leach, every item of behavior, every potential evidence of change, may be explained away as another incompetent performance, leaving the model intact and thereby avoiding the question of determining when the model, or the story, has changed.

Herrnstein-Smith (1980) goes too far in the other direction, however, for in her emphasis on the social context of the telling she dispenses with the concept of story. My position is that the story is prior to, but not independent of, the discourse. We abstract the story from discourse, but once abstracted the story serves as a model for future discourse. Each telling depends on the context, the audience, and the conventions of the medium. A retelling is never an exact duplicate of the already told story, for it takes account of previous tellings, the conditions of which are never identical. Thus, diachronically considered, the story is transformed and transformative, its inherent possibilities are explored, as in the unfolding of an art style, and the pure play and delight in its various combinations are made manifest. In his retelling of the story of Beckett, for example, Turner (1974) was very sensitive to the dialectic between root metaphor and historical experience; and the same sensitivity is shown by Schafer (1980) in his analysis of psychoanalytic dialogue. In ethnography, we need the concept of story to serve as a "model for." To paraphrase Barthes (1974:16), there is no primary, naive, phenomenal understanding of the field data we later explicate or intellectualize. No ethnographer is truly innocent—we all begin with a narrative in our heads which structures our initial observations in the field.

There is a dialectic between story and experience, but in the production of ethnography we are continually oriented toward the dominant narrative structure. We go to the reservation with a story already in mind, and that story is foregrounded in the final professional product, the published article, chapter, or monograph. If we stray too far from the dominant story in the literature, if we overlook a key reference or fail to mention the work of an important scholar, we are politely corrected by such institutional monitors as thesis committees, foundation review panels, or journal editors. At the beginning and the end the production of ethnography is framed by the dominant story. Most of the time there is a balance to research innovation—the study is new enough to be interesting but familiar enough so that the story remains recognizable. There are those who are ahead of their times—Bateson did publish *Naven* in 1936—but we usually define research with reference to the current narrative and report back our particular variation of that narrative to our colleagues, most of whom already know the plot structure in advance. The process is self-reinforcing and reconfirms everyone's view of the world (Kuhn 1962).

Most interesting is what happens in the middle of the ethnographic research process, in the field, where we find much folk wisdom. Sol Tax used to advise his students to write the first draft of their dissertations before going to the field; another view is that the research proposal does not really matter, since we usually end up studying something different anyway. We can all agree, however, that the field situation initially presents itself as a confusing "galaxy of signifiers" (Barthes 1974:16). It is alien, even chaotic; there is so much going on, all at once, that the problem becomes one of making sense of it. How do we accomplish this? I am reminded of Abrahams's (1977:99) statement about hijacking: "A common reaction of people involved in airplane hijackings, when asked how they felt and what they did, was 'Oh, everything was familiar to us; we had seen it in the movies already.'" Previous ethnographic texts and the stories they contain are the equivalent of the movies. Narrative structures serve as interpretive guides; they tell us what constitute data, define topics for study, and place a construction on the field situation that transforms it from the alien to the familiar. Even when we are settled in, however, feeling comfortable in our new surroundings, there is still the problem of going back from the lived experience of the field situation to the anthropological literature, to our final destination.

In the field we turn experience into discourse by what I refer to as the three tellings of fieldwork. First we tell the people why we are there, what information we are seeking, and how we intend to use the data. We do this directly, by explaining our project and by our behavior, by the questions we ask and the activities we attend. As the people respond to our questions, we begin the ethnographic dialogue, the complex interactions and exchanges that lead to the negotiation of the text. In the second telling we take this verbal and visual information and process it, committing it to writing in our field diaries. This transcription is not easy. Every ethnographer is painfully aware of the discrepancy between the richness of the lived field experience and the paucity of the language used to characterize it. There is necessarily a dramatic reduction, condensation, and fragmentation of data. In the third telling the audience consists of our colleagues, who provide feedback as we prepare our materials for publication, and here the story becomes even more prominent. There is, of course, a fourth telling—when other anthropologists read what we have written and summarize it in class lectures and in their own publications. We all retell the same stories, even the very old ones such as the progressive development of culture from the simple to the complex and the diffusion of traits from a center to a periphery. Retellings never cease; there is an infinite reflexivity as we go from experience to discourse to history. Eventually, all experience is filtered out and we end where we began—with the story.

Our ethnographies are coauthored, not simply because informants contribute data to the text, but because, as I suggested earlier, ethnographer and informant come to share the same narratives. The anthropologist and the Indian are unwitting co-conspirators in a dialectical symbolic process. In suggesting that narratives are shared, I acknowledge that the case is obviously stronger for American anthropologists and Native Americans, as they are members of the same larger society. I know that many stories do not apply to culture change, that alternative stories exist simultaneously, that the sharing is not complete, that there are variations of the basic plot, and that individuals manipulate stories. But stories *are* shared. Let me turn now to an example.

In New Mexico and Arizona during the summer of 1980, the tricentennial of the Pueblo Revolt of 1680 was celebrated by a series of events, including a reenactment of the original revolt, feast days at various pueblos, an arts and crafts show, foot races, ceremonials, and a proclamation by the governor of New Mexico. The narrative guiding these events was clearly the current story of resistance and ethnic resurgence, as is evident in the following quote from an article in *New Mexico Magazine*, based on a document issued by the Eight Northern Indian Pueblos Council: "The Pueblo Revolt of 1680 was the first successful rebellion on American soil. [It] expressed unyielding determination to safeguard ancient traditional beliefs and practices [and] will stand forever as a symbol of encouragement to all oppressed peoples everywhere in search of freedom and self-determination" (Hill 1980:54).

The Pueblo Indians are performing our theory; they are

enacting the story we tell about them in the pages of our pɪ
sional journals. We wonder if it is their story or ours. Which is ᵥ
inside and which the outside view, and what about the distinctioɴ
between emic and etic? I question these oppositions, just as I
question the notion that the Indian story is resistance and the
white story is acculturation. My position is that both Indian
enactment, the story they tell about themselves, and our theory,
the story we tell, are transformations of each other; they are retellings of a narrative derived from the discursive practice of our
historical era (Foucault 1973), instances of never-ceasing reflexivity. The story of exploitation, resistance, and resurgence goes
beyond American society, of course. It is an international story
that I have heard in Sumatra and in India; it is retold almost
daily in debates at the United Nations.

Some scholars make a sharp distinction between the ethnographer as subject and the native peoples as the object of an investigation. To the extent that we see the ethnographer as an outsider
looking in, the privileged stranger who can perceive patterns not
apparent to those within the system, then we further magnify the
separation between anthropologist as subject and indigene as object. We have long recognized that it is difficult to obtain an accurate description of the object, to know the true nature of the outside world. And we have been concerned with the accuracy of our
ethnographic accounts, especially when confronted with conflicting interpretations of the same culture (e.g., Redfield and Lewis).
The question of what is really out there then emerges. We have
recognized a problem with the subject, the anthropologist, but this
tends to dissolve into details of personal bias, individual personality traits, and selective perception—after all, we are only human.
We also have dealt with subject-object relations in another way,
by suggesting that the object of our ethnography is constituted by
a Western mode of thought, by our language, and that we have
created the category of the native or the concept of the primitive.
Said (1978) argues, for example, that Orientalists in western
Europe have represented and constituted Orientalism as a
mechanism of domination.

I wish to offer a different interpretation of subject-object relations. Borrowing from Barthes and Foucault, I take both subject
and object as problematic and dissolve the sharp distinction between them; I see both anthropologist and Indian as being caught

in the same web, influenced by the same historical forces, and shaped by the dominant narrative structures of our times. In a personal communication Bill Sturtevant remarked that this essay seems "to undermine the entire enterprise," and his statement deserves to be taken seriously, especially since he has devoted most of his professional life to editing the monumental *Handbook of the American Indian*. Ethnography, as I have described it, does seem less privileged, less the authoritative voice about native peoples. The ethnographer appears not as an individual creative scholar, a knowing subject who discovers, but more as a material body through whom a narrative structure unfolds. If myths have no authors (à la Lévi-Strauss), then in the same sense neither do ethnographic texts. Cassirer has argued that when we think we are exploring reality we are merely engaging in a dialogue with our symbolic systems (see Grossberg 1979:201). My point is that both anthropologist and native informant participate in the same symbolic system. Not that our cultures are identical; rather, we share, at least partially, those narratives dealing with intercultural relations and cultural change.

Marx, in that famous first sentence of the Eighteenth Brumaire, quoted Hegel to the effect that all the great events of world history occur twice, the first time as tragedy and the second as farce. In a sense, the Pueblo Revolt occurred twice—in 1680 as tragedy, and in 1980, if not as farce then at least as play, as ritual enactment. To look at it another way, the Pueblo Revolt is an example of intertextuality, in that the 1980 text contains or quotes the 1680 text. The 1980 enactment is a story about a story, the production of a text based on another text. What is created in 1980, however, is not the original event but another version of reality, for the meaning of the tricentennial is in the 1980 telling, not in the origin or source. We tend to go back to 1680 to interpret the actions of the first Pueblo revolutionaries and their Spanish conquerors, and this may be important for historical scholarship. But the Pueblo Revolt, for us, is constituted by the contemporary telling based on the contemporary narrative of resistance. Once enacted, of course, the tricentennial reinforces that narrative and revitalizes everyday Pueblo life. I do not see a 300-year continuity to the story of resistance; the peaceful people chose to celebrate a 1680 rebellion at a 1980 tricentennial but not at a 1780 centennial or an 1880 bicentennial. Whether they commemorate the revolt in

2080 remains to be seen—much depends on the ideological dynamic of the twenty-first century and the narrative structures of that time.

If stories are shared, as I claim, there are many implications for the production of ethnographic accounts. For if the story is in our heads before we arrive at the field site, and if it is already known by the peoples we study, then we enter the ethnographic dialogue with a shared schema. We can fit in the pieces and negotiate the text more readily; we begin the interaction with the structural framework already in place. It is as if our informants know, in advance, the chapter headings of our unwritten dissertations. There is, of course, considerable variability and factionalism within any population, so the task of the anthropologist is to select his or her informants carefully. This we have always done, but I suggest here that the concept of "my favorite informant" may be less a question of personal compatibility than of shared narrative structure. We choose those informants whose narratives are most compatible with our own—just as, I am sure, informants select their favorite anthropologists based on the same criterion of compatibility.

The final question I will raise concerns how narratives, or models, change. If the narrative is transformed with each retelling, then how much transformation can occur before the story is no longer acknowledged as being the same? And where do new stories come from? In part, this is a question of perspective, for we can look back over the various tellings and stress either continuity or discontinuity: continuity, or incremental change, in which the old story is continually modified; or discontinuity, or structural change, in which a new story emerges. The first is experienced as evolutionary change and the second as revolutionary, as a rupture in the social fabric.

In the first process, stressing continuity, the telling takes account of the context, previous tellings, and the relationship between narrator and audience; thus, the story is modified incrementally. Each retelling starts from the old story and encompasses new conditions, but it is recognized as being the same story. In structural change a new narrative is seen, as in the change from assimilation to resistance, because the old narrative can no longer be stretched to encompass the new events. The key to structural change is a radical shift in the social context. New stories arise when there is a new reality to be explained, when the social arrangements are so different that the old narrative no longer seems adequate.

New narratives do not arise from anthropological field research, as we sometimes tell our graduate students, but from history, from world conditions. The Indian acculturation story was part of the American dream, the expansion of the frontier, the conquest of the wilderness, and the Americanization of immigrants. After World War II the world changed, with the overthrow of colonialism, the emergence of new states, the civil rights movement, and a new conception of equality. Narrative structures changed accordingly.

Before World War II the acculturation story was dominant. Although the resistance story was told, it was not yet prominent in the larger discourse. After World War II the story of oppression, resistance, and ethnic resurgence was told in an increasingly louder voice and applied to many different peoples. As the old story became discredited and was labeled reactionary, the new story was articulated by new organizations, leaders, and prophets. With the early telling of the resistance narrative, new "facts" began to emerge which the acculturation story could not explain. For a time the two stories overlapped, but as the new story achieved dominance, the old story increasingly appeared to contradict common sense. It had lost its explanatory power and credibility.

During the period of competition between the two stories, there was a change in the role of the Indian in discourse. New narratives open up new spaces in discourse that arise precisely from the gaps and silences of the previous era (Foucault 1973:207). Let me characterize the difference, although for purposes of emphasis I shall overstate the case. In the past we had the cigar store Indian, the traveling troupe in full ceremonial dress representing the quintessential American Indian, on display at the sideshow at county fairs, carnivals, and rodeos (Mead 1932:67). Indians were mute, like museum specimens, a disappearing breed. It was not that they had nothing to say; rather, they were denied a space in discourse and hence had no power. Now, however, we have a new narrative. Indians march on Washington, become legal experts on water rights, and come to our universities to lecture. They speak directly in the political arena, not just in ritual and expressive domains, and stress such new themes as the value of Indian culture for white society, tribalism and ecology, and how to live in harmony with each other and with nature.

Because of its new role in discourse, the new narrative can be forcefully articulated. It is eventually accepted, not piecemeal, bit-by-bit, but whole, all at once, as a story. It takes time, however, for a new narrative to become dominant. For such change to occur there must be a breakdown of previously accepted understandings, a perception that a once familiar event no longer makes sense, a penetration of the previously taken-for-granted. Stories operate not simply in the realm of the mind, as ideas; to be convincing they also must have a base in experience or social practice. It is the perceived discrepancy between the previously accepted story and the new situation that leads us to discard or question the old narrative; and it is the perceived relevance of the new story to our own life situation that leads to its acceptance. Tricentennial enactments, political conflict, and social dramas play a key role in precipitating the sense of behavioral contradiction that leads to the acceptance of new narratives.

I conclude by noting that narrative structure has an advantage over such related concepts as metaphor or paradigm in that narrative emphasizes order and sequence, in a formal sense, and is more appropriate for the study of change, the life cycle, or any developmental process. Story as model has a remarkable dual aspect—it is both linear and instantaneous. On the one hand, a story is experienced as a sequence, as it is being told or enacted; on the other hand, it is comprehended all at once—before, during, and after the telling. A story is static and dynamic at the same time. And although I have focused on American Indian change in this paper, as an example, I trust the thesis of ethnography as narrative has wider applicability.

Stories give meaning to the present and enable us to see that present as part of a set of relationships involving a constituted past and a future. But narratives change, all stories are partial, all meanings incomplete. There is no fixed meaning in the past, for with each new telling the context varies, the audience differs, the story is modified, and as Gorfain writes in her essay in this volume, "retellings become foretellings." We continually discover new meanings. All of us, then, anthropologists and informants, must accept responsibility for understanding society as told and retold.

NOTES

Cary Nelson, Claire Farrer, Phyllis Gorfain, Kay Ikeda, Larry Grossberg, Norman Whitten, Nina Baym, William Schroeder, Barbara Babcock, and the members of my Fall 1980 graduate seminar provided generous assistance.

1. For similar studies see White (1973), Boon (1977), Said (1978), and especially Schafer (1980). I am heavily indebted to Foucault (1973, 1978).

2. Work in the field of narratology by French structuralists (Barthes 1974; Genette 1980) and the almost simultaneous appearance in 1980 of special issues on narrative in three different journals (*New Literary History, Poetics Today, Critical Inquiry*) testify to the recent intererst.

3. These definitions are based on Genette (1980). In this essay I have not had space to consider a number of important issues, for example, is storytelling universal and is narrativity a Western concept? I believe the answer to both questions is yes, but the issues are complicated (e.g., see Becker 1979).

REFERENCES

Abrahams, Roger D. 1977. "Toward an Enactment-Centered Theory of Folklore." In: William Bascom (ed.), *Frontiers of Folklore*, pp. 79–120. Boulder, Colo.: Westview Press.

Barthes, Roland. 1974. *S/Z*. New York: Hill and Wang.

————. 1977. *Roland Barthes*. New York: Hill and Wang.

Basso, Keith H. 1979. *Portraits of "the Whiteman."* Cambridge: Cambridge University Press.

Bateson, Gregory. 1936. *Naven*. Cambridge: Cambridge University Press.

Becker, A. L. 1979. "Text-Building, Epistemology, and Aesthetics in Javanese Shadow Theatre." In: A. L. Becker and Aram A. Yengoyan (eds.), *The Imagination of Reality: Essays in Southeast Asian Coherence Systems*, pp. 211–43. Norwood, N.J.: Ablex.

Boon, James A. 1977. *The Anthropological Romance of Bali*. Cambridge: Cambridge University Press.

Bruner, Edward M. 1953. "Assimilation among Fort Berthold Indians," *American Indian* 6(4):21–29.

————. 1961. "Urbanization and Ethnic Identity in North Sumatra," *American Anthropologist* 63:508-21.

————. 1974. "The Expression of Ethnicity in Indonesia." In: Abner Cohen (ed.), *Urban Ethnicity*, pp. 251–80. ASA Monograph 12. London: Tavistock.

Chatman, Seymour. 1978. *Story and Discourse*. Ithaca, N.Y.: Cornell University Press.

Clemmer, Richard O. 1970. "Truth, Duty, and the Revitalization of Anthropologists: A New Perspective on Cultural Change and Resistance. In: Dell Hymes (ed.), *Reinventing Anthropology*, pp. 213–47. New York: Random House.

Culler, Jonathan. 1979. "Derrida." In: John Sturrock (ed.), *Structuralism and Since: From Lévi-Strauss to Derrida*, pp. 154–80. Oxford: Oxford University Press.

————. 1980. "Fabula and Sjuzhet in the Analysis of Narrative," *Poetics Today* 1(3):27–38.

Deloria, Vine. 1969. *Custer Died for Your Sins*. New York: Macmillan.

Foucault, Michel. 1973. *The Order of Things*. New York: Vintage Books.

————. 1978. *The History of Sexuality*. New York: Pantheon Books.

Geertz, Clifford. 1973. *The Interpretation of Cultures*. New York: Basic Books.

Genett, Gerard. 1980. *Narrative Discourse*. Ithaca, N.Y.: Cornell University Press.

Grossberg, Lawrence. 1979. "Language and Theorizing in the Human Sciences." In: Norman K. Denzin (ed.), *Studies in Symbolic Interaction*, vol. 2, pp. 189–231. Greenwich, Conn.: JAI Press.

Herrnstein-Smith, Barbara. 1980. "Narrative Versions, Narrative Theories," *Critical Inquiry* 7(1):213–36.

Hill, Joseph. 1980. "The Pueblo Revolt of 1680," *New Mexico Magazine* 58(6):38–43, 52–54.

Jorgensen, Joseph G. 1972. *The Sun Dance Religion*. Chicago: University of Chicago Press.

Kermode, Frank. 1967. *The Sense of an Ending*. New York: Oxford University Press.

Kuhn, T. S. 1962. *The Structure of Scientific Revolutions*. Chicago: University of Chicago Press.

Leach, Edmund. 1976. *Culture and Communication*. New York: Cambridge University Press.

Lévi-Strauss, Claude. 1966. *The Savage Mind*. Chicago: University of Chicago Press.

Linton, Ralph (ed.). 1940. *Acculturation in Seven American Indian Tribes*. New York: Appleton-Century.

Lurie, Nancy O. 1961. "The Voice of the American Indian: Report on the American Indian Chicago Conference," *Current Anthropology* 2:478–500.

Mead, Margaret. 1932. *The Changing Culture of an Indian Tribe*. New York: Columbia University Press.

Province, John. 1954. "The American Indian in Transition," *American Anthropologist* 56:389–94.

Said, Edward W. 1975. *Beginnings*. Baltimore, Md.: Johns Hopkins University Press.

————. 1978. *Orientalism*. New York: Vintage Books.

Schafer, Roy. 1980. "Narration in the Psychoanalytic Dialogue," *Critical Inquiry* 7(1):29–54.

Turner, Victor. 1974. *Drama, Fields, and Metaphors*. Ithaca, N.Y.: Cornell University Press.

————. 1980. "Social Dramas and Stories about Them," *Critical Inquiry* 7(1):141–68.

Vogt, E. Z. 1957. "The Acculturation of American Indians." In: *Annals* (American Academy of Political and Social Science), pp. 137–46. Philadelphia.

White, Hayden. 1973. *Metahistory*. Baltimore, Md.: Johns Hopkins University Press.

————. 1980. "The Value of Narrativity in the Representation of Reality," *Critical Inquiry* 7(1):5–28.

PART THREE

Images

7

The Argument of Images and the Experience of Returning to the Whole

JAMES W. FERNANDEZ

Culture... taken in its widest ethnographic sense is that complex whole which includes knowledge, belief, art, morals, law, custom, and any other capabilities and habits acquired by man as a member of society.

E. B. Tylor, *Primitive Culture*

Metonym celebrates the parts of experience while the more eloquent metaphors refer back to the whole for significance.

Claude Lévi-Strauss, *The Raw and the Cooked*

The essential problem for contemporary thought is to discover the meaning of wholes.

Louis Dumont, *Homo Hierarchicus*

A ROOM FULL OF MIRRORS

In this paper I wish to bring materials taken from work with revitalization movements in Africa to bear on this "essential problem for contemporary thought": the discovery of the meaning of wholes.[1] In particular I will be concerned with giving an account of the mechanisms that lead to the conviction of wholeness primarily, but not only, in these revitalization movements. I will label the work of these mechanisms, in the most general way, as "the argument of images" and will argue that the conviction of wholeness is the product of certain kinds of imaginative—that is, visualizing or pictorializing—activity.

The discovery of the meaning of wholes is a problem for contemporary thought because of the atomization and economic individualization of modern life; because of our harried existence, trying to manage an overload of information; and, as a consequence, because of the appeal of lowest common denominators and utilitarian all-purpose currencies that generalize shared experience at a very reduced and impoverished level of reality. We are better understood, it is said, as "dividuals," rather than "individuals," negotiating multiple and often incompatible memberships in separate self-contained associations.[2] The ideological promotion of our individuality, the defense of our freedom for self-actualization, stands in compensatory contrast to the dividedness of our commitments.

All this makes us agnostic when any whole is suggested. The plenitude of any overarching entity is regarded as illusory, medieval, something achieved by Cabbalistic or Thomistic conceits that have little to do with our daily ongoing efforts at competent management and pragmatic adaptation to the succession of abruptly changing circumstances. It stands in contrast to the affliction, in Durkheimian terms, of our endless profanity.

If we are unable to believe or be persuaded in our present particulate existence by the whole, we are yet prepared to recognize the possibilities of its achievement in other times and other cultures. Indeed, there is an old orthodoxy in anthropology, Durkheimian in tone and argument, which sees this matter in evolutionary terms; it sees human consciousness and powers of mind as evolving from synthetic to analytic capacities, from an easy and dynamic access to mystical participation in the presence of collective representations to the present state of sedate individuation in the presence of predominantly personal symbols.

Ernst Cassirer is a recent thinker who has articulated this orthodoxy most persuasively. His views, as the founding philosopher of symbolic forms, should be all the more interesting to a contemporary symbolic anthropology that is persuaded, like Cassirer, by the constitutive power of symbols. Picking up on observations present in the work of Durkheim and, more polemically, in the work of Lévy-Bruhl, Cassirer (1960) discusses the "consanguinity of all things" which prevails as the fundamental presupposition of mythical thought in the mythopoeic societies. "Life," he tells us, "is not divided into classes and subclasses. It is felt as an unbroken continuous whole which does not admit of clear-cut and trenchant distinctions. Limits between different spheres are not insurmountable barriers. They are fluent and fluctuating . . . by a sudden metamorphosis everything can be turned into everything. If there is any characteristic and outstanding feature of the mythical world, any law, it is this 'law of metamorphosis' " (1960:108).

There is an ambiguity in Cassirer, as there often is among those who address themselves to this old orthodoxy, as to whether we are dealing with rule-bound thought whose laws we can discover or whether it is simply the play of emotion . . . a sympathetic process. "Myth and primitive religion are by no means entirely incoherent, they are not bereft of sense or reason" (1960:108). But their coherence depends much more on a unity of feeling than logical rules. To be sure, Cassirer does not want this ambiguity to lead to an identification of his ideas with those of Lévy-Bruhl. On a facing page he gives instances of the powers of observation and discrimination, vis-á-vis the natural world, that are characteristic of primitive beings: "All this is scarcely in keeping with the assumption that the primitive mind by its very nature and essences is undifferentiated or confused . . . a prelogical or mystical mind" (1960:109). Obviously, Cassirer would have been much better served by more explicit reference to the Durkheimian argument, particularly to Durkheim and Mauss's *Primitive Classification* (1963).

But we are not concerned here with the long debate over the discrimination of parts in the primal and archaic mind; Lévi-Strauss's (1966) discussion of the intellectual impulse in totemism has pretty well laid that issue to rest. We are concerned, rather, with the relatively easy access to the whole that is characteristic of the primitive mind. What interests us, to use Cassirer's terms, are the principles of consanguinity and metamorphosis that are essential to the access to the whole and that make it, in effect and by virtue of symbolic statement, greater than the sum of its parts. In brief, we are concerned with the mechanisms that lead to the conviction of wholeness.

We should not pretend that the excess meaning of symbolic wholes has not been explored since Durkheim's day, or that "consanguinity of thought" or metamorphosis have since been neglected. It is just this relation of consanguinity, understood in the broadest sense, to metamorphosis (or transformation) that Lévi-Strauss has recurrently explored in his oeuvre. Still, seminal thought is not always fully clarified thought, and Lévi-Strauss's discussion of what he calls the "totalizing savage mind" is often complex and difficult to decipher. As an example, consider the "roomful of mirrors" he offers to us as an "aide pensée" in thinking about the knowledge of totality achieved by the "savage mind": "The object [of savage thought] is to grasp the world as both a synchronic and diachronic totality, and the knowledge it draws therefrom is like that afforded of a room by mirrors fixed on opposite walls which reflect each other (as well as objects in the intervening spaces) although without being strictly parallel. A multitude of images forms simultaneously, none exactly like any other—none furnishing more than a partial knowledge—but the group is characterized by invariant properties expressing a truth" (1966:263). The truth expressed is that of the whole, but it is a very "complex whole," indeed—one that is expressed for Lévi-Strauss in an interreflecting congeries of "imagenes mundi," as he calls them, or, as I would like to call it, by an "argument of images" (Fernandez 1978).

TUNING IN TO THE MUSIC OF SOCIAL SPHERES: THE EXPERIENCE OF RELATEDNESS

Cassirer's phrase "the consanguinity of things" reminds us that "the whole," whatever else it may be, is a state of relatedness—a kind of conviviality in experience. Societies so largely adversarial as the modern ones are, by nature, alienated from the possibilities of such overarching conviviality; and they neglect the fundamental problem of relatedness—which is, we might argue, the central problem of the whole. But revitalization movements of the kind I wish to consider here—and perhaps all religions—*are* fundamentally interested in restoring the relatedness of things.

It is argued frequently enough in the anthropological literature that our social animality—that is, our empathetic (or antipathetic) species' preoccupations with matters of domination and subordination, inclusion and exclusion, sympathy or empathy—which is further to say, our preoccupation with the restricted codes of our solidarity in interaction—must be the points of departure for any study of any institution or more elaborated code. We fool ourselves, in this view, if we posit the construction of these institutions on utilitarian and material needs, on cupidity in the appropriation of surplus value, or on an aesthetic or idealistic drive.

Fundamentally, what men and women are doing in life is taking expressive and rhetorical action against or in the service of these preoccupations. As Justice Douglas, in the Holmesian tradition, used to argue about the law, it is a magnificent edifice based not on the lofty search for truth but on an endlessly fertile rationalization of some quite simple and self-interested predilections. Many scholars, without mentioning Durkheim, have fastened on matters of relatedness as elemental. Bateson (1972) has pointed up the existential preoccupations about relatedness in animals and human animals. Cooley (1909) founded his sociology on the "face-to-face" situation. For Malinowski (1923), the "context of situation," that is, prevailing solidarities and divisiveness, preceded and underlay communicative acts which, in important measure, evoked these situations even if they did not refer to them directly. For Sartre (1963), "le regard"—looking at and being looked at— was the *point de répere* of all social life. And for Schutz (1951), whom I have mainly in mind here, it was the "mutual tuning-in relationship" that was antecedent to all communication. He was, incidentally, pessimistic about our ability to illuminate these inchoate matters: "All communication presupposes the existence of some kind of social interaction [he meant the mutual tuning-in relation] which though it is an indispensable condition of all possible communication does not enter the communicative process and is not capable of being grasped by it" (1951:84). Schutz consequently turned to music, to the nonverbal, to understand this "tuning-in."

Schutz's view that these elemental matters of relatedness are not capable of being grasped by the communicative process requires some qualification, I believe: first, in respect to the way it may privilege the needs elemental to social interaction, and second, in respect to the view of language implied. Recall that Malinowski's attempt to identify basic needs and thus found basic and secondary social institutions on them was effectively countered by Lee (1948), who showed how needs themselves were a reality subject to cultural shaping. (A recent work in the same vein is that of Sahlins (1976), who shows how the empirical world of individuals posited by utilitarians and materialists as a reality on which to found institutions of production and exchange is itself a creation of bourgeois culture.) We cannot privilege the preoccupation with relatedness from cultural shaping; neither can we exclude it from the founding moments in our study of institutions.

Of greater interest is the view of language implied in Schutz, for it points to, though it does not sufficiently describe, a view taken here that a narrowly grammatical view of language is insufficient. To understand the tuning-in that occurs in social situations, we have to go beyond what is manifestly contained in the language events themselves, for these will tell us only so much about the emotions of relatedness that underlie the communication and the images evoked by it. They will tell us only so much about the general knowledge—virtually encyclopedic, from the point of view of formal linguistic analysis—that accompanies ongoing interaction and is essential to the meaning of the language situation. The ethnography of a social situation requires, as we now well recognize in anthropology, that we go much beyond the given language information. Giving primacy to the imagination, I wish to refer to this ongoing interaction as the "argument of images" that lie behind and accompany behavior. Some of these images have their source in language; many of them do not. The relatively accessory nature of the grammatical system itself is well expressed by the linguist Einar Haugen:

It is at least the experience of this writer that many ideas do come in extralinguistic form, as images, patterns, relationships, flashes of illumination. That they are extralinguistic does not mean that language is not involved . . . but most of the meanings we wish to convey are not conveyed by the grammar at all. If my shepard comes running to tell me that a wolf has eaten my sheep, there are three basic facts to be conveyed and for these I need a common vocabulary: "wolf," "eat," "sheep." A statement NP (actor) – V (action) – NP_2 (goal) is merely an empty schema into which he can, if he has the time, fit the words. But he need only cry "wolf." . . . I therefore contend that the grammatical system as such has a minimal connection with any formulation of ideas whatever. (1973:11)

We all recognize that powerful images may repose in lexicon alone and that the sincere cry of "wolf" or "fire" can have powerful tuning-in consequences. We teach our children accordingly. But we also assiduously—and often with an established sense of propriety—teach our children grammar. We might better teach them about the argument of images which lie behind and accompany such established things as grammar. Yet if we teach them grammar, it should be the grammar by which these images are conjoined and transformed. That is, to recall Cassirer, we should teach them about the consanguinity that can be seen to prevail among classifications and the metamorphosis in social life attendant on the discovery of that consanguinity. For it is in that process that proprieties, the sense of acceptable relatedness, are established.

How, then, are we to proceed in an academic essay when we must go—as anthropologists are required to do—so far beyond the information linguistically given? Schutz argued that the experience of the "we"—the foundation of all possible communication—could only emerge from extended mutual "tuning-in" of the primordial kind we get through long mutual involvement at the perceptual level—(i.e., hearing, seeing, touching, tasting) in primary groups, families, ethnic groups, fraternal or sororal associations, and so on. If we do not have these things to begin with, we have to somehow recreate them by an argument of images of some kind in which primary perceptions are evoked. Of course, in many academic essays (unlike this one—and mathematics is the best example, though this will occur with any discipline that employs metalanguages and has high-level theory) the virtually imageless manipulation of abstract concepts can be sufficient. But in most human situations, particularly when we are trying to demonstrate how wholes are constructed, we must in some way pictorialize our topic, visualizing as we can the context of situation of the several religious movements whose reconstructive play of tropes we wish to consider.[3] We are obliged to deepen our participation with the help of "imagenes mundi."

What I should like to do, then, is to verbally visualize aspects of certain African religious movements which relate to the return to the whole. Pictorializing in this way we can inspect the organizing images that are at play in ritual performance and see how microcosm and macrocosm, inner things and outer things, centers and peripheries, upper things and lower things, time-present and time-past, are related. For out of such parts are wholes constructed.

Picture if you will a new community of largely wattle-and-daub thatched buildings set on the semiarid plain amid the dry forest of the southern Volta region of Ghana. This is New Tadzewu, a religious community of the Apostle's Revelation Society of Ghana. In the center of this community is the three-story

Prophet's house; it contains, on the first and second floors, the school, meeting rooms, and the archives. Close by is a long low-lying shed containing administrative headquarters. On the long porch is a row of blackboards on which has been written the Prophet's most recent dreams and revelations. And in the very center of this community is the church, much like any village church of western Europe. As we walk around this community we see several things: its boundaries are well demarcated, it is sub-divided into quarters named after the tribes of Israel, and the offi-cials of this religion are dressed in spotless white uniforms with red piping. In our walk we hear and see many groups, particularly schoolchildren, marching to and from within to drumbeats and bugle call. During a day's time these marching groups will have "knit together," as it were, the whole community. Members of this society see themselves most fundamentally as the tribes of Israel and as Christian soldiers—spiritual soldiers who are ever watchful for the appearance of the devilish apparitions without.

Moving east on the Guinea Coast to Togo and Dahomey, pic-ture a wide beach of white sand under a brilliant sun, next to the dark blue sea. Here, under a cluster of three palm trees, is a group of Celestial Christians in their resplendent white and gold uni-forms, kneeling around a deep hole dug in the sand, at the bottom of which a small trace of ocean water has seeped up. Close by are bottles of holy water and fruit to be poured and placed in the hole as an offering, after which the Bible will be read and prayers will be said. Then the hole will be filled in with the whitest sand and the group members, covering themselves with the whitest sheets, will lie on their backs and go to sleep around the hole. The divine force of the heavens, which they worship, and the sea and earth, which they have just propitiated, will now ebb and flow through them without disturbance and with purificatory and healing power. When we return to their sacred precincts behind raffia walls, inland on the outskirts of Cotonou, we see other people lying out on the ground on mats with a lighted candle burning at their heads and pineapples and other fruit around the candle. These Celestial Christians see themselves as channels between sea, earth, and sky. They are healed and rendered whole when they experience themselves as pure and perfect conduits who do not in any idiosyncratic way impede the flow of these overarching and underarching forces in their endless circulation.

Next, picture the thick equatorial forest of Gabon, Western
Equatorial Africa, and a long narrow village with two lines of huts
facing each other. The village was slashed out of that forest some
time ago, and the vegetation is starting once again to lean back
over the village. At one end of the village, close by the forest, is
the chapel of the Bwiti religion. During the day, when the sun
beats down on the dusty courtyard, at precisely 3:00 P.M., a
phalanx of the membership, in rows of three abreast, in a series of
entrances, dances from far out on the peripheries of the courtyard
into the center of the chapel. They are dressed in red and white
flowing uniforms—white on the pure upper half of their bodies
and red on the impure and passionate lower half. Men and women
are dressed exactly alike, with two exceptions: the leader—The
Parrot's Egg, The Great Hunter—of the chapel is dressed all in
red, and the guardian of the chapel as well as the player of the
harp are dressed all in white. The leader, who takes away the sins
of the members, dances on the left side of the phalanx, the female
side; the guardian of the chapel, who maintains the purity of the
night, dances on the right side, the male side. This sidedness is
repeated over and over again in the all-night ceremonies, for there
is a male side of the chapel and a female side, a men's secret
chamber and a women's. Further, a totality of worship can only
be obtained by dancing on both sides of the chapel and by coun-
terdancing men on the female side and women on the male side.
We must also know that the chapel is visualized as a sacred body
that can only be brought into being—embodied, as it were—by
the totality of these entrance and exit dances. The exercise of the
orifices of this microcosmic chapel, the interactive celebration of
its parts, its sidedness, together create the religious macrocosm.

We must picture as well the vertical dimension: the red-
barked adzap tree, the loftiest tree of the equatorial forest, in a
grove not far behind the chapel. This tree is the route of the ancestors: they proceed to and fro between the above and the below.
Their route and this tree are represented by the central pillar, one
that is laden with symbolic meaning thick with sculpted representations whose full reading—a reading of all available associations—would virtually lead out to the Bwiti universe. During the
night dances, members frequently touch this pillar, for it keeps
them in contact with the below and the above, just as their entrance dances and counterdances keep them in contact with the

two horizontal dimensions of their quality space. Exactly at midnight, just outside the chapel, the members gather in a long line, each holding a candle. Slowly, led by the cult harp, they dance in file out into the thick forest along precut paths. They are soon swallowed up by the forest, and all we can see and hear is an occasional glimmer of a candle, a floating chord from the harp. Later they return; and proceeding just within the entrance and beside the central pillar, they begin fifty strong to wind a tighter circle until all members are pulled together and the candles now held above their heads form one large dancing flame. This is *nlem mvore*, one-heartedness, one of their main images of the wholeness of their communion—an experience otherwise achieved by the dancers as they dance together into one whole village and forest, microcosm and macrocosm. Worship ends with a final circle just before the sun rises. And then the members gather in a thatched pavilion in a state of high euphoria and conviviality for a morning meal of manioc.

Finally, we move to the seaside savannah and the semiurban zones of Natal, Southeast Africa. This is Zululand, although in the city of Durban the Zulu do not have permanent permission to reside. On Sunday afternoon, gazing out on the vacant spaces of that city, not yet built on or since abandoned, we see countless small groups of Zionists setting up their blue and white flags, which whip about in the constant Indian Ocean breeze, beside dusty circles worn deep in the grass. The main spiritual force these Zionists seek to evoke is the Holy Spirit, Umoya Oyingwele, or Holy Wind; they do so by running breathlessly for long periods around these circles. If the runners are pure, they are eventually drawn into the center of the circle for final purification and incorporation with that powerful wind; but if they are impure, they are cast out of the circle into the peripheries often in a state of possession, and must be purified before they can begin to run again in the circle. Eventually, with any luck, they will return as in previous weeks to the center of the circle. The whole worship arena is an image of the Zulu kraal. Here, too, as in West Africa, members periodically go to the beaches for baptism in the crashing surf of this active ocean. Far out into the water they go—every year some drown—for complete immersion, for the ocean is the home of the Holy Wind and those immersed in it become, like those drawn into the circle, at one with this holy agency. Later, the group gathers on the shore in the image of the Impi, the Zulu regiments of yore. Chanting and stomping on the beach in the pincher-like movement that is characteristic of the Impi, they surround those members of the congregation with especially resistant illnesses, fixing them at the center of this military encirclement so that the leader may lay his hands on them in the name of the community and with special power—the powers of the multitude of purified eyes focused on the afflicted one in the shadows.

It is important to my argument to thus visualize selected aspects of these movements. It gives us some of the basic images with which these movements revitalize . . . with which they reconstitute their world. It is true that from the perspective of the discovery procedures of a normal science of behavior, pictorialization may appear to be inadequate; we might expect instead to be shown the elementary ideas behind these images and their associated behaviors. It is my argument, however, that these very images are elementary and primordial.

THE MIX OF ELEMENTARY POSTULATES

Despite some feeling that the notion of elementary thought, *Elementargedanken*, like the notion of mystical participation, is nineteenth century in locus, it persists in various forms in the anthropological literature, whether as "themes" (i.e., "underlying dynamic affirmation"), "motifs" (the basic units of folklore), or "basic premises," "cultural axioms," or "existential postulates." In a more formal vein, with both Lévi-Strauss's "mythemes" and folklore models in mind, Dundes (1963) advances the "motifeme" as the basic unit. Subsequently and more relaxedly, he refers to "folk ideas" (Dundes 1971)—such things as the idea of linearity, the idea of circularity, the idea (Dundes prefers that word to "image") of limited good—as the basic units or building blocks of worldview. More recently, Witherspoon (1977:5) has argued in connection with his study of the Navajo universe that "all cultures are constructed from and based upon a single metaphysical premise which is axiomatic, unexplainable and unprovable."

Such elementary postulations are characteristically out of reach for ethnographic interview, but I would argue that the search for *Elementargedanken*, if not misplaced concreteness, inadequately assesses the experience of coherence and wholeness, which is an experience both horizontal and hierarchical, peripheral and central, interior and exterior—an experience of affinity and consanguinity, as it were. At the least this kind of inquiry assigns to deep thought processes—or to those thought processes having to do with relatedness—an ideational explicitness and clarity they do not possess. Participants may be within reach of such ideas, but their reach inevitably exceeds their grasp. Such things are inchoate. From the anthropological perspective, the search for elementary ideas risks being a schoolmasterish kind of inquiry if it presumes that such formulations are causal or controlling. In fact, they are emergent and consequent to a stimulating thickness in experience—to primordial forms of postulating and participation in which by subsequent abstraction supposed elementary ideas can be discovered to be embedded, but mostly by people of thought. Those actors in the revitalization movements I studied, whether under the pressure of my inquiry or the problematics of their situation, resurrected from the depths of their experience prototypical images that were persuasive to their well-being or apt for statisfying performance.

Of course, the search for *Elementargedanken* is understandable because the primary problem, if we are to understand any kind of formal or structural study, is to "find operational units which can be manipulated and on which logical operations can be performed (cf. Fernandez 1979). Since most well-schooled individuals in the modern world are intensively taught to perform operations on things (i.e., to be competent), it is understandable that we are driven to search for elementary ideas. But as Durkheim has shown, it is arguable—and particularly so if we are concerned, as we are here, with experience—that ideas are always emergent. We squeeze them out of embeddedness, out of participation, out of a relatedness of men and women. They do not have experientially the primacy we seek to give them. To make a much longer argument short (see Fernandez 1974), in my view the elementary forms are, in experiential terms, first the personal pronouns that point at the unities of our experience, and second the sign-images (metaphors and other tropes) that are predicated on them to give them actionable identity. These predications, in all their variety, are the elementary postulates that formulate and stimulate experience.

In respect to the religious movements we have been looking at, it is easy to recognize certain recurrent tropes—mostly metaphors but sometimes metonyms—which, since tropes are not only asserted but can be performed, satisfyingly organize considerable activity in the particular religious community. Table 1 presents the particular predications and the performative consequences of these movements. Earlier on in my thinking about the place of tropes in religious revitalization, I tended, like Witherspoon—though I was specifically influenced by Pepper's *World Hypothesis* (1942)—to argue for ultimate organizing metaphors. Remember that in Pepper's (1942:107) view there were

TABLE 1

Metaphoric Predictions	*Performative Consequences*
For the Apostle's Revelation Society:	
We are the tribes of Israel.	Each group, by manifesting its particularity, shows that it is part of a whole chosen people.
We are Christian soldiers.	By marching to and fro, we militate against devilish forces without and devilish disorder within.
For Celestial Christianism:	
We are the conduits between sea, earth, and sky.	By living purely and in tranquility, we will not disturb the forces which flow through us.
For Equatorial Bwiti:	
We are people of the forest threshold.	By gathering the forest around us and ceremonially making our way out into the forest, we can be reborn.
We are lost hunters of the forest.	
We are one heart.	We separate individuals can recapture our family identity.
For Zulu Zionism:	
I am the bull who crashes in the kraal. We are the regiments of the holy wind. We are the cattle of the Lord.	By moving faster and faster in tighter and tighter circles, we can recapture our inner purity and the security of supernatural tutelage.

four basic philosophical worldviews, each of which had one underlying hypothesis or metaphor to work out: "formism," "organi-
cism," "mechanism," and "contextualism." He argued for the in-
stability, dynamism, and eventual collapse of any system that
mixed metaphors. More recently, however, I have reexamined that
presupposition and the search it implied as being overly
philosophical in inspiration. The underlying unity found in religious culture cannot be expressed satisfactorily in any one
metaphor. Religious movements, if not any act of cultural revitalization and returning to the whole, always mix metaphors. It is
the dynamic interplay of these metaphors that is most interesting
and consequential and that gives the impression of coherence—of
the return to the whole. We turn now to this play of tropes—this
grammar, if by grammar we mean a series of predications on pronouns whose constituents are in both syntagmatic and paradigmatic relation (see Fernandez 1974).

THE PLAY OF TROPES

In considering how metaphors are mixed in revitalization—or better yet, how tropes are mixed because metonymy is present, as
well as occasional irony—we begin to make music. Or at least we
begin to see the music in our subject. It is complex polyphonic
music, the score of which can be difficult to follow in public presentation if we are not used to sight-reading this kind of music.
Here we are moving from simply "tuning-in"—referring back to
Schutz's use of the musical metaphor to get at the fundamentals
of relatedness—to something more symphonic: the symbolic symphony, if you will, which returns to the whole.

There are as many kinds of polyphonic composition as there
are varieties in the play of tropes. Lévi-Strauss, in the
Mythologiques, develops the possibilities of this variety with characteristic verve and resourcefulness as he begins *The Raw and the
Cooked* (1969) with an overture and conducts the reader through
arias, recitatives, variations, interludes, and the coda of Bororo
song. He presents a "Good Manners Sonata," a "Caitatu Rondo,"
a "Fugue of the Five Senses," an "Oppossom Cantata," a "Well-
Tempered Astronomy," a "Toccata and Fugue of the Pleiades and
the Rainbow," and finally, a "Rustic Symphony in Three Movements Including a Bird Chorus"—a symbolic symphony indeed.

But we cannot be interested here in such variety or in such adventurous use of the musical metaphor. Rather, our interest lies in the usefulness of music and, more specifically, in orchestral performance as a metaphor for ritual sequence and the conviction of totality.[4] In its own way this is profoundly structural, but let me alert the reader to two differences of approach. While most structural analyses regard myth or ritual as being generated primarily to solve a culture's problematic and unwelcome contradictions of a cognitive, sociological, or technological kind—it is, after all, a method intent on setting up and solving such contradictions—we will regard them, or at least we will regard the African revitalization rituals, as having two intentions: the intention to give definition to the inchoate, and the intention to return to the whole. At the same time we do have a structuralist sense of how the permutational dynamics of expressive statements are to be understood. This sense is in contrast with a narrative-oriented analysis in which the syntax of the narrative looms large and the agonistic surface arguments and denouncements are primary. Mine is a domain-oriented analysis in which paradigmatic shifts in the domain of interest are primary and, in the end, taken to be (experienced as) wholly convincing.

The sight-reading for this subject rests on the very old but so often poorly understood distinction (basic, in my view, to any anthropology) between associative relations of contiguity and associative relations of similarity. This is essentially the Frazerian distinction between contagious and sympathetic magic, that mix of manipulations that together move the whole realm of the unseen. It is essentially what is involved in the distinction between consanguinal and affinal relations, that mix of relations that together constitute the whole kinship system. Pertinent here are those phrasings of Jakobson and de Saussure. Jakobson (1956) clarified for us the way that metonym is an assertion of an association based on contiguity of relations, and metaphor is an assertion based on similarity of relation. De Saussure (1966) meant much the same thing in distinguishing between syntagmatic and paradigmatic relations in language communication, though the language-oriented understanding of contiguity-similarity relations to some degree inhibits our understanding as far as ritual sequences are concerned, which themselves are arguments of images and not fully syntactical in the linguistic sense.

In music, the same distinction is afoot in the contrast between harmony and melody. Melody is the sequential contiguity
of notes, while harmony is the paradigmatic association of different instruments or voices playing with their respective pitches and
registers. In symphonic music we are familiar with different instruments, which may have been all along in background accompaniment, being brought into focus as the melody progresses and even
with shifts in key to suit these instruments. This is comparable to
what happens in similarity-contiguity relations. We can choose or
are forced to see from another perspective what is contiguous in
our ongoing experience—in musical terms, we choose another key.
A contiguous or syntagmatic sequence can by transformed, by
paradigmatic permutation, into another mode of expression, and
vice versa. This metamorphosis, this transformative interaction of
syntax and paradigm, metaphor and metonym, is fundamentally
what is at play as parts are related to wholes, universalizations to
particularizations. And it is in sum wholly convincing.

It may be useful to remind ourselves of the Lévi-Straussian
analysis of these matters, which addresses itself to sequential
and paradigmatic arrangements of myths—a narrative-oriented
analysis. This method takes the contiguous narrative and first
breaks it up into a sequence of episodes. These episodes are then
arranged in such a way—into a paradigm—as to reveal the unwelcome contradictions being wrestled with and the transformation
of these contradictions being effected. Hence the paradigmatic permutation that underlies the myth.[5]

The particular approach I take to the symphonic play of associations assumes that the nether regions of the mind, whatever
structures it may have for organizing subsequent expression, are a
repository of images of former sociohistorical experiences actively
lived through or vividly described. Such an approach contrasts
with the usual structural approach in which the nether regions
are "always empty" or at least "alien to mental images"—merely
there to impose structural laws on inarticulated elements originat-
ing elsewhere. These images in their nether repository carry positive or negative signs according as the experiences associated with
them were positive or negative, gratifying or deceiving. And they
can be brought forward and predicated on the subjects of religious
experience and become the basis of ritual performance. I have
attempted to pictorialize some of these enacted images: the image

of the Zulu kraal or the Zulu Impi; the image of the threshold
tree of the Fang religious forest; the image of the tribes of Israel in
organically harmonious production; the image of Christian soldiers; the image of religious men and women mediating, interced-
ing, between earth, sky, and water. All of these images in either
autochthonous or creatively synthesized and synchronized form
are brought forward and, as ritual metaphors or metonyms, made
the basis of ritual performance. Practically any of these revitalization rituals can be seen as acting out a number of these images at
various levels of attention (see Fernandez 1977).

The consequences of the production and, often, the acting
out of these images is cosmological. That is, it returns to the whole
in at least three ways: by iteration, by the discovery of replication,
and by the creation of novel semantic categories of wide classification. Here it is important to keep in mind that this is a domain-
oriented approach. For each of these images derives from or is a
pictorialization of a domain of experience—the domain of forest
life, of domestic life, of military affairs, of supernatural relations.
Acting out these images restores vitality if only in expressive form
to that domain of activity, which has fallen into disrepute or questionable participation because of such transitional afflictions
associated with revitalization movements as status deprivation,
material exploitation, cultural deprecation, and so on. The performance of these images revitalizes a domain of experience and participation. The performance of a sequence of images revitalizes, in
effect and by simple iteration, a universe of domains, an acceptable cosmology of participation, a compelling whole.

To understand the second sense in which the acting out of
these images is cosmological, we must understand something more
about the way in which images are associated analogically and
the concept formation that goes on in this association. Here we
return as well to the interplay of melody and harmony, which is to
say the interplay of similarity and contiguity. Sometimes the association of images in ritual performance is that of continuous
analogy: $A : B :: B : C :: C : D \ldots$—people are to trees as trees are
to the forest as the forest is to the world. . . . But more often, what
we find is the production of a sequence of domains of performance
by discontinuous analogy: $A : B :: C : D$. Here the relational structure—the contiguities—existing in one domain of experience
suggests by analogy the relational structure existing in another

domain of experience: a person's relation to his or her clan is as the tree's relation to the forest; or, the heart is to the body as the center of the circle is to the circle, as the cattle kraal is to the Zulu homestead. In the play of discontinuous analogies in ritual, what occurs is that in performing the contiguous experiences of one domain, a sense of resonance or relation by analogy arises with some part or related parts of the contiguous structures of another domain. This produces, first, a shift from one domain of performance to another and, second, a sense of the coherence between domains—coherence by reason of analogous relational structures. In brief, the Order of Things in one domain comes to be perceived as somehow similar to the Order of Things in another. The expression "order of things" reminds us of Foucault's (1970) book by the same name—his historical archaeology in which he demonstrated at successive levels of historical time similar synchronic structures of ordering—epistemes—in the various domains of culture. It is the falling apart of these relational structures of ordering—these "structural replications" (Vogt 1965) in different domains—that produces the epistemological crisis that is one of the chief motives for attempts at revitalization by returning to the whole.

The third way the play of tropes returns us to the whole is through the "commanding image" (Read 1951) or the novel superordinate semantic category (Basso 1976). This commanding category is brought about by metaphoric predication of images on the inchoate subjects of our interest—the predications we have been speaking about. Metaphor, of course, is the statement of an association between things that are normally categorized in separate domains of experience. This association cannot be based on designative or literal defining features but rather on the figurative or connotative features the two things have in common. Connotatively there is something elephant-like about Frank and something Frank-like about an elephant—they are both ponderous, deliberate, and unforgiving—although literally they belong in different domains. When we make these associations on ostensibly connotative grounds, however, we also create, as Basso (1976:98–111) has shown, a superordinate semantic category to which both the animal (elephant) and the human (Frank) belong. This is a category characterized by the designative features "living being," "warm-blooded earth dweller," and so on.

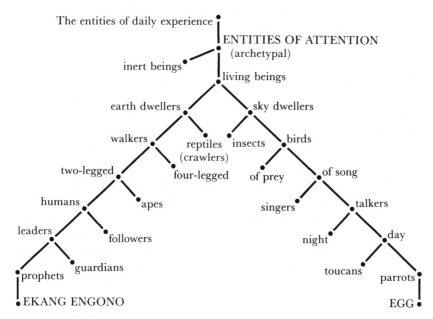

Figure 1. The Prophet as Parrot's Egg (Bwiti Religion)

One way—it is not the only way—to show the creation by metaphoric predication of a superordinate semantic category is by reference to a lexical hierarchy, or semantic tree (Figure 1), where, for example the referents of prophet and parrot, to take the leader of one of the revitalization movements, become members of the same domain at a very superordinate node of the hierarchy. The concept formed by metaphoric predication is always more inclusive than either of the categories involved in the predication. Metaphoric predication produces exceptionally wide classification and "symbolically coerces into a unitary conceptual framework" (Basso 1976:103) that whose designation was previously quite separated in our experience. The experience is of the collapse of separation into relatedness; it is the "shock of recognizing" a wider integrity of things, the recognition of a greater whole. Metaphoric predication, this central form of the argument of images, thus in its very nature impells a return to the whole, or at least to some whole that is significantly greater than the parts, be they elephants and hominids or parrots and prophets.

I must emphasize again that this wider classification is emergent and is not underlying in any behavioral sense. What we have from the behavioral view is the experience of the separation (or at least the variety) of domains into which we have classified experience and, at once, certain similarities, connotatively speaking, that exist between the members of separated domains. There is a state of tension in our experience. Because of the inadequacies of literal language—its constricted view of experience and the lexical gaps characteristic of it—we turn to metaphoric predication. The shock of recognition arises because, in making these predications, we suddenly become aware of a wider classification of things heretofore only implicit and embedded in experience. Particularly in times of stress, when literal routines break down and we are constrained by false or moribund categories, do we turn to figurative language and the argument of images for a wider and more transcendent view of things. These are the times with which ritual and revitalization are most associated. It is important to recognize how the play of tropes and the metaphoric language characteristic of these times of stress, by their very nature, return us to the whole.

To take up the musical metaphor again, the shift from domain to domain is like the shift from instrument to instrument in orchestral performance, each in their domain following the basic melody—the overall order of things in that culture—but each adding the different properties, the complementary qualities of their domain of expression. No instrument and no domain can "make music" alone, but performing together they create a vital—or revitalized—cosmological harmony out of iteration, replication, and wide classification.

SIMPLE AND COMPLEX WHOLES

I have been speaking about the conviction of wholeness obtained by the play of tropes—obtained, that is, by a complex transformative system of figurative predications on inchoate entities. The overall effect of these predications is to give these entities a plenitude of experience they could not otherwise achieve. In short, I have been speaking about a "complex whole," or at least a whole complexly achieved. We may wish to contrast this whole with the simple whole of the "communitas" experience of Victor Turner (1969: chap. 3) in his elaboration of the "liminality" phase of the rites of passage. Communitas is that "irrefragible genuineness of mutuality" (1969:137); that undifferentiated experience of communion, equality, poverty, openness to the other; that recognition of the "essential and generic human bond" that periodically occurs as an antistructural reaction to the hierarchical, differentiated and invidious relations of the structured everyday world. Turner (1969:107) contrasted the simplicity of communitas with the complexity of the status system in the structured world of everyday life. Communitas is an experience spontaneous and elementally existential.

However the final experiences of wholeness are to be compared, and Turner only in passing considered the "wholeness" in communitas,[6] here I have regarded the experience not as spontaneous or as instant and oceanic but as more elaborately achieved in an argument of images. In such an argument there is a productive tension between differentiated domains, on the one hand, and their collapse into wide classification, on the other. It may very well be that there are two kinds of wholes to which we return—the simple and the complex. Or it may be that Turner was approaching the communitas experience at a different point of its appearance. Or it may be that the communitas argument, in dichotomizing the structural from the antistructural experience, makes apparently spontaneous and not sufficiently emergent what is processually achieved in experience by complex argument (see also T. Turner 1978). Indeed, at several points in his discussion Victor Turner recognized the terms in which the argument for communitas must be cast—that is, in an argument of images: "Along with others who have considered the conception of communitas, I find myself forced to have recourse to metaphor and analogy" (1969:127). It was true, he noted, of the great figures such as St. Francis of Assisi who argued for communitas among their followers: "Francis is like many other founders of communitas-like groups . . . his thought was always immediate, personal and concrete. Ideas appeared to him as images. A sequence of thought for him . . . consists of leaping from one picture to the next" (1969:141). Indeed, Turner resisted any notion that communitas is merely instinctual. It involves consciousness and volition. It is, he said, quoting Blake, "an intellectual thing" (1969:188). Insofar as this is true, communitas is to be understood as a complex whole.

In any event, the "intellectual thing" in the return to the

whole is what I have tried to illuminate here. And more specifically, since mind is animated by adaptive intentions in specific
contexts, I also must seek to illuminate the strategic element in
the play of tropes and the return to the whole.

SYMBOLIC STRATEGIES

> Wholeness, holiness and adaptiveness are closely related
> if not, indeed, one and the same thing.
>
> Rappaport, "Sanctity, Lies and Evolution"

Until recently the very phrase "symbolic strategies" would have
seemed a contradiction in terms, for symbolic matters traditionally were seen as mainly expressive and adjustive, as epiphe-
nomenal. But this has changed, and the presence of symbolic
constraints has been shown for both common sense (Geertz 1975)
and practical reason (Sahlins 1976). The neo-Marxists, in their
effort to give us a more adequate grasp of the superstructure/in-
frastructure interaction, deprecate the old "vulgar materialism"
(Friedman 1974), with its exclusion of the symbolic, and make
common cause with the neo-structuralists (Hastrup 1978), who
arise out of the most symbolic of traditions. Even in such a preserve of positivism as medicine, the importance of the placebo
effect—symbolic healing, surely—is being reemphasized (Moerman 1979).

When we think of symbolic strategies, we usually think of the
use of symbols to manipulate persons and groups, most often for
deceitful, self-serving purposes. We are surrounded by an advertising environment that seeks to symbolically associate questionable
products, whether cigarettes or oversized cars, with desirable
milieus of activity or belonging. And many of us have lived
through catastrophic periods of history in which torchlit stadiums
and Wagnerian symbolism were used to animate a sophisticated
people to primitive deeds. In a later period, and in our own country, authentic symbols of the frontier were used to animate a far-
off and irrelevant war. We are, in fact, well aware of flag-waving
and pseudo-patriotism of all kinds in which symbols are used to
dominate and deceive.

But what about the ritual complex of symbols, the symbolic
symphonies I have been talking about? Rappaport's *Pigs for the*

Ancestors (1975) and subsequent studies influenced by it have been revelatory in tying ritual activity directly into systems maintenance. Flow charts drawn up on the basis of Rappaport's data integrate symbolic representations and ritual activities into the ecological model where they play their important part in preventing the Tsembaga system from passing beyond thresholds of carrying capacity and into a consequent production-population collapse (Shantzi and Behrens 1973). Thus, there is a whole set of activities involved in or generated by ritual that are adaptive for a society in its milieu and are strategic in the most crucial sense.

It is not really this action or systems adjustment aspect of ritual, however, that we have been concerned with here. Rather, our interest lies in the cosmological aspect—the reconstruction, or at least the intimation—of wholes accomplished by our symbolic symphonies. Could this reconstruction be strategic as well, or at least strategic in the adaptive sense? The epigraph for this section implies that it is and that, in fact, wholeness and adaptation are in significant relation.

In the separated (though really mutually nurturant) cells of our modern organic (to use the Durkheimian metaphor) forms of solidarity, individual reality looms very large and the study of strategy tends to be the study of "the manipulative ploys of individuals" rationally elaborating stratagems and enjoying spoils (Bailey 1969). Such an approach is even more persuasive for anyone imbued with a market mentality. Returning to the whole seems somehow beyond our reach, something that pertains to societies characterized by mechanical forms of solidarity, by strong feelings of consanguinity and affinity, and by real possibilities of mystical participation. And this would appear to be so. At the same time, we moderns feel ourselves faced with the "tragedy of the commons" and argue for holistic healing and the "whole earth." There are those who despair that analytic reason alone is sufficient to temper the ambitions of separated men and women so that they may subordinate themselves to such common interests. And those who are impressed with the reality of common interests tend to find just as illusory the self-sufficiency and autonomy ascribed to our individuality.

Rappaport (1979), whose touchstone is adaptation and consequently survival, is impressed by these issues. He argues that the "ultimate corrective operation inheres in systems as wholes" and that, in effect, the ultimate strategy may be that of returning to the whole:

Although humans are metabolically separate from one another, and although consciousness is individual, humans are not self-sufficient and their autonomy is relative and slight. They are parts of larger systems upon which their continued existence is contingent. But the wholeness, if not indeed the very existence, of those systems may be beyond the grasp of their ordinary consciousness. Although conscious reason is incomplete, the mode of understanding encouraged by liturgy may make up for some of its deficiencies. Participation in rituals may enlarge the awareness of those participating in them, providing them with understandings of perfectly natural aspects of the social and physical world that may elude unaided reason. (1979:236–37)

When we read such a passage we may be inclined to take it as a religious statement. Inasmuch as Rappaport began his field research nominalistically in counting the flow of kilocalories, there is a tendency to see signs of a conversion here. But in what way, really, is Rappaport's system allegiance any different than the system allegiance of those of us who, say, study symbolism as a cultural system? Is the cultural system we affirm more graspable to ordinary consciousness, more accessible to unaided reason, than the system Rappaport affirms? Perhaps it is, and certainly here I have tried to give a graspable account of the mechanisms by which revitalization movements return to the whole. But it may well be that I have only succeeded in giving a partial account, that I have only pointed at the whole but have not really grasped the nature of it, not to mention the experience of it. And it may be that the whole is never fully graspable. It is *there,* implied in our symbolic activity but inchoate. When we say "cultural system," then, perhaps we are making a symbolic statement, not a scientific one.

In any event allegiance to system is a characteristic of almost all anthropology and most of social science. Our discipline began, after all, as the opening epigraph indicates, with the affirmation of a "complex whole" to whose study we were dedicated. Of course, there have been periods of seeing culture as a thing of shreds and patches, periods of concentrating on isolated traits and their diffusion. But the overall strategy of most anthropology is to take the students' much individuated awarenesses and demonstrate system to them—in some sense to return them to the whole. And this is often to revitalize them.

With the concept of revitalization in mind, let me reemphasize finally that the play of tropes I have been speaking about here are those of "revitalization movements"—movements with a special and more open opportunity for creative ritualization, for a relatively unfettered argument and performance of images than is characteristic of most human situations, committed as they are to well-worn routines and the inertia of institutions. These movements are strategic in a special sense. Wallace (1956:265), who coined the phrase and identified the phenomena, clearly puts their strategy in terms of system allegiance:

A revitalization movement is defined as a deliberate, organized, conscious effort by members of a society to construct a more satisfying culture. Revitalization is thus, from a cultural standpoint, a special kind of culture change phenomenon: the persons involved in the process of revitalization must perceive their culture, or some major areas of it, as a system (whether accurately or not); they must feel that this cultural system is unsatisfactory; and they must innovate not merely discrete items but a new cultural system, specifying new relationships as well as, in some cases, new traits.

It must be clear as well that these movements arise from, and their strategies derive from, deeper prototypical levels of awareness than is characteristic of the daily routine and the everyday life we know in the space-time object world out there—the mastered world, that is, to which strategic understandings normally apply. Revitalization movements are responses to the hyper- and hypo-arousal associated with the collapse of accustomed masteries and the frustration of received strategies once applicable within and between the various domains of that object world. In such situations of epistemological crisis, dreams, visions, and deathlike excursions occupy an incipient and central part. They rise from the depths of experience with old or newly rehabilitated images with which to reclassify and reintegrate a world in which the personal pronouns can once again confidently move with the fullest sense of both the consanguinities of their context and their powers of transformation into something more—something more whole—than they are.

My argument has been that in these—during masterful times—forgotten depths of our experience there are always a plenitude of entities we can retrieve, entities with which we can construct an imaginatively integrated context—a stage—for satisfying performance. Such retrieval and construction is the ultimate and recurrent strategy of the human experience. It is the experience of returning to the depths—that room full of mirrors in which we can see ourselves—in order to return to the whole.

NOTES

This is a revised version of a paper presented at the anthropology section of the New York Academy of Sciences on May 19, 1980, entitled "Symbolic Symphonics and Symbolic Strategies: The Reconstructive Play of Tropes in Culture Revitalization." I have profited from comments made on this paper in the several places I have delivered it: at the New York Academy of Sciences, at Princeton University, at the University of Rochester, and at Indiana University. I thank particularly Warren d'Azevedo, Charles and Bonnie Bird, Hildred Geertz, William Green, Grace Harris, Michael Herzfeld, Ivan Karp, Daniel Moerman, James Spencer, and Aram Yengoyan.

1. The basic statement of the theoretical position I am taking here can be found in Fernandez (1974). Some parts of that argument concerning the mission of metaphor in culture were in need of clarification or amplification, and in several subsequent papers I have sought to do that: Fernandez (1977) clarifies the notion of "quality space"; Fernandez (1982) clarifies the relation of metaphor to the inchoate. This paper, therefore, is part of an ongoing argument and should not be read as a complete statement about all aspects of the revitalization movements discussed nor a denial of the celebration of parts even of the "unwholesome disorder" which occurs in phases of these movements. Indeed, I argue that it is the interwoven and alternating celebration of parts and wholes that constitutes the "total" symphonic experience of these movements.

2. This distinction has been made, however, for a much different culture (see Marriot and Inden 1974).

3. One shouldn't ignore the fact that there are differences among us. Some of us are visualizers, more readily convinced when we are shown a picture; others of us are verbalizers, anxious to be given by formal processes of argument those powerful concepts necessary and sufficient to the logic of our own theoretical vocabulary.

4. The usefulness of this metaphor is pointed up in Leach (1976:chap. 9).

5. Lévi-Strauss (1955) has produced a quasi-, or perhaps only pseudo-, algebraic formula to describe it involving Proppian functions. It has subsequently been an algebraic bone of contention, to say the least. The Marandas (1971) have offered an interpretation—really a considerable reinterpretation—which involves a mediating personage or type who brings about a transformation in the revealed contradiction. Crumrine and Macklin (1974) have applied the

Maranda interpretation to Mexican folk religious narratives and, in their paradigmatic rearrangement, discover the unwelcome contradiction to be that of death in the midst of life. Of relevance to our interest in revitalization is the transformation wrought by a prophetic mediator who sacrifices personal vitality to restore life to society.

6. He wrote, "For communitas has an existential quality; it involves the whole man in his relation to other whole men" (1969:127).

REFERENCES

Bailey, F. G. 1969. *Strategems and Spoils: A Social Anthropology of Politics*. Oxford: Oxford University Press.

Basso, K. 1976. "Wise Words of the Western Apache." In: K. Basso and H. Selby (eds.), *Meaning in Anthropology*, pp. 93–121. Albuquerque: University of New Mexico Press.

Bateson, G. 1972. "Problems in Cetacean and Other Mammalian Communication." In: *Steps Towards an Ecology of Mind*, pp. 364–78. New York: Ballantine.

Cassirer, E. 1960. *An Essay on Man*. Garden City, N.Y.: Doubleday/Anchor. (First published in 1944.)

Cooley, C. H. 1909. *Social Organization*. New York: Scribner's.

Crumrine, R., and B. J. Macklin. 1974. "Sacred Ritual versus the Unconscious: The Efficacy of Symbols and Structure in North Mexican Folk Saint's Cults." In: I. Rossi (ed.), *The Unconscious in Culture*, pp. 179–97. New York: Dutton.

de Saussure, F. 1966. *Course in General Linguistics*. New York: McGraw Hill.

Dumont, L. 1970. *Homo Hierarchicus: The Caste System and Its Implications*. Chicago: University of Chicago Press.

Dundes, A. 1971. "Folk Ideas as Units of Worldview," *Journal of American Folklore* 84:93–103.

Durkheim, E., and M. Mauss. 1963. *Primitive Classification*. Chicago: University of Chicago Press.

Fernandez, J. W. 1974. "The Mission of Metaphor in Expressive Culture," *Current Anthropology* 15(2):119–45.

———. 1977. "The Performance of Ritual Metaphors." In: J. D. Sapir and C. Crocker (eds.), *The Social Use of Metaphor*, pp. 100–31. Philadelphia: University of Pennsylvania Press.

———. 1978. "African Religious Movements," *Annual Reviews in Anthropology* 7:195–234.

———. 1979. "Edification by Puzzlement." In: I. Karp and C. Bird (eds.), *African Systems of Thought*, pp. 44–59. Bloomington: Indiana University Press.

———. 1982. "The Dark at the Bottom of the Stairs." In: Jacques Maquet (ed.), *On Symbols in Anthropology: Essays in Honor of Harry Hoijer*. Malibu, Calif.: Udena.

———. 1984. "Convivial Attitudes: The Ironic Play of Tropes in an International Kayak Festival in Northern Spain." In: E. M. Bruner (ed.), *Text,*

Play, and Story: The Construction and Reconstruction of Self and Society, pp. 199–229. 1983 Proceedings of the American Ethnological Society. Washington, D.C.

Foucault, M. 1970. *The Order of Things: An Archaeology of the Human Sciences*. New York: Pantheon.

Friedman, J. 1974. "Marxism, Structuralism and Vulgar Materialism," *Man* 93:444–69.

Geertz, C. 1975. "Common Sense as a Cultural System," *Antioch Review* 33:5–26.

Hastrup, K. 1978. "The Post-Structuralist Position of Social Anthropology." In: E. Schwimmer (ed.), *The Yearbook of Symbolic Anthropology*, pp. 123–48. London: Hogarth.

Haugen, E. 1973. "Linguistic Relativity: Myths and Methods." Paper no. 1871, Ninth International Congress of Anthropological and Ethnological Sciences, Chicago, August.

Jakobson, T. 1956. "Two Aspects of Language and Two Types of Aphasic Disturbances." In: *Fundamentals of Language*. The Hague: Mouton.

Leach, E. 1976. *Culture and Communication*. New York: Cambridge University Press.

Lee, D. 1948. "Are Basic Needs Ultimate?" *Journal of Abnormal and Social Psychology* 43:391–95.

Lévi-Strauss, C. 1955. "The Structural Study of Myth," *Journal of American Folklore* 78:428–44.

———. 1966. *The Savage Mind*. Chicago: University of Chicago Press.

———. 1969. *The Raw and the Cooked*. New York: Harper Torchbooks.

Malinowski, B. 1923. "The Problem of Meaning in Primitive Languages." In: C. K. Ogden and I. A. Richards (eds.), *The Meaning of Meaning*, pp. 451–510. London: International Library.

Maranda, P., and E. K. Maranda. 1971. *Structural Models in Folklore and Transformational Essays*. The Hague: Mouton.

Marriot, M., and R. B. Inden. 1974. "Caste Systems," *Encyclopaedia Britannica, Macropaedia* 3.1966:441–47.

Moerman, D. 1979. "Anthropology of Symbolic Healing," *Current Anthropology* 20(1).

Pepper, S. 1942. *World Hypothesis*. Berkeley: University of California Press.

Rappaport, R. 1975. *Pigs for the Ancestors: Ritual in the Ecology of a New Guinea People*. New Haven, Conn: Yale University Press.

———. 1979. "Sanctity and Lies in Evolution." In: *Ecology, Meaning and Religion*, pp. 236–37. Richmond, Calif.: North Atlantic Books.

Read, H. 1951. *English Prose Style*. London: G. Bell and Sons.

Sahlins, M. 1976. *Culture and Practical Reason*. Chicago: University of Chicago Press.

Sartre, J. P. 1963. *Search for a Method*. New York: Dutton.

Schutz, A. 1951. "Making Music Together: A Study in Social Relationship," *Social Research* 18(1):76–97.

Shantzi, S. B., and W. W. Berens. 1973. "Population Control Mechanisms in a Primitive Agricultural Society." In: D. D. Meadows (eds.), *Toward Global Equilibrium*, pp. 257–83. Cambridge: Wright Allen.

Turner, T. 1978. "Transformation, Hierarchy and Transcendence: A Reformulation of Van Gennep's Model of the Structure of Rites of Passage." In: S. F. Moore and B. Myerhoff (eds.), *Secular Ritual,* pp. 53–70. Amsterdam: Van Gorcum.

Turner, V. 1969. "Liminality and Communitas." In: *The Ritual Process,* pp. 78–104. Chicago: Aldine.

Tylor, E. B. 1871. *Primitive Cultures.* London: Macmillan.

Vogt, E. Z. 1965. "Structural and Conceptual Replication in Zinacantan Culture," *American Anthropologist* 67:342–53.

Wallace, A. F. C. 1956. "Revitalization Movements," *American Anthropologist* 63:264–81.

Witherspoon, G. 1977. *Language and Art in the Navaho Universe.* Ann Arbor: University of Michigan Press.

8

Performance
and the Structuring
of Meaning and
Experience

BRUCE KAPFERER

When R. D. Laing stated in *The Politics of Experience* (1967) that it is impossible to experience another person's experience, he was repeating one of the central problematics of much phenomenological and existentialist philosophizing and theorizing. This problematic concentrates on the essential aloneness and solitude of human beings in the world as lived. Phenomenology, taking solitude as a fundamental basis of human existence, directs much of its analytic attention to the processes whereby individuals overcome or transcend their aloneness in the world and come to share their lived experiences with others. It is an approach which both attends to the particularity, individualness, or uniqueness, of human experience and to it universalizing character. The relation of the Particular to the Universal and vice versa is a basic dimension of the dialectic of phenomenological analysis. Of course, phenomenologists share this concern with a great many others, among them anthropologists and sociologists, who do not necessarily pursue the same theoretical orientation.[1]

But let me return to Laing's postulate. If, as he claimed, it is impossible to experience another person's experience—a position I will modify subsequently—it is true nonetheless that individuals understand that aspects of their experience are shared in common with others. The world as we live it is not founded on some kind of solipsism which views only the individual self and self-experience as real. The everyday world of human action is not constituted after the manner of Mrs. Christine Ladd Franklin, an eminent logician, who, as Bertrand Russell (1948) reported, wrote in a letter that she was a solipsist—and was surprised that there were no others. The reality of oneself and the reality of individual self-experience—or to put it another way, a consciousness of being in the world—is formed within an experiential reality composed of consociates and contemporaries with whom individuals assume both a degree of commonality in experience and a shared framework of understandings through which they become aware of their own and other's experience. The basis of Mrs. Franklin's not unexpected surprise rested on the fact that the validity of her position depended on its being shared by others, an expectation that was contravened by the very position she took but that paradoxically confirmed her as a solipsist.

The structuring of social action and relationships constituted as these are by and within culture limits the likelihood of individuals sharing the same experience. Culture, as it relates to the ordering of life in mundane situations, is both particularizing *and* universalizing. It mediates the relations of individuals both to their material terms of existence and to each other. It is particularizing in the sense that the structuring of relations between individuals in terms of a framework of cultural understandings variously locates individuals in the mundane orderings of everyday life. It differentiates them and makes possible a variety of individual perspectives and standpoints on the everyday world. Individuals experience themselves—they experience their experience and reflect on it—both from their own standpoint and from the standpoint of others within their culture. This is what gives to the practical activity of everyday life some of its movement and process. Further, I do not experience your experience. Paradoxically, your experience is *made* mine; I experience my experience of you. The expressions revealed on your face, in the gestural organization of your body, through the meeting of our glances, are experienced through my body and my situation. "In being looked at by the other, I find his 'expression' not so much *on* his face as *through* my situation—in feeling admired, in sensing coolness, in apparent indifference, in being shamed or humiliated" (Natanson 1970:140).

Even so, the point remains that human beings as social actors in their cultural worlds take for granted that they are acting in relation to others who share a history and a set of common experiences and understandings of experience. We tend to others as fellow human beings, who are like us and unlike us in the cultural worlds we inhabit. Culture is universalizing even as it particularizes and differentially situates and roots our experience. As G. H. Mead (1934) argued, I become aware of myself, of my experience, and of the possibilities of my Self-hood, through the act of standing outside myself and reflecting my action through the perspective of another person—by taking the attitude of the Other and organizing this, processually, in accordance with rules of interrelation and of appropriateness, what Mead termed the Generalized Other. This Other profoundly influences our personal experience as it enters our awareness in the reflective act, such acts continually orienting and reorienting our ongoing and future action. While I understand my action and the experience of my action and the action of others through my situation in the world, the nature of my experience and what I might understand to be the experiences of others reaches clarity through a range of cultural and social typifications and idealizations of experience. This is the universalizing character of culture to which I point. Whatever uniqueness there might be in my experience is generalized and lost in a set of culturally constituted constructs, concepts, or typifications. These stand between me and my fellow human beings, between the immediacy of my experience and the experience of that other person. I understand the experience of the other directly through my experience and indirectly through the mediation of a variety of cultural constructs. These constructs, through their mediation, are vital both in the constitution of sociality and for what has been termed the intersubjective sharing of experience. What is shared, however, is not the experience of the other in its full existential immediacy. Rather, the sharing takes place at another level, at a degree removed from any immediate individual experience. The various concepts, constructs, and typifications, that are engaged in the action of sharing experience are *about* experience, integral to its comprehension and understanding rather than to the experience itself.

This entire discussion lends support to Laing's postulate concerning the impossibility of experiencing another's experience, but it is restricted to experience as comprehended and realized in the mundane world of everyday life. My argument now turns to the possibility of mutual experience in the sense of experiencing together the one experience. Such a possibility is present in many of the cultural performances we and those in other cultures recognize as art and ritual. Art and ritual share potentially one fundamental quality in common: the Particular and the Universal are brought together and are transformed in the process. The Particular is universalized beyond the existential immediacy of the individual's situation so that it is transcended, even while its groundedness and specificity are maintained, to include others in what is essentially the same experiential situation. Concurrently, the Universal "is given a focus, an experiential content, in the immediacy of the individual's situation" (Natanson 1970:126). The process that is actualized and revealed in art and ritual as *performance*, the universalizing of the particular and the particularizing of the universal, is one of the factors accounting for the frequently observed close connection between art and ritual and the common recognition that much ritual is art, and vice versa.

What is most often glossed as "ritual," as with the variety of arts in their independent formation in numerous cultures, is a complex compositional form as revealed through the process of performance. I stress this because the word "ritual," as applied to a completed cultural performance, such as the grail-like anthropological concern with discovering a unifying definition of ritual, often denies or obscures the significance for analysis of the many different forms that are actualized in what we call ritual performance. A great number of the rituals recorded by anthropologists are compositions that interweave such forms as (labeled here for convenience) the plastic arts, liturgy, music, song, narrative storytelling, and drama, among others. These manifest in their performance varying possibilities for the constitution and ordering of experience, as well as for the reflection on and communication of experience. Within specific cultures, and possibly across them, they are tantamount to different languages of expression and communication. But in addition, and apart from the communicational dimension of ritual, which has received the greatest emphasis in anthropological discussion, the languages of ritual contain varying potential for bringing together the Particular and the Universal. In the extent to which this is so we find the possibility for those organized in relation to them to *commune in* the one experience.[2]

At this point the concept of performance becomes critical to my discussion. I wish to go beyond the term in one of its major commonsense usages, that is, performance as the enactment of text. A commitment to an understanding that there is an essential separation between the text and its enactment lies at the root of much anthropological debate. It opposes *some* structuralist and semiological anthropological approaches to other anthropologies which stress an attention to the description and analysis of cultural and social action through the actual experiences, dynamics, and processes of cultural worlds as these might be lived and observed. Either way, exclusive attention to the properties of the text (e.g., as a complex of signs and their structural interrelation), or a focus on enactment independent of its formative or structuring aspects, risks a reduction. As Ricouer (1976), among others, has stressed, the structuralist analysis of a text loses key aspects of that text's meaning as it is communicated and experienced. The way a text reaches its audience is no less an important dimension of its structure. Similarly, a concern with enactment at the expense of the structural properties of the text as actualized through the specific mode of its enactment will likely overlook some of the salient constitutive properties of the particular enactment itself. Furthermore, such concern risks a retreat into subjectivism, in which the meaning and the nature of experience are simply the sum total of individual interpretive responses, the only constraining factor being the limits of the broad cultural world in which individuals are placed. A concern with the bones ignores the flesh and the blood, the spirit and vitality of form. But a concern with the spirit alone disregards the skeleton around which the form takes shape and which directs but does not determine the character of spirit and vitality. In my usage, "performance" constitutes a unity of text and enactment, neither being reducible to the other. More properly, it is what certain philosophers of aesthetic experience refer to as the Work, irreducible to its performances and yet graspable only through them or, rather, in them (Dufrenne 1973:27).

Additional and integral to my specific use of the term "performance" is a concern with the interconnectedness of the directionality of performance, the media through which the performance is realized, and an attention to the way it orders context. Performance always intends an audience, and in ritual this might include supernaturals as well as those from the mundane world—performers, ritual subjects, and spectators, among others. The media of performance, whether music, dance, drama, or a particular combination of these, for example, have certain structural properties which, when realized in performance, order in specific ways those engaged to the performance. The directionality of performance and the media of performance are structuring of the ritual context; together they constitute meaning of the ritual, variously enable the communication of its meaning, and create the possibility for the mutual involvement of participants in the one experience, or else distance them and lead to their reflection on experience perhaps from a structured perspective outside the immediacy of the experience. The approach I adopt here is broadly in agreement with Dufrenne's (1973:59–60) analysis of the work of art: "The work has the initiative. And forbids any subjectivism. Far from the works' existing in us we exist in the work. . . . The ideas it suggests, the feelings it awakens, the concrete images—*Ansichten*, as Ingarden calls them—which nourish its meanings vary with each spectator. But they vary like perspectives which converge at the same point, like intentions which aim at the same object. All these views only display or exfoliate its possibilities. . . ."

The elaborate exorcisms that Sinhalese perform in the south of Sri Lanka provide some grounding, as well as extension, of my argument. These rites continue throughout the night, from dusk to dawn, and are directed toward severing the malign and individually disordering and disorienting attachment of demons to a patient. Paradigmatically, the logic and structural process of exorcism ritual is constitutive and reiterative of principles that are central to Sinhalese Theravada Buddhist culture. The key dimensions of this paradigm underpin the structure of every key ritual event, in the ordering of symbolic articles and actions within them, and in the arrangement of events in the diachronic and syntagmatic progression of an exorcism performance. Thus, at the paradigmatic level and in accordance with the Sinhalese cosmological view and worldview, demons and ghosts are at the base of a hierarchy dominated by the Buddha and a host of major and lesser deities. The organizing principles of this paradigm, purity and pollution, attachment and nonattachment, knowledge and ignorance, to name but a few, articulate the cosmic hierarchy and variously locate supernaturals and human beings in its order. In terms of a structuralist analysis wherein the exorcism as a whole, or each ritual event in a syntagmatic progression, is examined at its deeper level, as an abstract system of signs, few transformations in structure or in meaning as a function of the structural interrelation of signs would be detected. As they progress exorcisms effect a reversal in the relation of demons to human beings. Throughout much of the rite, human beings—exorcist and patient—give demons offerings to signify their subordination to them. But at the close of the rite the demons give offerings to deities and to human beings, thus signifying the culturally agreed proper relation of subordination of demons to deities and to human beings within the cosmic scheme. This need not necessarily be interpreted as a transformation at the level of the deep structure of the rite. Rather, it is a final and completed revelation of the paradigmatic structure of the ritual action which has continually informed the logic of its progression. At all points in the rite the offerings given to demons are conceptualized as dead and polluting. The reversal is simply a rendering, as consistent, of the structural logic of the rite as it is present from the very beginning.

I definitely am not arguing that shifts and transformations do not occur in exorcisms. Their overt purpose is, after all, decidedly transformational. Exorcists, patients, and others assembled at exorcisms understand them to be effective ways to sever the malign relation between demons and patient, to move the patient from sickness to health, and to achieve important definitions and redefinitions by the patient and others of the reality in which they all are placed. Instead, I am directing attention to the level at which shifts and transformations in meaning, understanding, and experience are achieved. This is not at the level of the text, here identified as a combination of the structural principles ordering the rite as a whole and the rules governing both the syntagmatic progression of ritual events and the manner of their enactment. Rather, important definitions of reality by the patient and others assembled for the rite, and shifts and transformations in these definitions, are possible through the structure of performance.

I isolate two aspects of performance: as the structuring of standpoint and as the structuring of context through the medium of presentation. The analysis of both aspects is critical to an understanding of how ritual establishes and transforms meaning and experience for participants, and for understanding how ritual might create the potential for engaging participants in the one experience as well as enabling their reflection on that experience. Although I have distinguished analytically the structuring of standpoint within performance from the medium of performance, both are closely related in any one observed performance. Thus, Sinhalese exorcisms comprise a complex interweaving of performance modes—music, song, dance, and comic drama, to name but a few—and it is the nature of their interweaving, as well as their constituting properties as forms actualized through, and only apparent in, performance, which is integral to the structuring of standpoints and to the constitution of context. Through these aspects of performance, too, specific possibilities for the realization of experience and meaning, and their transformation, are created.

Major Sinhalese exorcisms vary from performance to performance, and this variation is related to the particular demands of clients and the exorcism tradition to which the exorcism specialists belong. Within the area I worked, however, there are certain invariant aspects of the performance structure which are apparent at the level of each specific performance. All performances, for example, regularly move members of the ritual gathering from positions in which their standpoints are largely structured in contexts external to that in which the patient is located, to positions *within* the context established around the patient. In addition, all major exorcisms concentrate specific media of performance at certain periods in the ritual progression. Thus, the elaborate performance of music and dance is most marked in the period known as the midnight watch—when the demonic is made present in its full dominating power and becomes manifest in the entrancement of exorcist and patient. Later in the midnight watch, usually after the entrancement of the patient, and throughout much of the morning watch, when the exorcism draws to a close, comic drama is the dominant medium of ritual presentation. This form often involves exorcists appearing in the masked guise of successive apparitions and demons.

In Sinhalese cultural understandings a demonic victim approximates what I refer to as an existential state of solitude in the world. The demonic as conceptualized by Sinhalese is similar to that which Goethe recognized from within the worldview of European culture as ultimately everything that is individual and separates one from others. Demons attack individuals who are understood to be in a state of physical and metal aloneness. Solitude and its correlate, fear, are among the key essences of the demonic. Exorcisms represent these as the condition of the patient and can,

as a logical possibility of the structure of their performance, reproduce and actualize the experience of the demonic in a patient and
in other participants.

The early phases of an exorcism involve exorcists in summoning the demons to the ritual site and in the construction of that
reality in which the patient is understood to be immersed. The
patient is isolated from others in the ritual gathering, and the
ritual action is directed and focused almost exclusively on the patient; other members of the ritual gathering are virtually irrelevant
to the ritual process orchestrated by the exorcists. While the patient is engaged in a reality in which the powers of gods and demons are invoked, the others who assemble at the rite are involved
in everyday action contexts. Some drink and play cards, while
others renew friendships and share everyday gossip and information. The maintenance, and to some extent development, of contexts of meaning and action outside of that in which the patient is
placed, but within the immediate setting of a performance, is in
part a product of the way exorcists organize their performance in
this early period. What I must stress here is the difference between
the standpoint of the patient, on the one hand, and the possible
standpoints of the rest of the participants, on the other, as these
are structured through performance. Patients are not just isolated
in a world of the exorcists' construction but are limited in movement. They are expected to remain seated, to refrain from conversation with others who attend the proceedings, and to concentrate
on the words and actions of the exorcists. Patients are limited in
the number of standpoints outside their immediate experience
which could be taken on the action. Indeed, they are restricted to
the standpoint of demonic victims as this is culturally defined.
What is understood to be the subjective world of the patient becomes objectified in the ritual action—the subjective is also objective, and vice versa. Imprisoned in a subjective world of struggling
supernatural forces in which Life and Death are held in balance,
and impelled to reflect on this world from a position within themselves, it is no surprise that patients should occasionally express
outward signs of terror and occasionally lapse into unconscious-
ness or manifest trancelike behavior.

In terms of the structure of performance, what is experientially possible for the patient is not so for those gathered for the
occasion. The other participants are placed outside the context of

the patient and, furthermore, are enabled to adopt a variety of standpoints on the ritual action in terms of rational, everyday constructs and understandings. Members of the ritual gathering are not confined within their own experience and understandings, but by their interaction they are able to stand outside themselves and interpret their experience through shared constructs and understandings constitutive of an everyday world not determined by demonic malevolence. Their experience, insofar as it is reflected from their own situated and reciprocally shared standpoints outside that of the patient, is made distinctive of the patient's, through the structure of performance. The patient's behavior, in that it is perceived through the particular experiences and structured standpoints of audience members in the world, is rendered potentially quite strange. The meaning of the patient's behavior might be conceptualized through constructs and typifications of the demonic, but members of the ritual gathering do not share in the immediacy of the patient's experience.

A significant shift in the structuring of contexts through performance occurs from the start of the elaborate presentation of music and dance in the midnight watch. For the first time exorcists use the entire performance area and direct their action inward to the patient and outward to the audience. What usually occurs is that most members of the ritual gathering become directly focused on the action and thus become individuated and separated from those mutual engagements in which everyday contexts of meaning and action were sustained. This change in the structuring of performance is one means whereby everyday contexts, hitherto part of the performance setting, can be suspended and members of the ritual gathering recontextualized within fundamentally the same context as the patient. Through their individuation, members of the audience are located in essentially the same relation to the central events as the patient. And by virtue of relocation, one condition is established for the potential engagement of audience and patient in the one experience—a common isolation in the world of experience.

Through the media of music and dance, members of the ritual gathering are further impelled in the direction of the patient's experience. The reality of experience constructed in music and dance reaches the senses directly through these media as aesthetic forms and in much the same way, given the extent to which members of the gathering are uniformly individuated and restricted from adopting standpoints outside the immediate experiential realm constituted in music and dance. Those who are directly and immediately engaged in the realms of music and dance experience in different ways. However, this ability to reflect on music and dance in the act of experiencing it requires, I would suggest, some capacity for individuals to disengage themselves from the experience while it is being experienced. It is largely only when the music or dance stops, or in some way interrupts its own flow and movement, that reflection and the treatment of experience as an object—a vital element of all reflection—becomes fully possible. Musical and dance form, as revealed in performance, are constitutive of subjective experience; they mold all subjective experience to their form.

A concern with the internal structuring properties of music and dance as forms revealed in performance makes possible some statements as to the parameters of experience constructed through them. Music and dance, for Sinhalese exorcists, are closely connected. The basic sounds out of which the structure of Sinhalese music is built also correspond to the fundamental body gestures and steps of the dance. In the Sinhalese system, dance fills out the time-structure of music and makes visible its movement and passage. An essential property of the time-structure of music and dance is that it constitutes a continuous present. Musical time is movement and passage filled out in its existential immediacy. Because of these aspects, members of the ritual gathering who are engaged within the musical context of the patient can share the same vivid and continuous present, which is an experiential possibility of music. Musical time is reversible, and it is in this reversability that the structure of music and dance finds it essential coherence. The time-structure of music and dance tends both forward and back in the very moment of its presentation to the senses.

The structural hierarchy of the Sinhalese cosmology is continually present in an exorcism. Demons are unambiguously subordinate within the cosmic order. It is through the power of the Buddha and the deities that the demons are summoned to the rite, that their hold over the patient is progressively broken, and that their polluting and illness-causing essence is withdrawn from the patient's body. The attitude of demonic victims, as this is culturally typified, denies the cosmological order. Patients are understood to see their reality as crowded by demons who determine their action and who vie with the powers of the gods. Contrary to the view of healthy Sinhalese, demons are seen to be in the same phenomenal plane of existence as the deities, and they evidence a similar relation to human beings.

The time-structure of music and dance, and their internal coherence in performance, contain the potential for creating such an experience for the patient and for extending this experience to the members of the ritual gathering. Music and dance, through their structuring capacity, can render as copresent and mutually consistent those dimensions of experience that might appear as distinct, opposed, even contradictory, from the rational perspective of the everyday world. In the music and dance of exorcism, both deities and demons are constituted of the same fundamental units of sound and gesture. They are made coexistent in the single and continuous flowing motion of music and dance. In the reversible time-structure of music and dance the deity can rise in the midst of the demonic, and vice versa. Through the form of music and dance the relation of the demonic to the deity is uncertain and unstable. At one moment one might appear to dominate, only to give way to the domination of the other.

In the music and dance of exorcism the Particular is universalized and the Universal is particularized; and the culturally understood subjective world of the patient finds external form. This subjective world, in turn, insofar as music and dance order the context of experience, is rendered capable of entering directly into the experience of the spectators who have hitherto stood outside the patient's experience. It is in the individuation of members of the ritual gathering in relation to the central ritual events and through the media of music and dance that the experiential state of the patient, alone and terrified in the world, is most nearly approached. The drama of exorcism which follows ends this isolation and destroys that particular accent on reality which is a potential of the structuring of context through music and dance. Drama, and especially the highly comic form it assumes in exorcism, can achieve this by virtue of its own structuring properties as revealed in performance. In its dialogic mode, and in contrast to music and dance, drama is intersubjective rather than subjective in its process. It does not appear to the senses so much directly, as in music and dance, but rather organizes its meaning—for the characters portrayed in it and for the audience—indirectly and at a distance, in accordance with the different structured standpoints the characters in the drama assume. Both the characters and their audience are enjoined to adopt perspectives outside their own particular subjective standpoint and to reflect on them. Drama is quintessentially reflexive as a property of its own internal form. In the drama of Sinhalese exorcism, the ritually constructed world of the supernatural is joined to the everyday world of Sinhalese action and understanding. Exorcists who appear in the masked guise of demons, for example, not only act these roles but also those of characters who figure in daily experience—politicians, police officers, government administrators, girls in search of lovers, schoolteachers, and so on. The drama of exorcism is conducted in the discourse of everyday speech, not in the specialized verbal forms apparent in the earlier phases of the ritual.

It cannot be overstressed that the drama of exorcism is comic in form. Through comedy, various meanings which lie within the structure of exorcism and which inform its process, but which are variously hidden or suppressed through the structuring properties of such performance media as music and dance, are revealed and subjected to examination. Comedy and the discovery of the comic finds its specific movement and process in the juxtaposition of opposites, in the linking of categories of experience and knowledge which in the everyday cultural world are understood to be located in different domains, and in the realization of contradiction. Of course, these are also features of other modes of discourse and symbolic action. The distinctiveness of comedy, however, is that even while engaging in these processes it invites those who attend to it to see such juxtapositions, oppositions, and contradictions for what they are: as absurdly, impossibly, and inappropriately linked in terms of the everyday typifications and understandings of the cultural world. Comedy finds its form in inconsistency as a guiding principle; and the enjoyment it can evoke is dependent on the realization by the audience of this essential inconsistency. The comic process itself reveals this inconsistency, but the recognition by an audience of the full potential of the comic is dependent on their being conscious and committed to their everyday world as it is culturally and socially typified. Patients are enjoined by exorcists and by other participants to laugh, and their laughter in the company of others is taken to be a sign that they have reentered the world as experienced by the normal and the healthy. To laugh at and with the comedy, as do all audiences in the comic drama of exorcism, is to share in a universally typified and comprehended world.

The comedy of exorcism, as a central structuring dimension of its performance, plays in word and action with structure ordering and reordering of the categories and relations in terms of which experience is understood and meaning is generated. If comedy is disordering, it is ordering at the same time, for in discovering and bringing to realization the absurd, it also points to that culturally defined proper order of things. The comic drama of exorcism is both an attack on limiting form—on that which hides, obscures, and restricts—and an attack on falsity and illusion, the handmaidens of limiting form. Demons, who in themselves are masters of falsity and illusion, are harbored and nurtured in the limiting form of music and dance and by the restriction on standpoint produced through the realization of these forms in performance. The comedy of exorcism breaks through such limitations, however; it frees individuals from the solitude of subjective experience, links them to others through the mediation of shared constructs and typifications, and demands that they take a variety of standpoints on the world as experienced and as it achieves its diverse meanings.

Demons and the demonic cannot live in the expanded world of everyday understanding created in the comedy. They represent, as part of the comic and in their own essential absurdity, a failure to unify to their being the world as experienced in its diversity of context and in its movement and process. And so the demons appearing in exorcism retreat from the stage of human action, and in their failure to unify they are replaced in their subordinate position in the cosmic schema. Through the comedy of exorcism the particularlity of individual subjective experience, and the danger of the solipsism of the demonic, is transcended and to some extent lost in the universality and legitimacy of agreed and shared cultural understandings.

Sinhalese exorcisms exhibit an essential joke form with demons as the ultimate butt, as Mary Douglas (1968) has noted more generally for ritual. A broad conception of exorcism ritual, one not too distant from that which exorcists themselves hold, might be that of a magnificent trap in which demons are ensnared only to be repelled for the moment from the cultural world of human beings. This trap is elaborately set through the various illusions created by form realized in performance. Demons and human beings are subject to these illusions of form, though in different ways. Yet when the illusions are finally dispelled, the demons are caught and subordinated in the very cosmic reality they have sought to subvert, and human beings are freed from their capricious control.

If there is one general point underlying my argument it is the critical importance of performance in the analysis of meaning and experience. Performance as the unity of text and enactment is realized in a variety of forms, aesthetic and otherwise, which carry with them, as a potential of their structure, their own possibilities for the realization of meaning and experience. They are not necessarily reducible one to the other.

Performance, in my view, is the structuring of structure, and it is this critical feature which makes performance essential to the analysis of ritual and other modes of symbolic action. Natanson (1974) has recently noted that the difference between some phenomenological approaches, on the one hand, and some Marxist approaches, on the other, was that while blood flows for the Marxist, the phenomenologist contemplates the essence of gore. Add a structuralist to this macabre gathering and we might have a person who cleans away the blood and gore only to reveal the bones. It is conceivable that in the analysis of performance all these approaches could combine to increase our understanding of the complexities and wonders of the cultural and social worlds of human beings.

NOTES

1. Theory in anthropology and sociology has continually been drawn to the central issue of the relation between the Particular and the Universal. It was one of the major concerns of Durkheim and underlies his final great work, *The Elementary Forms of the Religious Life* (1915). Enduring debates in anthropology revolving around cultural relativism, cultural determinism, and questions of individual freedom and the degree to which individuals exercise choice and control over their own action and experience, are all instances of this central concern.

2. Ritual is not just communication; it is many other things as well. The recent work in hermeneutics and phenomenology, particularly in the area of narrative form and poetics, has much to add to the anthropological analysis of ritual.

REFERENCES

Douglas, Mary. 1968. "The Social Control of Cognition: Some Factors in Joke Perception," *Man* (n.s.) 3:361–76.

Dufrenne, Mikel. 1973. *The Phenomenology of Aesthetic Experience*. Evanston, Ill.: Northwestern University Press.

Durkheim, Emile. 1915. *The Elementary Forms of the Religious Life*. New York: Macmillan.

Laing, Ronald David. 1967. *The Politics of Experience*. New York: Pantheon.

Mead, George Herbert. 1934. *Mind, Self, and Society*. Chicago: University of Chicago Press.

Natanson, M. 1970. *The Journeying Self*. Menlo Park, Calif.: Addison-Wesley.

———. 1974. *Phenomenology, Role, and Reason*. Springfield, Ill.: Charles C. Thomas.

Ricoeur, Paul. 1976. *Interpretation Theory*. Forth Worth: Texas Christian University Press.

Russell, Bertrand. 1948. *Human Knowledge: Its Scope and Limits*. New York: Simon and Schuster.

PART FOUR

Reflexivity

9

Play and the Problem of Knowing in *Hamlet:* An Excursion into Interpretive Anthropology

PHYLLIS GORFAIN

"In Dreams Begin Responsibilities"—a short story by Delmore Schwartz, 1938

"In Dreams Begins Responsibility"—the epigraph for *Responsibilities*, a book of poems by William Butler Yeats, 1914

"In Dreams Begins Responsibility"—old play, no date (the source given by Yeats for his epigraph)

Anthropologists may take *Hamlet* as an important cultural text, since Hamlet has become for readers the epitome of their deepest aspirations for self-knowledge, of their quests to penetrate the hidden truth of appearances, and of their sense of responsibility to right a world made corrupt by uncertainty. They may, however, overlook *Hamlet* as a mirror of their own anthropological enterprise—that of probing actions for the truth of their meanings but finding instead only other images of text making. As a text about the unclosable distance between behavior and its meanings, between the immediacy of experience and the shaping of experience into transmittable forms, *Hamlet* may mirror to anthropologists their own processes and those of the people they study. It depicts an unremitting series of inquiries and representations—reports, narratives, pretenses, games, dramas, rituals, and punning—as Hamlet attempts to close epistemic gaps between the past, present, and future, to secure the truth and authority of experience, and to direct its power through symbolic action. Yet no character can seize the original event behind any performance; each search yields only another shadowy text, a resemblance, a memory. Like Hamlet, anthropologists also find themselves poised between a reflexive knowing that their "knowledge" of society is always a kind of text, a construction based on constructed social forms, and a feeling that they bear a responsibility to penetrate beyond the appearances of social life to the truth of experience. But because meaning is always based on appearances, is always interpretive, and is never fixed or final, anthropologists can find in *Hamlet* a master text of their desire to know what they also learn will always elude them. Just as Geertz (1972:24–26) has explained how, for the Balinese, the cockfight may be read as their *Macbeth*, I wish to explain how, for anthropologists, *Hamlet* may be read as their Balinese cockfight.

I suggest that *Hamlet* is not only an expressive text through which our culture tells itself about itself, but also a reflexive text which anthropologists can study as a story about themselves as both makers and students of the texts they examine. I do not claim that *Hamlet*, or my reading of it, can show fieldworkers how to do ethnography or instruct theorists how to define a reflexive anthropology. As an inquiry into interpretive anthropology, this essay aims toward an anthropology of interpreting texts. That effort becomes a central exercise in the anthropology of experience, a humanistic science which interprets experience seen as, and in, texts. Such an anthropolgy tends to "read" experience (Geertz 1972, 1980). It postulates that experience becomes knowable only in performances and accounts; these productions are seen as interpretations which cultures present to themselves, and which the anthropologist then must interpret (Geertz 1972). Because deriving meaning requires making differences, we note the cultural choices that constitute meaning. We study how performers switch genres, select details, omit references, shift perspectives, or even transform ontologies, as they do when they move actions into the domain of the play. The "difference that matters" may, however, be experienced as the veil that always seems to fall between an authentic reality and a mere "version" of it. We may view the versatile differences which produce meaning as signs of our impenetrable complexity—as the drawn curtains in a theater signal that a stage action will be just a fiction. But difference may also signal an ongoing drama of inquiry. Seen in this light, the probing of culture becomes not a matter of truth or proofs, not a review of discrete events or fixed realities. The illusion that reality is set, or even a set of rules, dissolves before a sense of culture in production.

The interpretive method for studying culture as a process relies on paradoxes of reflexivity, for we must inevitably confront our own processes of interpretation when we deny that we can finally locate the "head and source" (*Hamlet*, 2.2.55) of our condition.[1] Promises that social truth may be found "though it were hid indeed / Within the center" (2.2.159–60) are made only by one as foolish as Polonius and are believed only by those with fatal purposes, at least in Shakespeare's drama. By contrast, *Hamlet* valorizes the playfulness to experiment with uncertainty and the courage to learn through not knowing.

As a mirror which exalts our own image yet also reflects its inability to provide no view beyond itself, *Hamlet* presents us with a consoling answer to this tautology, but *Hamlet's* consolation depends on the paradoxes of reflexivity. This reflexivity entails not just self-awareness or self-reference; it requires a consciousness of our means of self-consciousness and of our uses of self-presentation (Ruby 1980:156–57).

Like epistemology, reflexivity does not address *what* we know but *how* we think we know (Myerhoff and Metzger 1980:103). In reflexive examination we probe the techniques by which we reflect ourselves to ourselves: our stories and projections, our portraits and mirrors, our journals and novels, our games and pastimes. We study our reflections and speculations (Fernandez 1980) and thereby become the objects of our own subjectivity (Babcock 1980b:1–3) Such duplicity examines not only the objects in which we become objectified to ourselves but also the methods by which we see ourselves making ourselves in them. When we thus turn a mirror on the mirror, to examine mirror*ing*, we create a sense of movement, of resonance, of process. The exercise can produce the vertigo of infinite regress or an ascent into transcendence. In fact, the language of reflexivity is replete with metaphors of affect and spatiality. When we speak of a "meta-level" of self-knowing "above" or "beyond" the level we may at first have taken as real or privileged, reflexive positions may seem superior. But these constructions may also seem like the dreams from which we must awaken to live. If we imagine, spatially, that we have "jumped up" a level in metaphysical consciousness, we may feel that reflexive insight arrives at the "higher truth," in which case the dream is paramount and "life" is just the shadow (Herz 1977:390–93). Temporally, a distance seems to widen between the past we recall in present objects—those we use to fashion the future. Thus, we may seem to stand at the very junctures of ontology and time, at a moment so interstitial that we may feel we partake of eternity.

Because reflexivity promotes such paradoxical awareness through open artificiality, it makes sense that works of art regularly employ reflexivity. Since they already operate within the clear zone of artifice, fictions seem to illuminate, rather than deny, our sense of reality. For this reason fictions may most profoundly convey the double dimensions of reflexivity. Fictions that confess their own feigning do not so much threaten our faith in appearances as allow us a holiday; we are freed to play with the translucency of culture. The seeming opacity and permanence of social arrangements become refractable in the prism of a fiction or reflexivity. Even a tragedy can painlessly expose to us the limits and powers of our fabrications.

Hamlet acknowledges the epistemological dilemmas of any reflexive undertaking and also instructs us how to read both itself and the world. A reflexive reading of *Hamlet*, for anthropologists, might proceed first with a consideration of the drama as a fiction and then with a consideration of what happens in the drama. It resists the absurdity and despair which can beset us when we realize that our knowledge of social motives, meanings, and truths is confined within the scope of our languages of social meaning. But to understand the consolation *Hamlet* holds out to interpretive anthropology, we must learn more from *Hamlet* about the paradoxes of *using texts* for knowledge.

THE PROBLEM

My aim is twofold: to show anthropologists something about the relevance of fictions and play to problems of reflexivity and interpretation in anthropology; and to show how anthropological theories can clarify lasting puzzles in the interpretation of *Hamlet*. Both efforts can demonstrate the pertinence of fictions to anthropologists as players-readers and the power of anthropology in reading. One question, for example, concerns what we might call Hamlet's indeterminate madness. Is he mad, or is he feigning

madness? And why are we made so uncertain about his intentions? Another question notes the peculiar ending of the play, in
which a fake fencing match resolves the plot instabilities. Why is
this game which is not a game so apt an ending for this play?
How does the play teach us to think about fictions, such as games,
and deceptions, such as con games? We also must wonder why
Hamlet engages in this game when he must, by then, suspect it
may not be a game, and when he in fact senses that the game,
even as a game, may be potentially lethal. In this regard I will
connect fiction making and reflexivity to processes of play. This
configuration of concerns raises fundamental questions about the
relationship of fictions to making meaning and to undertaking acts
of responsibility.

HAMLET AS A FICTION

Hamlet assures us that we can use fictions to play with—to refor-
mulate and master—our problems of semantic penetration, discovery through mistaking, and the multiplication of meaning through
indeterminacy. These are the problems anthropologists make more
and more the objects of their analysis and theory, whether they
look at their informants or themselves constructing semblances of
social meaning. Indeed, anthropologists do not need Shakespeare's depictions of social ingenuity to admire how cultures fab-
ricate worlds of openly artifactual events, reflexive situations,
liminal processes, reframings, deceptions, and fictions. We hardly
require a reading of *Hamlet* to recognize the virtuosity with which
humans re-present reality to themselves in one imaginative substitution of experience after another, how we turn the flux of experience into narrative, narrative into drama, plays into replays,
and use all these means of interpretation and reinterpretation to
maintain and invent roles, generate power in spectacle and symbol, refashion expectations, and question the "givenness" of rules
and institutions. Readers of culture, like readers of literature,
know it is as difficult for social researchers as it is for Hamlet to
"pluck out the heart of . . . mystery" (3.2.366), to seize "what is
out there,"[2] to bestow on posterity their own versions of the problem of knowing social "reality." Because some social scientists,
such as the contributors to this volume, examine the works of
imagination with which people organize and reconstitute their ex-

perience, they also increasingly take up literary methods and metaphors to characterize the ways they and the people they study make meaning in their lives (Geertz 1980).

Shakespeare successfully bequeathed to us his version of that problem, for *Hamlet* teaches us about our ways of taking occasions as texts, of making texts into means for social learning and action, and of using other works of art to master those techniques. Yet, great works of art, like the myth of Narcissus, warn us that they may reflect on only their own reflecting, suffering the same outcome as Narcissus (DiSalvo 1980). So, too, does *Hamlet* enclose mirror within mirror, story within story, play within play, to suggest how works of culture and art express an ever-receding virtual reality, which fictions can bravely portray yet never really betray.

In his essay in this volume, Bruner argues that ethnographies may be best understood as narratives that anthropologists learn and tell as a means to organize and interpret events over time. The structure and ideology of dominant narratives, as Bruner shows, give informants and ethnographers a structure of discourse, roles, and sources of power in which they can locate their own significance in relation to the differences in a past-present-future to which narratives give shape. But these narrativized accounts of change and significance are not open fictions; that is, they may be taken as texts, as narrative structures, but not as admitted fictions. Ethnography may be predicated on theoretical models or it may perceive events in terms of conventions about social behavior which anthropologists teach each other and acquire from dominant discourses of knowledge (Bakhtin 1981; Foucault 1978); but it is taken as a descriptive and analytic account of life "as it is," not as a representation of life "as if." Ethnography is taken as factive, not fictive. Anthropologists frequently interpret play and fictions within ethnographies, however, and they often regard such expressive events as arteries reaching to the very heart of a culture—to its imagination of itself.

At one level, as a fiction *Hamlet* invites us to use it to see ourselves; at another level it forces us to question that very process by a process of self-reflection. Because of that self-reflection, which produces paradoxes about its own powers, *Hamlet* both exploits and assaults our faith that dramas, like mirrors, disclose the reality of social life.

When we read the text of this Shakespearean play, or watch it performed in the theater, a system of conventions about taking such experiences as "play" comes into operation. We assume that the events taking place on stage, or the incidents we read about, are not "the events themselves," nor are they a transcription of the actual occurrences. The words on the page and the enactments on the stage are taken as representations of imagined actions, so that the actions depicted are not themselves assumed to be "real." We take fictive actions as imitations of actions which might at some time occur, given what we know about human possibility (Smith 1978:14–40).

Hamlet, for example, is an artwork that uses the past (or rather, certain ideas about it) as a setting but does not offer itself as a reproduction or investigation of the historical truth of that past, irrespective of whatever history there may be about a Prince Amleth in Denmark is A.D. 600.[3] Fictional drama is unlike a ritual, which we place in sacred time and is taken as "real," as doing work—producing or recreating actual occurrences. Rather, fictional drama is taken as a fabrication of events placed in a representation of time and place. Although the performance or the reading takes place in a historical moment in a specific place—on the Globe platform in the summer of 1600, or in an Oberlin armchair in the summer of 1981—the world depicted by the drama is one the audience must conjure up, beyond the stage or the page. The virtual world of *Hamlet* (as distinct from the rocky ledges of the real Amleth) remains an imagined zone. The heterocosm created in a fiction is a realm that imitates existing or possible worlds but also remains an alternate "made" world. Designed both by the "poet's eye" and the imagination of the audience, which must "piece out" and "amend" that vision,[4] fictional worlds always remain incomplete and detached from the realms they point toward. For its many actors, directors, readers, and audiences in performances, rehearsals, rereadings, and parodies over the last four hundred years, *Hamlet* shows not the events of Amleth, Feng, and Horwendil in seventh-century Jutland; instead, it enacts a set of incidents placed in a fictive domain which resembles or refers to that period and locale, yet it can also pertain to other contexts because of its fictional dislocation and atopicality.

Fictions build believable worlds for us, but never ones we take as actual. The virtuality of the mimetic world may render it no less compelling or even less convincing than the actual world, though it always remains, at some level, distinct from that world. Smith (1978:33–34) explains the difference: "Shakespeare composed the play, let us say, in 1603, but in what year did Hamlet kill Claudius? In one sense, he kills Claudius every time the play is performed, . . . but in another sense the slaying of Claudius is an act that never did, never will, and never can occur *in the historical world*." In Bateson's (1972) language, when we class an event as fiction or play, we designate something about how we take the event. When we indicate "this is play," we make the event a metacommunication which "says" we are to "take this signal to signify what *X* commonly signifies and take this signal to not signify what *X* commonly signifies." Moreover, we also assume that what *X* commonly signifies may itself be imagined. Observing a puppy's behavior, Bateson could see that the puppy knew a "nip" did not signify what a "bite" does; and the nip represented "a bite," though not an actual, particular bite (1972:179–80).

When Hamlet stages a play of murder as a court interlude, he reassures his royal audience that the actors only play at murder: "They do but jest—poison / in jest—no offense i' th' world" (3.2.134–35). He makes the obvious point that in a play the appearance of murder does not signify what the appearance of murder commonly signifies; and the audience may also safely assume that what this appearance of murder signifies may be a fictive event. The play does not mime any real murder; or, at any rate, it may be taken as if it doesn't. For the audience watching it, the sight of murder becomes a pastime; the immediate issue is what the *image* of murder means. Yet for those who watch Hamlet's jest, a murder of just this sort has been committed. That "extradramatic" fact adds a brilliant irony in the larger dramatic world which encloses the entertainment. There, the king who watches a fiction of regicide has himself committed an act of regicide and has used deception to cover the offense. Hamlet uses art to suggest "no offense i' th' world." But, of course, Hamlet also hopes his play will offend—not the body but the conscience. He aims the play as a jest and as a moral barb.

Later I shall discuss the expanding meanings of this scene within a scene, but for now I wish to point out the level on which Hamlet's disclaimer is true. For those whose consciences enable them to play, for those whose imaginations can take play with a playful spirit, drama is a jest, a gesture, incomplete, a sign about signs. The metacommunication "made by" fictive statements is, in fact, one the interpreter places on them. Play is a process of interpretation, not a matter of the intrinsic conditions in a situation or thing. Therefore, we cannot list the events we take as play or the objects we treat as toys. We make play by the way we frame an action as play. In terms of communication, a statement is being made on one logical level; at another level we take the discourse to be a representation of discourse. To put it another way, we understand the event framed as a play event. The metaphor of a "frame" suggests that a boundary defines the incident as mimetic. But the event includes its frame, so to speak. The double discourse of play makes communication double; the doubling occurs in the form of a metacommunication about meaning. As a discourse about its own meaning, play then centers not on any specific meaning but on the general issue of meaning, which it foregrounds as a playful problem.

Play events, then, produce a special process of interpretation, a process which uses the same means for interpretation that we use to understand natural events, but which are distinct from that process. We do not interpret a fictive statement to uncover a speaker's actual intentions or to formulate choices for consequential action. "No longer mourn for me, when I am dead" is not a request from Shakespeare (Sonnet 71, line 1) to be acted on when we read his words. We do not probe into the historical context of the utterance to ask ourselves if the writer—as distinct from the persona who fictively "says" this—was at that moment afraid he would die. When we begin the open-ended interpretation of this utterance as a fictive utterance, we construct a series of plausible, yet imaginary contexts into which we can situate a variety of readings of the lines, as spoken by a fictive poet/lover. This process of hypothetical readings makes the interpretation of fictive speech a process that, like the interpretation of everyday speech, considers speech in relation to speakers, social contexts, and consequences, though the contexts remain fictive. The process of interpreting a play event, then, plays with the process of interpretation used in "natural speech" (Bakhtin 1981; Smith 1978). We engage in a series of inconsequential conjectures.

Play interpretations also free us from making responsible choices based on the acts that are enacted or on the fictive utter-

ances that are spoken. Unlike the way anthropologists might respond to overhearing informants recall a deception they have perpetrated, we do not ask, after a play is over, "What shall we do
now that we know what happened?" What we learn about what
happened from "overhearing" *Hamlet* is something we use to enrich our understanding of what happens in the world. We do not
add it to our store of information of what has happened to actual
people. Moreover, we do not think that *Hamlet* requires us to make
judgments or choices in our world; we do not feel we must decide
if the real Gerutha of history knew that the real Feng killed her
husband before she married him. Our uncertainty about Gertrude's complicity, in Shakespeare's play, is not experienced as a
problem in judging a historical person for the sake of historical
truth. Instead, we enjoy the problem as a means for considering
general processes of suspicion and self-delusion, an illustration of
our lasting obstacles in knowing fully the motives of others. The
problem in the play world becomes the representation of real problems with knowledge in our world; the fictive problem enables us
to contemplate those problems in a specific setting but independently of any need to make "responsible" interpretive or moral
choices. The play becomes a mirror of problems of inquiry, but it
does not make an inquiry itself. Our interpretation of fictive events
is then a process of play, resting on both the play of what is presented and the play of judging and choosing among the meanings
of what is shown. Play events create a process of both interpretation and judgment which is itself playful.

Anthropologist who interpret the appearances of quotidian
activities inevitably confront the same indeterminacy in social life,
but their understanding becomes a matter of consequentiality and
negotiation:

In any social relationship, including the anthropologist/informant one,
actors constantly test the accuracy of their inferences and imputations,
and the process by which they do so is extraordinarily complex. They
read other peoples' behavior as meaningful activity, picking and choosing
among different possible interpretations of it available to them. If the
parties to the interaction create widely divergent interpretations . . . , they
can nevertheless continue to think their definitions are shared until evidence to the contrary no longer fits a hypothesis of consensus. At such
points, actors can either renegotiate a consensual definition . . . or they
can terminate the relationship. . . . (Karp and Kendall 1982:263)

Reducing uncertainty, locating intention, and deciding on meaning in social acts, for both participants and analysts, is not the playful art of reading fictions, however. Fieldworkers who may marvel at the meanings generated by the deliberate ambiguities and multivocality in everyday events differentiate this engagement with hermeneutic potential from the paragrammatic possibilities invited by fictive events. *Hamlet* is not simply a recreational and reflective version of doing anthropology or puzzling through life. As a reflexive engagement with knowing, this play helps us to discriminate between the problems of interpreting events and those of using fictions. Thus, it discloses the special ways in which fictions clarify the indeterminacies in all that we imagine we know.

Hamlet permits us to play with, to manipulate and reconsider without the consequences of mistakes, the very problems that beset a reflexive and interpretive anthropology. In both *Hamlet* and anthropology the problem of truth remains indissoluble. But in the playful process of interpreting a fiction, the process of pursuing meaning becomes a source of grandeur. As a character like Hamlet shows us the nobility and necessity in our searches for authority, we gain both a sense of our omnipotence over and the dangers inherent in the semantic worlds we construct. Mistakes about meaning and worth in the fictive world become matters of expansion and possibility, even as the fictive world pictures for us how mistakes in our world can be fatal and irreversible. *Hamlet* thus brings us closer to the chaos from which it protects us, even while it displays the epistemological paradox it presses: knowing through not knowing.

This knowing–not knowing paradox is related to the paradox of reflexivity (Babcock 1980b). When we use a play like *Hamlet* to create an "objective" or "other" self by which to see ourselves, and when the play helps us to examine that same process, the examination is conducted by the same faculties we hope to examine. The inquiring subject become the scrutinized object; the object becomes the subject. When the process involves a fiction, the problem is even more acute. Borges (1964:46) writes: "Why does it disquiet us to know that Don Quixote is a reader of the Quixote and Hamlet is a spectator of *Hamlet?* These inversions suggest that if the characters in a story can be readers or spectators then we, their readers or spectators, can be fictions."

Bateson (1979:8, 9) addresses the opposite, but structurally identical, problem in terms of play. Explaining that play is "communication *about* communication," he elaborates:

Now, what we began to discover is that the word "play" is a classifying term within the life of the creatures—or the natives, or whomever you're going to talk about; ourselves. If that is so, then of course it is quite different, from the acts which constitute it; or if it is *not* different, if the message, "This is play," is itself a playful message, then the roof blows off and you don't know where you are and somebody is either going to laugh, or be hurt.

You will create the Paradox of Epimenides when the message, "This is play," becomes itself playful. This is the hazing common in initiations, when initiators may conceal the fact that the message, "This is play," is playful, and may make it into a pretense of discipline.

Conversely, play may be the pretense, and under its cover real discipline may be perpetrated. For example, you might disarm an opponent by inviting him or her to join in a surrogate form of conflict—say, an organized game such as a fencing match—but then abrogate the play message by "playing for keeps" with a secretly untipped sword. This sort of cheating does not play with the "play message," however. A fake game destroys, rather than parodies, expectations and conventions; hence the violation of play at the finale of *Hamlet*. Laertes, the son whose father Hamlet has killed, tries to avenge his father's murder by pretending to engage in a fencing match with the prince. Laertes covertly wields an unbated and poisoned sword, but when the foils are accidentally exchanged during a skirmish, he kills not only Hamlet but himself.

In actual life, this kind of fraudulent play produces horror; its effect is not primarily a playful meta-metacommunication about play and pretense. In the drama, however, we can react with both regret and ironic understanding. The event is viewed with the protective lens of fiction, as a play message about play and deception. While someone in the dramatic world does, indeed, get hurt, no wounds are made in our world. *Hamlet*, if not the fencing match, remains intact as play. However, Shakespeare then turns the tables on us in another way, so that the frame of the drama itself is played with. Within the play the spectators to a game of death become witnesses to acts of murder; outside the play we may realize that we are watching a work that is playing with death and that could, like the fencing match which is concealing a duel, be just the *appearance* of a fiction.

The new meta-metamessage does not make the fictive action real, however. No actual murder is committed before us, as it is before the dramatic characters. Rather, the new cognitive level introduces a new frame of reference—in effect, the "roof blows off"—and we experience the exhilaration and sense of transcendence that such reframings and play may induce. The boundaries of fiction open up to include our action of spectating within the class of play. We then see both ourselves watching the play and the play together *sub specie ludis*.

By identifying our irresponsible position outside the play world with the position of witnesses to a disrupted play world within the play, even while distinguishing the two zones ontologically, *Hamlet* maintains its play-ness and yet implies how play becomes consequential. It also suggests that our "real" world has ludic character as well, for we begin to watch our own watching with the same kind of attention and analysis we bring to the drama. If we sense that our world may be framed, we may wonder by whom. Who else than ourselves, we must answer. The meta-metacommunication dissolves any privileged position as more "real" by making us part of the play world, objects of our own play vision. Yet we stand outside the mirror, subjects of our play world. It becomes now a world on which we can no longer gaze idly; we have been given a responsible engagement with our uses of fiction. We can see more specifically how this happens by looking closely at the drama.[5]

LOOKING AT WHAT HAPPENS IN *HAMLET*

The plot of *Hamlet* follows a course of events in the medieval Danish court following the sudden death of its warrior king, Hamlet. Prince Hamlet has returned home from his studies at Wittenburg to witness, within two months of his father's funeral, a wedding between his mother, Queen Gertrude, and his father's younger brother, Claudius. Hamlet watches his uncle assume the kingship and declare legitimate his marriage to the woman he publicly calls his "sometime sister" (1.2.8). In Shakespeare's England, a younger brother's marriage to an elder brother's widow was considered incestuous if the elder brother left a surviving son (Rosenblatt 1978). To claim the acceptability of this marriage, then, was tantamount to declaring Hamlet dead, since his existence should have outlawed the marriage. Hamlet's presence thus

betrays the personally arbitrary quality of the king's rules—
clearly, he uses them to serve his own will. But Claudius's sentences, state acts when pronounced by him as king, openly display
that what should be absolute is really manipulable. He under-
mines the fiction that social conventions are natural law when he
shows that, especially for one who wields the sway of king, all
rules are just rulings. Moreover, as Claudius redirects the conventions of mourning, marriage, and language to dictate new social
proprieties, he shows that such systems are like the rules for
games. Yet like the fiction we watch, his verbal and political feats
do not change brute facts: King Hamlet is dead; Prince Hamlet is
not. Similarly, in our lives, Shakespeare's craft is no more potent.
As convincing as we find their reality on stage, neither Hamlet
nor Claudius lives or dies before our eyes. Claudius's actions, even
if they are only "acts" he performs to disguise reality, *can* transform the way his world reads itself, however. Such craft, whether
in the hands of arrogant rulers like Claudius or in the service of
open fiction like *Hamlet*, can *alter* social reality as it portrays for us
its roles, expectations, interpretations, and judgments of events.

This world of fabrication leads Hamlet to view all appearances as shows and to be troubled when appearances he wishes to
disbelieve are proved true. His discovery that social meaning is
communicated in signs that may be merely acted is perhaps his
most paralyzing insight, for he learns that even his behavior cannot be one with what it signifies. The gap between social expressions—clothing, gesture, visage, language—and what they mean
becomes a hazard to a full interpretation of others and a block to
complete communication of oneself. Hamlet voices this realization
in his initial speech, when we first see him isolated in the court;
he is silent and the only person wearing black. His first statement
to the court defends his mourning but also discloses one cause of
his grief: his awareness that all behavior appears as sheer acting
in a world of social theatricality.

This is the same dramatic realization that anthropologists
face when they recognize that "fieldworkers do not observe subjects behaving; they interpret human actions" (Karp and Kendall
1982:261). For Hamlet, action becomes divorced from meaning
when his mother's hasty marriage cuts short the transitional phase
of mourning; that union which usurped the funeral rites ironically
divorces motive and intention from behavior. Where play questions rules, ritual orders them (Handelman 1977). So the "maimed

rites" (5.1.219) of Denmark revert back to disorder and do not re-reverse reversal (Turner 1969). Hamlet's sure sense of order then becomes corrupted into supposition and suspicion. Such fractures, not only in rites but also in social conventions and expectations, frequently create reflexive moments for the members of society and for those who study them. We examine the artifices by which we accomplish social order whenever appearances become evident as merely shows of social order (Goffman 1975; Babcock 1980a; Bruner 1980; Karp and Kendall 1982; Handelman and Kapferer 1980).

In *Hamlet*, Gertrude evokes such reflections when she urges her son to "cast thy nighted color off" (1.2.68). She argues that Hamlet's apparel "seems" to mean his loss is "particular," as if he is the only son to suffer the death of a father. Hamlet seizes on her word "seems" to draw a metalinguistic and philosophical difference between "seems" and "is"; the distinction becomes one between appearance and reality. Hamlet's commentary on his lonely costume rips open all the seams between expression and meaning:

> Seems, Madam? nay, it is, I know not "seems."
> 'Tis not alone my inky cloak, good mother,
> Nor customary suits of solemn black,
> No, nor the fruitful river in the eye.
> Nor the dejected 'havior of the visage,
> Together with all forms, moods, shapes of griefs,
> That can denote me truly. These indeed seem,
> For they are actions that a man might play,
> But I have that within which passes show,
> These but the trappings and suits of woe.

(1.2.76–86)

Rupturing our confidence in knowledge and questioning how we know become increasingly the method and subject of this play.

Because "trappings" can so easily trap our understanding,[6] Hamlet's mourning generalizes into grief for all the values lost between what we note and what it can "denote . . . truly." As Hamlet considers the same problem anthropologists do—how to determine "that within which passes show"—his melancholy leaves him unable to act. If acts become nothing more than "actions that a man might play," the means to enact his own identity have become merely ludic.

Hamlet's dubiety about meaning sharpens into terror when a

ghost appears, claiming to be his father, and tells him a ghastly tale of having been murdered by Claudius. Now Hamlet's suspicions about Claudius are proved true. Yet Hamlet's doubts about what "seems" are also confirmed, for he notes that "one may smile, and smile, and be a villain" (1.5.108). Stricken by such discrepancies between acting and actions, Hamlet uses theatrical metaphors to understand the nature of life as staged. At this point he is burdened with an equally difficult moral charge, one that requires him to take action in accord with a set of conventions he finds as formulaic as an outmoded stage play. The ghost enjoins Hamlet to revenge, to kill the king to avenge his father's assassination. This terrible injunction raises even deeper questions about the authority of the ghost, whose disclosure reveals the falseness of Claudius's reports about King Hamlet's death yet may itself be no more valid. A ghost's ontology and reliability were both problematic in an age that raised doubts about one's perceptions of evil and at the same time warned of the manifold and misleading forms evil might assume. The ghost itself could be a deceptive appearance, no more reliable than a stage illusion; and its authority might not be that of Hamlet's father but as counterfeit as the assumed authority of the usurper, Claudius.

Both ambiguity and contradiction press Hamlet's uncertainty about appearances into a profound epistemological and moral dilemma. His problems in knowing match and lead to his problems in responsibility, where he is caught in another structural contradiction: the ghost extracts from Hamlet a pledge to exact revenge, which sacred law reserves for God alone, at least in Renaissance cosmology. As a result, Hamlet encounters a double bind (Bateson 1972:194–308) created by a supernatural obligation to his father's ghost and a superordinate rule which contradicts that charge. He responds in a way appropriate to his equally double awareness that all acts are just acting and rules are just rulings: by engaging in what he warns his friends is an "antic disposition" (1.5.173).

From the perspective of Bateson's theories of play, this role uses the paradoxical structure of play as communication operating on two logical levels, each of which negates the other. Like the paradox of the Liar, the antic disposition creates endless puzzles about how to assess the truth of what is said within a metamessage that denies itself as well as the member of the class to which it belongs. If I say, truthfully, "Everything I say is a lie," then my statement must be a lie for it belongs to the class of "everything I say"; but if it *is* a lie, then I am telling the truth and lying at the same time. Only if I am telling the truth is the statement a lie. This produces an impossible logical contradiction, but it is the kind of paradox we love to play with.

Similarly, the Fool's statements, because they are wise and true observations about the foolishness of others, can be spoken outright only by a fool. So, too, the truth of the mirror the Fool holds up to us, in which we see ourselves as fools, is always negated on the logical level, for we see that the mirror is held by a fool. The utterances of the Madman, even if they are true and wise, are always logically framed, as are lies and play and foolishness. Logically, if Hamlet is mad, then his statements cannot be taken as sane and thus can be discounted. But if he only acts mad, then the court is uncertain how to take his statements. His indeterminate madness and foolishness play with the paradox frames of play. Socially, Hamlet doubles the problem, making it one of identity. If he is mad, then he is "not Hamlet"; it is a madman who speaks. The Fool and the Madman become "symbolic types" (Grathoff 1970; see also Handelman 1979, 1980; Handelman and Kapferer 1980), which, along with the Clown and the Demon, emerge at fractures in social expectations and order. Person and role become absorbed in a pure symbol, which does not represent another figure but penetrates the immediate cultural construction to make a "direct superimposition on social action . . . and through this medium, social discontinuities are objectified and recontextualized" (Handelman 1979:86–87).

Hamlet uses such a mode to transform both himself and the very context in which he finds himself; under his constructions the court becomes a theater in which deception and uncertainty are exposed. In the licensed position of Madman and Fool, Hamlet can speak the truth and test it with safety; he is not held liable for his acts. At the same time the court can absorb his acts, equally free from punitive response by the allowances accorded the Madman. Just as play operates within a metacommunicative system which communicates that it does not count, actions taken as mad are judged according to superordinate rules which deny the force of ordinary sanctions, interpretations, and reactions (Raz 1975). The fact that there is "such method in't" (2.2.208) makes

Hamlet's antic disposition as dangerous for the court as the crimes of the court are impenetrable for Hamlet. Like play, and like the dilemma of revenge, his indeterminate madness creates a duplex discourse, the structure of the double bind. His acts become just "acts," which implicitly refer to themselves as well as what they seem to refer to. Hamlet's puns, disjointed speech, insults, incoherence, and impertinence speak of the world and of himself speaking. As a result, Hamlet's play and Shakespeare's *Hamlet* refer to their own meanings, thus calling meaning itself into question.

Nardo (1979) has analyzed Hamlet's antic disposition using Bateson's theories of play, but her approach emphasizes how Hamlet uses the ludic stance to mirror back to the court the fact that it faces the same epistemological questions he does. Ludic behavior becomes what Schwartzman (1978) calls "saying play": play which is communication both about itself (as communication) and about the world it transforms in play. From this perspective, we may see more precisely how Hamlet's indeterminate madness plays with what is real. He both says and disclaims responsibility for saying that he is at one with a court that only pretends to be what it seems. Hamlet's questionable identity then allows him to test how identity and social reality are constructed and changed.

Handelman (1979:1980) discusses such ludic behavior as a transparent mask that admits a view of what it seems to hide. Donning the mask suggests a similar masked or illusory quality in the behavior with which it is in dialogue. Since I am playing with you, you must be playing with me. Schwartzman (1978:232–47) also considers playing roles as a way of saying something about the roles and powers of players. She presents playing as a process of negotiations in which players both deny and express their social identities. When Linda (a young informant) organizes her playmates to play house, and makes herself "the mommy," she expresses her powers as a social manager and theirs as her collaborators; in her role as "mommy" she also becomes the "not-Linda" who is within her. Vygotsky (1979) ruminates on the ways playing with reality denies, and thus comments on, the organization of reality. He analyzes the play of two sisters who play that they are sisters. In such play the girls can pretend that they are not sisters, and their behavior thereby communicates the *rules of being sisters*, not that they *are* sisters.

Thus, on the one hand, Hamlet's antic disposition denies his identity and qualifies the meaning of all that he says, while on the other hand it amplifies his identity and discloses the equally ludic quality of the entire court. His "madness" uses ambiguity and paradox to occupy a ludic position from which he can assert, in "saying play," the illusory nature of court behavior as the counterpart to his own masked mode. In this context of political, moral, and cognitive contradiction, Hamlet's use of the liminal institutions (see Turner 1969, 1974) of Fool and Madman addresses the disorder of his world.

When a group of professional players arrives at the court, Hamlet finds in their performances and roles another set of reflections on role playing and a new means by which to test, and reflect, court appearances. The genres of drama, the process of rehearsal, the manipulation of revisions, the study of audience responses—all become additional techniques in Hamlet's use of play as a means for control, discovery, and escape. Not unlike the disrupting ghost, this company of actors arrives in Elsinore, unbidden, from another plane of reality (McDonald 1978). With the other interruptions, and with the maimed rites and mistakes, which will increase, these figures make a liminal opening in the organization of time and space. And on that edge the play of meaning may be placed.

As a court entertainment, Hamlet asks the actors to stage an old play, "The Murder of Gonzago," an Italianate court intrigue of royal murder and queenly remarriage. The performance of this piece for the Danish court creates for them a mirror of their own doings and for us a play-in-a-play with a complex set of metadramatic and metaludic statements. The play depicts events precisely like the ones in the ghost's tale, and so the inner play matches the court world, the ghost's story, and Shakespeare's play, which we are now aware of as a play. To us, it reflects not our crimes but our playing.

At the same time, Hamlet is showing the court its own masks. Characters may not be who they seem. At one point Hamlet identifies the murderer of the Player King as "one Lucianus, nephew to the King" (3.2.250); we may have taken the poisoner to be Claudius, brother of the king poisoned. Seeing the regicide as nephew to the king suggests that he may (also) be taken as a replica of Hamlet, present nephew of the present king. Here Hamlet uses the mirror play not only to investigate the truth of the past, by observing the guilty reactions of his audience, but also to shape a view of the future, by warning his audience about a possible world. Because the image contains such ambiguities in its multiple referentiality, it serves both for retelling and foretelling. The play reinterprets the past and shapes expectations about the future. Thus, it becomes more than a mirror and more than a rehearsal: it is an active means for constituting the future through a process of expectation.

Dubious about the meaning of this mimetic event, the king initiates a new series of deceptions. He has Hamlet summoned to his mother's dressing room for a seemingly private interview. But the intimate conversation becomes a performance, watched by an audience—a spy the king has placed in the room. Throughout the play the meaning of events takes on new perspectives as we see them watched, overheard, and directed. The events become scenes, the actions performances, as nearly all "by indirections find directions out" (2.1.66). The analogies between fiction, conventions in social life, and deception do not identify all social enterprises as isomorphic likenesses. And we note the differences that matter, for *mistakes* about what genre of situation you are in and who is filling what role can be fatal. At one point during his interview, Hamlet angrily threatens his mother, and the old courtier, Polonius, stationed behind a curtain, calls out, "What ho! Help!" (3.4.23) Taking the ambiguous appearance for the king, Hamlet impulsively stabs the shape behind the screen. This mistake is played on in Hamlet's ironic compliment to his unintended victim: "I took you for your better" (3.4.33). All the problems of taking that which is cloaked behind the interventions of signs are here revealed. Can any inquiry penetrate the other side of the curtain?

"I took you for your better" reverberates with ironic meaning at several levels; it becomes a hermeneutic statement about "taking," about differences and identifications between likenesses. As a moral judgment it might indicate that Hamlet had expected better, or more, of Polonius than this trick; that he had taken him to be a better man than he proved himself to be by standing in for the king. As a social statement it refers to rank, not morality; the mistake about social difference rings another irony in this statement about mistaken likenesses. That Polonius is a substitute for the "rightful king" creates an almost farcical version of the tragic usurpation Claudius commits. But at some level Polonius, as the king's surrogate, is not so different—and he has made himself liable by "standing in" for one who himself is a stand-in. So Hamlet has "taken" Polonius in the most fundamental usurpation of all, an usurpation of his life. Hamlet's language emphasizes to what extent he has aimed at a shadow, in aiming at Polonius's "better"—whatever that may be. Hamlet's efforts at a resolution of knowledge have instead hit a man, one whom Hamlet nonetheless takes, even now, in relation to what he is not. Once the rightful king is dead, we are left to measure value by difference and mistake. Such is the process of knowing.

Hamlet's pun on "taking" emphasizes the tragedy of mistakes which has now begun, for this is the turning point in the drama. If the Greek term for *hamartia* is best translated not as "tragic flaw" but more literally as "a mistake," having "especially to do with the identity of the person with whom the action has to do" (Else 1957:378–86), then Hamlet's misfired aim quintessentially embodies such tragic acts. They do not necessarily begin in some moral defect of character but result from active choices and interpretations which, like the aiming of an arrow, can easily miss their mark. A tragedy of knowledge is a tragedy of mistaking, a work which confronts our predicaments of uncertainty and ambiguity.

Earlier Hamlet's puns, as part of his antic disposition, created a comedy of mistaking. As a form of play with speech, puns take mastery over problems of ambiguity by making confusion deliberate (Philips 1975). They also create, by linguistic doublings, an awareness of simultaneity and indeterminacy in our making of sense(s), in several senses of that word. When we pun we both speak, using language, and play with speech, using the rules of speech. The simultaneous doubleness in punning then joins the stasis of interpretation with the movement of actions. Thus, Hamlet's puns exaggerate and discount the potentially dangerous problems of slippage in language as a system and of manipulating meaning in social exchange. By pressing his points in play, his puns allow him, with impunity, to "speak daggers . . . , but use none" (3.3.404). Moreover, many of the puns are themselves reflexive about punning, as they implicitly comment on their own toying with mistaking and control. Yet Hamlet's rash act, however mistaken, is one of murder; he uses a dagger, not speech. Death cannot be reversed by the fictions of play. The redirection of values he attempts in his pun on "taking" and in the ironies of "better" finally display, but cannot rectify, the finalities of death. Here lies the tragic problem of action which the drama confronts.

The irreversibility of death, despite the reversibility that play represents, makes Hamlet the object of a new revenge plot. Laertes, the son of Polonius, now becomes Hamlet's "foil" (5.2.256), as Laertes becomes another revenger of a father's murder. By murdering Polonius, Hamlet also pushes the king into a lethal exchange. Claudius can no longer simply spy on Hamlet; reconnaissance becomes absolute, for Hamlet's intentions are now clear. His sudden act of murder makes him the object, not just the subject, of revenge. The king's indirect pursuits of knowledge become indirect pursuits of murder; Hamlet, too, passes from playing as a means of knowing into an active engagement with death.

Meanwhile, Laertes mistakenly suspects that the king has eliminated his father, and he pursues his own revenge by rushing directly into the king's chambers, threatening to assassinate Claudius. But the wiley monarch quickly deflects Laertes's anger into an action that will substitute covert murder for open revenge: he redirects Laertes's course against Hamlet. Claudius asks Laertes to "be ruled by me," thus subordinating familial action to a state service, replacing the father with the king. Specifically, Claudius proposes that Laertes fight Hamlet in a deceptive fencing match, using court entertainment to disguise a duel. In place of the tipped foil used in fencing, Laertes will insinuate a bare blade. For double assurance Laertes offers to "anoint" his sword with poison. In a condensed mode, the strategies for a false game become the means for perverting life and rule, not for recreation. Once again the king has found a surrogate for his desired aggressions. He intends to use the social institution of play to escape the consequences of his legal act. The creativity of his wrongdoing perverts the structure of not doing in play. Claudius's plots do not play with reversibility but instead work actions which cannot be undone.

The fencing match, like the play we watch, should play with death, but it becomes a hidden duel which literally acts out the figurative fencing throughout the play's action. The game thus en-capsulates the agonistic acts of the court which thus far have been masked as playful interrogations; the match, as a counterfeit game which only seems to be a representation, summarizes all the other counterfeits at court. In the duplicity of lies, the con game mocks and illuminates the double language of play. The paradoxes of play are reversed in the paradoxes of action masquerading as a game.

To assure even more certainly that the fraudulent game will do its work, the conspirators plan that if its moves do not occasion death, then the scoring procedures will. Scoring creates the differ-ence between hits in a fencing match, where the hits are tallied because they "don't really count," and those in a duel, which count in more bloody ways. The king arranges that when the scores are made, social interludes will be added: they will take time out to toast the first two hits made by Hamlet. Into Hamlet's goblet the king will drop a disguised poison, and thus a salute to Hamlet's hits will ironically strike him down. If not by sport then by its celebration, the player-prince will be de-luded, killed by an illusion of playing.

Claudius works with a contestive, outcome-centered game to disguise the act of murder, while Hamlet commits himself to the free spirit of play. Each of these approaches to the ludic mode demonstrates something about their characters and about the ways in which game and play may figure as different world con-structs. The organized play of a game proceeds according to stata-ble rules; by contrast, informal conventions govern the improvisa-tional process of free play. The formal rules of games perform many functions, but ultimately the most essential rules create (1) a contestive structure, with two sides (even if one plays against oneself, or a goal, or some time limit), and (2) a measurable out-come with either a winner and a loser or some other interpretable ending (Avedon 1971). Through scoring, timing, and a series of moves, games model an end-centered world construct which con-trasts sharply with the open-ended flow of play. Claudius hopes that a game with death will legitimize and disguise an act of death; his scheme leads to the resolution of the action in a way that Hamlet's metacommunicative stories, dramas, puns, indeter-minate madness, and other ludic modes of free play could not. Claudius uses the appearance of a game to accomplish *an irreversi-*

ble act; Hamlet uses the freedom of play to explore, without consequence, the *meanings* of action. Ironically, Hamlet's interpretive
mistakes become irreversible actions, and Claudius's attempts to
control life with games confront the uncontrollable aspects of play.

Waiting with Hamlet for the start of the fencing match, his
friend Horatio warns the prince:

HORATIO:	You will lose this wager, my lord.
HAMLET:	I do not think so. Since he went into France I have been in continual practice. I shall win at the odds. But thou wouldst not think how ill all's here about my heart. But it is no matter.
HORATIO:	Nay, good my lord—
HAMLET:	It is foolery, but it is such a kind of gain-giving as would perhaps trouble a woman.
HORATIO:	If your mind dislike anything, obey it. I will forestall their repair hither and say you are not fit.
HAMLET:	Not a whit, we defy augury. There is special provi-dence in the fall of a sparrow. If it be now, 'tis not to come; if it be not come, it will be now; if it be not now, yet it will come. The readiness is all.

(5.2.210–24)

In taking this existential position, Hamlet renounces control of a
universe he declares as beyond human certitude. He rejects a system of augury by which we can *read* events as signs about the
future. In denying a readable universe, however Hamlet does not
predicate a universe without a plot. If a "special providence"
makes the fall of a sparrow no accident, then Providence accounts
for all outcomes. But the operations of Providence cannot be
explained by our discourses or ordered by our interpretive systems. In this view, outcomes simply are. Understanding must rely
only on the facts of outcomes, and choices must not rest on the
illusion that we can ensure endings.

Hamlet's entry into the fencing match now becomes not only
a substitute for revenge but also an engagement with the ludic
quality of the universe. His choice to *play* a game, moreover, becomes identical with his choice to act, no matter what the indeterminacies are, no matter how unpredictable and uncontrollable the
outcomes. Hamlet quietly embraces a universe he treats like a true
game—with an outcome that cannot be plotted. His view of the
game, and of the universe, differs radically from Claudius's, how-

ever. The false ruler uses rules to abuse power rather than accepting play as a means to refashion power. Using games to usurp rules rather than as models of order and disorder (Sutton-Smith 1976), the king's game becomes a con, to defy the open-ended universe Hamlet accepts. Each of their constructs defeat the other, yet both models remain compelling readings of the way the world goes. Shakespeare's drama uses the game to clarify two modes of responding to death and desire.

Once the fencing match begins, Hamlet confounds the script implicit in the king's plot; he defers drinking his wine and instead insists on uninterrupted play, and goes on to make a second hit. Hamlet's mother, warm with pleasure in her son's skill, toasts him with his own glass. Quickly Claudius tries to prevent her from drinking the lethal cordial, but she insists that she will honor Hamlet and swallows the poisoned drink. Helpless, the king watches the show, which he no longer directs. The game he has tried to fix remains, at some unfixable level, a game with its own momentum and an unpredictable outcome. Trapped by his safety as a spectator, the hidden author of death is ironically confined by his role as audience. The game exposes the limits to our controlling either outcomes or meanings. Claudius cannot prevent Gertrude's death without betraying his own treachery. The open-ended process of this false game displays the more open-ended character of authentic games and the analogous unplottability of life.

While life and games are open to subterfuge, cheating and deception may, in turn, be subverted by accidents. Indeed, at this juncture Gertrude's mistake may propel Laertes into one of his own, for he rushes at his opponent, inflicting a wound, and in the unruly scuffle their weapons are exchanged. The order of the false game now gives way to an open duel. When Hamlet discovers that he has wounded Laertes with an untipped sword, the spectators call out, "They bleed on both sides" (5.2.305). The audience to this sport becomes a witness to murder. Hamlet realizes that Laertes was wielding a real, not a tipped, sword, and he also learns that his mother has died, poisoned with a drink intended for him. Calling for the doors to be closed, Hamlet announces, "Treachery! Seek it out" (5.2.312). Once again the search for origins and truth begins. The openings are now closed, but the initial fact and crime are made no clearer. Laertes delivers his version of the story: Hamlet holds the treachery in his own hands; his sword is unbated and envenomed; he has no more than half an hour's life remaining, and Laertes soon will die as well. "The King's to blame" (5.2.321), his pawn concludes. At last Hamlet stabs the source of treachery with the poisoned blade and forces Claudius's own medicine down his throat. "Exchange forgiveness with me, noble Hamlet" (5.2.330), Laertes offers with his last breath. The two revengers thus find release from the code of vengeance in the ethics of forgiveness.

Even while all the plots spring back on their makers' heads, the play folds over on itself. The fiction becomes an event, the actual admission of its own enactment of a story. At the same time the boundaries of the fiction expand to include our event of watching this enactment within the story itself. Following the death of Laertes, the dying prince turns to "You that look pale and tremble at this chance, / That are but mutes and audience to this act" (5.2.335–36). He wishes to give them (and us) his account, but death, "a fell sergeant" (5.2.337), allows him no time. Turning to his friend Horatio, whose name indicates his functions as orator, Hamlet notes the crucial difference between life and death as the ability to rectify the past:

> Horatio, I am dead;
> Thou livest; report me and my cause aright
> To the unsatisfied.
>
> (5.2.340–41)

Horatio seeks his own satisfaction in death, reaching for the poisoned cup, but Hamlet beseeches him:

> O God Horatio, what a wounded name,
> Things standing thus unknown, shall live behind me!
> If thou didst ever hold me in thy heart,
> Absent thee from the felicity awhile,
> And in this harsh world draw thy breath in pain,
> To tell my story.
>
> (5.2.345–49)

Witnesses to death become once again an audience to a performance. As the play imitates it own fictive origin, the audience is made aware that it has become witness to a drama that is an open action, a drama that examines itself as a dramatized telling of Hamlet's story. Although those present, including the audience, have seen the very event, Hamlet cannot trust them to truly know it, for they (we) do not know its cause. His name will be as wounded as he is without the remedy of truth—of motives, of "that within which passes show." Like a ghost, Hamlet bequeaths to his survivors a legacy, but not a call for revenge; he wants the "time out of joint" to be made right in a report. The revenger begs the orator to become his surrogate, a storyteller.

The epistemic problem is at once evident. The report that Horatio has been enjoined to tell has just been dramatized in the play, now clearly the latest version of his account, if ever such a one as Horatio told the story. Drama does not reveal its teller, as does a tale; actors' creations of enacted incidents produce fuller illusions of reality than does the storyteller's narration. Genres are not identical; differences matter. But this drama seems to unfold its connections to tellers and sources. Behind the compelling illusions of this play we *seem* to discover the truth. But all we have really seen are images of such truths, reminders of our quest. *Hamlet* again portrays how we make fictions of authority and origins. Yet, in its open admission of its own fictionality and of our uses of fictions, the play does achieve a paradoxical authority. It is a self-declared image of our searches for origins, sources, parents, truth, motives—and of how we find them in stories and in play.

Even as the plot seems to come into focus when Hamlet calls for it to be told as his story, a motive for the story is revealed: to right the past for "the unsatisfied." Yet surely that unsatisfied audience has persisted, and it includes us. We have learned how uncertainly fictions may fix outcomes or meanings; we have seen how feebly they control the future. If we have learned as well that fictions may shape expectations and constitute reality, then we may see again the blankness between certain knowledge and the origin of action. In fact as soon as Horatio begins his tale,

> . . . let me speak to th' yet unknowing world
> How these things came about. So shall you hear
> Of carnal, bloody, and unnatural acts,
> Of accidental judgments, causal slaughters,
> Of deaths put on by cunning and forced cause,
> And, in this upshot, purposes mistook
> Fall'n on th' inventors heads . . .

(5.2.380–86)

we feel the abstraction and partialities of the telling. Our theatrical experience of the original events of Hamlet now becomes just a story which we imagine has become the drama *Hamlet*. Still, all remains enclosed in the fiction of *Hamlet;* the world remains yet unknowing. The fiction now becomes one which includes us, its audience. Through the retelling and replaying of the past—in the critically different forms of drama, story, pretense, or ritual—we participate in making both history and understanding. We do not recreate *original* events, but we do create a genealogy of audiences by making meaning through re-visions. In *Hamlet* we contemplate ourselves alongside the survivors of Hamlet, united with them in the role of audience and witness to both the world of play and the world as performed.

Our inclusion in the heterocosm of play, however, does not nullify our sense of reality. We see ourselves all the more clearly, although in a ludic light, as we consider the audience in the play to be our counterparts, though not ourselves. A double consciousness separates us from them and thus permits us to contemplate both. Somewhere between the fiction we watch and the fictive world it depicts hangs the shadow of an unknowable past that can be imagined but never retrieved. The cycle of repetition in representations may seem as unending and inevitable as the killing of kings and avenging their deaths. But the cycle of repetition in art admits its differences from its references, acknowledges its ontology as a substitution. Thus, drama makes its recoveries in an art of separation, which accepts, as Hamlet does, the mobility of play, the cancellation of exchange in perfect forgiveness, the possibility of learning through mistaking, and the rectification of understanding in the limits and freedom of play.

CONCLUSION

Hamlet shows us our desires to revoke the finalities of death, to domesticate the wilderness of desire, to captivate the flight of time, and to manage the fate of our social selves. These cravings are shown to be both noble and tragic, for they can be realized only in the confinements of play, games, and dramas, and in the limits of social expression which may do no more than interpret and manipulate our views of reality. These means are powerful; they can determine the course of life and death, but they cannot revoke death. The order they make is the order of discourse. Hamlet recognizes the universe of discourse that play offers, and he finally submits to it rather than trying to plot it. In his submission we find a paradoxical release of freedom, which traces an arc of our aspirations for both reflection and action. Against that spirit stands the equally compelling truth of Claudius, whose transformations seize the channels of social power to serve his individual will. Yet in the last act "he is justly served" (5.2.328). His assertions of control are no more lasting than the systems he destroys. Both figures compose our recurring human history, our dreams and our lives, and both must be comprehended in the texts we tell about ourselves. We are Hamlet and Claudius, or at least we must know both to know ourselves. Each represents a different version of using play and game; the drama shows us how to cherish one and to recognize the other. In the end, the play places us in the position of neither Hamlet nor Claudius; instead, we are their audience, playing our roles by judging them as versions of human possibility. The play presents them and their modes of play for evaluation, not just examination. By giving them to us in a play world where we are free of the consequences of making choices, the drama allows us a playful exercise in the use of both interpretation and judgment as forms of conjecture.

Anthropologists may learn to fulfill their responsibilities to know the limits of knowing in the spirit of Hamlet when they *use* the equally illusory and real aspects of both fictions and social life. The ruptures produced by ethnographic interpretation, by mistakes, rites, mirrors, stories, and plays, can create for us moments of stasis. In these pauses for reflexive knowledge we may learn, as Hamlet finally does, how to overcome the paradoxes and paralysis of such self-knowing. *Hamlet* shows that the licensed learning of play becomes the basis of creative knowledge and action when we use the freedom of reflexivity to undertake consequential and committed interpretations, however mistaken or subject to illusion such attempts at knowing may be.

NOTES

This paper is based on earlier essays presented at the American Folklore Society meeting in 1980 and the Association for the Anthroplogical Study of Play meeting in 1981. Both efforts were supported by a fellowship from the American Council of Learned Societies and partially funded by the National Endowment for the Humanities. I wish to thank Jack Glazier, Edward M. Bruner, Ana Cara Walker, Güneli Gün, Diana Kahn, Anna K. Nardo, and Sandra Zagarell for their help in this work.

1. References are to act, scene, and line. This and all such quotations are from the 1963 Signet edition of *Hamlet*, edited by Edward Hubler and published by the New American Library.

2. This phrase is used by Bruner in his essay in this volume.

3. Various sources of *Hamlet* indicate that Shakespeare amalgamated many literary and oral traditions in his play, including a legend which itself combined many narrative strands and themes from Scandinavian and Celtic myth and lore. The major written source is an early thirteenth-century Danish history written by Saxo Grammaticus, in Latin. Belleforest's sixteenth-century *Histoires Tragiques* revised Saxo's story in French. Basically, the older versions give other accounts of very shadowy events set in seventh-century Jutland, where two brothers vie for power. Horwendil, Amleth's father, is killed by his jealous brother Feng (the spellings, of course, vary as do transcriptions of medieval Scandinavian languages). Feng marries Gerutha, the widow of his brother and victim, and veils his crime with cunning. Amleth feigns dullness and an utter lack of wits to ensure his own safety at court. Employing his own cunning, he devises a way to kill the king and eventually does so, but only after a series of dangerous tests perpetrated on him to reveal his pose as a distracted half-wit. Amleth succeeds to the throne following a tricky means of achieving vengeance for his father's murder. See Bullough (1973), Hansen (1887), Gollancz (1920), Armory (1977).

4. These are phrases from Shakespeare's play *A Midsummer Night's Dream*, which also teaches its audience about their complicity in the creations of art.

5. The summary and analysis that follow leave out some crucial incidents but none that are central to this study. Omissions include all mention of Ophelia, Fortinbras, Rosencrantz and Guildenstern, and Hamlet's shipboard adventures.

6. The term "trap" becomes a central image and symbol in the play. Hamlet calls a drama he presents "The Mousetrap" (3.2.243), for "the play's the thing / Wherein I'll catch the conscience of the King" (2.2.616–17). In the end, nefarious plots in the play become fatal both for their victims and their perpetrators when "purposes mistook [are] / Fall'n on th' inventors' heads" (5.2.385). As one remorseful trapper admits, "Why, as a woodcock to my own spring . . . / I am justly killed with my own treachery" (5.2.306).

REFERENCES

Armory, Frederick. 1977. "The Medieval Hamlet: A Lesson in the Use and Abuse of a Myth," *Deutsche Vierteljahrschrift für Literaturwissenschaft und Gerstesgeschichte* 51:357–97.

Avedon, Elliot M. 1971. "The Structural Element of Games." In: E. M. Avedon and B. Sutton-Smith (eds.), *The Study of Games*, pp. 419–26. New York: John Wiley.

Babcock, Barbara A. (ed.). 1980a. *Signs about Signs: The Semiotics of Self-Reference*. *Semiotica* (special issue) 30(1/2).

———. 1980b. "Reflexivity: Definitions and Discriminations," *Semiotica* 30(1/2):1–14.

Bakhtin, Mikhail. 1981. *The Dialogic Imagination*. trans. Caryl Emerson and Michael Holquist. Austin: University of Texas Press.

Bateson, Gregory. 1972. *Steps to an Ecology of Mind*. New York: Ballantine Books.

———. 1979. "Play and Paradigm." In: Michael Salter (ed.), *Play: Anthropological Perspectives*, pp. 7–16. Proceedings of the Association for the Anthropological Study of Play. West Point, N.Y.: Leisure Press.

Borges, Jorge Luis. 1964. *Other Inquisitions, 1937–52*. trans. Ruth L. C. Sims. Austin: University of Texas Press.

Bruner, Edward M. 1980. "Image and Reality: Toward a Reflexive View of Social Life." *The Crescent* 43(7):7–10.

Bullough, Geoffrey (ed.). 1973. *Narrative and Dramatic Sources of Shakespeare*, vol. 7. London: Routledge and Kegan Paul.

DiSalvo, Marilyn. 1980. "The Myth of Narcissus," *Semiotica* 30(1/2):15–26.

Else, Gerald. 1957. *Aristotle's Poetics: The Argument*. Cambridge, Mass.: Harvard University Press.

Fernandez, James W. 1980. "Reflections on Looking into Mirrors," *Semiotica* 30(1/2):27–40.

Foucault, Michel. 1978. *The History of Sexuality*. trans. Robert Hurley. New York: Random House.

Geertz, Clifford. 1972. "Deep Play: Notes on the Balinese Cockfight." *Daedalus* 101(1):1–37.

———. 1980. "Blurred Genres: The Refiguration of Social Thought," *American Scholar* 49:165–79.

Goffman, Erving. 1975. *Frame Analysis: An Essay on the Organization of Experience*. New York: Harper and Row.

Gollancz, Sir Israel (ed.). 1920. *The Sources of Hamlet, with an Essay on the Legend*. London: H. Milford, Oxford University Press.

Grathoff, Richard H. 1970. *The Structure of Social Inconsistencies*. The Hague: Martinus Nijhoff.

Handelman, Don. 1977. "Play and Ritual: Complementary Frames of Meta-communication." In: A. J. Chapman and H. C. Foot (eds.), *It's A Funny Thing, Humour*, pp. 185–92. Oxford: Pergamon Press.

———. 1979. "Is Naven Ludic? Paradox and the Communication of Identity," *Social Analysis* 1(1):177–91.

———. 1980. "Rethinking *Naven*: Play and Identity." In: Helen Schwartzman (ed.), *Play and Culture*, pp. 58–69. Proceedings of the Association for the thropological Study of Play. West Point, N.Y.: Leisure Press.

Handelman, Don, and Bruce Kapferer. 1980. "Symbolic Types and the Transformation of Ritual Context: Sinhalese Demons and Tewa Clowns," *Semiotica* 30(1/2):41–71.

Hansen, George P. 1887. *The Legend of Hamlet, Prince of Denmark*. Chicago: Charles Kerr.

Herz, Judith. 1977. "Play World and Real World: Dramatic Illusion and the Dream Metaphor," *English Studies in Canada* 3(4):386–400.

Karp, Ivan, and Martha B. Kendall. 1982. "Reflexivity in Fieldwork." In: Paul Secord (ed.), *Explaining Human Behavior: Consciousness, Human Action, and Social Structure*, pp. 249–73. Los Angeles: Sage Publications.

McDonald, David J. 1978. "*Hamlet* and the Mimesis of Absence: A Post-Structuralist Analysis," *Educational Theatre Journal* 30:36–53.

Myerhoff, Barbara, and Deena Metzer. 1980. "The Journal as Activity and Genre: Or Listening to the Silent Laughter of Mozart," *Semiotica* 30(1/2):97–114.

Nardo, Anna K. 1979. "Hamlet, a Man to Double Business Bound." Unpublished ms.

Philips, Susan U. 1975. "Teasing, Punning, and Putting People On." Working Papers in Sociolinguistics, no. 28. Austin, Tex.: Southwest Educational Development Laboratory.

Raz, Joseph. 1975. *Practical Reasons and Norms*. London: Hutchinson.

Rosenblatt, Jason. 1978. "Aspects of the Incest Problem in *Hamlet*," *Shakespeare Quarterly* 29:349–64.

Ruby, Jay. 1980. "Exposing Yourself: Reflexivity, Anthropology, and Film," *Semiotica* 30(1/2):153–79.

Schwartzman, Helen. 1978. *Transformations: The Anthropology of Children's Play.* New York: Plenum Press.

Smith, Barbara Herrnstein. 1978. *On the Margins of Discourse*. Chicago: University of Chicago Press.

Sutton-Smith, Brian. 1976. "Games of Order and Disorder." In: *The Dialetics of Play*, pp. 151–63. Schorndoff, West Germany: Verlag Hoffman.

Turner, Victor. 1969. *The Ritual Process: Structure and Anti-Structure*. Chicago: Aldine.

———. 1974. "Liminal to Liminoid, in Play, Flow, and Ritual," *Rice University Studies* 60(3):53–92.

Vygotsky, Lev S. 1979. "Play and Its Role in the Mental Development of the Child." In: J. Bruner, A. Jolly, and K. Sylva (eds.), *Play: Its Role in Development and Evolution*, pp. 537–54. New York: Basic Books.

10

Symbols, Sylphs, and Siwa: Allegorical Machineries in the Text of Balinese Culture

JAMES A. BOON

Cultures operate in certain respects like texts. This now familiar proposition in symbolic anthropology pertains to institutions and practical life just as much as rituals and performative events. Any culture (even when it's not Bali) can be defined as a system-in-motion of signs and symbols that establish senses of equivalence and contrast in diverse sectors of experience. These senses are neither pat nor static; rather, they are constituted through, not despite, the passage of time.

Let me be more precise about signs and symbols. According to de Saussure (1966), a *sign* is the connection between a signifier and a signified, each a position in an entire set of signifiers and an entire set of signifieds. The total set of signs comprises a language; thus, meaning in language operates by implicit contrast. Every signifier signifies every signified by being *not* the other signifiers that could occupy its position (these form its paradigmatic set at the level of *langue*). Likewise, every signified is the relationship of difference from the other signifieds that could occupy its position. Taking the province of color categories as an example: in a three-category system black means not red or white; and three categories establish discontinuities of color in a different way from four categories, or seven, and so on. Another example is the sound continuum set into oppositional differential positions, such as "do-re-mi-fa-sol-la-ti," or any other conventional "scale." In the extensive elaborations of such differential relations that de Saussure calls language, the system is always changing; yet at any analytically designated "moment," communication is presumed to occur as if the system operated out of time, that is, synchronically.

According to Peirce (1955), a *symbol* is something that replaces something for someone. I would designate the entire set of replaceables the "culture," whose symbols are most readily observed in complex performances staged by diverse social actors. In Bali, obvious examples occur whenever the choreography of dance replaces the thematics of shadow theater, or when narrative replaces ritual, or when any institutional arrangement replaces another. But such special events are actually intensifications of general cultural processes. And in Peirce's terms, it is less a matter of replacing than of two things being conventionally regarded as replaceable for each other: word for idea; *hochsprache* for low, narrative for event, melody for mood, one language for another.

The approaches to signs and symbols consolidated by de Saussure and Peirce, respectively, have greatly enhanced our sense of complexity, specificity, and systematics in the comparative study of cultural meaning. I consider these two views of signs (as contrastives) and of symbols (as replaceables) to be compatible. Yet the two views—one stressing the differential remove of systematic meaning, the other stressing its performative richness—must certainly be distinguished. Here, I simply wish to define culture in general and Balinese culture in particular as the shifting system of signs and symbols that articulate equivalence and contrast across different provinces of social life: language, literature, kinship, ritual, mythology, economy, polity, art . . . at whatever level and whether present, future, or past. Indeed, signs and symbols are the means of constituting such provinces themselves, as well as any sense of present-future-past or other alternatives: eternal, cyclic, cycles within cycles, contrasting rates of time.

WORK/TEXT, MACHINERY/CULTURE

To approach Balinese culture as a text is neither to prettify nor to stabilize it—quite the contrary. As many recent theorists of cultures and texts—including anthropologists, critics, philosophers, and historians—have insisted, a text is in a state of continual production; it is not a fixed re-production of something outside itself that it merely refers to (such as life, event, context). Moreover, a text (i.e., a culture) is always interpreted, never simply experienced, both by those "living" it and by observers "reading" it. To take just one example of a serious reexamination of the nature of the text, consider the arguments of Barthes (1977:156–59), who opposed the text (*le texte*) to the work (*l'oeuvre*):

The difference is this: the work is a fragment of substance, occupying a part of the space of books (in a library for example), the Text is a methodological field....

... the Text tries to place itself very exactly *behind* the limit of the *doxa....* Taking the word literally, it may be said that the Text is always *paradoxical.*

... the work—in the best of cases—is *moderately* symbolic (its symbolic runs out, comes to a halt); the Text is *radically* symbolic: *a work conceived, perceived and received in its integrally symbolic nature is a text.* Thus is the Text restored to language; like language, it is structured but off-centered, without closure.... The Text is plural. Which is not simply to say that it has several meanings, but that it accomplishes the very plural of meaning: an *irreducible* (and not merely an acceptable plural).

A "work" is characteristically construed as a "fragment of substance"; it is typically explained by situating it in a process of filiation. Its sources and influences are traced and its author is acknowledged as proprietor of his or her own work. Barthes radically opposed to this exercise the interpretive reading of a text, "itself being the text-between of another text" (1977:160). The text reveals a "paradoxical idea of structure: a system with neither close nor center" (1977:159). Or, to couch the matter in an interrupted aphorism: A text's unity lies not in its origin (traced along a filiation) but in its destination. This view shifts the interpretive onus and opportunity to a work's language, or its readership, or the cumulative history of its readings, rather than leaving credit or blame with its presumable author. (One immediately wonders what might be the analogous shift when cultures are treated as texts.)

I cite Barthes here to accentuate paradox, irreducible plurality, decentering, text-betweenness, systems without closure, radical symbolics, and related properties. Many scholars in symbolic interpretations, semiotics and semiology, and hermeneutics—Burke, Detienne, Eco, Genette, Geertz, Lévi-Strauss, Ricoeur, V. Turner, to name several at random—have stressed similar issues although in very different ways. Here I wish to sidle a concept of culture alongside Barthes's criteria of textuality to facilitate a review of symbolic dimensions of Balinese society and to hazard some suggestions concerning its aspect as text. These textlike properties do not pertain solely to the wordy side of Bali—to the shaped, selected speaking and writing continually emitted (often with music) as ingredients of ritual and everyday life. Components of Balinese culture that many observers would wish to prove are text-external—its institutions, social arrangements, political strategies, infringed taboos, and actuated ideals—are as irreducibly plural, decentered, paradoxical, and *therefore* regulated (systems without closure), as are its mantras, conversations, grammatical (hierarchical) speech, or conventionalized writing (which all writing is). There is more to the text of Balinese culture than the culture's texts. And the best evidence of Balinese culture-as-text is not necessarily its most conspicuous symbolic expressions.

Balinese culture contains things that are often taken for the culture itself; or they are taken for the religion, or the particularly symbolic sphere (although still often construed as only moderately symbolic); or they are proclaimed as the center of myth and ritual, or the domain of the quintessentially Balinese. Readable scholars like Covarrubias (1937) have tended to designate the domain as Balinese "belief," or more vaguely as what "Balinese say"; things like: "The Balinese say that a house, like a human being, has a head—the family shrine; arms—the sleeping-quarters and the social parlour; a navel—the courtyard; sexual organs—the gate; legs and feet—the kitchen and the granary; the anus—the pit in the backyard where the refuse is disposed of" (1937:88). Clearly, many Balinese do say (and write) things like this, as do other Indonesian peoples who like to compare domiciles to crocodiles, ships, selves, macrocosms, and other bodies. And even where sayings (or writings) like this are lacking, certain kinds of scholars will themselves find things like this to say. Again, I cite Covarrubias (whose work has influenced so many subsequent studies on Bali, my own included—it can't be helped): "Like a continual undersea ballet, the pulse of life in Bali moves with a measured rhythm reminiscent of the sway of marine plants and the flowing motion of octopus and jellyfish under the sweep of a submarine current. There is a similar correlation of the elegant and decorative people with the clear-cut extravagant vegetation; of their simple and sensitive temperament with the fertile land" (1937:11).

When simile-makers make similes from the makings of simile-makers, it all starts to sound suspiciously figurative. Another variety of scholar tries to avoid compounding similes; its representatives designate things such as Covarrubias says the Balinese "say" as religion, particularly if such things are inscribed in writings employed by Balinese high-caste priests (*pendanda*) or in manuscripts codifying rituals of other priests. A preeminent example is C. Hooykaas, longtime doyen of Balinese philology, who concentrated on this seemingly patently symbolic domain in his vast commentaries on traditional Balinese manuscripts. Although such works were neither standardized by monastics nor thoroughly centralized by a dominant court, Hooykaas sought something like a regimented canon and set liturgies behind the products and activities of scribes. In a summary study of *Religion in Bali* (1973), he forthrightly deemed the domain as he perceived it.

I take nothing away from the domains that Covarrubias called Balinese belief or "saying" or that Hooykaas ultimately called religion; but I do insist that these domains—if they are domains—are neither the essential nor even a privileged arena of Balinese signs and symbols. Compare each domain or expression thereof to a work, not the text. Isolated as fragments of substance, such bits of allegory remain largely unread. To mistake such images or their respective domains for what makes Balinese culture symbolic would avoid the fullest implications of construing a culture—all of it: ethereal and everyday, subsistence and surplus, *humilitas* and *sublimitas*, written and oral, classificatory and instrumental, traditional cum contemporary, conceptualized and performed, high caste and low—as text, as components of a decentered, dialectical methodological field. I shall accordingly designate fragments of such domains as neither belief, nor religion, nor other ultimate-sounding spheres; rather, I shall borrow a less sublime term from Pope (1960 [1712]:xi): "The *Machinery*, Madam, is a term invented by the Criticks to signify that Part which the Deities, Angels, or Daemons, are made to act in a Poem: For the ancient Poets are in one Respect like many modern Ladies: Let an Action be never so trivial in itself, they always make it appear of the utmost Importance. These Machines I determin'd to raise on a very new and odd Foundation, the *Rosicrucian* Doctrine of Spirits."

The Augustan Pope thus explained how he attached an apparatus of Gnomes, Sylphs, Nymphs, and Salamanders from Earth, Air, Water, and Fire to the superficially inconsequential event of the "rape" of Arabella Fermor's lock of hair by Lord

Petre. The Machinery is the intricate set of simile and metaphor woven through any semantic fabric (like this one). It is most conspicuously a level of personification, deification, or "demonization" situated (allegory-like) within, over, or under the action itself. The Machinery projects into mirrored realms, both elevated and degenerate, the here and now. Pope lampooned the kind of Machinery that prevailed in masques, dramas, and poetic conventions of an earlier day. For every trivial act and sentiment he devised a puffed-up concomitant in his mocking throwback to humoral theory.

> The *Peer* now spreads the glittering *Forfex* wide,
> T'inclose the Lock; now joins it, to divide.
> Ev'n then, before the fatal Engine clos'd,
> A wretched *Sylph* too fondly interpos'd;
> Fate urged the Sheers, and cut the *Sylph* in twain,
> (But Airy Substance soon unites again)
> The meeting Points the sacred Hair dissever
> From the fair Head, for ever and ever!
> Then flashed the living Lightenings from her Eyes,
> And Screams of Horror rend th' affrighted Skies.....
>
> (Canto III, 2.147–56)

> For, that sad moment, when the *Sylphs* withdrew,
> And Ariel weeping from *Belinda* flew,
> *Umbriel*, a dusky, melancholy Sprite,
> As even sully'd the fair Face of Light,
> Down to the Central Earth, his Proper Scene,
> Repair'd to search the gloomy Cave of *Spleen*.
>
> (Canto IV, 2.11–16)

Now, I would be the last to subscribe to Pope's mockery—the anthropologist in me rejects all aloof, moralistic, belletristic disparagements of such conventions. Nevertheless, we can employ the exaggerated sense of Machinery in the parodic *Rape of the Lock* to emphasize these devices and conceits. And we might thereby avoid the opposite extreme of isolating any allegorical Machinery as the meaning of meanings, the essence of "being," or the symbolic system par excellence, thus mistaking "work" for "text." If, then, Balinese culture is our text (analogous to Pope's poem), what might be said of its Machinery?

The Machinery, Madam (and Sir), is abundant. Bali's undersea ballet virtually bubbles over with Machinery, even without the help of Covarrubiasian commentary. Like Majapahit Java, ancient Polynesia, traditional India, and other highly ritualized, hierarchical cultures, Bali's deities, angels, and demons bedazzle us. Every marriage is a little Siwa-Parvati; at burial, cremation, and recremation every corpse is divine king for a day. Each well-formed houseyard echoes principles of palace cosmography; each sector of activity—from wet-rice irrigation to human birth-through-burial; from local ritual space to islandwide politics—revolves around bespirited temple ceremonies. These, in turn, coordinate with Indic mythology, permutational and lunar calendrical systems, ancestor worship, exorcism, and esoteric principles of the sacred-dangerous qualities of ironsmith groups and other ritually charged occupations. And they coordinate as well with dramatic forms realized as dance, shadow-puppet theater, visual icons, and sundry genres of manuscript, some embodying in their writing or reciting socioliturgical forms in their own right, some regulating the proper manner of other such embodiments. A particular episode of myth or epic, courtly legend, or folk narrative can thus materialize as choreography, speech, script, drama, or icon, often coordinated as well with the percussion, string, and song of gamelan orchestral cycles. But the episodes also materialize *as social forms:* ascendant ancestor groups, auspicious marriages, courtly intrigue.

Like a thousand "Popish" parodies, Balinese institutions, rituals, dramatic arts, and scribal traditions allude to each other in a perpetual reflexivity, a process that Geertz (1973:chap. 15) has aptly deemed metacommentary. Everywhere in Balinese ideals and practice we must look beyond any allegorical Machinery to the dialectical field (the text) from which it emerges. I shall demonstrate this point in the province of spatial codes and symbols, after some illustrative remarks on status.

Studies of Balinese society long retained unexamined assumptions that its indices of rank should add up to a fixed stratificational scheme (cf. Boon 1977:pt. 1). Nineteenth-century military men and missionaries, and twentieth-century colonial administrators, construed Balinese hierarchy as work, not text. Their mistake was to overemphasize one or another of the status Machineries littering Balinese life, including: (1) Indic *warna* categories: Brahmana, Satria, Wesia, Sudra. (2) Historical legends tying noble houses to heroic ancestors and many commoner houses to distinguished origin-points as well. (3) Titles that convey the corporate status of partly endogamous groups (some members typically make auspicious marriages with first or second patriparallel cousin). A group holds rights to special administrative and ritual tasks, either refined or polluting, in the well-ordered sphere of courtly influence. (4) Hosts of sumptuary laws regulating appropriate temple heights and associated ritual regalia, often as Polynesian-looking as Indic. Traditionally, such regulations might be imposed locally by residential hamlet or irrigation society, by court officials, or by priests performing ritual duties for their clients.

Complex sanctions supporting sumptuary codes continue to operate throughout Balinese society, particularly in competitive factions of temple memberships. An example demonstrates the system's complexities: *Pesaji* is the name of a group now residing in western Bali; their title (3) is *I Gusti*, although some neighbors refuse to so honor them. They lack a prestigious court task, but they have a story (2) tracing their predecessors to a northern Balinese district where they belonged to the Wesia *warna* (1). Rights to attend specific temples sporting twice-born components in architecture and ceremony (4) would confirm these claims in their area of origin.

Everything in Bali is tinged with rank: male/female, elder/younger, wife receivers/wife providers, and so on. Yet Bali's plentiful Machineries of status symbols do not simply stack up; nor should we presume that they ever did. Rather, they seem made for contradiction and variable constructions to satisfy different parties, each interpreting to its own advantage. What rivals share is a set of hierarchical principles that form the ground rules for the ongoing cultural argument. As Geertz and Geertz (1975) have shown for Bali, contrary to conventional functionalist assumptions, such multiple indices are not "normally" congruent either in action or in ideal. Elsewhere I have documented status indices that operate like mythic contradictions, poetic oxymoron, dramatic tension, social dialectics, or religious paradox (Boon 1977, 1982a, 1982b, 1982c). By any such standard a simple logic of mutual reinforcement cannot obtain. Balinese *warna* schemes and twice-born (*triwangsa*) values, for example, radically distinguish ritual purity from political power and declare them mutually irreducible; in this respect Bali recalls Dumont's (1980) view of Indic hierarchy. In every activity characterized by Brahmana/ Satria-Wesia distinctions, the social category charged with nurturing elevated purity (Brahmana) stands above the category charged with promoting political prowess. (Whether this latter is designated Satria or Wesia, or by the title *Dewa* or *Gusti*, depends on the kingdom and its legendary histories of origin from other kingdoms.) The entire system of title-caste produces not a faulty scheme of would-be correlation but an irreducible logic (aesthetic?) of contradiction. Most generally: "Titles help establish the cultural problem of pragmatically earned versus divinely endowed status [a traditional topic in Balinese legend and cosmology]. If the titles simply offered a redundant index of political power, they would ring hollow.... Balinese titles, like Hindu *varna* categories, perpetuate a contradiction that would not be there unless they were" (Boon 1977:184).

Precolonial Balinese rank was probably never as rigid and permanent as Dutch officials made it appear. Nevertheless, certain Machineries, in particular the *warna* scheme complemented by principles of hypergamy, portray social strata as fixed. And the culture provides the parties espousing this view, both natives and outsiders, with materials to argue their case. My point is not merely that Balinese culture changes too, but that specific properties of its symbolic conventions likely characterize other so-called traditional civilizations as well. However dynamic, expansive, and decentered the culture, when read from an artificially centralized "top" down, it will appear inflexible. Finally, I insist that no projection of social strata in Bali is a simple distortion of something external, such as prestige, wealth, power, or ambition. Rather, the assortment of Machineries guarantees that status never becomes a singular quality; Balinese hierarchy has remained in this respect largely "unreformed." Neither prestige nor power can simply re-present each other. The Machinery produces paradox, systematically.

THE DESITUATION OF SIWA

Since the mid-nineteenth century, scholars have documented Bali's religious organization of space, which interrelates directional qualities, geomantic and tellurian codes, the choreography of ritual processions, and both horizontal and vertical cosmo-graphic axes. Space in Bali coordinates with divinity, particularly in a famous set of transformations: (1) a self-inclusive panoply of distinctions as "center" (Siwa); (2) two around a center (tripartite Brahma/Wisnu/Siwa; (3) four around a center (Iswara/Brahma/ Mahadewa/Wisnu/Siwa); (4) eight around a center (Iswara/Rud-ra/Brahma/Maheshwara/Mahadewa/Sangkara/Wisnu/Sambu/ Siwa). Now "center" is in effect a spatial way to pose the Siwa factor in such schemes. It places Siwa at the logical-middle of the triad, or at the conjunction of cardinal East, South, West, and North; or at the heart of the lotus-like rose of the winds (East, Southeast, South, . . .). But other registers reveal that Siwa is not precisely "center": rather, he is all-at-once, or what might more appropriately be called generic. Thus, the color equivalents for the cardinal scheme (fivefold) and the lotus scheme (ninefold) make Siwa polychrome: all distinctions at once (but not blended). On the other hand, as part of the Brahma/Wisnu/Siwa triad, echoing the totality of the sacred *a/u/m* syllable, Siwa becomes white versus Brahma-red and Wisnu-black. This shift in color un-derscores the fact that Siwa recurs in every elaboration of the dif-ferential scheme and that the difference between tripartite Siwa (versus Brahma/Wisnu) and four-around-the-center Siwa (versus Iswara/Brahma/Mahadewa/Wisnu) is *like the difference* between white (versus black/red) and polychrome (versus white/red/yel-low/black).

Swellengrebel (1960:46) has argued that in the tripartite scheme Siwa is not precisely a center, in the spatial sense: "In this triad, then, the third element is less the linking, intermediary member than it is the higher, synthesizing unity of which the other two are individual aspects." I would go further: Siwa is less syn-thesizer of unity than generic opposition. Siwa conveys the rela-tional creative/destructive properties of the polarized schemes and generates the "shifts" across varying degrees of differentiation. While Siwa implies all the distinctions, he can only be manifest in a set of distinctions, each set straining toward another set—an odd "center" that, as such, can only vanish; an odd "unity" that ultimately can only be absent. This view, I should add, is both logically and epistemologically distinct from conventional philological summaries of these systems. For example, "Siwa is the all-encompassing unity. Brahma, Wisnu and Iswara are indi-vidual aspects of his creative power" (Ramseyer 1977:108).

Such "spatialized" Machineries extend beyond divinities and colors to metals, directions, demons, descent lines, attributes (thunderbolt, snake snare, discus, lotus, etc.), musical tones, days of the cyclic weeks, numbers, and so on. Western scholars, and more recently Indonesian scholars concerned with rationalized Balinese religion, have often construed the Machineries as means to reduce one component to another: Brahma is red is *paing* is nine is seaward is copper.... But consider the entire system of distinctions and its logic of transformation: all-difference-in-one; threefold, to fivefold, to ninefold, operated by Siwa's generic capacity (plus the underworld and human-world analogies of every divine lotus). Viewed as totalizers, none of the Machineries is redundant, yet each throws the other off a bit, and the whole set cannot precisely collapse into a united synthesis. At the risk of oversimplification, consider the following example: there cannot be a center (even a vanishing point!) of colors, any more than there can be a polychrome of space. Or consider color alone at the level of tripartite distinctions: white is the ultimate negative (not-red, not-black); when transformed into five, white becomes one among the other negatives (not red, black, or yellow), allowing polychrome to become the ultimate negative. Color, then, works in an inverse fashion to deity, where Siwa remains the ultimate level in both the tripartite and four-around-the-center schemes. Thus, the difference between color and deity can be represented as the following shift: it takes two colors (white and polychrome) to fill the role of one deity (Siwa) in the transformation between tripartite and four-around-the-center schemes. Siwa remains the "center" because Iswara replaces him in the cardinal deities. White shifts down to the cardinal colors to be replaced by polychrome at the center. The Machineries establish not redundancy but interrelated irreducibles.

My point, familiar to students of anthropological structuralism and symbolic interpretation, is that the multiple Machineries organize categories relationally and not substantively, or in Burke's (1970:24n) terms, their symbols are polar, not positive. Consider again the Brahma/Wisnu/Siwa tripartition. While Siwa can be put at the center—Brahma/Siwa/Wisnu—that does not make Siwa the substantive middle, or the compromised, consolidated sum and unity. Rather, the middle term is neither the first nor the third, just as the first is neither the third nor the second, and the third is neither the second nor the first. If I am correct, rather than privileging the middle as a substantive in-between, Balinese Machineries pose first, second, and third each as an in-between of the other two. I have developed this point for the related tripartite distinction of demonic/human/divine (or in cosmographic terms, underworld/earth/heaven). The human world is not a blend of heaven and hell or some Manichaean composite; rather, each category is the mutual opposition of the other two. This fact is pronounced in the province of *kama/artha/dharma* values that distinguish and interrelate demonic passion, political prowess, and ancestral duty (Boon 1983:chap. 6).

Such relational properties pervade spatial Machineries as well. Just as locality in Bali traditionally was not perceived as territorial, so space itself is not perceived substantively. Yet scholars tend to slip into substantivist, even "territorial," views of space, *even* while appreciating polar codes. An example is Tan's (1960) stimulating review of the cosmological schemes behind Balinese domestic architecture—priestly, noble, and commoner. Tan plots Heavenly/Worldly/Demonic components along with the ninefold plan, laid out as three-by-three squares, which yields three rows across by three rows down *and* eight squares around a center. Moreover, any division is itself so divisible, in an infinite regression of ninefolds.

Although Tan does not make the point, we can see that the architectural ground plan cannot precisely coincide with either deity or color. The idealized nine squares might appear as actual, walled-off courts in fully elaborated palaces (*puri*), or remain merely implied by the placement of shrines and facilities related to the nine components of domestic life, including ancestor temple, conjugal (and sometimes unmarried daughters') beds, passage rite site, guest quarters, kitchen and granary, and so on (in contrast to uncoordinated components such as ingestion and bachelor sleeping). Regardless, the scheme intrinsically codes both three threes and eight-around-a-center. Polychrome cannot, in and of itself, doubly totalize in this way, but only by its conventional association with the ninefold scheme.

I would emphasize as well the shifting complexity of Siwa: cosmographically located as the middle square (or its vanishing center), and ritually located as the northeast temple square, Siwa as generic deity actually implies the whole scheme, both ninefold lotus and tripartite cosmography, whether horizontally or vertically. That left/right and up/down is ultimately tripartite (squared into threes) is true of male/female as well. This point is paramount in tying cosmography to social structure. We can glimpse this fact from Tan's (1960:449) comment on the *kamulan* shrine (here Siwa appears as Iswara, i.e., in his "East" manifestation): "The *sanggah kamulan* is divided into three compartments, each with a little door, dedicated to the deified ancestors, who are sometimes identified with the *trimurti*, the trinity Brahma-Ishvara-Vishnu. Brahma is associated with the male ancestors, Vishnu with the female. This is the shrine a man builds himself when he marries." Ishvara is not a middle between male/female but a spatial embodiment (in the material of the *kamulan*) of male/female distinction activated as Brahma on the one side, Wisnu on the other.

Further on, Tan (1960:457) continues a proclivity of many predecessors ultimately to substantivize space, particularly juxtaposed places: "The first attempt at a description of a typical *puri* was made by Moojen, amended by Van Romondt, and further revised for our present use. The ground plan is divided into nine courts, in this case not imaginary, but substantiated by high solid walls. We recognize again the well-known triadic division into sacred, intermediate and profane parts." This kind of sacred/intermediate/profane gloss is a Durkheimian formulation that was converted to more consistently polar terms by Mauss, other members of *L'Année Sociologique*, and their successors. Such a gloss makes the central term a blend rather than a mutual distinction among three. For the case in point, the central row might be spatially intermediate, but cosmologically it cannot be merely intermediate because it is the generic heart of the ninefold lotus (and in royal houses the site of the king's *ukiran* pavilion). Moreover, the lower row is more than profane: it is categorically demonic, in polar distinction to both ancestral duty (upper row) and political prowess (middle row). *Even in space the center is tripartite-polar rather than intermediate.* Propinquity or juxtaposition implies less intermediacy than another level of contrast (a point I could argue for temple layouts as well). In cosmological terms, everything stretches across *three extremes*—Divine/Worldly/Demonic—not along a gradual continuum running from ordinary-profane, through some compromised sector, to ultimately charged-sacred.

Finally, consider the famous three-temple clusters that represent the full elaboration of Balinese organizational ideals: origin temple (*pura puseh*), death temple *(pura dalem)*, and *pura bale agung*, often glossed awkwardly as "meeting house temple." The last is particularly hard for "rationalized" observers to grasp, because we think of political and civic sectors as secular rather than as another extreme, a liturgy, so to speak, in its own right. Just as Balinese cosmography coordinates extremes of ancestral/demonic/ political prowess, so does Balinese locality coordinate origin, death, and civic-subsistence "liturgies."

SPATIALITY IN MOTION

What may appear as arcane quibbling over symbolic meanings in fact pertains to fundamental issues in Balinese (and Indonesian) organization of space and topography. My view, again, is that no Machinery redundantly re-presents another; nor do they all simply index something external. Just as status Machineries are not distortions of a uniform prestige, neither are spatial Machineries a contorted nature, nor a hit-and-miss geography, nor a quaint landscape geometry. Rather, they establish the interrelated irreducibility of directions, ritual landscape, and associated dimensions. Like many Indonesian peoples, Balinese distinguish sunrise-orientation/sunset-orientation (*kangin/kauh*) and also mountainward/seaward (*kaja/kelod*). Thus far no cardinal points are necessarily implied, however much we automatically tend to insinuate them. Let us isolate this scheme to ponder what it implies *as a symbol system.*

Through the year the *kangin/kauh* dimension will slowly shift with respect to geography. Similarly, the *kaja/kelod* shifts (directionwise) perpetually as one moves through space (notoriously, in North Bali seaward is north; in South Bali seaward is south; etc.). Partial pan-Bali "standardization" of the *kaja/kelod* dimension can be achieved east to west only by switching mountains (as in fact kingdoms do). The scheme produces a uniform, unfluctuating radial *standard* only when perceived from the center, as if Bali were a perfect circle with its sacred mountain as its central vanishing point, like a rose of the winds. But even then *kangin/kauh* would fluctuate.

These aspects of Balinese Machineries prove troublesome to commentators who consider them cardinal directions manqué—although patent cardinal points figure explicitly as Machineries in their own right (and, as usual, cosmological properties accrue: northeast is sacred, like mountain-ward; southwest is demonic, like seaward; etc.). Scholars seeking "profound" symbolic redundancy inevitably adopt a centralized vantage of Balinese space, with the sacred mountain lying northeast. It is true that the Machineries can reinforce one another if posed from a bird's-eye pan-Bali vantage that sights (and sites) a capital (Bedulu, then Gelgel) along a southwest line from sacred *Gunung Agung*. But the Machineries do more than confirm a maharaja (*Dewa Agung*) and his court in proper relation to northeast (*Gunung Agung*) as ultimate center and coordination of Balinese society. They simultaneously guarantee that if we keep the same sense of "center," from any other vantage the Machineries are unhinged; yet by shifting the sense of "center," they can be realigned.

It would seem that the fuller social and cultural significance of the Machineries is that no centralized synthesis emerges with any stability. The symbolic values of *kaja/kelod, kangin/kauh,* topography, and cardinal attributes (northeast sacred, southwest demonic, etc.) are (1) that exceptionally everything can mesh, and (2) that inherently everything does not. Recalling Barthes, the symbolic of such Machineries does not run out at topography, or geography, or rational cardinality (which would make them mere works). Rather, they establish, arguably, topography, geography, and cardinality as sets of convertibles. Moreover, they do so in a continual dialectic between relative center-mountain/periphery-sea, every point on a periphery in turn a conceivable "center." Call such schemes not mere re-presentational "works" but the constellations of the text of what I have elsewhere characterized in ethnographic detail as Bali's "ever receding peripheries of Hinduized time and space" (Boon 1977:158).

To construe culture as text is by no means to eschew apparently pragmatic components of Machineries (although it is to deny isolubility of any patent pragmatics). Pragmatic Machineries have all the symbolic importance of any other Machinery. Yet, to the discomfort of both functionalist and Marxist approaches (at least in the more utilitarian moments of both), such Machineries cannot be reduced to materialist explanations. This fact is clear from Geertz's (1980) recent interpretation of the ritual, political, judicial, commercial, and irrigation functions across competitive spheres of influence in the traditional Balinese state (*negara*). Over time, influential court centers gravitated (almost literally!) toward an optimal point between sea drainage and mountain springs. The position apparently facilitated arbitration of conflicts along an entire irrigation sector (a macro-*subak*), all of whose paddies, thanks to gravity and a complex traditional irrigation technology, received water from the same source, making lower-lying levels vulnerable to interference with the water supply by higher levels.

Now the pragmatics of location here coincide with other spatial Machineries; for example, the capital court between upper (mountainward) and lower (seaward) is in another register highest (as center vs. periphery). But culturally, pragmatics are never pure and simple. Geertz demonstrates how Balinese rituals of state, intertwined in spatial Machineries, established a politics that was noncentralized while idealizing a center, that was nonterritorial while obsessed with the attributes of every locality, and that operated more through the competitive management of loyalties than any superimposed despotism—although this fact hardly makes Balinese rank or power a pretty, victimless picture. I would add that the many Machineries allow any particular development—say, the shift of a court or an ancestor group to a more advantageous location—to be nestled in sustained relations with past locations and its temple groups. Thus, the plethora of Machineries and their fundamentally disputatious significance helps to explain Balinese cultural dynamics cum traditionalism at every level, including local mobility, irrigation expansion, and ancestor worship (Boon 1977:107–15; see also chap. 4 and pt. II).

Finally, to demonstrate the importance of these points for understanding everyday life and domestic routines in Bali, let me at once salute and question a recent account of Balinese ritual space. Hobart (1978:5,6) wisely rejects any static dualistic scheme in tracing "interesting connections between ritual purity and the flow of water." He occasionally allows for coordinated contrasts in the significance of symbolic schemes: "Appropriately, the burial site for the three high castes, *triwangsa*, lies slightly to the north-east of the commoners' graveyard, to the south of which a small group of Chinese tombs faces open ricefields. (Apparently, this satisfies both Balinese ritual and Chinese geomantic requirements simultaneously!)" (1978:10). (This kind of simultaneous satisfaction is more frequent in Bali, even between native social segments, than Hobart's exclamation point would suggest [cf. Boon

1977:134–40, 220; see also chap. 4].) Hobart reviews and expands evidence of an east/west axis (and *kangin/kauh*) tied to "the socially recognized stages of human life," with vibrant diagrams of the "movement between sites in rites of passage" and the consequent nine-vector choreography of ritual space linking death temple to houseyard:

The proper place for birth, the rebirth of an ancestral spirit, and its attendant ceremony of *pekumel* is in the *meten*, even if this is not always practicable. As the descent group deities are worshipped from the *sanggah*, this implies a movement of the soul downwards and to the west, as divine essence is incarnated in humble and perishable human form. . . . The site for the subsequent rituals—*lepas aon*, held on the fall of the umbilical cord; *ngerorasin*, the twelfth-day naming ceremony; and *kambuhan* on the forty-second day, which terminates the mother's impurity—is moved due south and down again, as the pollution of birth sets in. From the 105th day onwards, the location is shifted yet again to the *bale dangin*.This coincides with the child's release from *kumel*. Only at this stage may a village priest, *pemangku*, officiate, for previous ritual is the duty of the less pure birth-specialist, *balian manakan*. The remaining ceremonies in life occur here, to ensure individual welfare and the reproduction of the group, through birthdays, *oton*, tooth-filing, *mesangih* and marriage, *mesakapan*. The more subtle distinctions of status are expressed in the secular [*sic*] use of living space mentioned. Death should also take place in the *bale dangin*. (1978:16)

Hobart's valuable account shows how spatial Machineries imply ordered movement and sequence as well as idealized ground plans. Yet he stops short of the *text*, preferring to pose Balinese conceptions of space as works whose symbolic runs out. He acknowledges that *kaja/kelod* is radial and bears "little relation to the compass points" (1978:7); nevertheless, he calls the island's extremities (e.g., due north where *kaja* is south) problems that must be "suppressed" for the system to work. For additional spatial axes Hobart (1978:12) also reports "difficulties in interpreting movement and relative position," as if such "difficulties" were not the point of schemes that pose shifting position relationally and multiply. When plotting upstream/downstream, inflow/outflow, purity/pollution, male/female, and so forth, Hobart anticipates congruence, avoiding points where Machineries produce their own contradictions; for example, locales with lowly, noncremating Bali Aga, residing upstream, sometimes construed in special sacred-dangerous ties with headwater regions.

Surprisingly, Hobart (1978:13) suggests that spatial attributes—particularly upstream/downstream = purity/pollution—may reflect or re-present natural phenomena: "Nor is this selection apparently arbitrary in a society which practices irrigated rice agriculture and is dependent upon water and sunshine for the successful harvests of its staple crop." Now, setting aside all those sunny isles that do not code upstream as hierarchical purity, how far might we go here? If symbols should be "good for" subsistence production, then why do Balinese conceptions deflect their attention from the bounty of the sacred-dangerous sea, receptacle of corpse ashes (an antideterminism paradox celebrated by Covarrubias himself)? Hobart borrows a notion of "natural symbols" from Douglas (1970), but he gradually eliminates any sense of oxymoron—vivid in at least portions of Douglas's works—from his view of symbol systems: "Nature may provide convenient objects by which to represent social values, or society itself (Douglas 1970), but its symbolic significance may stem also from the fact that certain aspects are in no way dependent on society. Water, after all, does not flow downhill because some collective representation states that it must" (1978:21).

Water merely flowing downhill is hardly the issue. In Bali, irrigation water indeed flows downhill—but through channels routing it, indirectly, from one paddy to another through waterworks not individually owned—precisely because collective representations state that it must. And for similar reasons women bathe downstream relative to men. Nor can this fact be merely pragmatic for the upstream men, since the "purer" water they merit is in actuality the downstream outflow of a relatively upstream village area. Water *keeps* flowing downhill; but the symbolic fact is that purity/pollution relations *shift*, to be reapplied relationally at every point, despite the natural fact that the next purity/pollution index lies absolutely downstream from one upstream. Moreover, that ultimate downstream—the sea—is a sacred-dangerous object of ritual attention in death rights; but it is also marked by the "purer" index of even demonic forces, the ocean temples (*pura segara*). Purity/pollution may be like upstream/downstream, but if there is anything it is meaningfully *not* like, it is nature's flow of water.

Further on, Hobart (1978:21) offers a more interesting insight into water types and social types by paraphrasing a Balinese just-so explanation of hypergamy: Just as water cannot flow uphill, semen cannot flow up-caste. No question here of a "natural fact," only of a simile from nature. But these Balinese Machineries, too, are more radically symbolic than Hobart implies. Connections between Bali's complex typology of water and semen (there are types here as well) perhaps even relate to ideals of the mythic notion of transposing husband's ashes into brother's sperm in rituals that seem, retrospectively, to convert high-caste wives into sisters, in line with positive values on incest glimmering out of many Balinese traditions (Boon 1982a; 1977:chap 6). To point even momentarily to the facts of gravity as "after all" some presumable base to all these symbols recalls comic comments by inveterately practical-minded servant-clowns in *wayang*, who also like to pose cultural facts as disguised natural facts.

Hobart (1978:18) feels that high castes are carried on to "the conspicuous display of wealth and support," and few would quarrel with this point. But do low castes differ except by degree; and at what point does Balinese ritual display become conspicuous (versus, I presume, "productive")? Following theoretical suggestions of Bloch, Hobart wants to attribute a kind of false consciousness to high castes, or perhaps to Balinese ritual symbols in general. He talks about "obfuscations" in which "purity and pollution are presented as realities of the same order as life and death, with a legitimacy conferred by appearing as natural" (1978:21). Reluctant to name the culprit, he couches the quasi-accusatory charges in the passive mode: ". . . emphasis is shifted. . . , discrepancies are hidden. . . , through this formalization a synthesis is produced. . ." (1978:21).

Hobart contends that Balinese symbols disguise discrepancies. I contend that all these Machineries, rather than furnishing society with a "semblance of naturalness," usher nature onto the plane of symbolic discrepancies and irreducible codes, posed and counterposed in contests of advantages and rivalry. Of course, particular Machineries advance ideologies serving particular interests. But Bali's masses, we should note, play this cultural game too.

CONCLUSION

No culture is a mere "work" deflected from something natural or disguising true labor production. As components in a culture-text, the Machineries of Bali are reducible to nothing less contradictory, indeed conflictual, than their symbols are: neither to brute power, nor to pure prestige, nor to just productivity or redistribution, nor to the natural flow of water from mountain-high to ocean-low even as the celestial sun moves inevitably east to west. Moreover, in its institutions and performances Balinese culture (this text) produces the means of exposing all of its allegorical Machineries, not as disguises (for there is nothing True underneath) but as masks. Indeed, everything is masks all the way down, and their symbolics never run out.

Balinese Machineries, even construed as works, are interesting enough, for there are sufficient sylphs and gnomes to keep enthusiasts occupied for the foreseeable future. But I would insist that Balinese Machineries ushered into the moving methodological field of its cultural text are more interesting still. In conclusion, then, I offer four semiotic guidelines for discerning the culture (text) tacit in every Machinery (work): (1) Any Machinery, including societal ones, is inherently transposable or convertible into others. (2) Machineries involve not replication but contradiction, and their terms tend less to reinforce each other (to stack up) than to offset each other in a meaningful way. (3) Machineries represent neither what an allegorically inclined people "believe" nor what they necessarily "say"; rather, they comprise the symbolic basis of a cultural argument engaged in by various parties, but never disinterested ones. (4) Any Machinery is bound to be grasped in different ways by various actors (and interpreters); it is the implicit terms of their evolving discourse that constitute the culture as text. Thus, the Machinery becomes paradoxical, irreducibly plural, and both within and beyond Bali dialectic.

NOTES

Besides E. Bruner, V. Turner, C. Geertz, R. Abrahams, and the other participants on the AAA panel at which this volume originated, I wish to thank J. Culler, L. Waugh, R. Paul, B. Mertz, R. Parmentier, B. Lee, S. Errington, B. Tedlock, D. Tedlock, and other colleagues and students kind enough to have commented on or at least listened to portions of this paper. The theoretical background I allude to here is more fully developed in Boon (1972, 1983).

Limitations of space preclude broaching other realms of Balinese Machineries, particularly tantric codes of sexuality, performative conventions that I associate with Menippean satire, mythic and historical images of twinship, and the contrast between Balinese social forms and those of neighboring islands.

I have treated all these issues in those of my publications listed in the references, and particularly in two recent papers: "The Other-Woman: Comparative Symbols of Society Beginning with Balinese Twins" (1982b) and "In Praise of Bali's Folly: Remarks on the History of Interpreting Performance in a Parodic Culture" (1982c).

REFERENCES

Barthes, Roland. 1977. *Image, Music, Text.* trans. S. Heath. New York: Hill and Wang.

Boon, James A. 1972. *From Symbolism to Structuralism: Lévi-Strauss in a Literary Tradition.* Oxford and New York: Blackwell's and Harper and Row.

———. 1977. *The Anthropological Romance of Bali, 1597–1972: Dynamic Perspectives in Marriage and Caste, Politics and Religion.* New York: Cambridge University Press.

———. 1982a. "Incest Recaptured: Some Contraries of Karma in Balinese Symbology." In: C. Keyes and E. Daniel (eds.), *Karma in the Popular Traditions of South and Southeast Asia*, pp. 185–222. Berkeley: University of California Press.

———. 1982b. "The Other-Woman: Comparative Symbols of Society Beginning with Balinese Twins." Paper prepared for the conference on "Feminism and Kinship Theory," Bellagio, Italy, August.

———. 1982c. "In Praise of Bali's Folly: Remarks on the History of Interpreting Performance in a Parodic Culture." Paper prepared for the Wenner-Gren conference on "Theater and Ritual," Asia Society, New York, August.

———. 1983. *Other Tribes, Other Scribes: Symbolic Anthropology in the Comparative Study of Cultures, Histories, Religions, and Texts.* New York: Cambridge University Press.

Burke, Kenneth. 1970. *The Rhetoric of Religion: Studies in Logology.* Berkeley: University of California Press.

Covarrubias, Miguel. 1937. *Island of Bali.* New York: Knopf.

de Saussure, Ferdinand. 1966. *Course in General Linguistics.* trans. Wade Baskin. New York: McGraw-Hill.

Douglas, Mary. 1970. *Natural Symbols.* New York: Vintage Books.

Dumont, Louis. 1980. *Homo Hierarchicus: The Caste System and Its Implications.* rev. ed. Chicago: University of Chicago Press.

Geertz, Clifford. 1973. *The Interpretation of Cultures.* New York: Basic Books.

———. 1980. *Negara: The Theatre State in Nineteenth Century Bali.* Princeton, N.J.: Princeton University Press.

Geertz, Hildred, and Clifford Geertz. 1975. *Kinship in Bali.* Chicago: University of Chicago Press.

Hobart, Mark. 1978. "The Path of the Soul: The Legitimacy of Nature in Balinese Conceptions of Space." In: G. B. Milner (ed.), *Natural Symbols in Southeast Asia*, pp. 5–28. London: S.O.A.S., University of London.

Hooykaas, C. 1973. *Religion in Bali.* Leiden: E. J. Brill.

Peirce, Charles S. 1955. *Philosophical Writings.* ed. J. Buchler. New York: Dover.

Pope, Alexander. 1960. *The Rape of the Lock*. New York: Dover Books.

Ramseyer, Urs. 1977. *The Art and Culture of Bali*. New York: Oxford University Press.

Swellengrebel, J. L. 1960. "Bali: Some General Information." In: *Bali: Studies in Life, Thought, Ritual*, pp. 3–76. The Hague: W. van Hoeve.

Tan, Roger Y. D. 1960. "The Domestic Architecture of South Bali," *Bijdragen tot de Taal-, Land- en Volkenkunde*, 442–75.

11

"Life Not Death in Venice": Its Second Life

BARBARA MYERHOFF

The whole earth is the sepulchre of famous men and ordinary men, and their story is not graven on stone, but lives on woven into the stuff of other men's lives. . . .

Pericles's funeral speech.

The power of breadth of our own life, and the energy of reflection upon it is the foundation of the historical vision. It alone enables us to give second life to the bloodless shades of the past.

Dilthey, *Pattern and Meaning in History*

In a recent article on "the refiguration of social thought," Geertz (1980:178, 167) points out the growing vitality of interest among social scientists in "the anatomization of thought" as indicative of "a move toward conceiving of social life as organized in terms of symbols . . . whose meaning we must grasp." How people make sense out of themselves, for themselves, and how we as anthropologists develop our interpretive skills in unpacking their symbolic systems becomes a central concern in our discipline.

One of the most persistent but elusive ways that people make sense of themselves is to show themselves to themselves, through multiple forms: by telling themselves stories; by dramatizing claims in rituals and other collective enactments; by rendering visible actual and desired truths about themselves and the significance of their existence in imaginative and performative productions. Self-recognition is accomplished by these showings and is, as George Steiner says, a "formidable, difficult, and perpetual task." More than merely self-recognition, self-definition is made

261

possible by means of such showings, for their content may state not only what people think they are but what they should have been or may yet be. Evidently, interpretive statements are mirrors for collectivities to hold up to themselves; like mirrors, such statements may lie, reverse, and distort the images they carry, and they need not be isomorphic with "nature."

In this paper, I will present two instances of cultural mirroring, one event which I call a "definitional ceremony," the other an inscribed text, a self-portrait of a collectivity. Both of these are found in a highly self-conscious community which continually interprets, depicts, and performs its self-determined reality; both forms are strikingly symbolic and can be unpacked to elucidate the community's understanding of itself; and both are reflecting surfaces and reflexive, demonstrating the creators' consciousness of their own interpretive work.

The cases I cite, ceremony and inscribed text, were exceptionally successful in the persuasions about the reality they asserted. Their success may be judged by the fact that they reached beyond convincing and moving their own members about the claims they made. They succeeded in interesting and captivating outsider-witnesses as to the validity of their interpretations. These outsider-witnesses—anthopologist and the media—served as further reflecting surfaces, broadcasting, re-presenting what they had been shown, and thus enlarging the people's original interpretations and giving them a greater public and factual character than they had in their primary form. By pressing into service others who believed, to restate their versions of themselves, they amplified their claims. The people involved eventually succeeded in bringing about actual changes, in reversing to some degree their political impotence and invisibility, by the canny deployment of their symbols, consciously manipulated; by their skillful operation on public sentiments; and by their sheer conviction that although they understood their manipulations fully, they were innocently, utterly correct. Ultimately, they displayed "facts" of their life and their meaning, knowing full well that the facts they portrayed were about life not as it was but as it should have been.

"LIFE NOT DEATH IN VENICE": BACKGROUND

In 1971 I began an anthropological study of ethnicity and aging, concentrating on a community of very old immigrant Jews from Eastern Europe, whose social life was focused on the Israel Levin Senior Adult Center in Venice, California.[1] My work there brought to my attention a singular and dominant theme: the people's severe invisibility and the consequent disturbing psychological and social consequences of being unnoticed. It is a truism that severely marginal people are stigmatized and neglected by the mainstream society, subject to dismissal that is usually not even the result of hatred or conscious disdain. Often, it is merely that such people are not *seen;* they are treated as invisible.

Among very old people—those with fading sensory acuity, deprived of natural intergenerational continuity, and hence unable to transmit their natal culture or personal histories to their absent, acculturated progeny—people who are facing death and utter disappearance, the problem of social inattention is especially serious. They may come to doubt not only their worth and potency, not only their value, but the very fact of their existence. It became clear to me that these particular elders were intent on presenting themselves to the world and being noticed; on interpreting the meaning of their history and culture to a wider outside world that would remember them after they had died; on possibly transmitting something of their lives to younger people. Many of their struggles were intractable: extreme poverty, poor health, inadequate housing and transportation, insufficient medical care, dangerous surroundings, loss of social roles, and outliving spouses, family, and friends. But their invisibility proved not to be irreversible. Through their own ingenuity, imagination, and boldness, aided by outsiders who publicized their activities, they learned to manipulate their own images, flying in the face of external reality, denying their existential circumstances.[2] They displayed and performed their interpretations of themselves and in some critical respects became what they claimed to be. By denying their invisibility, isolation, and impotence, they made themselves be seen, and in being seen they came into being in their own terms, as authors of themselves.

The elders had created an entire culture of their own making, one of great complexity and richness that was shot through with contradictions, paradoxes, and fantasies. It had been built up over the course of some three decades spent together on the beach in Venice. The had come to this neighborhood in their mid-sixties, after retirement, leaving the industrial centers of the North and Northeast, where most of them had lived and worked since emigrating to America from Eastern Europe around the turn of the century. Here, in an age-homogeneous ethnic enclave, surrounded by the carnival-like life along the boardwalk, they revived some features from their childhood history in the cities and shtetls of the Old World. Particularly important was their return to their natal language and culture, Yiddishkeit, and to some extent to the religious practices they had discarded on arriving in America, when rapid assimilation for themselves and education for their children were their most singular concerns.

The culture they had invented to meet their present circumstances in old age was bricolage in the best sense—an assortment of symbols, customs, memories, and rituals, blending in a highly ecumenical spirit; they used something from all the layers of their history: Old World, Yiddish, Jewish, modern, American, Californian, secular, and sacred. They knew that improvisation and invention were essential, but like all people they also needed to convince themselves that these solutions were proper, authentic, believable, and occasionally traditional. Their need for such persuasions, and for being visible, coincided with their naturally performative bent, resulting in a highly dramatic self-presentational culture that was extroverted and often touched with the frenzy of desperation. (And, of course, things had to be loud, clear, and exciting since most of these people were in their mid-eighties to mid-nineties; it was often difficult for them to see and hear some of the quieter displays. The way of life devised by these elderly Jews was a major accomplishment, one that proved successful in dealing with their everyday circumstances and with numerous internally and externally generated crises.

Exegesis and self-examination were ancient religious and secular customs for the elders; textual analysis was taught them as part of the Scripture. A long history as pariah people, at least since the biblical Dispersion from Israel, in the Old World, and repeated now in their old age, further heightened their self-consciousness. Performance and self-commentary were natural to them. Life in a constructed world (one that they knew to be constructed) was characteristic of their past as well as their present. The power of the imagination, when publically stated and collectively experienced, was understood by many to be a necessity, a gift, and a potential danger.

Following a precariously contrived ceremony that wedded an

Old World religious event with a secular modern one (with which it had little in common), a great argument ensued among some of the Center's elders as to whether or not the ritual had been "proper," "successful," indeed, whether it had been "real" (Myerhoff 1980:106). "This is nonsense, completely made up. Nothing like this could ever happen," protested Shmuel. Moshe's comment was finally accepted as authoritative, however.

This is a story I am getting from Martin Buber, the great Hasidic philosopher. I am showing it to the ones who say [the ceremony] was not proper. It tells about two men who are worried about the holiness of the Sabbath. "What is it that makes something holy?" they ask. They decide to make a test to see what happens when they have Sabbath on a weekday. So they make the Sabbath in the middle of the week. Everything they do is right, and it feels the same way as on Saturday. This is alarming, so they take the problem to the rabbi to explain. Here is what the rabbi tells them: "If you put on Sabbath clothes and Sabbath caps it is quite right that you had a feeling of Sabbath holiness. Because Sabbath clothes and caps have the power of drawing the light of the Sabbath holiness down to the earth. So you need have no fears." (1980:68)

On another occasion, the dangers of a life lived imaginatively were discussed vividly by Shmuel, who described his childhood in a little town in Poland:

Now it is strange to say that we belonged there. . . . The beautiful river, forests, none of these are ours. What did we have but fear and hunger and more hunger? Hidden in a foreign land that we loved and hated. A life made entirely from the imagination. We say our prayers for rains to come, not for us here in Poland but for the Holy Land. We pass our lives to study the services in the Temple. What Temple? Long ago finished. Where do our priests make offerings? Only in our minds. We feel the seasons of Jerusalem more than the cold of Poland. Outside we are ragged, poor, nothing to look at, no possibilities for change. But every little child there is rubbing elbows with the glorious kings and priests of the Holy Land. . . . In this we find our home. . . . Would you say this is insanity? It could be. If we lived more in Poland and not so much in the Holy Land, would all our people now be buried in pits along the river? (1980:69)

Here, then, are two illustrations of the group's capacity to describe their lives imaginatively and consciously, questioning their own inventions while proceeding to believe in and enact them. Alongside their verbal reflections, however, was their often startling capacity to shape their physiological lives no less than their thoughts and acts. It was remarkable that they continued to survive, as individuals and as a collectivity, far beyond the norm, beyond predictions of sociology, history, and physiology. And not a few proved able to tailor their deaths as well as their lives, according to their own designs, dying naturally but precisely in the moments and manners of their choice. These people inscribed their self-interpretations on the spaces and surfaces they touched—walls, neighborhoods, media—sometimes even pressing their own bodies into service as statements of meaning, the most final and most dramatic of all.

DEFINITIONAL CEREMONIES

Definitional ceremonies are likely to develop when within a group there is a crisis of invisibility and disdain by a more powerful outside society. Let me state briefly why visibility was such a critical issue among these people. As immigrants, they had no natural witnesses to their past lives and culture. They lived in a world of strangers who "had to be told everything." Moreover, since the Holocaust had eliminated their natal culture, these elders felt an especially great obligation to transmit their firsthand experiences in Eastern Europe to others. They were the last ones who could explain "what it really had been like." And because their children were assimilated into another culture, there was no one to receive and preserve their memories and tales. Also, because they were marginal, disdained people, outsiders knew nearly nothing about them. The absent witness/missing progeny feature, then, was a serious, multidimensional problem.

While marginality, extreme age and the proximity of death, the shock of immigration and the loss of a natal culture (suggesting personal and collective obliteration) all contribute to a sharp self-consciousness, pain and discontinuity are essential contributors as well. Only through the assimilation of experience into a form that endows meaning can such a history be rendered bearable. "Because both our fortunes and our own natures cause us pain, so they force us to come to terms with them through understanding. The past mysteriously invites us to know the closely-woven meaning of its moments" (Dilthey 1961 [1910]:100). But the sense of continuity, of being a member in a chain of being with an inherited history that can be transmitted, may contribute as much to reflexive consciousness as rupture, pain, and loss.

This point emerged very clearly in a discussion[3] with some of the elderly artists who participated in the cultural festival (see note 2). Sherrie Wagner, a graduate student in history, queried the artists about their sharp awareness of being "in history," saying:

One of the things that I often asked my grandmother was what she thought about historical events, like Pearl Harbor, the Second World War, and things like that. She never really had a sense of having been a part of history or a part of the important events of her time. I could never get her to talk about where she was or what she felt. It was as though they had no impact on her. But the people sitting here today seem to have a much clearer sense of history and I wonder if it is because they are painting and sculpting and that makes them more aware? Or is it being in this show? Do you now have a greater sense of being part of history?

Ida Bernstein replied: "Well, to tell you the truth, I had it before, I always had this very strongly. This may sound very pompous, but I have to say I am very conscious of the fact that I have certain traditions, values that I can transmit."

Not being noticed by children or the outside "serious world" was exacerbated among these elderly by the loss of some of their sensory acuity. Clarity of consciousness tended to fade, memories fused with the present, dreams with desire, sleep with wakefulness. There were few kinesthetic cues as to their continuing vitality since there were no kin, spouses, or children to hold, and it was not their custom to embrace each other. Sensory deprivation was often severe. When both the outside and the inner world deprive us of reflections—evidence that, indeed, we are still present and alive, seen and responded to—the threat to self-awareness can be great. Definitional ceremonies deal with the problems of invisibility and marginality; they are strategies that provide opportunities for being seen and in one's own terms, garnering witnesses to one's worth, vitality, and being. Thus, it was the custom for Center members to display and dramatize themselves in many forms, informal and formal, planned and spontaneously: by storytelling, creating difficulties, making scenes; by positioning themselves to be noticed, recorded, listened to, and photographed.

Definitional ceremonies were the elders' most regular and

formal patterns of display. These were quite predictable, marked by considerable momentum leading up to a crisis, after which, when things had settled down, it appeared that nothing had been accomplished. No internal conflicts were settled, no social realignments made. At first these events seemed to resemble what Turner (1974) described as social dramas—they had a natural sequence, a beginning, a middle, and an end, and there was the same progression from breach of a norm to crisis and resolution, with displays of common, powerful, binding symbols. Certainly the style was agonistic; much adrenalin had flowed and a good fight indeed offered clear-cut evidence of continuing vitality. Heroes emerged, pro- and con-, and there were antagonists, accessories, and always a sizeable chorus. Parts were discovered and developed so that everyone was heard from, seen, authenticated. And as with Turner's social dramas, the ends of these affairs were always marked by the enunciation of the participant's collective symbols, reiterating their common membership and deepest shared commitments. That the ceremonies changed nothing was signal, and is what distinguished them from social dramas. It seemed, in fact, that their purpose was to allow things to stay the same, to permit people to discover and rediscover sameness in the midst of furor, antagonism, and threats of splitting apart.

Here, the performative dimension of definitional ceremonies was the critical ingredient. Within them claims were made that were frequently unrelated to any palpable "reality," which was often evident to all of those involved. To merely assert such claims would be ludicrous and utterly unconvincing; but to enact them was another thing. Mounted as dramas they became small, full worlds, concrete, with proper masks, costumes, gestures, vocabularies, special languages, and all the panoply that made them convincing rituals. Our senses are naturally persuasive, convincing us of what the mind will not indulge. Presentational symbols have more rhetorical power than discursive ones (the latter require exceptional skill and some veracity); in ritual, doing is believing, and we become what we display. Detail may substitute for artfulness. Kenneth Burke might refer to definitional ceremonies as another example of "dancing an attitude." Like string quartets and Balinese cockfights, as Geertz (1973) points out, such symbolic dramas are not "mere reflections of a pre-existing sensibility, analogically represented"; they are "positive agents" in the creation and maintenance of the subjectivity they organize into a proper, coherent tale. Considering the frequency with which this particular population engineered such opportunities for appearing and enacting their dreams, we are tempted to describe definitional ceremonies as more like stages than mirrors. They did not merely show the people to themselves; rather, they provided scenes into which the people could step and play their parts. If others were watching, so much the better. Their attention, belief, and possibly recording would become evidence in the future of the "truth" of the performance, solid corroboration of what began as desire and through enactment came into the world as fact. If no one else noticed, the Center members watched each other and themselves, bearing witness to their own story.

THE PARADE

The boardwalk which the Center faces had been used for some time by bicyclists, though a local (unenforced) ordinance prohibits wheeled traffic. More recently, roller skating enthusiasts have joined the stream of bicyclists, making the boardwalk as heavily trafficked and dangerous as a major street. Several collisions have occurred; old people have been struck down and injured. All of them were growing frightened and angry, but no one had succeeded in seeing to it that the law against wheeled traffic was enforced. Old and young competed fiercely for space, dramatically enacting their opposing concerns in regular shouting matches:

"This isn't an old people's home, you know!"
"I worked hard all my life. I'm a citizen. I got to have a place to put down my foot also."

Thus the stage was set for the precipitating event that lead to a crisis. A bicyclist struck Anna Gerber, aged 86, as she left the Center one Sunday morning. The youth who hit her was reported to have said in defense of himself, "I didn't see her." His statement outraged the old people, for Anna evidently had been directly in front of him. Clearly, it seemed a case of "death by invisibility." When Anna died as a result of her injuries, the Center members organized a protest march. The event was carefully staged and described in advance to the media, which appeared to cover it. An empty, unmarked "coffin" made from a paper carton painted black was in the middle of the procession. Members carried placards reading "S.O.S. = Save Our Seniors," "Let Our People Stay," and "Life Not Death in Venice." Two blind men led the procession, and people with walkers and canes placed themselves prominently alongside the coffin. The members dressed in particularly bright, nice clothing, "so as not to look poor or pathetic," said one member.

Roller skaters, bicycle riders, and the concessionaires who rented skates and bikes all heckled the elders, who spoke up sharply to be sure that the television cameras and microphones caught the moral outrage they articulated: "See this sign, 'Let Our People Stay'? That goes back to the Bible, you know. We were driven out from Europe already. We don't want to be driven out from here." The group proceeded several hundred yards down the boardwalk, to the small orthodox synagogue that recently had been acquired by a group of young people. The elders did not regularly visit the synagogue because most were not observant and many objected to the orthodox practice of separating women and men during prayer, regarding it as "too old-fashioned, the kind of thing we got away from when we left the Old Country." Now everyone crowded into the little shul. Men and women were seated together, Jew and non-Jew, young and old, members and media people, as many of those who had joined the parade as could fit inside. It was a splendid moment of communitas, a profound and moving celebration of unity, as the prayers were said to "bind up the name of Anna with the ancestors."

The ceremonies did not end there, however. The members returned to the Center for an afternoon of dancing to celebrate the birthday of Frances Stein, aged 100, a woman of singular strength, a symbol of successful longevity, always in good spirits, clear-headed, unencumbered by cane, hearing aid, or illness. The continuity of life was acknowledged as vividly as the presence of death had been earlier in the day. "It's a good way to finish such a day," people agreed, clearly aware of the symbolic propriety of juxtaposing a funeral and a birthday to assert their continuing vitality and power despite injury and loss. The ceremony had been an enactment of their historical vision and their rejection of the assigned position of helpless victim. It was a profoundly reflexive occasion, the kind that, as the opening epigraph by Dilthey notes, gives human experience its "second life."

What were some of the specific symbols deployed in the definitional ceremony? Most were clearly identifiable with the peoples' layered, long history, ranging from ancient times to the most recent developments. "Let my people stay," the reference to the Jews' exodus from Egypt, came from the oldest layer of history, signifying their capacity to achieve freedom and leave slavery behind in a return to their homeland. Certainly the motto referred as well to the repeated form, a procession, or in recent terms, a protest march, a demonstration. That freedom in ancient times meant "going out" and in contemporary times meant "staying put" was a satisfying bit of opposition that gave that motto a pungent, ironic flavor. The placard that became "the name" for the parade, "Life Not Death in Venice," similarly reasserted the life-over-death message and was in response to a newspaper clipping announcing the coming protest march under the heading "Death in Venice." Some members became irate by this suggestion of defeat and, recognizing its danger, used a counterslogan; they employed placards, printed words speaking to other printed words (the newspaper headline), as a means of erasing or out-shouting the statements made by outsiders about them. It was another instance of literally "making a scene" to make sure that their message was seen and heard.

The use of the prayer for Anna, "binding her up with the ancestors," came from a historical layer that was equally old. The Jewish prayer for the dead, Kaddish, makes no reference to death. It is a statement only about continuity and perpetuity; it elevates the individual who has died to the quasi-sacred position of the Patriarchs and Matriarchs, mythic figures with whom he or she becomes bound, suggesting the removal from history and time, sounding again the theme of renewal and transcendence, of deathlessness. Note as well that no official reference was made to the most recent and powerful historical episode of all: the Holocaust. While it was briefly, obliquely cited verbally, it was not used on a poster or displayed in any way. It is my impression that, as a rule, these people avoid using that experience or exploiting it, except in rare circumstances, and then usually to each other but not outsiders. The experience seems too strong and sacred to put to immediate practical purposes.

The note of renewal and denial of death were repeated in the association of a coffin and a birthday party. The incorporation of the synagogue into the procession was a fortunate choice, for it symbolized the inclusion of all of Judaism in this local event and touched the particular circumstances with sacrality. That outsiders and nonmembers were included within the synagogue was a fine symbolic note that their cause went beyond them, beyond other Jews or old people. It was essential that outsiders be brought into the protest for the definitional ceremony to succeed. If it were limited to only those like themselves, there would have been no audience to register the elders' message. While they might have succeeded in convincing themselves, there would have been no hope of making the impact they aimed for on the outside world.

Finally, within the procession the elders displayed themselves as symbols, dramatizing precisely how they wished to be and how they wished to be seen. They exploited signs of their fragility—canes, walkers, blindness—but deliberately dressed well. They wished to be viewed as strong presences, angry but not defeated; yet they were too cagey to omit the message about their vulnerability and the implicit accusation it stated. At once they dramatized strength and weakness in a brilliant, accurate paradox. Moral superiority and structural inferiority so commonly deployed by liminal people, as Turner has pointed out, was particularly well stated here.

The comment made by the youth on the bicycle after he struck Anna was often repeated and called to the attention of outsiders as highly symbolic. All the old people knew why he hadn't seen her; their determination to make themselves visible was the specific impetus for the parade. That they succeeded in altering more than their own version of themselves was beyond question when a few weeks later barricades appeared on the boardwalk, on either side of the Center, providing a four-block section where the old people could walk without fear of traffic. A limited but decisive victory. The elders had transformed their assigned role as helpless, unseen people into their chosen one as people to be reckoned with. The definitional ceremony had defined them as such and was sufficiently convincing to outsiders as well. All entered into collusion to agree that the elders did indeed exist and should be seen.

It was, of course, real or anticipated popular pressure that finally caused local politicians to erect the barricades. This pressure was generated by media coverage that amplified the elders' visibility, making it larger, clearer, and more public than it would otherwise have been. Hence, the media must be included in this analysis of reflecting surfaces. Publicity afforded by the parade was a significant mirror that showed the old people's culture to themselves and to outsiders. Nevertheless, the elders originated the image that was broadcast, and it was to their image that they successfully drew their witnesses. They not only created an imaginary existence for themselves but for those who watched them. Geertz has described ritual as that form which allows the "dreamed-of" and "lived-in" orders to fuse. Indeed, they fused in this event. The authors of the ritual stepped into the single reality made of the two orders and took part of their audience with them.

THE CENTER MURAL: AN INSCRIBED TEXT

Paul Ricoeur tells us that "inscriptions fix meaning." A social event read as a text is slippery, as though the words flew off the page before we could finish reading them. An "inscribed" social text is easier to read, however. Like an object, it sits still while we look at it; it allows us to re-present it to others, as I do here in discussing the meaning of the second symbolic form used by the group of elderly Jews in California.

The Center members all came from a tradition that forbade portraiture and the depiction of images. Nevertheless, many were attracted to visual art and themselves enjoyed painting. Their self-expression in this form was encouraged by their art teacher, Mrs. Betty Nutkiewicz, herself an Eastern European Jew and a refugee from the Holocaust, somewhat younger than most of the members but still what Americans would call a senior citizen. She organized some of the most enthusiastic students in her regular art classes in the Center to paint a mural the length of one hall there (see Figure 1). Many people participated in the project, but three of the members were the major designers and artists. Those who did not paint instead witnessed, criticized, kibitzed; and finally the painting took shape. It is not possible to determine precisely how many or who contributed particular themes and ideas, though Mrs. Nutkiewicz remembers some especially striking contributions. The mural is unquestionably a collective self-portrait, showing the elders' social history freely interspersed with their myths.

The mural begins at the west end of the hall with a drawing

of the Mayflower. An American flag flies on top, jutting out of the confining frame. Mrs. Nutkiewicz notes: "This was Bessie Mintz' idea though I do not think that most people in this group came over on the Mayflower. She made the boat very big because it had to carry so many Jews here."[4] The next scene depicts the Statue of Liberty; like the American flag a beloved symbol to these immigrants, marking the beginning of a new life of freedom. Mrs. Nutkiewicz comments: "You notice they made Miss Liberty a little heftier than usual. You might think that is because she is strong. That's true, but also because the artist who made it thought that women who were a little bit fat looked healthier, more attractive."

A market scene in a village square, fusing New York and Eastern Europe, follows, prompting Mrs. Nutkiewicz to tell us: "What is interesting here is that these little houses you wouldn't really find in New York. They brought them from their past probably. They carried these ideas and memories from their little shtetls and put them right up here on the wall." The secular associations of Yiddish and the sacred associations of Hebrew are eluded to by two written signs in the scene: "Fresh herring can be bought here" in Yiddish over one of the stalls in the marketplace scene; "Synagogue" in Hebrew over the House of Prayer. She continues: "This scene you would find in the Lower East side, all right, it's mixed up with Europe. [The Center elders] identified themselves with these people. Some had sisters, mothers like this, sitting all day in front of a little pile of fruit, vegetables. And of course, there are peddlers. You see one very talented artist made that horse, a beautiful skinny horse, had to be skinny because it shows that everyone was poor."

Next is a segment on the elders' middle years in America, in the sweatshops where so many passed most of their working lives and which represents a significant portion of their collective social history; whether or not experienced individually, the experience is "borrowed" as a historical moment and regularly incorporated into accounts of personal histories. (The same is true for having lived as a member of a shtetl rather than in a town or city. When pressed, many members indicate that they were not actually born or raised in shtetls, those largely Jewish hamlets and villages of Eastern Europe. Rather, they use the term to signify their childhood experiences as members of a religious community of their

Figure 1. Mural at the Israel Levin Senior Adult Center in Venice, California. The woman in the photograph is a member of the Center who refused to move for the photographer, so she has been included, which is in keeping with the spirit of this essay. Note that the ship is the Mayflower, which dates from 1620, but that it is carrying an American rather than a British flag; also note that the flag breaks the frame at the top of the mural. This and the sequence of photographs on the following pages are courtesy of Andrew Bush.

own people, in contrast to their later lives in secular, pluralistic America.) Mrs. Nutkiewicz remarks: "And this is, you know, the Liberation movement. It started to grow up at this time. Here are the suffragist women with their signs, 'Strike,' 'Fight,' 'Eight Hours of Work,' 'Arbeiten,' all in Yiddish. You see, they are in long dresses, heels, the old-fashioned dress but they are modern people, fighting for the improvement of their working conditions. Because after the sweatshops come the unions. That was their doing. They fought for themselves, for freedom and social justice, but everyone benefitted." The merging of strikers and suffragettes is an interesting note, suggesting the peoples' identification with common causes for which they must struggle in their pursuit of freedom and social justice. Trade unions and the fight for women's rights merge here. That primarily women are depicted in the protest march is not unusual when we consider that all the painters of the mural were women. Clearly, it is the privilege of artists

everywhere to personalize and localize their great themes, embuing the Great Tradition with the specific forms and personnel that give the Little Tradition its vivacity.

The portion of the mural that follows this displays the citizens as middle-aged people in the sweatshops. "This has a great history in the life of the Jewish people," says Mrs. Nutkiewicz. "Because you see here the worker sewing, in very poor conditions, on the sewing machine. And you see standing over them, the foreman who is supposed to be very strict, selfish. You can see how hard everyone works. But at least we are together."

Then come the elders in Venice, already retired, dressed in modern American garb and seated outside the Israel Levin Center on the boardwalk benches.

Here you see the people sitting on the benches. Look, one is feeding a hungry dog. You see the woman is almost falling down but she didn't want to sit because she had to feed the dog. They painted this picture but they were unhappy with it because they identified themselves with this picture. You see they are a little apart from each other and they look kind of desolate. So what can we do to make the picture happy and the conditions happy? So somebody said, "Let's make the Israel Levin Center." And here we began to build a center.

Now here is something interesting, I would say almost surrealistic. People walk through the Center and the Center became almost transparent. You see one figure is inside, one figure is half outside. But they

show that they are going through the Center. Even the figure is still in the Center but we can see it. And naturally, they dance, the "eternal Hora" dance, and they're all happy. And it was Friday. We finish with the Oneg Shabbat (the welcoming of the Sabbath) with the blessing of the candles. The hallah (braided Sabbath loaf) is there, and the beautiful table cloth with fringes.

The half-inside-half-outside figures are two individuals who are holding hands, drawn in outline, not colored, shaded, or given any detail. They look unfinished. Indeed I assumed that someone had simply failed to complete them, until I heard them referred to as the "ghosts" or "spirits" in the mural. Explained one of the members: "We have here ghosts because, you see, even though we are old, we are not yet finished. We still come into new things and could change yet a lot before we die." Intrigued, I asked several other people about the possibility of ghosts, and there were various interpretations: "These are not ghosts. No, it's because you see, people don't come fully into their life without holding their comrades' hands. This we learn from our history. United we stand. You can see how lonely they look over there [on the benches] before they took hold of each other."

A woman standing nearby overheard our conversation and countered: "You always got to put politics into things. It was much simpler. I know the woman who did this part of the painting. Esther Wolfe was her name. You would be standing outside

and so naturally you couldn't see the people inside the Center already. So you have to show them coming out into the world, which they couldn't do with their bodies. So they don't get their bodies until they come out into the sunshine." Mrs. Nutkiewicz didn't like the suggestion that these outlined figures were in any way "not real":

Oh no! They are not ghosts or spirits. They're very real. They are the people going through the Israel Levin Center. And our artists are primitive, I would say. They didn't know how to solve the problem to show that the person is inside and you can see the person, half in and half out, if you are standing outside looking in. But they are real. Real living members of the Center, not ghosts, everything is real. If someone wants to say they see ghosts, all right, but that would be gloomy. They are very much alive.

Here's another thing. You can be naive but it doesn't mean you are always realistic. Chagall would have a cow flying in the sky. That doesn't make it senseless. So maybe if the people weren't inside or weren't dancing the Hora, they are pale, a little anemic you could say. They became alive when they join hands and danced in a group. This could be, too. Esther said that in the Center when they participate in the activities, they look much brighter. I thought this was very interesting. You see, one person inside is really pale, like a shadow, and the other one joined hands and became already colorful. It is like a little fantasy.

This carries over into the Oneg Shabbat. You see how everyone here is inside now. Everyone is together and peaceful and very happy.

This is a significant set of comments. The overall discussion at several points makes explicit the elders' free interpretation of history, shaping and idealizing it, bringing it to the level of near-myth. Many of their most strongly held ideals are portrayed, particularly working for others through social change and philanthropy, which is somewhat pathetically expressed by the woman feeding a hungry dog even though she herself was too frail and poor to stand alone. Another important theme is the returning to the peace of the Sabbath, the sacred, expressed primarily in the realm of women and the home, usually at a heavily laden table. The importance of community is another theme that is implicit throughout the mural. And Mrs. Nutkiewicz's statements are interesting for their near explicit claim that the mural does not merely reflect, it actually creates the peoples' reality: "They painted this picture but they were unhappy with it because they identified themselves with this picture"; and later, by "making the picture happy the conditions depicted are also made happy."

The argument about ghosts is, however, the outstanding element here, establishing with certainty a truly reflexive attitude on the part of the creators of and witnesses to the mural. Their analysis and argument, sorting among the possible symbolic impli-

cations of the empty figures, is a metatext, a commentary on the original commentary. In more abstract terms, it is a second-order signification. The mural becomes fully contextualized in this argument, for we hear the creators' exegeses of it. Texts require multiple contextualization to be well read (see Geertz 1980:176–77). In this segment we have such contextualization: the relation of the parts to each other within the text; to the creators of the texts; to the realities lying outside the text; and to those associated with it. What, then, is the meaning of the ghosts? All the suggestions made are valid and germane: the people are unfinished; they continue to grow and change and therefore have a future, for which they need each other, coming fully into their humanity only when they are seen in public, though they never stray too far from the place of their beginning, to which they always return—the Center and all that is associated with it: Yiddishkeit, home, hiddenness, and community.

THE PARADE COMMENTS ON THE MURAL, AND VICE VERSA

Since both the parade and the mural are regarded here as symbolic statements, as texts to be read, it is suitable now to read each in relation to the other, intertextually. Do they merely repeat the same message? Do they distort, contradict, reinforce, expand,

refine, or shift each other's messages? Do we find in them any information about differences between performed and inscribed texts? Since one is behaved and the other is a picture of ideas, can we draw any conclusions about the relations between action and ideas? Can we go beyond considering both as mirrors and attribute causality or influence of one statement to the other? Finally, can anything be said about the relations of these texts to the existential circumstances in which they occur? These are some of the more interesting questions raised by the data, and they are worth noting, though not all of them can be fully answered or explored in depth with the materials on hand.

Both statements, Parade and Mural, were made for the same purpose—self-knowledge, self-creation through display—and roughly by the same people. Presented diagramatically (see Figure 2), it is clear that both the mural and the parade have a parallel form. In each case the members depart from the safety and familiarity of home, here associated with childhood, family, and exclusively Jewish communities and made sacred through local custom and deep embedding in culture. These are the profoundly familiar and intimate settings in which daily life takes place. With all its limits, poverty, and conflict, unquestionably it is *home* in the fullest sense. The people depart for a zone of strangers, a secular world to which they do not truly belong but which they try to improve nevertheless through protest for social justice. They are active, re-

Figure 2. Diagram of the Parade and Mural

	Departure from "home" *Primary ties* *Exclusively Jewish* *Sacred; familial*	*Protest for* *social justice* *Public activity* *Secular, amid* *strangers*	*Liminal zone* *Venice community* *Neighbors,* lantzmen *Strangers, intimates*	*Return "home"* *Primary ties* *Exclusively Jewish* *Sacred; familial*
PARADE	Center	March with coffin, placards	Synagogue	Center: celebrating life (birthday party)
MURAL	New York/shtetl	March with placards	Boardwalk benches	Center: celebrating life (Sabbath)

Note: I have begun this reading with the New York/shtetl scene instead of the Mayflower/ Statue of Liberty because of the fusion of New York and shtetl, New World and Old. The story which the mural tells is about America, but it suggests the peoples' reluctance to omit or leave behind their past in Europe. Read as a pilgrimage, the mural suggests a set of nesting circuits: from the Old World to the New, from the East Coast to Venice; and in miniature, the same form is enacted whenever they depart from the Center for an outside public event in which they enact their self-definition, and then return to the Center. The format and message are reiterated.

solute, and performing. Then they pass into a liminal zone, be-twixt and between, partaking of public and private, strangers and intimates, in their made-up community in Venice where they live with neighbors and *lantzmen* (fellow immigrants). They are mid-way between inside and outside, somewhat lost. The benches are not truly theirs, nor is the synagogue (for reasons too complicated to discuss here; see Myerhoff 1980). They are described and de-picted as "desolate," sitting apart from each other in the mural, not yet having established the Center. In the synagogue they are similarly uncomfortable, partly because they are not habitual vis-itors, partly because it is being used for secular as well as sacred purposes and includes a great many non-Jews. In both cases the elders are passive, witnessing the activities of others rather than performing themselves.

The circuit is completed in both cases by a celebration back "home" in the Center. At the end of the march a birthday is marked, that of an exceptionally vital, exceptionally old person, a clear rejoicing in ongoing life. Similarly, the end of the mural shows a celebration, the Oneg Shabbat, a holiday customarily celebrated at home which includes women and children and is associated with all that is intimate, safe, and loved. The Sabbath begins when the woman of the house lights the candles, bringing in the Sabbath and with it a foretaste of Paradise, for a Jew enters Paradise for this twenty-four-hour period.[5]

Together, the mural and the parade sketch the same shape: birth, struggle, and death; movement from home, into the world, and returning home; a rite of passage showing separation, liminality, and reaggregation. These are variations on the same theme, marking the movement through the primary stages of life, individually and collectively, macro- and microcosmically.

Clearly, we are justified in noting that the mural and the parade replicate each other; the mirrors show the same image. As texts, they are redundant. The performed text, the parade, was preceded in time by the inscribed one, the mural, which may have had some influence in shaping behavior. Certainly, no one consciously constructed the parade to conform to the mural. But remember that these people spend all day, every day, within walls that broadcast messages about who they are, what they do, how they do it, where they have come from, and where they are going. This must make a silent, steady impact on them. One might say that the idea of the mural shaped the behavior of the parade; but it is more fruitful, I think, to see them both as symbolic statements, performance and icons ricocheting off each other, dual reflecting surfaces that do more than merely mirror. The parade and the mural are mutual shapers of thought and action.[6]

In these texts we see a group of people creating themselves. The inner world, the more real one, they know they have made up. It is invisible to the outside world, sometimes even invisible to them, as many of its most important features are shadowy memories from the remote past. The membrane that separates the real invisible world from the unreal daily world of the present is permeable, like the curtain that separates the Balinese Topeng dancer from his audience, or the Indonesian *wayang kulit* screen on which shadows appear and dance, reflections of the "real" invisible world of heroes, gods, and demons. Just before he leaps into view, the Topeng dancer daringly shakes the curtain that separates the daily world from the world of illusion. When he bursts forth, we are reminded of the fragility of such boundaries. The imagination incarnated in action does not give us time to pause and consent. It is palpable and must be addressed. No matter how secular the setting, stepping from one world into another is a numinous moment, a hierophany, when the sacred shows through.

These old Jews know exactly what they are doing. Their highly developed reflexive consciousness does not impede their capacity to believe in their creations. Long ago they learned to make hidden, safe, self-determined worlds from within. To quote Shmuel again on his little town in Poland: "In that little town, there were no walls. But we were curled up together inside it, like small cubs, keeping each other warm, growing from within, never showing the outside what is happening, until our backs made up a stout wall." This was an important lesson, one that serves them well in America in their old age. Here, they do not remain inside, however. By enacting their dreams publicly, they have altered the world in which they live. As a result of their ceremonial parade, something has changed externally; through self-display, their commentary has persuaded outsiders to their own truth. Skillfully using strong symbols drawn from relevant, abutting social fields, the old Jews have managed to convey their statement to outsiders, to witnesses who then amplified and accredited their claims. Quite literally, they were taken in. A self-fulfilling prophecy and then some: the reality created by the elders' imaginative statements is not limited to their own minds and beliefs but has become true for nonbelievers, for nonmembers. As a result, the real world has been brought into conformity with imagination, by means of imaginative statements.

Lansing (n.d.) describes the Balinese as remarkable for their ability to "make up an invisible world, watching themselves make it up and still believe in it so strongly that they can enter it." These old Jews do likewise, separating the curtains between real and unreal, imagined and actual, to step across the threshold and draw with them, pulling behind them, witnesses who find, often to their surprise, that they are somehow participating in someone else's drama. They may not "believe" in the claims being made, nevertheless they are incorporated. Having stepped over the threshold, they become the "fifth-business," witnesses who push a plot forward almost unwittingly; their story is not wholly their own but lives on, woven into the stuff of other people's lives.

NOTES

This project was part of a larger study entitled "Social Contexts of Aging," funded by the National Science Foundation and administered through the Andrus Gerontology Center of the University of Southern California. A full description of the group appears in Myerhoff (1980). A film about the group, entitled "Number Our Days," was produced and directed by Lynne Littman for public television station KCET, Los Angeles, based on my fieldwork. The cultural festival referred to in note 2 was entitled "Life Not Death in Venice," after the parade. I would like to acknowledge the people who made it possible and to thank them for their generosity in helping to produce the festival and for assisting me in gathering the written and visual materials I needed to do this preliminary analysis. At the University of Southern California, Center for Visual Anthropology: Alexander Moore and Denise Lawrence; College of Continuing Education: Barbara Perrow; Department of Anthropology: Sherrie Wagner and Vikram Jayanti. Partial funding for portions of the festival was provided by the Ford Foundation and the California Council for the Humanities.

After much deliberation I decided to use real names in this paper, for the Center, the community, and the pertinent individuals. This is not consonant with general anthropological practice, which seeks to preserve the anonymity of the populations it studies. In this case, however, the groups' urgent desire to be recorded suggests that it is appropriate to name names; it is also consistent with the approach that they have pressed me to take and that I have agreed is suitable. In view of the wide distribution of the film about them, anonymity is not genuinely possible, in any case. Since I live in close proximity to these people and continue to be in contact with them, I regularly submit my writings and photographs to them for comment. There is usually some disagreement about my interpretations; sometimes I amend the original statements, sometimes I merely note that our views do not concur.

1. When I first began my work here, there were approximately ninety official members, though a great many more used the Center. At present there are close to four hundred members, due in part to increased publicity and activity and in part to the Center's relatively recent provision of daily, hot, inexpensive meals. At its farther reaches, the community of elderly Eastern European Jews within walking distance of the Center is estimated at between three and four thousand; thirty years ago there were approximately eight to ten thousand. Inadequate housing has helped to diminish the population and prevents others like them from moving into the area. The recent surge in membership of the Center does not represent recruitment either of people outside the neighborhood or of younger people. New members seem to be formerly peripheral individuals, nonjoiners, and the like who have decided to become affiliated for a variety of reasons.

2. Aware that these people sought attention above all, my own efforts were naturally directed toward promoting their visibility within the community and in relation to the outside society. By establishing life history classes and the like at the Center, I was able to offer additional arenas for them to present themselves

to each other. By sending my students to work with them, further channels for publicizing themselves were opened. The publication of my book about them helped, as did the "Life Not Death in Venice" art and cultural festival held at the University of Southern California in 1980, where the elderly and their art works, and scholars and artists who had worked in the same Eastern European cultural traditions, were brought together. The older people served as docents to their art works, and their life histories, collected by students, were presented along with the art. The subtext of this festival was to provide circumstances not only for the elderly to be seen and appreciated, but for them to be there when this occurred, seeing the public, artists, and scholars *seeing them*, thus assuring them of some of the cultural transmission which they so ardently sought. Perhaps the most important aspect of this part of my work came through the KCET film, shown on national television several times, which portrayed this community of elderly Jews to the largest audience available. The film sensitized outsiders to their presence, their difficulties, and their accomplishments, but it did not give the members the direct experience of becoming visible in the eyes of people immediately around them; hence the arrangement for this offered in the festival.

3. The discussion was organized and videotaped in connection with a grant from the California Council for the Humanities, to assess the impact of the artists and scholars involved in the festival on one another and to evaluate the effects on the artists of both themselves and their works being displayed in public.

4. This commentary was recorded on videotape and transcribed for inclusion of excerpts in this essay.

5. The association of fire, the lighting of the candles, with entering Paradise is very widespread. Here Paradise is clearly associated with a symbolic set: renewal, the transcendence of time and change, *illud tempus*, the return to eternal beginnings and origins, completion, fulfillment, and finally death, at least in mortal, temporal terms.

6. In a Nov. 1, 1982, letter to Ed Bruner, in response to his editorial suggestions, I wrote: "Certainly feel free to say that the parade and mural are not isomorphic—that is quite accurate. There is a metaphoric relation between them, with possible modeling of behavior—the parade—based on an image or story— the mural. Influence and metaphor, but not cause or isomorphism. And by all means do stress the openness and tension between these two forms of expression. That is indeed what makes it complex and interesting."

REFERENCES

Dilthey, Wilhelm. 1961. *Pattern and Meaning in History.* ed. H. P. Rickman. New York: Harper Torchbooks. (First published in 1910.)
Geertz, Clifford. 1973. *The Interpretation of Culture.* New York: Basic Books.
———. 1980. "Blurred Genres: The Refiguration of Social Thought," *American Scholar*, Spring, pp. 165–79.
Lansing, Stephen. n.d. "Reflexivity in Balinese Aesthetics." MS. Author's files.
Myerhoff, Barbara. 1980. *Number Our Days.* New York: Simon and Schuster.
Turner, Victor. 1974. *Dramas, Fields, and Metaphors: Symbolic Action in Human Society.* Ithaca, N.Y.: Cornell University Press.

PART FIVE

Enactments

12

Patronage and Control
in the
Trinidad Carnival

JOHN STEWART

Officially, the Trinidad carnival is a moveable feast which takes place annually on the weekend immediately preceding Ash Wednesday. However, this weekend is only the climactic period of a much longer season that begins with a few band fetes right after Christmas. During the weeks leading up to carnival Tuesday (*mardi gras*), the fetes increase in size, variety, and number. Social, ethnic, cultural, and sports clubs, service and civic organizations, diplomatic units, and many individual citizens are the sponsors; while some fetes are small at-home parties catering to groups of relatives, friends, and selected invitees, others are mass events held in large halls, parking lots, and other open spaces. For some fetes there is no charge to the revelers; others are investment affairs on which sponsors plan to realize a profit. All feting is marked by abundant drinking, eating, and dancing to the season's calypsos, in an atmosphere of festive release.

Along with the fetes, the carnival season is marked also by other display and performance events, several of which are competitive. Calypso tents are open nightly, beginning in the second week after New Year's. Here, in a concert-theatrical context, new compositions are rendered-performed. Tents compete with each other for patrons, and individual calypsonians compete against one another for popularity, acclaim, and nomination as the national calypso king of the season. Lesser calypso competitions are also organized among schools and various employee groups. Organized carnival costume competitions are held at both the child and adult levels. Children compete as individuals, as members of school bands, or as members of informally organized bands patterned after the main bands which take part in the national competition on carnival Tuesday. Many business and commercial establishments run "queen" competitions among their employees, in which individuals win honors for costume and personality displays. There is also a national carnival king and queen of the bands competition, featuring several elimination events from which winners then go on to the final contest on carnival Sunday (*dimanche gras*). A steel band competition—"panorama"—is similarly organized, with elimination rounds held in various parts of the country during the season and those winners playing in the final competition on the Saturday of carnival weekend. In the rural areas where stick-fighting (*calinda*) is still performed, *gayals* open on the weekend after New Year's, and the drums then play every weekend until the grand Tuesday. When the recently developed series of "after-carnival" shows and entertainments—designed mainly for tourists but heavily patronized by locals—which extends into the middle weeks of Lent is taken into consideration, it becomes clear that for almost one-third of the year carnival accounts for a significant share of all public events in Trinidad. In fact, carnival is unsurpassed by any other form of public festivity.

Preparation for all the various carnival competitions and performances constitutes a bustle of activity which begins long before the opening fetes of the season. Costume design, the assembling of materials (much of which must be imported), and the mobilization of necessary sculpting, tailoring, and construction skills; the preparation of drums and the practice of performance pieces among steel bands; the preparation of sticks among stickmen; the composition and arrangement of new songs by calypsonians and their specialist assistants; the production of printed materials for advertising and other purposes; the organization of time, space, and committees of judges for the various competitions—all of these involve much preseason and in-season activity which spreads the influence of carnival into time and performance contexts far beyond those of the actual celebration.

There are those who regard each Ash Wednesday as the first day of preparation for the next carnival. Such extremists betray an addiction to the festival experienced by many Trinidadians, especially those who live abroad, to one degree or another. Wherever Trinidadians have settled in sufficient numbers—Toronto, Harlem, Brooklyn, London, the outskirts of Caracas—they have taken carnival with them. Yet great numbers troop back home annually from these and other places for the master celebration. For them, carnival stands as a time of renewal, of self-affirmation, which can occur in no other way. To miss carnival is to be diminished.

By contrast, an increasing number of locals, even while they enjoy the fetes, calypsos, and pageantry as social or aesthetic events, place neither psychic nor symbolic burden on the festival. They treat it as a series of happenings to be enjoyed, perhaps, but then abandoned—or ignored altogether—with no profound engagement of the self in the process. For them, to analogize carnival as street theater (Hill 1972; Manning 1978), the suspension of disbelief which lies close to the heart of theatrical success is not suitably attained. In the past, many Trinidadians who abstained from the carnival did so for religious reasons—it was licentious and therefore evil. Recent withdrawal has less to do with religion than with a feeling of encroaching emptiness in the festival.

A factor which may be contributing to this alternate way of experiencing the carnival, that of partial but uncritical withdrawal, is the increased politicization of the festival. The Trinidad carnival has never occurred in an atmosphere of political neutrality; but whereas in the past the festival construed an alternate context with reflexive and rebellious potentials, in recent times it has become more openly an extension of a moderating (modernizing) process central to the overall objectives of current political leadership. These objectives may be summarized as follows: (1) to maintain control over leadership offices; (2) to manage public belief and sentiment toward a continued recognition of influence and power in these offices; and (3) to cultivate the imagery of a society transcending the culpabilities of racial, social, and cultural divisiveness inherited from the colonial past. These objectives are not in themselves unique to Trinidad, but the particular historical and sociocultural circumstances underlying their adumbration in the carnival make for an interesting case.

During the eighteenth century the Spanish, who had not accomplished much in developing Trinidad as a colony, revised their immigration policies to allow Catholics from friendly nations to enter the island as settlers. Many colonists from Grenada, Guadeloupe, Haiti, Martinique, Dominica, and other French-controlled territories took advantage of this policy and relocated in Trinidad. French and Creole planters with their slaves, many free colored, came in such rapid numbers that by the last decade of that century the Francophone settlers constituted more than 75 percent of the island's population (Pearse 1956).

Bringing with them a patois, a Creole cuisine, and a generally vigorous level of economic and social activity, these settlers quickly transformed Trinidad from a backwater Spanish colony into a lucrative economic base, with a popular culture in which the "bon vivant" was idealized (Ottley 1974). With the use of increased African slave labor they established several successful sugar plantations, and some assumed leadership roles in the business and civic communities. The French and Creoles were, in fact, the dominant cultural and civic force in the colony when the Spanish ceded it to the English in 1797 (Williams 1962).

Class stratification and a color-caste system were well-known features of the social structure in Franco-Caribbean territories during the eighteenth century (Leiris 1955; James 1963). Along with the major color categories "white," "black," and "gens de couleur," whites were further subdivided into "grand-blancs" and "petit-blancs," and gens de couleur into as many as 128 subdivisions based on the degree to which white ancestry was integrated into a particular lineage (James 1963:38). Blacks and whites were integrated into the social system as economic, cultural, and political opposites; the mulattoes ranged between these two poles (James 1963; Harris 1964). As Trinidad passed from Spanish to British sovereignty, the population enlarged and became more diversified both racially and culturally. In the eleven years preceeding the census of 1808, the African slave population more than doubled, from 10,000 to 22,000 (Williams 1962). In that same period a number of Chinese, Corsicans, Germans, and other Europeans entered the colony as laborers or settlers (Wood 1968). They were followed in the next decade by small numbers of freed blacks from the United States, demobilized Creole and African recruits from the West Indian regiments, and émigrés from Venezuela (Laurence 1963), each group bearing its own set of ethnic traditions. Even for the West Indies the ethnic mix in Trinidad during the early nineteenth century was remarkable. In spite of the British attempt to impose an Anglican culture through institutional means, the island "was taking on the cosmopolitan, almost Levantine atmosphere which it has never lost and Port-of-Spain was becoming a restless Caribbean Alexandria where people of different cultures came together and where the texture of life was quite unlike that of Kingston, Bridgetown, Fort-de-France, or even Havana..." (Wood 1968:44). In this milieu the caste system based on racial, religious, and national characteristics was nevertheless quite seriously maintained.

Within the upper class, the British distinguished themselves from the French, whom they labeled as "foreigners" and "interlopers," even though the French had a longer presence in the colony. Ascription was the prerogative of those in power, and the system of discrimination imposed by the British emphasized color-class discontinuities to a degree much greater than had previously been the case. This was felt particularly by the middle-class *gens de couleur.* They continued to hold themselves aloof from the blacks politically, socially, and culturally, but their own assumed inferiority provided a basis for successive British governors to systematically challenge, and in some cases reduce, the rights they had enjoyed under the Spanish (Campbell 1981). The Chinese and other nonblack laborers fell above blacks on the color scale, but by virtue of their economic status and cultural differences were regarded as inferior by both whites and the colored middle class. At the bottom of the society remained the blacks, both slave and free, with the former a source of serious concern to the upper-class planters and property holders on the eve of their emancipation in the 1830s.

Not only were the planters, English and French, concerned about the loss of property and labor which emancipation entailed, they were concerned as well over the potential loss of cultural control in the colony. They had consistently advocated a process which through criminal labeling and other forms of intimidation had prevented African culture from attaining public legitimacy (Trotman 1981); and now, with emancipation would come a challenge to the hegemony they had constructed (Burnley 1842). So serious was the fear of "savage retaliation" on the part of former slaves that authorities took armed precaution on the day emancipation was announced (Trotman 1981). Apart from a mild gathering in the capital city of Port-of-Spain, however, there was no mass violence following the official announcement. Instead, many of the freed laborers turned their backs on the sugar field and became independent squatters on crown lands (Burnley 1842). To replace them as a reliable source of cheap labor, East Indian indentures were brought in.

Between 1845 and 1917 approximately 142,000 East Indians

were indentured to various estates throughout the colony (Weller 1968). Initially, they were restricted to the estates to which they were assigned and were housed, fed, and clothed in a manner reminiscent of that endured by the former slaves. This placed them immediately at the bottom of the social hierarchy. As latecomers, and also because of their racial and cultural differences, East Indians were heavily disparaged and discriminated against by all other groups in the society. For their part, they returned much of the discrimination. Unlike the black descendants of African slaves, they were not generations removed from an original and highly developed culture. Many had migrated from India as families, and they had a sufficiency of population and cultural specialists to constitute themselves as a separate community. On the sugar estates where they were isolated both socially and politically, and as long as they did not constitute a "public nuisance," they were relatively free to maintain what they could of their own culture.

After their period of indentureship, many Indians settled villages of their own adjacent to the estates which continued to provide them employment. Some became landed peasants. Together they maintained practically self-contained communities where their religions (Hinduism and Islam), marriage and culinary customs, and to some extent their language and dress were retained with much integrity. A few were converted to Christianity, but on the whole the East Indians maintained their own ritual calendar, celebrating festivals such as Muharram (Hosay), Diwali, Phagwa (Holi), among others (Jha 1973). The pattern of isolation and internal cultivation of an ethnic identity lasted well beyond the end of indenture in 1917, and so the Indians thrived. By the 1950s, Indians comprised approximately one-third of the island's population. They had improved their economic and social statuses significantly and had developed a strong religious-political leadership. An inspiration behind their development and improvement was a sense of themselves as isolated aliens in a hostile milieu. They maintained an intense identification with mother India: "The independence of India in 1947 and the inauguration of the Republic of India in 1950 was celebrated with jubilation by the Indians of Trinidad. Now that their mother country was free they would not suffer from an inferiority complex. Soon new Indian youth and other organizations were set up. Hindu and Muslim schools started teaching Hindi, Urdu and religion. . ." (Jha 1973:46).

During the last years of the 1950s, the changes that would lead from a colonial to an independent government in Trinidad also came to a climax. A populist movement following World War I and then a strong union movement in the 1930s had succeeded in both organizing workers in the major industries (sugar and petroleum) and in providing a form of political representation for the working class who essentially had no voice in the colony's formal legislature. Adult suffrage, granted in the late 1940s further accelerated the organization of politically oriented associations among workers and other interest groups. By 1955 the popular appeal for a voice in government graduated to a call for complete independence from colonial rule. This independence movement, spearheaded by a cadre of black intellectuals, led directly to the emergence of a broad-based political party, the People's National Movement (PNM). Strong support among nonwhite Creoles throughout the society was quickly mobilized, but the main Indian leadership and the Indian masses, as well as expatriate whites and other elites, either opposed the independence movement or were neutral. Several competitive political parties came into existence, including one headed by the old union leadership, but the one that emerged as the best-endowed opposition to the PNM was the Democratic Labor Party (DLP), a substantially Indian organization.

With the coming of party politics, the quest for control of the political process led to a rallying of entrenched racial, cultural, and social antipathies. Politically, the society fissioned into three major factions directly linked to its racial, cultural, and social discontinuities: an elite alliance including mostly whites with a few upper-class Asiatics and mulattoes; an Indian faction integrating various economic and social classes but based on racial and cultural solidarity; and a nonwhite Creole faction including various classes but based on racial and social-cultural affinities. The anticipation of dramatic change within the society during the late 1950s promoted a generally liminal atmosphere centered around the electoral process. Election campaigns were heated mixtures of scholarship, demagoguery, and satirical debate. Racial slurring between Indians and nonwhite Creoles was acrimonious and led in some instances to outright violence.

In urban and rural areas, neighbors who had quietly adjusted themselves to their place in the social, cultural, and economic hierarchy under colonialism swiftly became antagonistic party supporters. Calypsonians composed songs extolling the character of certain political leaders and ridiculing others. In their public debates, political candidates adopted a folk-rhetorical style and language to emphasize their identification with the masses. Political parties "invaded" each others' neighborhoods and financed much fete and feasting. Motorcades crisscrossed the countryside, and flamboyant spokesmen entertained crowds with witty assaults against opposing candidates.

When local control of the government was achieved in the late 1950s, the predominantly nonwhite Creole political party won the right to leadership. The Indian party formed the opposition, and the elites had already begun to withdraw from institutional politics. Political leadership in the newly independent but culturally and socially plural state was confirmed as a sectional property. And while sectional integrity may have been a convenience during the colonial regime, it was clearly an obstacle to the image and achievement of independent nationhood. The black leadership therefore acquired at once the problem of protecting the offices they had achieved, in a mistrusting atmosphere, while promoting a belief system that could be the basis for widespread cooperation and development of a cohesive society. This is reflected in the phrase coined as a national motto in those early days: DISCIPLINE, PRODUCTION, TOLERANCE. This motto at once expresses an ideal and the pathway to achievement of that ideal.

The black political leadership has been able to maintain itself in power for more than twenty years without interruption. The strategies underlying this dominance have often played on traditional racial and social rivalries between blacks and Indians, particularly since the opposition remains a predominantly Indian party. At the same time, the effort has been to cultivate a national cultural presence based on remnant traditions and contemporary elements from African, European, American, and Asiatic sources. Functioning as the stem for this cultural alliance is the broadly Afro-based Creole heritage, and nowhere is this pattern more clearly elaborated than in the carnival.

Social divisiveness, economic dependency, and cultural underdevelopment have long been recognized as serious problems in West Indian societies (Smith 1965; Mintz 1974). Absentee ownership and multinational corporate control over the economy (Beckford 1972), a tyrannous but regenerate middle class (Guerin 1961), mental and psychological colonization (Fanon 1967), and a debilitating ethnic competition over slender resources (Despres 1975) have all been postulated as explanations of the poverty, pluralism, cultural conflict, and political corruption observed in the region, as well as the tensions they manifest. Every West Indian society is challenged by racism, class and color discrimination, sexism, and alienation between the business and political leaderships and the masses. While tensions are not so wholly formalized in Trinidad as to rigidly oppose black against white or mulatto, Creole against Indian, rurals against urbanites, rich against poor, lower class against upper class, the mildly subterranean conflicts are nevertheless quite real and involve shifting discretions and alliances linked to particular issues. For instance, Creole and Indian businessmen would combine their efforts to determine or defeat government regulations, while at the same time being very discriminating in their conduct—business and social—with each other on the basis of race, class, ethnicity, or color. Residential neighborhoods and schools carry class and cultural insignia, even though they may be interracial with no viable social contact between races—except insofar as representation or defense of the unit may be at issue. Individuals prize and maintain great sovereignty over their allegiance and recognize separate interactional domains such as the personal, the intimate informal, the public informal, and the public formal, as contexts each with its own level of discretion. In such an atmosphere friendship stands out as a relational category which often transcends or balances the constraints of family, race, neighborhood, and background, but seldom class. Privately, Trinidadians often complain about the pressures they experience in negotiating their everyday lives. They complain of the constant need to be assertive, the constant vigilance they must practice to avoid being misused or abused, the unrelievedly ad hoc and competitive texture of their society.

Fetes are a good and standard way to relieve this tension (Freilich 1970). In the throes of a fete it is not unusual for Trinidadians to assert, particularly to strangers, that theirs is a free and easy society, with no formidable hostility between races such as in the United States or South Africa; no religious intolerance such as in India or Iran; no ethnic wars such as in Nigeria or Southeast

Asia. They will point to the very ease with which the corruption that pains them takes place and goes unpunished in the society as evidence of its "open" nature, its "sweetness." Indeed, the ethos of openness and sweetness is a central characteristic of the fete. Fetes are social events at which the experience of friendship is enacted; they are events at which friendship may be initiated or vitalized. But they are also events at which pseudo-friendships may be instrumented on behalf of some practical need. If your child is having difficulty getting into a particular school, give the teachers and other officials a fete. If you want to cultivate the support of a particular person or social group for business, social, or political purposes, give that person or group a fete. And so on. The fete therefore becomes an arena in which Trinidadians both endorse themselves and exploit each other. One's presence at a fete, while a satisfying experience in itself, may also produce an aggrandized awareness of oneself and one's value to others. And the grandest fete of all, that in which the ethos of an "open" and "sweet" society is gloriously and dramatically presented, is the carnival.

When the carnival bands parade through the city streets of Port-of-Spain on carnival Monday morning (*jouvet*), and then again on carnival Tuesday afternoon, they create a panoramic view of thousands of men, women, and children, all bearing African, Asiatic, European, or mixed features, dancing to the same music. Obviously, not all of these people enjoy the same social or economic circumstance, but they appear as a people who find too great a joy in being themselves to entertain rancour against their neighbors. All racial and color groups are represented in the parade. Dressed down or dressed up, in costume or casual attire, they share food and drink, they strut, they "wyne," they jump and march to the beat of steel bands, brass bands, and amplified recorded music, chanting refrains from the season's calypsos. They hug each other openly, and although miscues may cause brief and minor altercations, by far the greatest emphasis is on submission to the music, the dance, the motion of liminal conviviality. The carnival has not always been this way.

According to the accepted records (Hill 1972), carnival was brought to Trinidad by the French and French Creole settlers during the 1780s. Among them were planters, entrepreneurs, and bureaucrats who developed a comfortable colonial lifestyle, with some pretensions to a gay and witty haute société. Dividing their time between their rural estates and city residences, they dressed in the courtly or popular French manner, maintained salons, and toasted themselves with imported wines. They hosted lavish dinners, balls, soirées, and hunting parties, and institutionalized the fete as the most important form of social entertainment (Ottley 1974).

Between Christmas and Ash Wednesday they observed a social season of ritual merrymaking and elegant divertissements which began with celebrations surrounding the nativity and culminated with the *mardi gras*. The Spanish may have celebrated a carnival prior to the influx of the French, but it was with the latter—and particularly as an aspect of their flair for good living—that the carnival developed into an event of consequence (Ottley 1974). The fat days (*dimanche, lundi,* and *mardi*) were observed with excessive feasting and entertainments principally among the island's elites; carnival was essentially an urban festival of the salon. Military bands performed, and there were street masquerades in decorated carriages and on foot, but costumed balls and festive play took place mainly in private and semiprivate ballrooms and in the salons and courtyards of the leading citizens. Revelers engaged in comic buffoonery, witty verbal encounters, and other mischievous play with one another (Hill 1972).

In this seminal period of the carnival, African and Creole slaves were barred from participating in the festival. The free colored were permitted to have separate celebrations, but these were limited to lesser imitations of the elite fetes. Costumes and dances borrowed from the European gala dominated the balls and pageant, although some individuals among the planter class did disguise themselves in the dress of their male garden slaves and their female servants.

The *nègre de jardin* (garden slave) costume, consisting of rags (or fine garments converted into rags) decorated with bits of ribbon, beads, and colored stitches, eventually became a popular costume in those early days. The mulattress costume imitated the flamboyant extravagance of mulattress dress—a bright madras head-kerchief, colorful scarf, long-sleeved bodice, and long high-waisted skirt over several billowing petticoats trimmed with lace. Bunched earrings, strings of beads around the neck, and various bright pins completed this costume. While in real life the *nègre de jardin* was the human chattel whose labor made the earth productive, the mulattress was recognized as the arch seductress—the secret or not so secret concubine, the mistress of occult powers who could bewilder, bewitch, and dominate even the most astute man.

Cannes brulées, or runaway cane fires, were in real life alarming occurrences. Fire was used to prepare canefields for harvesting by removing excess cane blades as well as snakes, wasps, and other vermin which habitually nested in the fields. But fields that were burned before they could be promptly harvested yielded a net loss in sugar. The runaway cane fire therefore threatened not only the fortune of the individual planter but that of the society as a whole, since the general economy was based on sugar production. When such fires occurred, they precipitated a great deal of excitement: "... slaves on the surrounding properties were immediately mustered and marched to the spot, horns and shells were blown to collect them and the gangs were followed by the drivers cracking their whips and urging with cries and blows to their work" (Hill 1972:23). Sometime in the early nineteenth century a performance which caricatured the *canne brulée* was added to the carnival. For this performance elite males wore the *nègre de jardin* costume and the women masqueraded as mulattresses. They danced to African drum rhythms and carried open torches through the streets in a nighttime procession (Hill 1972).

Following the emancipation of slaves in 1838, the laboring class developed a commemorative festival of their own which integrated some elements of the elite fete with forms and performances that were discretely of slave or lower-class Creole origins. At this festival, which occurred in August, "kings" and "queens" were selected, religious ceremonies were performed, and the *canne brulée*—localized as *canboulay*—soon became the centerpiece of a street parade. The commemorative festival itself came to be known as *canboulay*. In this celebration lower-class blacks introduced the traditions of *calinda,* a plantation dance, and stick-fighting, a ritual combat form grafted onto the *calinda,* into the public domain.

While both men and women danced the *calinda,* stick-fighting emerged as a masculine ritual form, a medium through which individual men could express their power and dominance over others. It is not clear whether stick-fighting was brought to the

West Indies by African slaves or whether it was borrowed from the Amerindians. In any case, combattants armed with hardwood sticks faced each other in pairs, and to the accompaniment of *calinda* chants and drumming strove to deliver the most telling blows to their opponents' heads or other parts of the body. Stick-fighting and *calinda* were combined into a single form within the *canboulay;* and the dramatic power of this combined form was great enough so that it tended to dominate the celebration. When, sometime in the mid-nineteenth century, celebration of the *canboulay* was shifted from August to coincide with the pre-Lenten carnival, the fighting and general misconduct among *canboulay* bands overtook the carnival. The upper classes complained, and steps were taken to curb the *canboulay*.

The earliest government restrictions against *canboulay* bands were passed during the 1840s, and over the next forty years, by ordinance after ordinance, the police were empowered to prohibit revelers from wearing face masks, blowing horns, playing noisy instruments, carrying torches, stick-fighting, drumming, and singing obscene songs. The *canboulay* bands did not readily submit to these prohibitions and instead vigorously struggled to maintain their style of celebration. Consequently, during the latter half of the nineteenth century, carnival became a period marked by rioting as bands resisted the police who sought to enforce official prohibitions. Violence on carnival days made the streets truly unsafe, and by 1869 "the ruling class and the white community had taken themselves completely out of the carnival" (Elder 1966:97). Serious confrontation between the bands and the authorities came to a climax in a legendary "battle" of 1881. Rebellious masqueraders, led by stick-fighters, stood against a combined force of police, local military units, and soldiers from a visiting warship. Many people were severely injured. And although several stickmen fought valiantly, the bands lost the confrontation. In 1884 *canboulay* was officially abolished.

With the *canboulay* bands in check, the elites gradually returned to participating in the street masquerade on carnival days, but they remained aloof from lower-class elements. They turned out in carriages, cars, and as small bands in decorated lorries (Hill 1972:100). For the greatest part they returned to enjoying carnival as an indoor event fashioned around masquerade balls, house parties, and social club affairs. British colonial officials were

prominent in this form of celebrating. Balls were led by the governor and his entourage, which included visiting dignitaries and
military officers. Historical characters and court styles from the
past reappeared at these costume affairs, and a staged pageant
highlighted by a series of acts around historical or courtly themes
eventually came to be a regular feature of this renewed elite
carnival.

Although *canboulay* bands were outlawed, the black laboring
class did not give up participation in the carnival. They continued
to enjoy their own fetes and developed a number of masquerades
in street performances. The "midnight robber," the "jab-jab," the
"pierrot," all masques whose performances emphasized competition in speech and mock combat, became popular (Crowley 1956).
So too did the "devil" masquerade in which revelers painted their
naked bodies in black, red, or blue and wore tails and horns in
fearsome caricature of the arch demon. Other supernatural
characters such as the vampire and the diablesse made their appearance. The stilt dancer (*moko jumbie*) also became a popular
street masque, and calypso came increasingly to be the music of
street dancing (Elder 1966; Hill 1972).

Like the *canboulay* procession before it, *jouvet* came to comprise
the ritual opening up of the streets at dawn on *lundi gras*. The
central inspiration in the *jouvet* was ribald mockery. Dressed in
rags, bed sheets, and banana leaves and other branches, players
presented graphic caricatures of high-profile personalities and officials in the colony. Men dressed in women's clothes and women
dancing in men's clothes parodied the relations between the sexes.
Others in diapers or ethnic garb parodied childhood and ethnic
peculiarities. With the *calinda* drum banned from the public domain (although the *calinda* itself had not entirely disappeared, and
stick-fighters with their drummers still played where the police did
not disturb them), *jouvet* bands accompanied themselves with
"bamboo-tamboo" (bamboo drums) or tin-pan bands. Upper-
and middle-class bands also appeared in this parade.

Despite the role reversals and other kinds of play acted out
in the *jouvet*, as a result of the actual separation between classes in
the society, the early twentieth-century carnival developed on two
distinct planes: as a rowdy, superstitious, always potentially
violent carnival of the masses, and as a carnival of glitter and
stiff-backed decorum among the upper classes. With the latter, the

carnival continued to be approached as an extension of European culture; while among the masses, the forging of a locally based and nurtured celebration remained the dominant pattern. Among the "cultured" middle class, carnival reflected the cultural ambivalence which affected them and came to be an important context within which this ambivalence could be addressed. From early on they had mixed attitudes toward the *canboulay* carnival, as indeed they had toward much of local culture. The agony of this class was the discrimination it suffered at the hands of whites who ignored the coloreds' deep desire to be recognized as equals in both culture and citizenship. In accounting for the absence of a tradition of assertion among the colored middle class in Trinidad, it has been observed that, "On rare occasions they would make a protest and, the ultimate pitch of rebellion, go to the Colonial Office. They did not do any more because all they aimed at was being admitted to the ruling circle of expatriates and local whites. More than that they did not aspire to. . . . For generations their sole aim in life was to be admitted to the positions to which their talents and education entitled them, and from which they were unjustly excluded" (James 1973:82).

In the carnival, the Creole middle class could share in the powerful spirit of fete as expressed by their social inferiors, but they balked at the extremes in expression. They had little taste for fighting, bloodletting, and public eroticism. They were among the most virulent critics of these "vulgar" elements of the street festival. At the same time, an invitation to the upper-class ball was for many of them a social achievement. It gave them the opportunity to locate, if only temporarily, in the social atmosphere to which they aspired. Others, considered by class affiliates as derelict or perverse, took their places in the street festival as players, band organizers, and on occasion as stick-fighting aficionados.

Carnival was banned for a short period during World War I. In its revival between 1919 and 1941, the separate levels of celebration were maintained but the middle class took a more active role. Although they still appeared in the *jouvet*, their great concentration came in the carnival queen contest on *dimanche gras* and the fantasy and historical bands of the *mardi gras* pageant. It is in this era that the street celebration assumed a sequencing characterized as "acts" (Hill 1972:85). *Jouvet* bands opened the streets on carnival Monday and dominated them until mid-morning; then followed the traditional masques—clowns, minstrels, maypole dancers, etc.—parading in small groups or as individuals until noon. Military bands and small bands wearing original costumes came out in the early afternoon, followed by the big historical bands in fine satin costumes and the individual depictions extraordinaire, which dominated until dusk. From dusk until midnight, daytime bands partially broke up and throngs gathered around the best musicians for the night's "jump-up." When elites and the "cultured" middle class participated in the street parade, they did so in bands comprised of their own cohorts. They seldom appeared in the mid-morning or midday "acts," and they seldom remained in the streets for the night's "jump-up."

On carnival Tuesday there was no *jouvet*. Individual masques and small fancy bands came out during mid-morning, and by noon the historical and grand fantasy bands were on the streets. Beginning at dusk there was again a general "jump-up" which lasted until midnight. During this last "jump-up," or *las lap*, particularly, fraternizing between the classes approached its most daring. Under cover of darkness and lost in the throng, people struck up acquaintances they seldom would have in other circumstances, and often promptly ceased to observe them once the carnival was over. Such fraternizing was a highly personalized matter; it seldom included expatriate whites and other elites but was mainly an affair of the blacks and mulattos from among the working and middle classes.

During World War II carnival celebrations were again suspended. Following their resumption in 1946, the steel band quickly replaced the "bamboo-tamboo" as the festival music among the lower classes. As with the earlier *canboulay* bands, steel bands came to be an organizational focus for black males, a mechanism for the expression of dominance and intimidation at both the individual and group levels. Neighborhood rivalries and the cultivation of individual reputations brought steel bandsmen into direct confrontation with each other in the streets, and once again the festival was marked by serious fighting. Heavily influenced by an American military presence on the island during the war, and by films depicting Allied heroisms, steel bands adopted names such as "Casablanca," "The Cross of Lorraine," "Invaders," "The Fighting Free French," and "Tokyo." Unlike the *battoniers* of an earlier era who fought with sticks, these bandsmen fought with knives, cutlasses, rocks, and razors.

There was a general outcry against these bands, and as before the police were called on to subdue them. Steel-bandsmen spent a good deal of their time in the late 1940s and early 1950s combating the police or facing the law in magistrates' courts. Old arguments which identified drum beating and working-class violence as retardant hooliganisms resurfaced, and it was several years before steel band music came to be broadly accepted. But this music, made initially from discarded oil drums, bits of pipe, and old car hubs, developed into an internationally accepted form.

By the emergence of cabinet government in 1959, the steel band was being established as Trinidad's unique gift to the musical world. Simultaneously, the calypso, that other lower-class musical form associated with the carnival, was gaining in acceptance and respectability. Acceptance of the steel band and the calypso was facilitated through local support by a few elites and professional promoters, and by acknowledgment of both forms in England and the United States as unique expressions of Trinidadian culture. Such recognition encouraged the local middle class to take pride in both forms and to claim them as expressions of a cultural genius belonging to the society at large.

With their escalating acceptance as indigenous alternatives to colonial culture, the steel band and calypso presented themselves as the nucleus around which a cultural movement mirroring substantiating the political movement for national independence could develop. Both steel band and calypso came together in the carnival. Therefore, the shift in cultural taste, as well as the politically charged context of the carnival itself, had an important bearing on both festival policy and performance as these developed under the independent political leadership. In the late 1960s the Trinidad government recognized that "there is also lacking institutional means of strengthening the psychological and cultural identity of the people of the Nation, such as indigenously owned and controlled mass media, publicly sponsored institutions for promoting indigenous culture, a distinctive architectural style, etc." (*Third Five-Year Plan* 1970:3).

In the policy designed to correct this deficiency, bolstering of a national cultural identity was pragmatically linked with development of the tourist trade. Local culture was conceptualized as both industry and commodity within the entertainment field, and government planners were confident that this approach would produce enviable results: "With our unique and vibrant culture, it is not too much to expect that over the years Trinidad and To-bago will become as noted for its Annual Festivals as other places" (Third Five-Year Plan 1970:264). Under this policy, the main annual festival, carnival, was to be pursued as a venture in cultural patriotism under the direction of a central carnival development committee (CDC).

The success of the centralized CDC has had an undeniable effect on carnival as a national experience. During its twenty-five years under this committee's guidance, the national festival has evolved into a series of staged, competitive performances for both adults and children. There are islandwide competitions for steel bands, costuming, and calypso singing. These competitions begin with preliminary or elimination contests weeks before the carnival weekend, and preliminary winners must also win in semifinal competitions before advancing to the finals, which are judged during carnival weekend. Some preliminary and semifinal events are scheduled for the outlying areas, but most of the staged competitions take place at a single venue: the Queen's Park Savannah in Port-of-Spain. National television coverage, however, brings all events into the homes of viewers around the country as television ownership is widespread.

In the steel band competition prizes are awarded in two categories: old-time steel band, or "pan-around-the-neck," and conventional steel bands; a grand prize is awarded to the winner in the conventional category at the Panorama finals on carnival Saturday night. Among calypsonians eight finalists appear in the finals at the Dimanche Gras show on carnival Sunday night, and the winner is declared calypso king for a year. In costuming, there is a competition among "kings," another among "queens," and another among bands in several categories. Among the "kings" and "queens" eight finalists are selected during elimination contests, and overall winners are declared after these eight appear on stage during the Dimanche Gras show. The best bands competitions take place on days when street parades are allowed. The children's bands parade takes place on carnival Saturday, and adult bands are judged on both carnival Monday and Tuesday.

For the bands competition prizes are awarded in twenty major costume categories, a best-band-of-the-day category, and three categories according to size—small bands (25–250 members), medium-sized bands (251–600 members), and large bands (601 or more members). The largest bands number between 3,500 and 4,000. Apart from the competition among "kings" and "queens," there is also an individual costume competition in which prizes are awarded in twenty-six categories. Bands receive prizes for being judged first, second, third, or fourth in the competition. Individuals receive prizes up to seventh place in each costume category and up to tenth place for overall male and female winners. Prizes are also awarded in eight skills and design categories: wire skills—two dimensions; wire skills—three dimensions; metal skills; aluminum skills; molding; carving; bands designer; and individual designer.

All prizes are cash payments, and while not large, they are many. In 1983, for example, 516 prizes were awarded, with the lowest at $130 for seventh place in the individual "sailors-on-shore-leave" costume category. Among other prizes, the king and queen of carnival winners received $2,040 each, while the calypso monarch received $8,800. All entrants in the CDC finals received an appearance fee: for calypsonians, $600; "king" and "queen" competitors, $1,000 each; large bands, $750; and individuals (costume), $150 each (*CDC Guide to Participation* 1983). Along with prizes and appearance fees, the CDC paid transportation fees for competitors and absorbed all the site preparation, utilities, and service costs involved in actually staging the competitions.

The inducing subsidies of cash and acclaim are to some extent balanced by a series of constraints for all those who participate in the CDC competitions. Competitors are required to "obey and comply with all instructions given by the Stage Manager or Stage Director or the authorized official of the Carnival Development Committee in and concerning the presentation of the show in which the competitor takes part," on pain of being disqualified with no appearance fees and no eligibility for being judged in the competition (*CDC Guide to Participation* 1983). Contestants whose costumes are judged to be "substandard" are not permitted to participate, and immediate disqualification is faced by those whose stage presentation is judged to be lewd, vulgar, or obscene. These inducements and constraints, along with easy access to the broadcast media and control of the main venues by the CDC have brought about a uniformity in the carnival which some find unrewarding.

Along with the CDC venue, there are two other sites in Port-of-Spain where bands may compete on carnival days. In outlying municipalities local "carnival improvement committees" conduct competitions based on the CDC Port-of-Spain model, for which they receive some subsidy from the central committee in the way of services and minor funding. Committee membership in both the development committee and the improvement committees tend to reflect membership or other supportive relationships with the ruling political party.

Altogether, official competitions account for a sizable percentage of time, energy, and attention given to the carnival, which has resulted in near complete domination of the public festival by these staged performances. When a local editor complained that "the time has come to return carnival to the streets" (Boyke 1981:9), he was voicing a sentiment felt by a growing number of Trinidadians against the overwhelming domination of the staged carnival and the constraints it imposes on certain traditions. One tradition in particular about which many are concerned is the parade of steel bands, sometimes in costume, through the streets on carnival Monday and Tuesday: "Only a few steelbands still produce costumed bands for Carnival. . . . By Monday afternoon though, pan is almost totally disinherited, still the outcast, its followers lost to funk, punk, reggae and rock. Yet, a steelband has won the Band of the Year title in competition with all time great mas men. Can this ever happen again?" (Boyke 1981:9). Described as "an endangered carnival species," the steel band has faded from the street parade to such a degree that a group of entrenched panmen were leaving Trinidad on carnival weekend 1984 for a concert appearance in Minnesota (Cliff Alexis, 1984 personal communication). Yet, the steel band was at the core of another old tradition which has itself also gone into decline—the *las lap*, or postpageant street dancing from dusk to midnight on carnival Tuesday.

The absence of steel bands in the street parades is linked to a long-standing disaffection between the CDC and the steelbandsmen organization, Pan Trinbago, over appearance fees and other awards associated with participation in the carnival. Many panmen who regard their music as the centerpiece of the carnival cultural complex feel that steel bands deserve more money and finer consideration for their participation in the festival. Also, among masquerade bandleaders and others associated with the costumed bands competition, many cite problems with fees, personnel management, and choreographic display as reasons why they choose the more compact sound truck (live or electronic) over steelbands for their accompanying music.

The limited capacity of the Queen's Park stage has led to a second frustrating aspect of the official carnival. Most bands begin their parade through the street on Tuesday morning between 9:00 and 11:00. By early afternoon there is a general convergence at the Queen's Park Savannah, and the route leading onto the stage is jammed with thousands of players waiting their turn to cross before the judges. They must wait, pressed by thousands of spectators outside the gates, because a single large band with 3,500 members divided into several sections sometimes takes longer than an hour to get on and off the stage. The impulse to excess and ribaldry during this wait must also be contained because costumes must remain fresh and the masqueraders ready to perform their dance before the judges. But for many, waiting in some semblance of order to "jump" across the Queen's Park stage before the judges and television cameras is not what "playin *mas*" is truly about. Some of those who have suffered the frustration of getting costumed by mid-morning, then standing in jammed lines waiting until 4:00 P.M. before they can cross the stage and enter into that time when they may truly cavort as they please, have dropped out of the masquerade altogether.

Coincidental with the decline of the street festival, the fixed stage events have been elevated to unprecedented levels in the carnival. Under the patronage and control of the middle-class Creole leadership, carnival has evolved into a grand spectator event. It is "Trinidad & Tobago's biggest crowd puller. . ." (*Caribbean Contact* 1984). Large audiences attend all competitive events, and much larger still is the stay-at-home television audience. Given the elaborate preparations required for the successful staging of events, spontaneous participation has all but disappeared from the festival, and there is limited participatory flow across the space that separates performance specialists from the audience.

Such "distancing" in the experience of the carnival has led to new concerns in the critical appraisal of the festival. Lewdness, wanton licentiousness, vulgarity, obscenity, and antisocial violence were generally regarded in the past as the carnival's chief faults.

Lately, however, the carnival is increasingly being criticized for its public wastefulness and the missocialization that cumulates from the festival as a national rite. Some of the criticism is vocal: "Many participants feel that the carnival needs to be decentralized ... and the emphasis on competition weakened. It is not a spectator event, devotees argue, it is a communal activity that needs to be freed up from bureaucratic interference and commercial exploitation" (*Caribbean Contact* 1984). But another form of criticism is to be observed in the changing attitudes and performances among players and local spectators alike.

An increasing number of Trinidadians spend the carnival weekend abroad, vacationing in Barbados or Miami. Others who do not go abroad spend the time away from the city on local beaches, where they fete in isolation from the tourists and the sterile masquerade put on largely for their (the tourists') benefit. Those among the urban masses who cannot afford out-of-town vacations, but who find that the official carnival is without vitality, are returning to the streets to celebrate, often without costume or other trappings of a masquerade. They go as individuals to outdoor block parties in their own neighborhoods, where they eat, drink, dance as they please to recorded music, and ignore the big parade. Even among those who go to the Queen's Park Savannah with picnic baskets to spend the day(s) watching the bands parade, many sit passively before the staged procession, appearing rather bored or cynical, even as they carry out the duty of attendance.

Among some players, attitudes toward the carnival have become heavily intellectualized. The level of research and the commitment to authenticity in costume design and construction is intense. And at least in the work of one major bandleader/designer (Peter Minshall), the thrust into overt thematic symbolism in costuming and dance is powerful enough to constitute what some regard as a fresh level of consciousness for the festival. Minshall has won several awards, but his work remains controversial to the extent that it mixes class and ethnic insignia in designs that are as mentally challenging as they are emotionally awakening. Many regard the poetic standards and symbolic sovereignty of this work to be excessively intellectual and receive it with reserve.

The experience of the carnival, then, clearly varies with the orientation and background brought to a participation in or observation of the festival. Players themselves may be divided into two categories: the "old-time" players and the younger, or "new" players (those who came into carnival during the postindependence period). Among the old-time *mas* men, carnival is still a time for extreme individualistic expression. They tend to favor extraordinary costumes and are less concerned with feting themselves than with making an impact on those who see them. Younger *mas* people tend to cluster in the throngs of players who wear costumes almost as though they were uniforms. In many bands, apart from the "king," "queen," and other extraordinary characters, many players wear the same costume design. For many old-time players, the carnival is a dramatic event which culminates in their individualized display and impact during the bands parade. For many of the younger players, however, the carnival experience is grounded in the fete, the jamming with friends, the sporting encounter; and for them, satisfaction comes principally from "having a good time."

Spectators also may be divided into two categories: the visitors and the locals. Visitors, mainly tourists, could have a carnival without leaving their hotel. The hotel will have public dances that bring throngs to it, and it will have television sets in the rooms and lobby on which may be seen whatever is taking place at various competition venues. Or visitors may venture out to calypso tents, the steel bands' final performances, and to the Queen's Park stands for the parade of the bands. One-time visitors could enjoy the mixtures of peoples, the costumes, the music, the dancing, drinking, and eating, and the casual encounters, with little or no awareness of the tensions and contradictions at work in the festival. By contrast, local spectators may be more directed in their support for one band or the other, or for particular players. They too will fete and enjoy themselves, but not without some critical appraisal in which costumes, calypsos, and steel band arrangements will be compared to those of previous festivals. The videotapes that are run and rerun on television tend to encourage such appraisal. There will be self-congratulatory remarks of a national order—"Trinidadians real good for themselves, oui!"; "Trinidad sweet too baad..."; "Where else could people fete like this?"—but none of these will have anything to do with the abridgment of social barriers. That concern is left to the pundits on society and culture, editorialists, and other commentators. Carnival is a personal affair, and nobody much cares what commentators have to say about it.

It has been shown that carnival belongs to a species of communication systems that not only reflects but shapes a people's ideas about themselves and their societies (Lavenda 1980; Le Roy Ladurie 1979; Davis 1970; Duvignaud 1976). In Trinidad, the carnival clearly is an event in which society takes the opportunity to make rash, sometimes in the extreme, comments about certain aspects of itself, while seducing any impulse to retaliatory gesture with an illusion of universal ecstasy. As is the case with other institutional forms in Trinidad's Creole culture, the carnival is itself an eclectic system burdened with satisfying multiple, sometimes also contradictory, social impulses and objectives. Geertz's (1983:40) observation that "any particular ritual dramatizes certain issues and mutes others" applies especially well here, because it is in the changes of what is dramatized or muted over the years that the carnival, more successfully than any other institutional form in Trinidad, maintains a dominant position in the local culture.

The African, Amerindian, Asian, and European traditions which cluster at the base of what might be regarded as a formative Trinidadian Creole culture, and which in varying degrees still foster different propositions about meaning in life, expressed and maintained through ethnic diversity, constitute a resourceful change potential—and the carnival is well suited to the maintenance of traditional remnants, particularly those of a nonmaterial order. *Calinda* persists in some rural districts. Warriors and supernatural beings from the African and Amerindian past, Asian dynasties and dragons, European courts, all recur in the annual pageants, and with them is taken up, as it were, all challenge against the exercise of free choice. At the same time, the contradictions which necessarily occur where free choice is possible stimulate what might be regarded as social movements within the carnival; for example, the *calinda* and steel band movements. These movements and the official responses to them represent instances in which contradictions of a social order were not glossed but, indeed, violently acted out in the festival.

Changes in the carnival, then, may be recognized as occurring between the two poles of social ideal and social reality, with a tendency to reject insistence on either extreme. Where the underlying tensions that are a fundamental part of everyday social relations appear too boldly, are too fully expressed, the carnival declines from ritual to mere disorder. By contrast, where there is overemphasis on the ideal of harmonious integration, such as is the case with the current festival, one result is the loss of ritual vitality. In their interpretation of the festival, Trinidadians resist either being too fully subjects of their carnival or being too heavily subjected to it. The desire is for a voluntary experience of the tensions between ideal and real, balance and excess, permissiveness and control, and various other oppositions. The suppression of distinctions in such a field constitutes a challenge to the creative energies vested in the festival. The historical eruptions against constraint in the *calinda* and steel band movements, and expansion of the performance categories resulting from such eruptions, attest to an abundantly creative energy at the heart of the carnival. Such an energy may, to some extent, actually thrive against constraint.

The experience of the carnival, then, is grounded in a system of paradoxes which link socially defined opposites at both the societal and the individual levels. Such linkage simultaneously announces a submission to and transcendence of certain dominant constraints in the society. Race, color, class, wealth, institutional power—the carnival blatantly expresses each of these socially significant criteria, simultaneously endorsing and criticizing them as principles of social organization. Certain trends dominate from period to period, but such dominance becomes itself a stimulus for the emergence of countertrends.

In a field of such eclectic possibility, individual and group patterns of experience have considerable room for variation. Yet at the core of the carnival experience remains the tension between license and constraint. Whether stimulated by a critically ironic detachment, such as is evident in the "aesthetic movement" currently championed by Minshall, or the intoxicated absorption in momentous revelry exhibited by disencumbered street dancers, license, the attribute that gives carnival its special meaning, must await the proper conjunction and intensity of constraints to graduate from mere individual eccentricity to a socially powerful "transcendent ecstasy" (Turner 1982:23). Of course, the deception which leads to such a state must be individually experienced, and the potential for such experience is necessarily conditioned by knowledge and disposition. Political sponsorship of the festival (the CDC) has as an unacknowledged objective control over both knowledge and disposition on behalf of an integrated but compartmentalized model of society. Whether such a model overdetermines the spirit of the festival remains an issue that increasingly affects the direct experience of the festival itself among Trinidadians.

Those who most enjoy carnival in Trinidad these days are the visitors (returnees and tourists), who by their very journeying have already assumed a status of license and who have no knowledge of the burdening encumbrances carried by local traditionalists and innovators. Their approach to the festival is singularly individual. In increasing numbers they don costumes and "jump" in the "best" bands. They sweat, eat, drink, and cavort exotically. Then, on the day after, they return home weary but vitalized, carrying images and memories which stir a sense of individual possibilities not otherwise stimulated. They are not affronted by anything in the carnival, where they have no interest in the politics of the occasion. They are not concerned with whether the CDC awards are distributed fairly. Certainly, many Trinidadians themselves recall older days when this was the quality of their carnival experience, and hope for the return, once again, of such an illusion.

REFERENCES

Beckford, George. 1972. *Persistent Poverty.* London: Oxford University Press.
Boyke, Roy. 1981. "Parties, Politics, Pan and Peter." In: *Trinidad Carnival,* pp. 8–9. Port-of-Spain: Key Caribbean Publications.
Burnley, William Hardin. 1842. *Observations on the Present Condition of the Island of Trinidad, and the Actual State of the Experiment of Negro Emancipation.* London: Longman, Brown, Green, and Longmans.
Campbell, Carl. 1981. "Ralph Woodford and the Free Coloureds: The Transition from a Conquest Society to a Society of Settlement, Trinidad 1813–1828," *Caribbean Studies* 2(2/3):238–49.
Caribbean Contact. 1984. "Is Carnival at the Crossroads?" vol. 11, no. 11, Apr.
CDC Guide to Participation. 1983. Port-of-Spain, Trinidad and Tobago: Carnival Development Committee.
Crowley, Daniel J. 1956. "The Traditional Masques of Carnival," *Caribbean Quarterly* 4:194–223.
Davis, Natalie Zemon. 1970. "The Reasons of Misrule: Youth Groups and Charivaris in Sixteenth Century France," *Past and Present* 50:41–75.

Despres, Leo. 1975. "Ethnicity and Resource Competition in Guyana." In: *Ethnicity and Resource Competition in Plural Societies*. The Hague: Mouton.

Duvignaud, Jean. 1976. "Festivals: A Sociological Approach," *Cultures* 3(1):13–25.

Elder, J. D. 1966. *Evolution of the Traditional Calypso of Trinidad and Tobago: A Sociohistorical Analysis of Song-Change*. Ann Arbor, Mich.: University Microfilms International.

Fanon, Frantz. 1967. *Black Skin, White Masks*. New York: Grove Press.

Freilich, Morris. 1970. "Mohawk Heroes and Trinidadian Peasants." In: *Marginal Natives: Anthropologists at Work*. New York: Harper and Row.

Geertz, Clifford. 1983. *Local Knowledge*. New York: Basic Books.

Guerin, Daniel. 1961. *The West Indies and Their Future*. London: Dennis Dobson.

Harris, Marvin. 1964. *Patterns of Race in the Amercias*. New York: Walker and Co.

Hill, Errol. 1972. *The Trinidad Carnival*. Austin: University of Texas Press.

James, C. L. R. 1963. *The Black Jacobins*. New York, Vintage Books.

———. 1973. "The Middle Classes (1962)." In: David Lowenthall and Lambros Comitas (eds.), *Consequences of Class and Color*, pp. 79–92. New York: Anchor Books.

Jha, J. C. 1973. "Indian Heritage in Trinidad, West Indies," *Caribbean Quarterly* 19:28–49.

Laurence, K. O. 1963. "The Settlement of Free Negroes in Trinidad Before Emancipation," *Caribbean Quarterly* 9:26–52.

Lavenda, Robert H. 1980. "From Festival of Progress to Masque of Degradation: Carnival in Caracas as a Changing Metaphor for Social Reality." In: Helen B. Schwartzman (ed.), *Play and Culture*, pp. 19–30. New York: Leisure Press.

Leiris, Michel. 1955. *Contacts des Civilisations en Martinique et en Guadeloupe*. Paris: UNESCO.

Le Roy Ladurie, Emmanuel. 1979. *Carnival in Romans*. New York: George Braziller.

Manning, Frank E. 1978. "Carnival in Antigua: An Indigenous Festival in a Tourist Economy," *Anthropos* 73:191–204.

Mintz, Sidney W. 1974. *Caribbean Transformations*. Chicago: Aldine.

Ottley, Carlton R. 1974. *Slavery Days in Trinidad*. Trinidad: published by the author.

Pearse, Andrew. 1956. "Carnival in Nineteenth-Century Trinidad," *Caribbean Quarterly* 4:175–93.

Smith, M. G. 1965. *The Plural Society in the British West Indies*. Berkeley: University of California Press.

Third Five-Year Plan, 1969–1973. 1970. Trinidad and Tobago: Government Printery.

Trotman, David. 1981. *Crime and the Plantation Society: Trinidad 1838–1900*. Ann Arbor, Mich.: University Microfilms International.

Turner, Victor. 1982. *Celebration*. Washington, D.C.: Smithsonian Institution Press.

Weller, Judith Ann. 1968. *The East Indian Indenture in Trinidad*. Rio Piedras: Institute of Caribbean Studies, University of Puerto Rico.

Williams, Eric. 1962. *History of the People of Trinidad and Tobago*. Trinidad: PNM Publishing Co.

Wood, Donald. 1968. *Trinidad in Transition*. London: Oxford University Press.

13

Modeled Selves:
Helen Cordero's
"Little People"

BARBARA A. BABCOCK

I don't know why people go for my work like they do.
Maybe it's because to me they aren't just pretty things
that I make for money. All my potteries come out of my
heart. They're my little people. I talk to them and
they're singing.

Helen Cordero, interview

Whatever the receptive and inventive powers of the
mind may be, they produce only internal chaos if deprived of the hand's assistance.

Henri Focillon, *The Life of Forms in Art*

When Helen Cordero, a Cochiti Pueblo woman, began making
pottery twenty-five years ago, she turned her hands to figurines
because her bowls and jars "were crooked and didn't look right."[1]
In so doing, she happened on what was to become a perfect embodiment of personal and cultural experience. All the "little
people" she has shaped—whether a Drummer, a Nightcrier, a
Turtle carrying children on his back "to learn the old ways," or
one of the Storytellers with which her name has become synony-
mous—are modeled selves, representing and recreating images of
personal history and family life, of Pueblo life and ritual, and of
Keresan mythology. Through her ceramic creativity, Helen
Cordero has made one of the oldest forms of native American
self-representation her own, reinvented a long-standing but
moribund Cochiti tradition of figurative pottery, engendered a
revolution in Pueblo ceramics comparable to those begun by
Nampeyo of Hopi and Maria of San Ildefonso, and reshaped her

316

own life as well as that of her family and her pueblo. Her "little people" have become prize-winning and world-famous collectors' items. Storytellers and related figurines are now being made by no less than 200 other potters throughout the Rio Grande Pueblos, and she has become—and has had to come to terms with what it means to be—"a big Indian artist." For the past six years, I too have been learning to deal with what that means, learning to describe and interpret the dialogic relationship between Helen Cordero and the people she makes and talks to and about, and which in turn make her by situating them within the dialogues— with ancestors, with ceramic tradition, with cultural patterns and values, with personal and social experience, with present and future generations—of which they are simultaneously the product and the expression. This essay is a small portion of that effort, focusing as it does on personal meanings, on the relationship between self and modeled selves.

At least fifty years ago, Dewey (1934:3) argued against separating art objects from human experience: "Since the actual work of art is what the product does with and in experience, the result is not favorable to understanding." He further asserted that the primary task of anyone who would understand the fine arts is "to restore continuity between the refined and intensified forms of experience that are works of art and the everyday events, doings, and sufferings that are universally recognized to constitute experience." If the essays in this volume are any indication, we have come a long way from the formalist and autotelic conceptions of art that Dewey decried and have taken sizable steps toward restoring and understanding crucial continuities between the order of events and the order of expression. And yet, as the majority of contributions to this volume again demonstrate, when we do examine how and in what forms peoples reflect on their own experience, construct a sense of self, and interpret life events, we tend to focus on verbal and performative genres. I would argue, however, that cultures and the individuals within them not only constitute, reflect on, and reconstitute themselves through what they say and what they do but through articulations of the material world as well. "Transactions between people and the things they create constitute a central aspect of the human condition" (Csikszentmihalyi and Rochberg-Halton 1981:ix), for objects are used not only to represent experience but also to apprehend it and to interpret it, to give it meaningful shape. All textualization is not verbal. Objects do speak and should be heard as significant statements of personal and cultural reflexivity, as shapes that "materialize a way of experiencing" and "bring a particular cast of mind out into the world of objects, where men can look at it" (Geertz 1976:1478).

As a sensuously perceptible and enduring form of culture, Pueblo pottery is a case in point. It is impossible to ignore the pervasiveness of pottery in Pueblo life, but it is easy to forget that pottery making involves a transformation of the natural world into commodities of cultural value and personal significance as well as economic necessity. In traditional Pueblo belief, clay itself was a living substance; and, according to Cushing (1886:510–15), a pot acquired a kind of conscious and personal existence as it was being made. "In other words, a pottery vessel was not thought of simply as an inert manufactured object. Rather, it was active, endowed with a life of its own. As a receptacle for water and food, it held, and was in turn, a source of life" (Hardin 1983:33). This is not an easy concept to accept for scholars "trained in the Western traditions in which to distinguish between animal, mineral and humankind is a mark of sophistication" (Taylor 1980:29). It is all too easy for us to dismiss such notions as "primitive" animism and to eschew these problematics of meaning for the formalities of design and the pragmatics of use.[2]

Unfortunately, with the notable exceptions of the Zuni work of Cushing, Bunzel, and most recently Hardin, this is exactly what Pueblo ethnographers have done, if they have dealt with pottery at all. It is not at all uncommon to read full-length ethnographies of Pueblos long-famous for their pottery and find but a paragraph or two about ceramics, and that usually in a section on economics. Perhaps the most telling example in Keresan ethnography is White's (1935:27) monograph on Santo Domingo, in which pottery is dealt with as follows: "Considerable pottery is made in Domingo. Women, children, and old men erect bowers (for shade) along the nearby highway and sell pottery to passing tourists. They also sell it to traders. Considerable income must be derived from this source." Regrettably, this situation has not improved much. In his overview of material culture studies, Fenton (1974:26–27) remarks: "In neglecting the material basis that underlies, limits, and to a degree determines social life, anthropology is not fulfilling its mandate to study whole cultures. . . . With all the studies we have of Pueblo ceremonialism and politics, we are still in the dark about the material culture of the Keresan Pueblos." And even in those studies concentrating on pottery and its manufacture, it is surprising how little attention has been paid to social and cultural contexts and meanings, as well as to the less than obvious ways in which pottery is a container of "life," of cultural value.[3]

In the absence of other cultural manifestations with which ethnographers deal, pottery *is* a privileged text for archaeologists. Much of the story, both substance and sequence, they reconstruct of prehistoric Pueblo culture is based on ceramic remains. Although they recognize that modeled clay is an informed substance, the archaeologists' primary concern has not been with the ways in which pottery gives shape to experience and meaning to social behavior, but with what these objects record and reflect· of the society in which they were produced and used. This perspective has changed somewhat with increasing interest and work in ethnoarchaeology, but even here, as Hodder (1982) points out, the relationship between ceramics and culture tends to be construed in passive rather than active, reflective rather than reflexive, terms.[4] For all that sherds have "told" us of the past, the dynamic human aspects of these man-made and man-used products have been neglected. In the last analysis, Pueblo "potteries"[5] are seldom thought of as other than mere things or lifeless artifacts; they are rarely conceived as the symbolic forms that they are, "through which and in which [Pueblo] conceptions of the person, the social order, and the cosmology are articulated and displayed" (Rabinow and Sullivan 1979:19).

Given the conceptual complexity of clay things from the Pueblo point of view, the unthinking materialism of most ceramic studies is distorting and demeaning. It has long since been forgotten that "thing" in our own cultural tradition originally meant a gathering, an affair or matter of pertinence, the nexus of a manifold of sensations, or that "techne" (art or craft) originally denoted a mode of knowing.[6] If, as I and others have remarked, we use things as well as words "to build up culturally constituted modes of existence" (Hallowell 1953:603), then why should the problem of "arriving at the significances of material culture objects" be one of anthropology's "most profound dilemmas"

(Weltfish 1960:169)? Over twenty years ago, Weltfish answered that "the question is deeply involved in our *own* dilemma of how man and material are related" (1960:161). My personal experience inclines me to agree with her and to argue that if we are ever to understand Pueblo pottery as an art shaped from experience as well as earth, and which in turn shapes personal and cultural experience, as something people have used to give meaning and structure to their lives as well as to carry water or to make money, we must bracket, if not discard, our common conceptions about the ontology of things. We also must recognize that most studies of material culture have ignored or oversimplified this problem. "If our study of material culture is to open up for us another world-view, the exposure of our ethnically-limited viewpoint upon common objects and material can be a more demanding discipline than most of us have realized" (Weltfish 1960:167).

Perhaps of all our ethnocentric viewpoints, Cartesianism dies hardest and continues to obstruct our understanding of the relationship of both things and selves to cultural experience. Dualisms of matter and mind, of individual and society, of self and world, cannot but distort the complex connections of pot and potter to each other and to Pueblo experience and worldview.[7] Yet they do persist and influence our conceptions both of art and of individual artists. I doubt that we will ever understand how individuals might use the resources of their own creativity to shape and interpret the roles society has presented to them, or to change their world by interpreting it, until we revise common assumptions about the "primitive" or "folk" artist as a self-effacing, naive, unreflective medium of tradition, or about individual creativity as alien to the expression of shared themes.[8] There is something very wrong in denying these artists the personal, aesthetic, and cultural self-awareness as well as the creative ability to invent and reinvent culture that we laud in modern Western artists. Unfortunately it is still true, as Marx observed in the 1840s, that "the chief defect of all previous materialism is that the object, actuality, sensuousness is conceived only in the form of the *object of perception*, but not as *sensuous human activity, practice*, not subjectively" (in Easton and Guddat 1967:400).

All life stories are not told in words. In countless ways, Helen Cordero has told me that her potteries are her autobiography and that her art has given her "the privilege to imagine, to recollect, to think, and to feel in *forms*" (Focillon 1948:47). The remainder of this essay is therefore an attempt to describe and understand in words and in images the relationship between the art and experience of this Cochiti Pueblo potter who invented the Storyteller doll, to describe not only how her clay figurines are shaped from her experience but also how her "little people" have reshaped and continue to shape her life. More particularly, I am concerned with how she herself understands the relationship between her art and her life and with what her structured self-images mean to her— with the essential unity of creator and creation. This is not to imply, as some have, that "unsophisticated," "primitive" artists do not make a distinction between art and life, or that art can and should be reduced to biography or personality. I do mean to imply, however, that Helen Cordero is as much what she has been as what she is able to imagine, and vice versa; and that through the medium of pottery, the life of its creator has become a cultural artifact, an object of shared experience.[9] Where necessary I have expanded on and contextualized her words and her work; but having already discussed my biases and assumptions, I have deliberately chosen not to appropriate her voice with models, theories, and analyses of my own. This is not a plea for absence of anlysis but a dialogic effort to understand her art in her own terms.

When Helen Cordero began making people of clay over twenty years ago, she was forty-five years old, the six children she had raised were grown, and she was doing bead- and leatherwork with her husband's cousin Juanita Arquero to earn a little extra money. Most of the profits went toward buying more materials. One day her husband's aunt, Grandma Juana, asked, "Why don't you girls go back to potteries? You don't have to buy anything; Mother Earth gives it all to you." And so Juanita, who had learned to make pottery as a child, "started up again," and Helen spent six months "under her," learning the ancient art. Her bowls and jars "came out crooked" and she despaired of ever "getting it right." Juanita suggested that she try figurines, and "it was like a flower blooming"—tiny birds and animals and eventually "little people" came to life in abundance. The first time Helen "showed them out" at a Santo Domingo feast day, folk-art collector Alexander Girard bought all that she had, urged her to make more and larger figurines, and commissioned a 250-piece Nativity set.

Thinking, perhaps, of the "singing mothers" made by Helen

Figure 1. Singing Mother. 5½″ h. 1960–61. Courtesy of Marjorie Lambert. Photograph by Glenn Short.

Figure 2. The first Storyteller with five children made for Alexander Girard. 8¼″ h. 1964. Courtesy of the Museum of International Folk Art, Museum of New Mexico, acc. no. A.79.53–41. Photograph by Glenn Short.

and several other Cochiti potters (Figure 1), Girard then suggested that she make an even larger seated figure with children. She recalls that when she went home and thought about it, "I kept seeing my grandfather. That one, he was a really good storyteller and there were always lots of us grandchildren around him." When she created that first Storyteller in 1964 (Figure 2), Helen Cordero added yet another voice and another shape to generation upon generation of clay children. For almost as long as Puebloan peoples have shaped utilitarian objects from the clay of the Southwest, they have produced ceramic images of themselves and their gods.[10] Despite the zeal of Spanish and later Anglo clergy in destroying these "idols," the figurative tradition survived. When the railroad brought numerous whitemen and their ways to New Mexico one hundred years ago, Rio Grande potters responded with both clay caricatures of the intruders and portraits of themselves. In quality and quantity, the most notable figurative pottery production in the past century has occurred in Cochiti, a Keresan Pueblo thirty-five miles southwest of Santa Fe. But even

Figure 3. Storyteller with sixteen children. 10¾″ h. 1971. Courtesy of Al Anthony, Adobe Gallery. Photograph by Glenn Short.

here, in the years between 1915 and 1960, fewer potteries were made and the human forms that were shaped were considerably smaller and simpler than their turn-of-the-century ancestors: a drummer, a dancer, a woman with a bowl of bread or a child. The last, a "singing mother," or "madonna," was the most common, but only a few women at Cochiti made them, and "for a long time pottery was silent in the pueblo." Helen broke that silence when she remembered her grandfather's voice and shaped that first Storyteller, with two significant modifications in the Singing Mother tradition: (1) she made the primary figure male rather than female; and (2) she placed more than a realistic number of children on him—the first Storyteller had five children; subsequent ones have had as many as thirty (Figure 3).

The consequences of her creation have been enormous. Almost immediately the Storyteller brought Helen Cordero acclaim and success, and with each passing year both her reputation and the demand for her work continue to grow. She has more "ribbons" and awards than she can count or remember, and more orders than she can fill in her lifetime. Like it or not, she has become a famous potter ("a big Indian artist") and her work has brought her substantial professional and material rewards. When

Figure 4. Santiago Quintana holding one of his eighteen grandchildren, ca. 1906. Photograph courtesy of the National Anthropological Archives, Smithsonian Institution, neg. no. 80–5499.

Figure 5. Helen Cordero shaping a Storyteller with twenty-five children. 1979. Courtesy of the Denver Museum of Natural History, neg. no. 4–79082–9A. Photograph by Dudley Smith.

asked about her success, she says, "I don't like to be called famous. My name is Helen Cordero. My grandfather, he's giving
me these" (Figures 4 and 5). But she does like to travel to openings and demonstrations, to meet new people and experience new
places, and to be able to remodel her house and buy a new car or
a refrigerator. "Sometimes I just can't believe it, all the nice
people my little people have brought to my house and all the
places like Chicago they have taken me. When my grandpa said
there would be things in the sky made out of tin cans, I never
thought I'd be flying in one. I'm so lucky and I thank him and
God and Grandma Clay for what they have given me. When I
picture back, we used to be so poor—no couch, no bureaus, no
table. There were eight of us then and only two rooms in this
house, so we were in here like sardines. We ate on the floor and
we put our clothes in orange crates. Now, I'm getting me what I
always wanted."

Given the changes that the Storyteller has made in the visible
surface of her life, and given the fact that all her potteries are
made for an Anglo art market, it is tempting to talk about both
her art and her experience in acculturative terms. But that would
oversimplify and overlook the substance of personal and cultural
experience that has not changed and that has, if anything, been
intensified since she learned to make pottery "in the old way."
Whatever their destination, those old and local beliefs, values, and
experiences determine the meaning and the shape of her potteries—they determine how she thinks about her "dolls" and what
they mean to her, and when and how they are made.[11] I began to
revise my own assumptions about art and acculturation after I
asked her how many figures she made every year and she replied,
"I really don't know. It's like breads. We don't count."

As I pondered that unexpected answer, and wondered on
many occasions how I could get the answer I wanted, I realized
that what mattered was not numbers or economics but meaning:
What does it mean to liken potteries, and by implication stories,
with "breads"? What does that statement reveal of her and her
culture's values and conceptions of pottery making, which is today
a highly lucrative enterprise? The answers to these and related
questions are still being discovered, and the implications go far
beyond the scope of the present essay. For now it should be said
that there are obvious technological similarities between these two

modes of cultural production and that it is not at all uncommon in Pueblo English to describe ceramic technology in the language of bread making. More importantly, in the Pueblo worldview clay, like corn, is regarded as a god-given, living, life-sustaining substance which one takes and makes and gives without counting and with thanks, and which one never handles lightly. Every stage of pottery making, from digging clay to firing, is accompanied by prayers and cornmeal offerings to Clay Mother. "I don't just get up in the morning and start making potteries. First, I go and talk to Grandma Clay."[12] Every piece of clay that is not used or that is sanded away or broken in the fire is carefully saved and taken back to the river—the repository for all sacred substances no longer of use. Helen will not work on Sundays or saints' days; she will fly home from a Scottsdale opening in time to make bread for All Souls' Day; and she will, without hesitation, attribute her success to the fact that she makes potteries "in the old way, the right way."

Helen also acknowledges that the strength and appeal of her figurines derive in large part from her personal involvement and from their direct relationship to her life: "I don't know why people go for my work the way they do. Maybe it's because they're not just pretty things that I make for money. They come from my heart. They're my little people. I talk to them and they're singing." When she says this, she is not speaking metaphorically, for she does, indeed, talk to her "little people" when she shapes them, when she paints them, when she fires them, or when she encounters those she made and sold years ago. One March day, in 1979, she was putting the white slip on a large Storyteller that had been ordered for a traveling exhibit of Pueblo pottery. After speaking to the figure in Keresan, she turned to me and said, "I talk to him. I tell him he's going on a long trip and lots of people will see him, so he has to come out real pretty" (Figure 6). And so he did; but when they do not, she says, "I'm sad, but I take them into my heart and take them back to the river." Another time, when a Drummer was successfully taken out of the fire at a demonstration at Pecos National Monument, a child asked, "What's he doing?" Helen replied, "He's singing, can't you hear him?" After putting her ear to its mouth, the child said, "No," for which she was gently admonished, "Then you're not listening" (Figure 7).

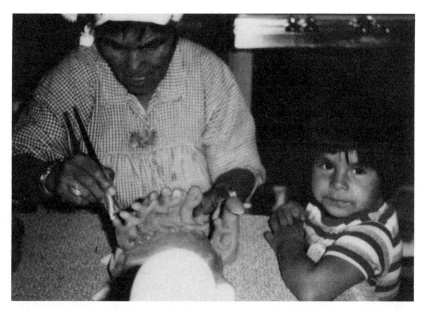

Figure 6. Helen Cordero with her granddaughter, Dina Suina, putting the slip on a Turtle and Storyteller (*foreground*), March 1979. Photograph by Barbara A. Babcock.

Figure 7. Trying to hear the Drummer singing. 1974. Courtesy of Pecos National Monument. Photograph by Tom Giles.

As well as telling stories about the past, Helen's grandfather Santiago Quintana used to relate prophetic anecdotes. One, which she interpreted literally as a child, was about children being born without ears. Now she understands what it "really" means and delights in recalling it whenever people question or deny that objects speak: "That one, oh, he knew so much. He was a wise man with good words." In addition to telling stories to his many grandchildren and being known in the pueblo as both as gifted storyteller and a leading member of one of the clown societies, Santiago Quintana was the valued informant for several generations of anthropologists: Bandelier, who made him one of the protagonists in his ethnographic novel *The Delight Makers* (1971 [1890]); Curtis (1976 [1926]), who greatly quoted and photographed him; and Benedict, who collected many of the *Tales of the Cochiti Indians* from him and warmly wrote of him in letters from the field. Writing to Margaret Mead on September 5, 1925, she described Santiago Quintana as follows: "My old man is ninety and a great old character . . . he's known all over this country as 'the Fair.' He speaks excellent Spanish and I can follow a good deal when he talks it—I am angry that I have to bother with interpreters at all, but I do. He hobbles along on his cane, bent nearly double, and is still easily the most vivid personage in the landscape—he has the habit of enthusiasm and good fellowship" (in Mead 1973:300). Like his granddaughter, he was an adventurer and a teacher. He reached out for experience and shaped it into the memorable narratives and pantomimes he gave to others. What he created with words and gestures, Helen Cordero recreates today in clay: "It's my grandfather. He's giving me these. His eyes are closed because he's thinking. His mouth is open because he's singing. He had lots of grandchildren and we're all in there, in the clay."

Family portraiture and the objectification of personal experience is not limited to the past, however. When people ask, as they frequently do, where Helen gets her ideas for the whimsical postures and gestures of all the little kids scrambling over the Storyteller, she points to one or another of her twelve grandchildren and says, "Just look at them." Or while prospective buyers are admiring a Storyteller in a Scottsdale gallery, she will turn and say, "That's a pretty one. He really came out good. Look at that face. It's Erica" (her eleven-year-old granddaughter). Whether ancestral or immediate family, her portrayals are not a matter of recollection but of presence. "We are," as she says, "all in there, in the clay."

Stories are thought to be "life for the people," and Helen Cordero's "little people," grandfather storytellers alive with children, are themselves statements of generation, procreation, and the power of the word as well as the hand. In the oldest and most sacred stories, Keresan origin myths, creation itself is described as occuring in part through the process of pottery making: Iyatiku ("bringing to life") and her sister Nautsiti ("more of everything in the basket") are sent up into the light, to this earth, with baskets crammed full of clay images and seeds from which they create all forms of life.[13] In the most recent Keresan narratives, Laguna poet and novelist Leslie Silko tells us that Pueblo storytelling embodies a vital dynamic of "bringing and keeping the people together," of maintaining a continuity from generation to generation, and of endless creation, for each story is the beginning of many stories—a "seed of seeds."[14] As conceived by Helen Cordero, the Storyteller is itself a material expression of regeneration: its very structure reenacts this reproductive dynamic; its proportions are indeed social proportions; and its subject is explicitly relationship—between generations, between past and future, and between words and things.[15] From the Pueblo point of view, stories and potteries, like kinship systems, constitute a "bridge between the reproductive aspect of generation and the cultural basis of thought, transmission" (Ricoeur 1983:30). Both are vital necessities, conceived in terms of (and themselves expressions of) fertility, the key symbol or root metaphor of Pueblo culture.[16]

For Helen Cordero, the life-giving and life-sustaining meaning of the Storyteller is also very personal. In 1968 and 1971, both her oldest son and daughter were killed in automobile accidents. At the time, recognition of her work was spreading and the ever-increasing demand for potteries, shows, and demonstrations helped her to deal with her loss. "When God took away my babies, he gave me my little people to keep me going. If I hadn't had my work, I think I would have just gone down myself, I still get sad when I think about it, and then I say, 'Look what he's given you, look at all those little people.'" Clearly, this statement and related remarks she has made to me imply that much more than vocational therapy was involved in her burst of productivity in the 1970s. Through the symbolic paradigm of clay people she

was able to exchange biological reproduction for cultural reproduction, to recreate her lost children, and in so doing to reconstruct her self and to "retrieve her identity."[17] There is a model for
this symbolic replacement in traditional Pueblo practices associated with rites and prayers of increase, especially those
associated with the winter solstice and/or Christmas. Small
figurines, usually unbaked and unpainted, made of cornmeal or
clay, are placed on kiva and/or church altars. Thereafter, in the
case of domestic animals, the images that are taken to be "the
seed from which the real objects will grow" (Parsons 1939:574)
are "planted" in the corral, "so that there will be more of them"
(Parsons 1919:279). A woman wanting children will make a clay
"baby," take it to the altar, and then place it on a miniature cradleboard in a special place in her home; alternatively, one of the
kachinas may give her a clay or wooden "baby" in a miniature
cradle, which she then cares for and regards as "the heart of the
child" (Dumarest 1918:141). Through her "little people" (which
her grandfather has given her), as well as her biological children,
grandchildren, and great-grandchildren, Helen Cordero has given
life to the people. In giving birth to these modeled selves, she has,
both literally and symbolically, culturally and personally,
answered mortality with natality and given the world a powerful
model of fertility and continuity.[18]

The innumerable clay people Helen Cordero has created are
not limited to these images of natural and cultural reproduction,
Singing Mothers and Storytellers, which I have presented thus
far. In the last fifteen years she has gone on to produce other
images of her experience, other family and cultural self-portraits.
Her other interesting re-presentation of storytelling is the Children's Hour (Figure 8), in which the children are grouped around
rather than placed on the Storyteller. "These are older kids listening to him. He used to say, 'Come children, it's time,' and I remember us all around him out at the ranch, and that's how I
thought of the Children's Hour." In addition to the physical impossibility of older children sitting on their grandfather, this
ensemble and her remarks about it connote integration with differentiation and individuation and a greater emphasis on the
grandfather's pedagogical rather than nurturant role, characteristic of an adolescent state of affairs.

The structural hierarchy of the Storyteller and the Children's

Figure 8. Children's Hour. Storyteller, 9″ h.; children, 2¼″–3½″ h. 1980. Courtesy of the Museum of International Folk Art, Museum of New Mexico, acc. no. A.80.27.1v. Photograph by Glenn Short.

Hour is inverted in the other multiple-piece scene that she regularly makes, the Nativity, in which the entire community—people, animals, foodstuffs, and goods—is organized around the infant. While this is the very essence of the traditional Christian scene, she emphasizes that unlike the first *nacimiento* she made for Alexander Girard, these are "Indian nativities"—all the figures are dressed in Indian costume, "what we wear when we dress up nice," and they carry "what we take to the Infant Jesus on Christmas morning." "The man with the sack over his shoulder is carrying what the boys use for their dancing. Costumes. The Indians knew that Jesus was a boy and would need what the boys use. The cows and horses are close to the baby to keep him warm. They all have the Cochiti brand" (Figure 9). The artistry of this scene is not realized entirely in clay. The cottonwood bows and arrows, the cradleboard ("For the newborn baby, we always use the cradleboard to lay him on"), and the stable are made by her husband Fred and her son George. Again, as in the case of the Singing Mother or Madonna, Helen has taken a traditional Christian image and transformed it into her own very personal and very Pueblo terms.

Figure 9. Nativity. 1½″–6½″ h. 1972. Courtesy of the Museum of International Folk Art, Museum of New Mexico, acc. no. FA.72.61–1–16. Photograph by Guy Monthan.

Many of her potteries, as well as their accessories, bear her husband's imprint. For several years in the beginning, when she was afraid to paint her people, Fred Cordero both taught her and helped her paint. Her Drummer (Figure 10) is her portrait of Fred, who in addition to being a fine drum-maker is the leading singer and drummer for the Pumpkin kiva and has held many ceremonial and political offices in the pueblo, including governor (Figure 11). Drums are the heart of Pueblo life and ritual and have kept its rhythm for centuries. Throughout the Pueblos, Cochiti has long been famous for its drums, which are made for and sold both to other Pueblos for ceremonial use and to Anglos for decorative purposes. In recent years the drum has become an important symbol of community identity—the landscape is dominated by two water towers painted to look like drums, and the end of every pew in Cochiti's St. Bonaventura Church is decorated with an incised drum. Like the Drummer, the Nightcrier is also a familiar Cochiti ceremonial figure. Sometimes Helen personalizes him with a governor's cane of office "so that he looks like Grandpa [Fred]." She made the first Nightcrier in 1976 after seeing an old (ca.1880–1900) Cochiti figurine at Fenn Galleries in Santa Fe. She

Figure 10. Drummer. 11¾" h. Courtesy
of Dr. and Mrs. Zigmund W. Kosicki.
Photograph by Glenn Short.

Figure 11. Fred Cordero with a drum
he has just made. ca. 1971. Photograph
courtesy of the Cordero family.

looked at it standing in its *nicho* on the stairway and said, "He's
sad. Nobody should sing alone." She measured it and went home
and made the first of these large standing figurines, who now sings
with his century-old friend (Figure 12).

Potteries are not only described as being, or being like, family
members or significant Pueblo personages; the reverse also occurs.
I have been struck on several occasions with the extent to which
Helen's works of art, as Focillon (1948:63) observed, "create formal environments which impose themselves on human environments." I once brought her a Parkhurst photograph taken of her
mother in the 1920s which I had found in the Museum of New
Mexico (Figure 13), and she responded, "Look at her. She's so
pretty. She looks just like my Water Carrier" (Figure 14). The
same sort of reciprocal interchange occurs with old Cochiti potteries, which sometimes, as in the case of the Nightcrier, are an
inspiration to Helen for a new shape or a new design. In other
cases, the older forms are evaluated and interpreted both techni-
cally and aesthetically in terms of her own work. While she acknowledges her debt to old Cochiti figurines, and frequently ad-

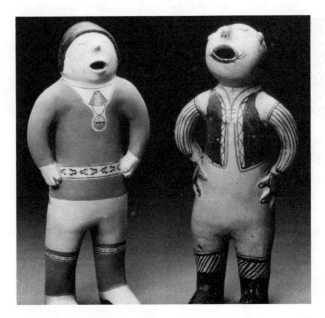

Figure 12. Nightcrier. 17½" h. 1976; and Cochiti *mono*, 17"
h. ca. 1895. Courtesy of Forrest Fenn. Photograph by
Glenn Short.

mires them, she is quick to point out that she differently conceives
and names her own figurines: "Those old ones, they called them
monos [Spanish: "monkey, mimic, silly fool, mere doll"]. Some
people here and some of the dealers still call them like that. I tell
them. 'No, these aren't *monos*. These are dolls. They're my little
people.' I don't like to call my potteries by that word because
they use that for the figures that you knock over and break with a
ball at the carnival."

One of Helen's more recent and very appealing creations is a
Turtle carrying children on his back. When she talks about this
figurine, it is clear that he is regarded both as a model *of* an important event in Keresan mythology and a model *for* a desirable
present occurrence. "He's not only a turtle. He's somebody who
helps out and he's very big in spirit. A long time ago when there
were wars and the people were fighting among themselves, the
turtle came and volunteered to take the kids away. Now, he's taking these ones on a long journey—very slow and very sure—to
learn the old ways" (Figure 15). Sometimes the shell of the turtle
is decorated realistically with a saddle blanket of Pueblo textile

Figure 13. Caroline Trujillo Quintana Pecos. ca. 1920. Courtesy of the Museum of New Mexico, neg. no. 2326. Photograph by T. Harmon Parkhurst.

Figure 14. Water Carrier. 9½″ h. 1984. Courtesy of Helen Cordero. Photograph by Barbara A. Babcock.

design; at other times it is treated like an inverted bowl and the edge is painted with traditional pottery rim designs representing seeds or rainclouds—designs, I should add, that are omnipresent in Pueblo iconography as prayers for rain and icons of fertility and by no means limited to ceramic design. Whether we are dealing with the relationship of her art to her personal and cultural experience or, as in this case, of her clay shapes to other forms of Pueblo art or systems of signification, it is no simple matter of representation and reflection but a complicated one of continuity and reciprocity in which all of the meanings are ultimately related.

There is no question that Helen Cordero has learned "the old ways" well and has used the knowledge and skill that her grandfather and Juanita Arquero have given her to see and hear and reshape her own experience and fashion her life situation into a language of forms. But if she has been given much, she has in turn given, and goes on giving, much both to her own people and to the Anglos who buy her work and come to watch her at dem-

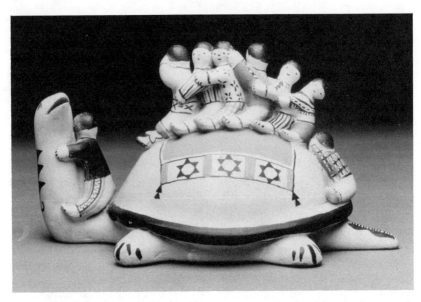

Figure 15. Turtle. 6¼″ h. x 11″ l. 1980. Courtesy of R. K. McCord. Photograph by Glenn Short.

onstrations. When I remarked on the patience she displayed in light of the repeated and sometimes rude questions she was asked, she replied, "They have to know what our ways and the old ways, the right ways of making pottery are. I have to tell them and share what I know." Both at home and in the outside world, Helen and her work have become exemplary, and one of the notable consequences of her creativity is the influence that it has had on other Pueblo potters. Her "little people" have initiated a remarkable revival of figurative pottery making both in her own pueblo and in other Rio Grande pueblos. By 1973, when the Museum of International Folk Art in Santa Fe mounted their "What is Folk Art?" exhibit, Helen's Storyteller had been imitated by at least six other Cochiti potters (Figure 16). Today, pottery is anything but silent in the pueblo, and no less than 50 potters, including several members of her extended family, are shaping Storytellers. The voice of the Storyteller is not limited to Cochiti, however, and can now be heard in differing accents from Santa Clara to Acoma. Over 140 potters in eleven other Rio Grande pueblos are presently making Storytellers and related figures, each in the clays, paints, and designs characteristic of her pueblo; and with each month the number increases.

Figure 16. Storytellers in Museum of International Folk Art exhibit. 1973. *Left to right:* Helen Cordero, Felipa Trujillo, Aurelia Suina, Juanita Arquero, Frances Suina, Seferina Ortiz, and Damasia Cordero. Courtesy of the Museum of New Mexico, neg. no. 70433. Photograph by Arthur Taylor.

Helen Cordero's first Storyteller has engendered countless "little people," her own and others', because among other things it speaks in terms of cultural constants—stories, generations, and the persistent problem of community organization and survival. Like telling stories, making and exchanging potteries has always been a vehicle for retelling family history and for expressing personal and tribal identity—a model of reproduction as well as a means of production. With the encroachment of an Anglo world and the expansion of an Anglo market for Indian objects, ceramic art has become increasingly important, not only as a source of income but as a cultural voice, as a container of Pueblo values. In addition to changing the shape and size of Pueblo ceramic production, Helen Cordero's Storyteller and his clay cousins and descendants have caused figurative pottery to be taken more seriously than ever before in the Anglo art market where they are bought and sold. For the first time since Anglos began collecting and buying Pueblo pottery, ceramic figurines are valued and respected as "art" rather than dismissed as exotic artifacts or primitive idols for the museum or quaint curios for the tourist.

Helen's response to this revolution she has given birth to is somewhat ambivalent. While she recognizes that imitation is a form of flattery and that she has done something important in terms of contemporary Pueblo ceramics, she does not like the endless reproduction of something so very personal and autobiographical: "They call them Storytellers, but they don't even know what it means. They don't know it's my grandfather." Nor does she like the fact that many of these potters do not make their Storytellers in a traditional manner, instead using commercial clays, paints, and kilns: "Today, everything is easy. Buy their clay, their paint, take them to big ovens in Albuquerque. Grandma Clay doesn't like it and most of them don't even know about Grandma Clay. To make good potteries, you have to do it the right way, the old way, and you have to have a special happy feeling inside." Whatever these other potters think they are making and however they do it, there is no question that there is a new and flourishing genre of Pueblo pottery. At the 1981 Storyteller Show at Adobe Gallery in Albuquerque, there were over 200 potteries by more than fifty potters. When I told Helen this she replied, "See. I just don't know. I guess I really started something."

Indeed she has. Her "little people" have irrevocably changed the shape of her own life and of Pueblo ceramics, attesting to the power of the individual imagination to remake reality and to create the terms of its existence. Beyond that, both the creator and her creations also remind those of us who traffic in the interpretation and analysis of cultural forms that works of art are "celebrations, recognized as such, of the things of ordinary experience" (Dewey 1934:11); that objects do speak and "art is a language by which the human mind gives utterance to its own integrity" (Hofstadter 1969:83); and that art is forever bound to our most mysterious and our most precious power, the power of creation (Rosenberg 1975:218).

NOTES

1. This statement, and those in quotation marks which follow, were, unless indicated otherwise, made by Helen Cordero in conversations with me between 1978 and 1982.

2. For further discussion of the problem of animism for Western scholars and the centrality of the belief in Pueblo thought that man-made things have life and spirit, see Babcock (1982:58, note 1).

3. As Foster points out in "The Sociology of Pottery" (1965) and Matson in "Ceramic Ecology" (1965), this observation is generally true of ceramic ethnography. For Pueblo historic pottery in particular, most existing studies consist of

descriptions of techniques and processes of manufacture, formal analyses of design, and chronological sequences of pottery types. Poets, novelists, and painters offer some rare and fleeting insights into the cultural meanings of clay things, but the business of cultural interpretation is generally ignored by ceramic scholars, many of whom, I should add, are not anthropologists. And anthropologists have not included things ceramic in their interpretations. As Csikszentminalyi and Rochberg-Halton (1981:1) have recently pointed out, "Social scientists tend to look for the understanding of human life in the internal psychic processes of the individual or in the patterns of relationship between people; rarely do they consider the role of material objects."

4. In addition to Hodder, see Richardson (1974), Gould (1978), and Longacre (1981) for discussions and examples of recent work in ethnoarchaeology.

5. Here and elsewhere in this essay I deliberately use the Pueblo English plural noun. As Margaret Hardin has pointed out to me, the proper collective noun, pottery, is inconceivable "from the native point of view," for each piece of pottery is a made being with a unique existence.

6. The implications of this etymology are discussed by Heidigger (1967, 1971) in his philosophical inquiry into the nature of things, the origin of the work of art, and what it means to ask, "What is a thing?"

7. For further discussion of the consequences of Cartesianism for social and cultural interpretation, see Singer (1980).

8. For critiques of traditional notions of "folk" and "primitive" art and artists as unreflective, unconscious, collective, and anonymous, see Solheim (1965), Glassie (1968), Biebuyck (1969), and d'Azevedo (1973). See also Boas (1955:155), who makes a similar critique and insists that "we have to turn our attention first of all to the artist himself."

9. For related discussion of the relationship between art and life, cultural artifact and individual creator, see Shiff (1979) and Duvignaud (1972).

10. Figurative pottery is found in all prehistoric Southwestern cultures and dates from at least A.D. 300. For discussion and illustration of prehistoric figurines and effigy vessels, see Morss (1954), Hammack (1974), and Tanner (1976).

11. In writing of the Pueblos over fifty years ago, Benedict (1934:57) observed, "Their culture has not disintegrated like that of all the Indian communities outside of Arizona and New Mexico. Month by month and year by year, the old dances of the gods are danced in their stone villages, life follows essentially the old routines, and what they have taken from our civilization they have remodelled and subordinated to their own attitudes." More recently, on the basis of his work in Cochiti, Fox (1973:275) has similarly remarked that the Pueblo acceptance of Catholicism is a matter of "accretion": "They have added it to their store of religious power. . . . they have added the saints to the *katsinas,* they have aligned God with the Sun Father and Mary with the Corn Mother; but all of these are in fact subordinate to the supreme deity of their pantheon, Spider Woman, who still sits in her cave spinning from her body the web of thought to fill men's heads—indeed, to make them men at all." For further discussion of the dynamics of Pueblo survival and the importance therein of both the ceremonial system and aesthetic traditions, see Ortiz (1976).

12. For discussion of both technological and symbolic connections between

breadstuffs and ceramics, see Cushing (1886, 1920). See also the etiological narrative, "The Institution of Pottery," in Benedict (1931), in which an explicit connection is made between these two modes of production.

13. For texts or summaries of Pueblo, and especially Keresan, origin myths, see Benedict (1931), Boas (1928), Cushing (1896, 1920), Parsons (1918, 1939), Stirling (1942), and White (1932a, 1932b, 1935, 1942, 1962). The motif of creation through the molding of meal, dust, or clay is not limited to origin myths but is widely found throughout Pueblo narratives.

14. Leslie Silko has made these statements and others about the power and importance of Pueblo stories and storytelling in several recent contexts: in *Running on the Edge of the Rainbow: Laguna Stories and Poems*, a videotape in the series *Words and Place*, documenting native American storytellers and artists; in a beautiful recent pastiche, *Storyteller* (1981a); in "Language and Literature from a Pueblo Indian Perspective" (1981b); and perhaps most importantly in her novel *Ceremony* (1977), which among other things is a story about the power of traditional stories. The storyteller who speaks in the title poem is described as follows: "He rubbed his belly. / I keep them here / [he said] / Here, put your hand on it / See, it is moving. / There is life here / for the people. / And in the belly of this story / the rituals and the ceremony / are still growing." (p. 2)

15. My remarks here are indebted to Weiner's (1980:71) "model of reproduction," which is based on the premise "that any society must reproduce and regenerate certain elements of value in order for the society to continue. . . . These elements of value include human beings, social relations, cosmological phenomena such as ancestors, and resources such as land, material objects, names, and body decorations; and to her more recent formulation of the configuration of "elementary cycling" consisting of "components associated with a primary encoding of sex, gender, and time" (1982:9). Whatever else it may be, Cordero's Storyteller is an exemplary embodiment of elementary cycling.

16. For discussions of fertility as *the* dominant idea or master trope of Pueblo culture, see especially Haeberlin (1916), Cushing (1920), and Benedict (1934).

17. See Csikszentmihalyi and Rochberg-Halton's *The Meaning of Things* (1981), especially chaps. 1–2, for an important discussion and elaboration of Arendt's (1958) argument that human beings make order in their selves (i.e., "retrieve their identity") by first creating and then interacting with the material world.

18. The concept of natality was introduced and developed by Arendt in *The Human Condition* (1958).

REFERENCES

Arendt, Hannah. 1958. *The Human Condition*. Chicago: University of Chicago Press.
Babcock, Barbara A. 1982. "Clay Voices: Invoking, Mocking, Celebrating." In: Victor Turner (ed.), *Celebrations*, pp. 58–76. Washington, D.C.: Smithsonian Institution Press.
Bandelier, Adolph F. 1971. *The Delight Makers*. New York: Harcourt Brace Jovanovich. (First published in 1890.)

Benedict, Ruth F. 1931. *Tales of the Cochiti Indians.* Bulletin of the Bureau of American Ethnology, no. 98. Washington, D.C.: Government Printing Office.

———. 1934. *Patterns of Culture.* Boston: Houghton Mifflin Co.

Biebuyck, Daniel (ed.). 1969. *Tradition and Creativity in Tribal Art.* Berkeley: University of California Press.

Boas, Franz. 1928. *Keresan Texts.* Publications of the American Ethnological Society, vol. 8. New York.

———. 1955. *Primitive Art.* New York: Dover Publications.

Bunzel, Ruth. 1972. *The Pueblo Potter: A Study of Creative Imagination in Primitive Art.* New York: Dover Publications.

Csikszentmihalyi, Mihaly, and Eugene Rochberg-Halton. 1981. *The Meaning of Things: Domestic Symbols and the Self.* Cambridge: Cambridge University Press.

Curtis, Edward S. 1976. *The North American Indian,* vol. 16. New York: Johnson Reprint Corporation. (First published in 1926.)

Cushing, Frank Hamilton. 1886. "A Study of Pueblo Pottery as Illustrative of Zuni Culture Growth." 4th Annual Report of the Bureau of American Ethnology, pp. 437–521. Washington, D.C.

———. 1896. "Outlines of Zuni Creation Myths." 13th Annual Report of the of American Ethnology, pp. 321–447. Washington, D.C.

———. 1920. *Zuni Breadstuff.* Indian Notes and Monographs, vol. 8. New York: Museum of the American Indian.

d'Azevedo, Warren (ed.). 1973. *The Traditional Artist in African Societies.* Bloomington: Indiana University Press.

Dewey John. 1934. *Art as Experience.* New York: Capricorn Books.

Dumarest, Fr. Noel. 1918. "Notes on Cochiti, New Mexico." Memoirs of the American Anthropological Association, no. 23, pp. 135–236. Lancaster, Pa.

Duvignaud, Jean. 1972. *The Sociology of Art.* trans. Timothy Wilson. New York: Harper and Row.

Easton, Loyd D., and Kurt H. Guddat (eds. and transl.). 1967. *Writings of the Young Marx on Philosophy and Society.* New York: Doubleday and Co.

Fenton, William N. 1974. "The Advancement of Material Culture Studies in Modern Anthropological Research." In: Miles Richardson (ed.), *The Human Mirror: Material and Spatial Images of Man,* pp. 15–36. Baton Rouge: Louisiana State University Press.

Focillon, Henri. 1948. *The Life of Forms in Art.* New York: Wittenborn, Schultz.

Foster, George M. 1965. "The Sociology of Pottery: Questions and Hypotheses Arising from Contemporary Mexican Work." In: F. R. Matson (ed.), *Ceramics and Man,* pp. 43–61. Viking Fund Publications in Anthropology, no. 41. New York: Wenner-Gren Foundation.

Fox, Robin. 1973. *Encounter with Anthropology.* New York: Harcourt Brace Jovanovich.

Geertz, Clifford. 1976. "Art as a Cultural System," *Modern Language Notes* 91(6):1473–99.

Glassie, Henry. 1968. *Pattern in the Material Folk Culture of the Eastern United States.* Philadelphia: University of Pennsylvania Press.

Gould, Richard A. (ed.). 1978. *Explorations in Ethnoarchaeology.* Albuquerque: University of New Mexico Press.

Haeberlin, H. K. 1916. "The Idea of Fertilization in the Culture of the Pueblo Indians." Memoirs of the American Anthropological Association, vol. 3, no. 13, pp. 1–55. Lancaster, Pa.

Hallowell, A. Irving. 1953. "Culture, Personality, and Society." In: A. L. Kroeber (ed.), *Anthropology Today: An Encyclopedic Inventory*, pp. 597–620. Chicago: University of Chicago Press.

Hammack, Laurens C. 1974. "Effigy Vessels in the Prehistoric American Southwest," *Arizona Highways* 50(2):33–34.

Hardin, Margaret Ann. 1983. *Gifts of Mother Earth: Ceramics in the Zuni Tradition.* Phoenix, Ariz.: Heard Museum.

Heidigger, Martin. 1967. *What Is a Thing?* Chicago: Henry Regnery Co.

———. 1971. *Poetry, Language, Thought.* New York: Harper and Row.

Hodder, Ian. 1982. *Symbols in Action: Ethnoarchaeological Studies of Material Culture.* Cambridge: Cambridge University Press.

Hofstadter, Albert. 1969. "On Consciousness and the Language of Art." In: James M. Edie (ed.), *New Essays in Phenomenology*, pp. 83–99. Chicago: Quadrangle Books.

Longacre, William. 1981. "Kalinga Pottery: An Ethnoarchaeological Study." In: I. Hodder, G. Isaac, and N. Hammond (eds.), *Patterns of the Past: Studies in Honour of David Clarke*, pp. 49–66. Cambridge: Cambridge University Press.

Matson, Frederick R. 1965. "Ceramic Ecology: An Approach to the Study of the Early Cultures of the Near East." In: F. R. Matson (ed.), *Ceramics and Man*, pp. 202–17. Viking Fund Publications in Anthropology, no. 41. New York: Wenner-Gren Foundation.

Mead, Margaret (ed.). 1973. *An Anthropologist at Work: Writings of Ruth Benedict.* New York: Equinox Books.

Morss, Noel. 1954. "Clay Figurines of the American Southwest." Papers of the body Museum, vol. 49, no. 1. Cambridge, Mass.

Ortiz, Alfonso. 1976. "The Dynamics of Pueblo Cultural Survival." Paper presented at the annual meetings of the American Anthropological Association, Washington, D.C.

Parsons, Elsie Clews. 1918. "Nativity Myth at Languna and Zuni," *Journal of American Folklore* 31(120):256–63.

———. 1919. "Increase by Magic: A Zuni Pattern," *American Anthropologist* 21:279–86.

———. 1939. *Pueblo Indian Religion.* 4 vols. Chicago: University of Chicago Press.

Rabinow, Paul, and William M. Sullivan (eds.). 1979. *Interpretive Social Science: A Reader.* Berkeley: University of California Press.

Richardson, Miles (ed.). 1974. *The Human Mirror: Material and Spatial Images of Man.* Baton Rouge: Louisiana State University Press.

Ricoeur, Paul. 1983. "On Thinking about the Unthinkable," *University of Chicago Magazine* 76(1):29–31.

Rosenberg, Harold. 1975. "Metaphysical Feelings in Modern Art," *Critical Inquiry* 2(2):217–32.

Shiff, Richard. 1979. "Art and Life: A Metaphoric Relationship." In: Sheldon Sacks (ed.), *On Metaphor*, pp. 105–20. Chicago: University of Chicago Press.

Silko, Leslie. 1977. *Ceremony.* New York: Viking Press.

————. 1981a. *Storyteller.* New York: Seaver Books.

————. 1981b. "Language and Literature from a Pueblo Indian Perspective." In: Leslie A. Fiedler and Houston A. Baker, Jr. (eds.), *English Literature: Opening Up the Canon,* pp. 54–72. Selected Papers from the English Institute, 1979. Baltimore, Md.: Johns Hopkins University Press.

Singer, Milton S. 1980. "Signs of the Self: An Exploration in Semiotic Anthropology," *American Anthropologist* 82:485–507.

Solheim, Wilhelm C. 1965. "The Functions of Pottery in Southeast Asia: From the Present to the Past." In: F. R. Matson (ed.), *Ceramics and Man,* pp. 254–73. Viking Fund Publications in Anthropology, no. 41. New York: Wenner-Gren Foundation.

Stirling, Matthew. 1942. *Origin Myth of Acoma and Other Records.* Bulletin of the Bureau of American Ethnology, no. 135. Washington, D.C.

Tanner, Clara Lee. 1976. *Prehistoric Southwestern Craft Arts.* Tucson: University of Arizona Press.

Taylor, Joshua C. 1980. "Two Visual Excursions." In: W. J. T. Mitchell (ed.), *The Language of Images,* pp. 25–36. Chicago: University of Chicago Press.

Weiner, Annette. 1980. "Reproduction: A Replacement for Reciprocity," *American Ethnologist* 7:71–85.

————. 1982. "Sticks and Stones, Threads and Bones: This is What Kinship Is Made of." Paper presented at the conference on "Feminism and Kinship Theory," Bellagio, Italy, August.

Weltfish, Gene. 1960. "The Anthropologist and the Question of the Fifth Dimension." In: Stanley Diamond (ed.), *Culture in History: Essays in Honor of Paul Radin,* pp. 160–80. New York: Columbia University Press.

White, Leslie A. 1932a. "The Acoma Indians." 47th Annual Report of the of American Ethnology, pp. 17–192. Washington, D.C.

————. 1932b. *The Pueblo of San Felipe.* Memoirs of the American Anthropological Association, no. 38. Menasha, Wis.

————. 1935. *The Pueblo of Santo Domingo.* Memoirs of the American Anthropological Association, no. 43. Menasha, Wis.

————. 1942. *The Pueblo of Santa Ana.* Memoirs of the American Anthropological Association, no. 60. Menasha, Wis.

————. 1962. *The Pueblo of Sia.* Bulletin of the Bureau of American Ethnology, no. 184. Washington, D.C.

14

Magnitudes
of
Performance

RICHARD SCHECHNER

How can performances be understood? A structural analysis, as proposed by some semioticians (see, e.g., Pavis 1982; Elam 1980), is, in my opinion, static. Classical semiotic study, founded as it is on linguistics, is not able to account for the processual flux of performance. Turner's exposition of "ritual process"—which took a sharply theatrical turn in the years before his death in 1983 (e.g., Turner 1982a, 1982b)—is more applicable to performance but is concentrated on public, social performances. Goffman (1959, 1963, 1967, 1969a, 1969b, 1971, 1974), in his series of works on social interaction, amply demonstrated the performative nature of face-to-face encounters. But none of these studies catches the whole problem: What are the sources of performance, and what are its full dimensions?

Ethologists and neurologists are giving performance theorists still more to think about. The waters will get a lot muddier before confused, conflicting particles of thought settle down, leaving mere lucidity. In one of his last writings, Turner attempted to come to grips with the relationship between brainwork and performance. After neatly summarizing his own ideas concerning ritual as not only a conservator of social values but a generator of new values through transformation, liminality, communitas, and antistructure, he outlined the triune structure of the brain: the reptilian "stream of movement," the old-mammalian "stream of feeling," and the new-mammalian "stream of thought" (Turner 1983:224–28). Then he asked "if ritualization, as discussed by Huxley, Lorenz, and other ethologists, has a biogenetic foundation, while meaning has a neocortical learned base, does this mean that creative processes, those which generate new cultural knowledge, might result from a coadaptation, perhaps in the ritual process itself, of genetic and cultural information?" (1983:228).

In several of my writings (see Schechner 1985) I have emphasized the analogies between the ritual process as defined by Turner and the workshop-rehearsal process as it is practiced especially in experimental Euro-American theater and dance. The task of the workshop is to deconstruct the readymades of individual behavior, texts, and cultural artifacts into strips of malleable behavior material; the work of the rehearsal is to reconstruct these into a new, integral system: a performance.

To what depth are there cultural readymades, and how much of human equipment/action is reconstructable? This really gets to the heart of Turner's questions. Part of the answer may be coming from laboratory experiments such as those conducted by Ekman (1983). Working from his earlier cross-cultural comparisons of emotion in the human face (Ekman, Friesen, and Ellsworth 1972), he is currently detailing relationships between the autonomic nervous system (ANS) and acting. Here I mean acting as done by professional actors, which may not be much different than what is meant by "ordinary behavior." The difference may simply be one of reflexivity: American professional actors are aware that they are acting.

Ekman's experiments show that six "target emotions"—surprise, disgust, sadness, anger, fear, and happiness—elicit "emotion-specific activity in the ANS" (see Figure 1). He elicited these data in two ways, using actors from San Francisco's American Conservatory Theatre. In one, subjects "were told precisely which muscles to contract" (1983:1209), "constructing facial

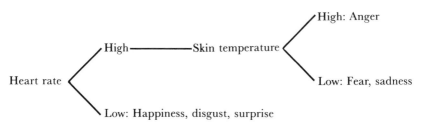

Figure 1. Emotions Ekman (1983:1209) distinguishes on the basis of heart rate and skin temperature differences. The figure is reproduced here by permission of the American Association for the Advancement of Science. Copyright 1983 by the AAAS.

prototypes of emotion muscle by muscle" (1983:1208); in the other, "subjects were asked to experience each of the six emotions . . . by reliving a past emotional experience for 30 seconds" (1983:1209). Reliving a past emotional experience is close to Stanislavski's classic exercise of "emotional recall" practiced at the beginning of the century and much refined by those following the methods of Lee Strasberg at his Actors' Studio in New York. Ekman wrote me, "The idea of studying actors was suggested to me by Lee Strasberg some years ago. Although I never met Strasberg, we corresponded at some length about how our research might be used to explore the nature of the physiological changes that can occur when the 'method' [Strasberg's system of actor training] is used" (personal communication, 1983).

The actors who made the faces were not aware of what emotion they were simulating; rather they were coached muscle by muscle as they looked at themselves in mirrors. Their work was flagrant demonstration of "mechanical acting"—the kind despised by most American performers, but exactly the kind learned by young boys studying Kathakali dance-drama in India. There, a most rigorous system of body and facial training is followed, one that more or less adheres to the ancient Sanskrit text on theater, the *Natyasastra*, which I will discuss later in connection with Ekman's study. What should be noted now, however, is that the facial and body displays practiced by students of Kathakali are not "natural" but exaggerated, wholly composed "deconstructions-reconstructions" of human behavior (see Figure 2). If the Kathakali displays also elicit changes in the ANS, might not the human genetic base lean toward learned transformation? That is, our species' "fixed action patterns" might be specifically transformative—a Batesonian play-frame resulting from the interplay among our three brains.

As I noted, reliving emotions from past experiences is an exercise familiar to anyone who has studied acting in America. It is so common, in fact, that many experimental theater people eschew it. Its clichés and its underlying mechanism are detested: the performer is drawn away from the actual present circumstances unfolding onstage and is concentrated on a "there and then" experience inserted or bootlegged into the present. As a theater director, I prefer performers to concentrate on what is happening "here and now" among them and between them and

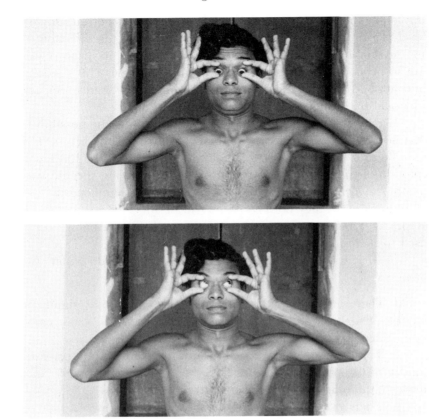

Figure 2. Kathakali eye training at the Kerala Kalamandalam, 1976. Photographs by Richard Schechner.

the audience. This urgency is what drew me to the techniques of Asian theater, which has the qualities both of present-centeredness and immense imaginative (nonnaturalistic) theatrical possibilities.

What is truly surprising about Ekman's (1983:210) experiment is not that affective memory or emotional recall work but that "producing the emotion-prototypic patterns of facial muscle action resulted in autonomic changes of large magnitude that were more clear-cut than those produced by reliving emotions." That is, mechanical acting worked better in getting the actor to feel. This is absolutely contrary to the Stanislavski-Strasberg canon. It also suggests that performance—or "deep acting,"[1] as Hochschild (1983) calls it—does exist at the level of the ANS. Acting is not only a neocortical event but one that penetrates to the level of the old-mammalian and reptilian brains; the direction of motivational flow does not come only from down up, from reptilian to neocortex, but also from up down. Actors hear instructions and act accordingly; their changes in musculature lead to, or are identical to, changes in their ANS.

Ekman rules out—but I emphatically do not—the possibility that seeing their own faces in the mirrors aroused the actors. He feels "that it was contracting the facial muscles into the universal emotion signals which brought forth the emotion-specific autonomic activity" (1983:1210). Why must he choose among the explanations when they both could be true? I am certain that a good actor can arouse in me a response in my ANS; and I know how I used to scare myself by making faces in the mirror.

Be that as it may, Ekman's experiment does add a new dimension to a growing body of evidence that suggests:

1. There are universal signals that not only repeat signifiers but signifieds: a "universal language," if you will, of "basic emotions" (see especially Eibl-Eibesfeldt 1979).

2. This "language of emotions" is nonverbal and consists mostly of facial displays, vocal cries, body postures (freezes), and moves (stamping, rushing, crouching).

3. There is a corresponding universal system present in nerve and brain process—and this system probably underlies what anthropologists have called "ritual" (see Turner 1983; d'Aquili, Laughlin, and McManus 1979).

And there's a twist to all this that Ekman's experiment confirms. Without denying the existence of "culture universals," or at least an underlying neurologically based ritual process, displays of emotion can be so well feigned by skilled performers as to make distinction between what is "really happening" and what is "skillfully pretended" or "mechanically induced" simply a matter either of social or aesthetic convention. "Lies like truth," director Harold Clurman said. Or to put it in the form of an old theater joke: The great acting teacher told his students, "Truth is all there is to acting. Once you learn to fake truth the rest is easy."

Ekman's machines detected no lies in skin temperatures or heart rates when his actors were simply following orders and putting on the masks of anger or happiness or other "target emotions." The only way we know whether they were "really feeling the feelings" or not was by what they tell us. And their ANS was telling us that they were really feeling the emotions.

Is all this just a restatement of the James-Lange problem: Am I running from the bear because I am afraid, or am I afraid because I am running from the bear? There are systems of performer training, both ancient and modern, that say the problem is no problem at all, because both circumstances are true. The human animal is complex enough so that emotions generate actions and actions generate emotions. What Ekman's experiment shows is that these two possibilities are operative independent of each other. Good theater acting elicits in both the performers and the spectators a very high state of participatory arousal exactly like Ekman's "mechanical acting" experiment. In fact, what Ekman's experiment measured at the level of ANS was "good acting."

The *Natyasastra*, compiled in India between the second century B.C. and the second century A.D., describes in great detail the various facial and bodily poses and expressions needed to perform the "eight basic emotions": love, happiness, sadness, anger, energy, fear, disgust, and surprise. (Humankind has countless gods, but I would be very surprised if there were not general agreement on the "basic emotions.") Love and energy are not on Ekman's list, possibly because they are considered, at least in our culture, to be "mixed" or composite emotions.

Ekman (1983:1208) states that the fear-face is made by raising the eyebrows and pulling them together, raising the upper eyelids, and then stretching the lips horizontally back toward the ears. The *Natyasastra* deals with several kinds of fear, and different classes of characters react differently to being afraid, but there are some generalizations. In Ghosh's (1967:144) translation: "Fear is to be represented on stage by . . . shaking of the narrow limbs, body tremors, paralysis, goose pimples, speaking with a choked voice." Regarding the eyes and surrounding musculature, of which Ekman makes so much, the *Natyasastra* states: ". . . the eyelids are drawn up and fixed, and the eyeballs are gleaming and turned up" (Ghosh 1967:155); and "the eyes are widely opened, the eyeballs are mobile in fear and are away from the center [of the eye]" (1967-157). Also, "the glance in which the eyelids are drawn up in fear, the eyeballs are trembling and the middle of the eye is full blown due to panic is called *Trasta* [frightened]" (1967:159). But the *Natyasastra* is not entirely consistent. Its author(s) are always quoting *slokas* (sacred couplets), and sometimes these say that fear is to be represented by half-closed eyes. Consider, though, the fact that the *Natyasastra* is not a scientific study but a compilation of centuries of experience by many actors in India. Specific gestures are suggested for a wide variety of emotions: for the eyes, eyelids, eyebrows, nose, cheeks, lower lip, chin, mouth, and neck. There are also sixty-seven gestures for the hands and many gestures for other parts of the body.

No one knows exactly how, in its day, the *Natyasastra* was put into action. Most probably it was a text—like Stanislavski's books on acting or Grotowski's (1968) *Towards a Poor Theatre*—that collected what was actually done. As such it serves as a node or transfer point linking previous practice with future practice. A hiatus of several centuries divides the Sanskrit theater of the *Natyasastra* from even the oldest of the still-performed Indian dance-dramas, Kutiattam of Kerala. But in Kutiattam, as in its sister genre, Kathakali, a rigorous training reflects and continues the tradition of the *Natyasastra*.

The *Natyasastra* insists on what Ekman shows—that there are definite links between "mechanical acting" and interior states of feeling; that the causal chain can go in both directions: feeling can lead to stage action (*abhinaya*) and the practice of specific stage actions can cause feelings to occur in the actor.

Now I shall speak of the *Bhavas* [literally, feelings]. Why are the *bhavas* so called? . . . *Bhavas* are so called because through Words, Gestures, and Representation of the Sattva [causes of feelings] they *bhavayanti* [infuse] the meaning of the play. . . . *Bhava* is an instrument of causation. (Ghosh 1967:119)

Sattva originates in the mind. It is caused by the concentrated mind. . . . Its nature: horripilation, tears, loss of color and the like cannot be mimicked by an absent-minded man. The Sattva is desired in a play because of its imitative human nature. . . . How can sorrow which has weeping as its basis, be represented on the stage by anyone who is not sorry? And how can happiness which has joy as its basis be represented on the stage by any one who is not happy? (1967:145)

Why is [acting] called *abhinaya?* It is said in reply to this that the *abhinaya* is derived from the prefix *abhi*, and the verbal root *ni* meaning "to cause to get." (1967:150)

It becomes clear that *abhinaya* is not only the means by which the audience gets the play but also the way in which the actors get it—the "it" being not only the mechanical gestures of a performance but the feelings as well, which are evoked by the practice of the proper gestures. Several chapters of the *Natyasastra* are devoted to detailed descriptions of *abhinaya;* and most of the training in contemporary Indian classical dance (consciously modeled after the *Natyasastra,* in many cases) consists of rigorous and repetitious practice of specific chunks of performance: *abhinaya.*

Take Kathakali, for example (I have described the training at the Kathakali Kalamandalam elsewhere [Schechner 1984]). It is enough to know that its basis is in mastering certain steps, gestures of the feet, torso, hands, and face—especially the mouth and eyes—in what to an American appears to be a very mechanical manner. Boys begin training somewhere between the ages of eight and sixteen. They train for six or more years as their bodies are literally massaged and danced into new shapes suited to Kathakali (see Figures 3–4). Even as they are learning the stories—taken mostly from the *Ramayana, Mahabharata,* and *Puranas*—their feet, hands, back, and face are learning by rote the sequences that make up the finished performances. These sequences do not "make sense" by themselves; they are somewhat a denial of the universal facial displays Ekman identifies with his target emotions. But these sequences can be thought of as further ritualizations of already ritualized "natural" displays. The Kathakali sequences make sense, carry specific meanings, when situated within longer performances—including hours-long finished performances of whole plays. As they begin their training the boys have little idea, except as spectators, about these finished performances. But somewhere along the way the training "goes into the body" (as the Balinese, who use similar methods, say). An illumination of sorts occurs.

What was rote movement, even painful body realignment, becomes second nature. The maturing performer now feels his role, experiences it from within with every bit of force equal to what a Euro-American naturalistic actor might experience. I expect that if such a Kathakali actor were tested for ANS variation the results from the composed, performed actions of Kathakali would not be different than those from the enactment of the "natural" emotions tested by Ekman. Acting penetrates deep into the brain. As Padmanathan Nair, one of the best Kathakali actors, told me during

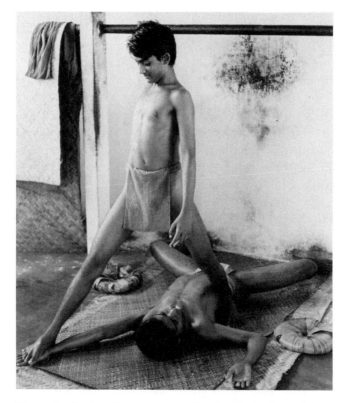

Figure 3. Kathakali massage at the Kerala Kalamandalam, 1976. Photograph by Richard Schechner.

an interview in 1976: "A good actor is the one who understands the character very well, thus becoming the character itself. . . . [But] we should not forget ourselves while acting. While acting half of the actor is the role he does and half will be himself." Bertolt Brecht would have been pleased with Nair's answer. But to achieve this kind of acting it is necessary to have mastered a total score: the exact details of performing. In Kathakali, at least, this score is first mastered mechanically, à la Ekman's experiment.

I now want to connect all of this to some of the work of d'Aquili and his colleagues. Their thesis concerns human ritual.

Human ceremonial ritual is not a simple institution unique to man but rather a nexus of variables shared by other species. All component variables have evolutionary percursers (or *analagen*) dating far back in

Figure 4. Kathakali performance in India. Photograph courtesy of Sangeet Natak Akademi, New Delhi.

hominid phylogenesis and beyond. Specifically, we would suggest that ceremonial rituals (ceremonies, rites) are strips of often complex ritual behavior that (1) are included in the collective E_c [cognized environment; see d'Aquili et. al. 1979:13] of a society, (2) are conceptualized by members of the society, (3) become a locus of symbolization for members of the society, and (4) may have effects on the E_o [operational environment; see d'Aquili et. al 1979:13], some of which are modeled within the E_c and some of which are not. . . . One may trace the evolutionary progression of ritual behavior from the emergence of formalization through the coordination of formalized communicative behavior and sequences of ritual behavior to the conceptualization of such sequences and the assignment of symbols to them by man. (1979:36–37)

Thus, just as performative behavior penetrates deep into the brain, so human ritual has its sources deep in evolutionary time. I take what is commonly called "ritual" to be a kind of performative behavior. D'Aquili's idea is schematized in Figure 5. Animal ritualization and ceremonial behavior not only phylogenetically precede human ritual but are more broad-based: they contain

A chain:

| Ritualization | Ceremonial behavior | Mythic, symbolic ritual |
| Animals | Primates and humans | Humans |

A set of concentric nests:

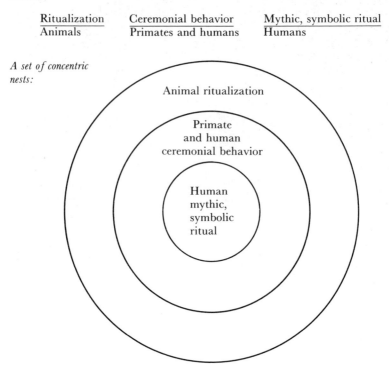

Figure 5. Two schematizations of d'Aquili's view of the evolutionary aspects of ritual.

human ritual. Humans do everything other animals do, and more. Humans ritualize, ceremonialize, and cognize; and these kinds of behavior occur in many combinations.

Human rituals are different from animal ritualization because they are cognitive; that is, they consciously try to explain or affect things. As Turner (1983:231) summarized the view of d'Aquili et. al.:

... causal thinking arises from the reciprocal interconnections of the inferior parietal lobule and the anterior convexity of the frontal lobes, particularly on the dominant, usually left side, and is an inescapable human propensity. They call this brain nexus "the causal operator" and claim that it "grinds out the initial terminus or first cause of any strip of reality." They argue that "gods, powers, spirits, personified forces, or any other causative ingredients are automatically generated by the causal operator." Untoward events particularly cry out for a cause.

Hence "human beings have *no choice* but to construct myths to explain their world," to orient themselves "in what often appears to be a capricious universe."

Turner pointed out that their reasoning goes back to Aristotle's "first cause that is uncaused." And if true, then their brain-based explanation explains not only performative behavior but every kind of cognitive speculation, from witchcraft to physics.

Turner (1983:231–32) argued that ritual works differently than myth:

Myths present problems to the verbal analytic consciousness. Claude Lévi-Strauss has made us familiar with some of these problems: life and death, good and evil, mutability and an unchangeable "ground of being," the one and the many, freedom and necessity, and a few other perennial "posers." Myths attempt to explain away such logical contradictions, but puzzlement remains at the cognitive left-hemispherical level. D'Aquili and Laughlin argue that *ritual* is often performed situationally to resolve problems posed by myth to the analytic verbalizing consciousness. This is because like all other animals, man attempts to master the environmental situation by means of motor behavior, in this case ritual, a mode going back into his phylogenetic past and involving repetitive motor, visual, and auditory driving stimuli, kinetic rhythms, repeated prayers, mantras, and chanting, which strongly activate the ergotropic system [left brain]. Ergotropic excitation is appropriate because the problem presented in the "mythical" analytical mode, which involves binary thinking, mediations, and causal chains arranging both concepts and percepts in terms of antinomies or polar dyads. These are mainly left-hemispheric properties and connect up . . . with the augmented sympathetic discharges [Ekman's ANS responses]: increased heart rate, blood pressure, sweat secretion, pupillary dilation, increased secretion of catabolic hormones, and so on. If excitation continues long enough the trophotropic system is triggered too, with mixed discharges from both sides, resulting often in ritual trance. . . . Presumably the frequent embodiment or embedment of the myth in the ritual scenario, either verbally in prayer or song, or nonverbally in dramatic action or visual symbolism continues to arouse within the ritual context the "cognitive ergotropic functions of the dominant hemisphere." If the experiences of participants have been rewarding—and ritual devices and symbolic actions may well tune a wide range of variant somatic, mental, and emotional propensities in a wide range of individuals (amounting to the well-known redundancy of ritual with its many sensory codes and multivocal symbols)—faith in the cosmic and moral orders contained in the myth cycle will obviously be reinforced. (1983:231–32)

And finally he pinpointed what is missing in d'Aquili's scheme—the one thing that can connect ritual to performative art: play. "But where does 'play' play a part in this model? . . . Play is a kind of dialectical dancing partner of ritual and ethologists give play behavior equal weight with ritualization. D'Aquili and Laughlin hardly mention the word" (1983:233).

Interestingly, Turner (1983:233) noted that "play does not fit in anywhere in particular; it is a transient and is recalcitrant to localization, to placement, to fixation—a joker in the neuroanthropological act." He went on to define play as "a volatile, sometimes dangerously explosive essence, which cultural institutions seek to bottle or contain in the vials of games of competition, chance, and strength, in modes of simulation such as theater, and in controlled disorientation, from roller coasters to dervish dancing." For Turner it may have been that play subverts the regular back-and-forth switching from brain hemisphere to hemisphere that d'Aquili says is the kernel of ritual action. Turner's (1983:234) play was "a liminal or liminoid mode, essentially interstitial, betwixt-and-between all standard taxonomic nodes, essentially 'elusive.'" But of course this begs the question, for play cannot be outside the brain. What it can be is all-relational, but no one has said exactly how this works neurologically.

All human behavior, from interiorized inexpressible, even unremembered dreams to great ceremonial ritual cycle plays like the Ramlila of Hindi-speaking India, relate both the triune brain, its hemispheric frontal lobes, and current human history, as acted out in various cultural performances, to a continuously recapitulated or laminated palimpset of individual human experiences. Some of these experiences are crystallized culturally in art, religion, science, and so on; and some are encoded neurologically and physiologically in the body-brain of each individual. Indeed, there may be room in the world for both Freud and Jung.

Erving Goffman spent much of his life studying the ways people greet each other, deceive each other, manager their "fronts," and play out their psychosocial roles both consciously and unconsciously. He himself was a superb, if laconic, gamester. What Turner saw in ritual process and d'Aquili et al. identify as part of brain process, Goffman (1959:73–74) tracked in everyday life:

The legitimate performances of everyday life are not "acted" or "put on" in the sense that the performer knows in advance just what he is going to do, and does this solely because of the effect it is likely to have. The expressions it is felt he is giving off will be especially "inaccessible" to him. But as in the case of less legitimate performers, the incapacity of the ordinary individual to formulate in advance the movements of his eyes and body does not mean that he will not express himself through these devices in a way that is dramatized and pre-formed in his repertoire of actions. In short, we all act better than we know how.

Just what the Kathakali performers perfect in a most conscious way, and what Ekman had his actors do, Goffman said we all do without knowing. I suppose that even unknowing actors, in the passion of their displays, are experiencing the suitable Ekman ANS fluctuations; and that, in d'Aquili's terms, the hemispheres of their brains are communicating through their corpus callosa. Remember that the Kathakali performers, for all the extreme formality and "unnaturalness" of their training, costumes, music, makeup, dance steps, and hand and face gestures, are "living their roles." But is one activity more "symbolic" than another? Is symbol making a conscious activity? And if so, what about dreams? "Perhaps dreams, like the ritual symbols I have analyzed, are laminated, accreting semantic layers, as they move from brain stem through limbic system to the right hemisphere before final processing or editing by left-hemispheric processes" (Turner 1983:240).

Humans live at the interface between culture (both immediate and historical) and genetics. Culture is the inevitable outcome of our evolution. Thus, nothing humans do is itself and nothing else. There is no strip of behavior—no, even of thought (whether dreamed, imagined, or conceived)—that does not nest within something else and thereby communicate at least two messages: that it "is" and what it "as ifs." The world is full of Goffmans and Turners ready to work on whatever comes their way.

Still, there is a difference between performances that are so because a Goffman or Turner tells us so,[2] and performances that are generally acknowledged as such. Could that difference be specified by what d'Aquili and his colleagues say about brain lateralization and ritual? Noting that the left side of the brain is

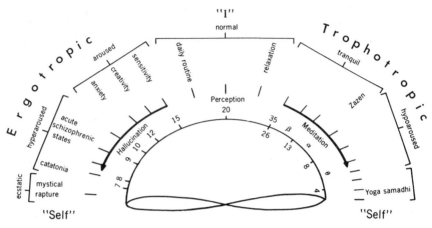

Figure 6. Fischer's (1971:898) "cartography of the ecstatic and meditative states."
He explains: "Varieties of conscious states [are] mapped on a perception-halluci-
nation continuum of increasing trophotropic arousal (*left*) and a perception-mediation continuum of increasing trophotropic arousal (*right*). These levels of hyper-
and hypoarousal are interpreted by man as normal, creative, psychotic, and ecstatic states (*left*) and Zazen and samadhi (*right*). The loop connecting ecstasy
and samadhi represents the rebound from ecstasy to samadhi, which is observed
in response to intense ergotropic excitation. The numbers 35 to 7 on the percep-
tion-hallucination continuum are Goldstein's coefficient of variation . . . , specifying the decrease in variablity of the EEG amplitude with increasing ergotropic
arousal. The numbers 26 to 4 on the perception-mediation continuum, on the
other hand, refer to those beta, alpha, and theta EEG waves (measured in hertz)
that predominate during, but are not specific to, these states." The figure is reproduced here by permission of the American Association for the Advancement
of Science. Copyright 1971 by the AAAS.

"ergotrophic" and the right side "trophotropic," they argue that
"there is something about the repetitive or rhythmic emanation of
signals from a conspecific that generates a high degree of limbic
arousal. . . . There is something about repetitive rhythmic stimuli
that may, under proper conditions, bring about the unusual neural
state of simultaneous high discharge of both [the sympathetic and
parasympathetic] autonomic subsystems" (1979:157). They go on
to assert that the excited ANS "supersaturates the ergotropic or
energy-expending system . . . to the point that the trophotropic system not only is simultaneously excited by a kind of spillover but
also on rare occasions may be maximally stimulated, so that,
briefly at least, both systems are intensely stimulated" (1979:175).
This is the feeling of the inexpressible. . . . It sometimes accom-

panies not only religious rituals but public performative gatherings of many different kinds—from football games to Beckett's plays, from Nazi rallies at Nuremberg to the soft but rhythmic panting-chanting I teach as part of a voice workshop.

In 1971 Roland Fischer devised what he calls "a cartography of the ecstatic and meditative states" wherein the spectrum of arousal is outlined from hypoaroused (trophotropic) states such as Yogic samhadi and Zen meditation, through normal "I" states of daily routine, on to hyperaroused (ergotropic) states such as acute schizophrenia and mystical ecstasy (see Figure 6). Like d'Aquili, Fisher (1971:902) speaks of a "rebound" from one extreme to another:

In spite of the mutually exclusive relation between the ergotropic and trophotropic systems, however, there is a phenomenon called "rebound to superactivity," or trophotropic rebound, which occurs in response to intense symapthetic excitation, that is, at ecstasy, the peak of ergotropic arousal. A rebound into samadhi at this point can be conceived of as a physiological protective mechanism. . . . Meaning is "meaningful" only at that level of arousal at which it is experienced, and every experience has its state-bound meaning. During the "Self"-state of highest levels of hyper- or hypoarousal, this meaning can no longer be expressed in dualistic terms, since the experience of unity is born from the integration of interpretive (cortical) and interpreted (subcortical) structures. Since this intense meaning is devoid of specificities, the only way to communicate its intensity is the metaphor; hence, only through the transformation of objective sign into subjective symbol in art, literature, and religion can the increasing integration of cortical and subcortical activity be communicated.

Fisher points out how strongly humans seek this kind of arousal. Not only do people get it from rituals, and so on, but also, and maybe even more strongly, from various drugs. The experience of "some" goes back to the earliest period of human cultural life. We are just now beginning to understand precisely how these psychotropic agents work; certainly, as Fischer (1971:902) argues, they are coexistent with religious, ritual, and artistic practice.

The hallucinatory constancies are "magical symbols," visible or audible metaphors within a structure of symbolic logic and language, the language of hyper- and hypoaroused hallucinatory states, and are at the base of the general tendency toward geometric-rhythmic ornamentalization. For example, both the rose windows of Gothic cathedrals and the mandalas of Tantric religious art are ritualized hallucinatory form constants. The tendency toward ornamentalization, however, is not reserved to visual imagery, but also governs the order of poetic and musical rhythm, imposing an all-pervasive metrum and harmony on the hallucinatory creative-religious states; the rhythm of music, poetry, and language corresponds to the geometric-ornamental rhythm of the visual realm.

But there is no "single source" for human creativity. Neither drugs nor play nor brain structure nor genetics nor culture ... nothing single can possibly explain what is doubtlessly an incalculably complex relational system—not to mention the old problem that the explainers are part of what is to be explained.

Yet it is also true that humans are driven to keep trying. In seeking experiences that provide "rebound" or "spillover"—simultaneous excitement of both ergo- and trophotropic brain systems—people have taken drugs, invented performances, participated in rituals. Whatever meaning such experiences have, they also clearly bring their own intrinsic rewards. Often enough, the leaders of such experiences exempt themselves from what they offer their followers. And in such abstention these leaders acquire much power.

In connecting human ritual experience to neurological function and brain lateralization, d'Aquili's work touches on Ekman's. Together we are offered not only a biological basis for ritual behavior but a species-wide system of emotions that can be artifically induced at a deep enough level to affect the ANS. And this is where performance—acting, as in a theater—comes in—as a joker, yes, but also as a confirmer of the theory. Performer training is designed to first identify, then to control, and utimately to freely manipulate (arouse, rearrange, edit, transform) the very systems Ekman and d'Aquili examine "in nature." What Turner (1983:236) said of play, I say of performer training:

Since play deals with the whole gamut of experience both contemporary and stored in culture, it can be said perhaps to play a similar role in the social construction of reality as mutation and variation in organic evolution. Its flickering knowledge of all experience possible to the nervous system and its detachment from that system's localizations enables it to perform the liminal function of ludic recombination of familiar elements in unfamiliar and often quite arbitrary patterns. Yet it may happen that a light, play-begotten pattern for living or social structuring, once thought whimsical, under conditions of extreme social change may prove an adaptive, "indicative mood" design for living.

This kind of training—playing with the ergo-/trophotropic dualities of the brain—has been going on for a long time. John Pfeiffer has been studying the cave art of southwest Europe and he and I have had several conversations concerning this art. In *The Creative Explosion* (1982), he tries to prove his belief that the caves were actually ritual theaters, sites of initiations/transformations. Pfeiffer (1982:174–90) assembles evidence of music and dancing: bones and antlers that could perhaps be percussion instruments; adolescent and adult footprints showing circular movement. But no one can know for sure what happened in those caves.

There is more definite evidence concerning certain caves in India studied by Richard Lannoy. For 1,300 years the main locus of art—and possibly of ritual performance—in India were man-made caves, dug between the third century B.C. and the tenth century A.D. and numbering more than 1,200. Of these Lannoy (1971:34) says, "The sites selected for excavation of sanctuaries were ideal retreats possessing all the characteristics of sacred *mana* or numen—and it is more than probable that these sites were already regarded as holy places by the local people." He argues that the human caves were "a conscious recreation of a primitive ethos, integrally part of the fertility theme" (1971:38); and that "the structure and ornmentation of the caves were deliberately designed to induce total participation during ritual circumambulation. The acoustics of one Ajanta *vihara*, or assembly hall . . . , are such that any sound long continues to echo round the walls. The whole structure seems to have been tuned like a drum" (1971:43).

In fact, the Indian caves, Ajanta especially, are ritual theaters, probably not unlike the cave-theaters of paleolithic Europe.

Ajanta should be seen in the early days of the monsoon when the trees are in flower. Only then can one appreciate the tremendous emotional release when color and fertility are restored to the dry soil after the long hot season.

. . . The caves of Ajanta offer the sole remaining opportunity to visualize the way a combination of color and form was originally fused in a wrap-around synaesthesia.

. . . There is no *recession* [of painted images on caves walls]—all *advance* towards the eye, looming from a strange undifferentiated source to wrap around the viewer.

. . . The Ajanta style approaches as near as it is likely to get to a felicitous rendering of tactile sensations normally experienced subconsciously. These are *felt* rather than *seen* when the eye is subordinate to a *total* receptivity of *all* the senses. Here the eye functions quite differently from its linear reading of a flat image. It explores the non-visual properties of spatial forms, creating a sign language or optical braille for the tactually educated. The seated queen with the floating hand is drawn so that we obtain information which cannot be had by looking at her from a single, fixed viewpoint to which we are conditioned by the artifice of optical perspective.

. . . The viewer scans it piecemeal—not in perspective but empathically.

. . . The closest to this method which Western art approaches is the medieval "continuous narrative," in which the same figure is portrayed within a single organized "frame" several times, to represent different moments in the narrative sequence. . . . It could be said that the Ajanta artist is concerned with the *order of sensuousness*, as distinct from the *order of reason.*

. . . The cave art forms part of a synaesthesia appealing to all the senses simultaneously, by chanting of Pali and Sanskrit verses in a magical, resonating echo-chamber embellished with frescoes and sculpture. This environment [quoting McLuhan 1964:357] "demands participation and involvement in depth of the whole being, as does the sense of touch." (1971:46–50)

The synaesthetic experience that Lannoy claims participants in Ajanta had is like the ergo-/trophotropic rebound experience described by d'Aquili et al. and by Fischer.

Lannoy outlines several affinities between the cave art and Sanskrit drama, the body of plays most directly related to the practice outlined in the *Natyasastra*. Sanskrit drama "amplified with words what was suggested in the visual imagery of the cave frescoes. . . . Both were refined products of a sensibility deriving from magico-orgiastic rites [dedicated to] Shiva, Lord of the Dance, god of creation and destruction" (1971:53). He then discusses affinities in narrative structure, spiritual outlook, and finally, "affinity in vision-inducing technique: words and images are used to draw the viewer into a vortex of multiple perspective" (1971:55).

Clearly, the theories of Ekman, d'Aquili et al., Turner, Pfeiffer, and Lannoy converge. They all say that ritual theater is coexistent with our species: it is wired-in, we are adapted for it—and we are labile enough to make many things out of it. Or, to put it in a less cybernetic way: homo sapiens have been evolutionarily selected for adaptability. More than any other creature, humans can live anywhere, creating artificial environments where the natural ones are hostile, eating almost anything—even, as in intravenous feeding, eschewing the ordinary ingestive organs—and on and on. Human adaptability is nowhere better demonstrated than in our stunning capacity to lie, simulate, pretend, imagine—to make art, especially performative art, that cannot be distinguished from the real thing even at the level of ANS response. Performances, when they are not con games (ranging from the shaman Quesalid described by Lévi-Strauss [1963:167–85] to those games that are never uncovered, and there are many), are strictly framed by rules—sometimes labeled ritual, sometimes labeled aesthetic convention—so that spectator-participants can be reassured concerning what is "actual" and what is "feigned"—though each society has its own often shifting definitions of these terms. I would say that everything imaginable has been, or can be, experienced as actual by means of performance. And that, as Turner said, it is by imagining—by playing and performing—that new actualities are brought into existence. Which is to say, there is no fiction, only unrealized actuality.

In other writings (Schechner 1985) I have described in detail the deconstruction–reconstruction process that is workshop-rehearsal. This process, apparent in different cultures under various names, is identical to the ritual process outlined by Arnold Van Gennep and explicated by Turner (1969). It may be that this way of acquiring new behavior—or, more precisely, rearranging old strips of behavior into new configurations—is exactly what d'Aquili et al. and Fischer describe: learning itself may have to do with ergo-/trophotropic stimulation. But this stimulation, and the subsequent submersion in experience, is only the deconstructive phase of learning, in terms of the individual's previous patterns of action—the "readymades" that are brought into rehearsals, the person-that-was who enters a rite of passage. These strips of behavior are deconstructed into more malleable bits, which is not only a term of computer jargon meaning the smallest piece of information, but a venerable theater term meaning the smallest repeatable strip of action. Bits are important to commedia del l'arte and to Stanislavskian deep acting. They are what the young boys learning Kathakali repeat over and over. Of the magnitudes of performance, a bit is the smallest exterior unit.

Once bits are freed from their conventional attachment to larger units of action, they can be rearranged—almost as frames of a film being edited are rearranged—to make new actions. This is the reconstruction phase. This phase is not mechanical, for it is accompanied by varying degrees of self-consciousness. In some cultures, only the masters are privy to this self-conscious, reflexive reconstruction. In contemporary experimental performance, where collectivity is prized, the whole group may be invited to participate in a "discussion about what happened" after the intense experiencing of workshop-rehearsal is over. D'Aquili et al. recognize, too, that one of the main achievements of human ritual is its cognitive aspect, its reflexive potentialities. They speak, in fact, of a "cognitive imperative": "Man has a drive (termed the 'cognitive imperative') to organize unexplained external stimuli into some coherent matrix. This matrix generally takes the form of a myth in nonindustrial societies and a blend of science and myth in western industrial societies" (1979:161). Workshops-rehearsals are models of myth making. Where the task of the performance group is to discover, invent, rearrange, or in some way "make" a performance, part of that task is to control the cognitive aspects, whether or not these are expressed verbally or in some other mode (sounds, images, movements, etc.).

Currently, I am working on a performance piece I call *The Prometheus Project* (or *Problem*). Part of this work is done in workshops where, with about ten other persons, different themes relating to the Prometheus story are actively investigated. By that I mean that narration is improvised or affective states evoked. The basic texts include fragments from Aeschylus's *Prometheus Bound* and Doris Lessing's *Shikasta* (1981). During the fall of 1983 we worked almost exclusively on Io's story. She is "troubled" by Zeus, who comes to her seductively in dreams. It is unclear whether or not she and the god make love, but clearly Zeus's wife, Hera, grows increasingly jealous. To protect Io from Hera, Zeus transforms the young woman into a cow. She begins her wanderings tormented by Hera's stinging gadfly and spied on by hundred-eyed Argos. Io wanders to the limits of the world: from the Bosphorus (names after her) to the Himalayas, from Arabia to the source of the Nile at Victoria Falls. Ultimately, she is healed at Canopus.

We did not "play" this story literally. But with the assistance of workshop members who played Haitian drums, violin, accordion, and with chanting, repetitive movements, and deep breathing, on several occasions people in the workshop entered a kind of trance where they experienced their own versions of Io's wanderings. I have these workshops on sound tapes. Listening to them convinces me after the fact of what I felt during the workshops: for many participants, entering Io's world was a very deep experience. I am certain that, had ANS tests been administered, the responses would have been most noticeable.

My work with the performers did not end with their "having an experience," however. That would be enough, maybe, if I were not also in the art-making business—an occupation that is as cognitively rigorous as it is experientially radical, to the roots. Also on tape I have the discussions of a cooling-down period that followed the intense phase of the workshop. During these discussions the performers first recounted in words—Wordsworth's "recollection in tranquility"—what happened to them. During the next forty-five minutes the participants came back to each other, to the present moment, to a state of mind that was more thinking than feeling (more left brain than right brain, more cortical than limbic). Not only did ideas that proved valuable to the *Prometheus Project* unfold during the discussions, but the performers were reassured from inside themselves that they could return intact to the ordinary non-Io world. This aftermath–cooling down–cognitive grasping of the experiential work was necessary if I expected them to undertake similar, yet even more extreme, work later on. And, of course, through discussions connections were made between their experiences, Io's story, and the performance we were collectively seeking.

Hence the "cognitive imperative." But there is more to it; namely, what Turner called play: the sheer thrill, pleasure, positive feedback, you name it, that untold thousands of rituals give to their participants the world over; the acting out of dangers within the frame of "as if." Obviously, there are people who seek actual dangers—mountain climbers and war-makers, for example. But I believe that a greater proportion of humankind is satisfied with experiences that thrill, even frighten, but which we can be pretty sure of returning from. We seek the kick of an ANS fluctuation and the extraordinary high of a double-brain rebound spillover.

In this essay I have explored aspects of the magnitudes of performance from the standpoint of individual experience. But individual experience is, in a sense, an illusion. We are a collective; we share a collective destiny. (I would go so far as to say that we are in the process of constructing that destiny.) The other extreme of performance magnitude would be great-cycle plays like that of the Orokolo (see Williams 1940; Schechner 1977) or the Ramlilas of Hindi-speaking north India (see Schechner 1985). At one end of the spectrum of performance, deep acting blends into ordinary behavior. For example, airline stewardesses, trained to be "nice," often absorb that training to their very core. A number of former stewardesses sued United Airlines, which fired them years ago because they had either married or turned thirty-two. According to Lewin (1984:D1): "Even on the witness stand, many behave more like hostesses than litigants. When the lawyer who is challenging their testimony stands up and says, 'I am Mark Bigelow, representing the union,' the witness is as likely as not to lean forward with a big smile and say, 'Hi!'" Perhaps at the other end of the performance spectrum are religious, civic, and political pageants where everything is so obviously planned, staged, arranged. In the middle are those vast areas of behavior where there is an ambiguity, or at least an ambivalence, between the composed and the spontaneous. Formal art and ritual apparently belong near the fixed end of the spectrum—I say "apparently" because more of art and ritual than one would suppose is actually spontaneous, is deep acting, not pasted-on routine.

Actually, this essay is—or ought to be—part of a much longer, more detailed and peculiar study of performance in all its magnitudes, from the interior events of the brain to bits of training—the deconstruction-reconstruction process—and on to public performances of varying sizes and duration—the end point being performances on a worldwide scale, such as the Olympics, the hostage crisis in Iran, the shooting down of KAL 007. These are media events, social dramas, performances. Whatever their magnitude at their points and moments of origin—a lone 747 trailed by a single fighter, say—they soon catch up hundreds of millions of people in their narrative and symbolic significances. So, to what degree and depth does our very survival as a species depend on how our peoples and their leaders "act," not only in the sense of comportment but also in the theatrical sense?

This brings us back to the basic paradox: humans are able to absorb and learn behavior so thoroughly that the new behavior knits seamlessly into spontaneous action. Performance magnitude means not only size and duration but also extension across cultural boundaries and penetrations to profound levels of historical, personal, and neurological strata. To be conditionable is also to be free is also to be susceptible to enslavement. What, then, is the "ordinary behavior" of humans? Neither this nor that, neither here nor there, but fundamentally betwixt and between. And deep enough to link all our brains, from the reptilian to the godlike.

NOTES

1. As used by Hochschild (1983), "deep acting" is acting done by a person with a "trained imagination." Using the work of Stanislavski as her guide, Hochschild discusses emotion memory, the particularly powerful exercise of Stanislavski's whereby a person imagines all the "given circumstances" of an event—the room, the temperature, the people present, the time of day, the smells, and so on—and soon the emotions of the event are being "spontaneously felt." Hochschild shows how deep acting is used in everyday situations: "In our daily lives, offstage as it were, we also develop feeling for the parts we play; and along with the workaday props of the kitchen table or office restroom mirror we also use deep acting, emotion memory, and the sense of 'as if this were true' in the course of trying to feel what we sense we ought to feel or want to feel" (1983:43). She then goes on to show how techniques of deep acting are used by corporations and other "emotion managers" who wish their employees—mostly people in service jobs—to actually feel what the institution wants them to feel. Hochschild contrasts deep acting with "surface acting," where "the expression on my face or the posture of my body feels 'put on'" (1983:36). Of course, Ekman's experiment shows that an expression well put on can affect the ANS every bit as much as a feeling deeply acted.

2. Both these great anthropologists specialized in locating within social life interactions which they saw as "drama" or "performance." Goffman's "self-presentation" and Turner's "social dramas" surely have qualities of theater. But to what degree are these qualities metaphorical—is a waiter waiting tables or the resolution of a conflict that is tearing a group to pieces "like" theater but "not really" theater? Surely, often enough the people doing the performing don't think of themselves as play actors—at least not until a Goffman or a Turner comes along and shows them what's going on. Still, is consciousness of action necessary before that action "is" something? I would say there are two classes of performances: those where participants and spectators know a performance is

going on, and those where there is ignorance or doubt regarding whether or not a performance is occurring.

REFERENCES

d'Aquili, Eugene G., Charles D. Laughlin, Jr., and John McManus. 1979. *The Spectrum of Ritual*. New York: Columbia University Press.

Eibl-Eibesfeldt, Irenaus. 1979. "Ritual and Ritualization from a Biological Perspective." In: M. von Cranach, K. Foppa, W. Lepenies, and D. Ploog (eds.), *Human Ethology*, pp. 3–55. London: Cambridge University Press.

Ekman, Paul. 1972. "Universal and Cultural Differences in Facial Expressions of Emotion." In: *Nebraska Symposium on Motivation, 1971*, pp. 207–83. Omaha: University of Nebraska Press.

———. 1983. "Autonomic Nervous System Activity Distinguishes among Emotions," *Science* 221(Sept. 16):1208–10.

Eckman Paul, Wallace V. Friesen, and Phoebe Ellsworth. 1972. *Emotion in the Human Face*. New York: Pergamon Press.

Elam, Keir. 1980. *The Semiotics of Theatre and Drama*. London: Methuen.

Fischer, Roland. 1971. "A Cartography of the Ecstatic and Meditative States," *Science* 174(Nov. 26):897–904.

Ghosh, Manomohan (ed. and trans.). 1967. *The Natyasastra* (ascribed to Bharata-Muni), vol. 1, chaps. 1–27. Calcutta: Manisha-Granthalaya.

Goffman, Erving. 1959. *The Presentation of Self in Everyday Life*. Garden City, N.Y.: Doubleday.

———. 1963. *Behavior in Public Places*. New York: Free Press of Glencoe.

———. 1969a. *Interaction Ritual*. Garden City, N.Y.: Doubleday.

———. 1969b. *Strategic Interaction*. Philadelphia: University of Pennsylvania Press.

———. 1971. *Relations in Public*. New York: Basic Books.

———. 1974. *Frame Analysis*. New York: Harper.

Grotowski, Jerzy. 1968. *Towards a Poor Theatre*. Holstebro, Denmark: Odin Teatrets Forlag.

Hochschild, Arlie Russel. 1983. *The Managed Heart*. Berkeley: University of California Press.

Lannoy, Richard. 1971. *The Speaking Tree*. London: Oxford University Press.

Lessing, Doris. 1981. *Shikasta*. New York: Random House/Vintage.

Lévi-Strauss, Claude. 1963. *Structural Anthropology*. New York: Basic Books.

Lewin, Tamar. 1984. "Ex-Stewardesses vs. United," *New York Times*, Feb. 24, D1, 15.

McLuhan, Marshall. 1964. *Understanding Media*. New York: McGraw-Hill.

Pavis, Patrice. 1982. *Languages of the Stage*. New York: Performing Arts Journal Press.

Pfeiffer, John. 1982. *The Creative Explosion*. New York: Harper and Row.

Schechner, Richard. 1977. *Essays on Performance Theory*. New York: Drama Books Specialists.

————. 1985. *Between Theater and Anthropology.* Philadelphia: University of Pennsylvania Press.

Turner, Victor. 1969. *The Ritual Process.* Chicago: Aldine.

————. 1982a. "Performing Ethnography," *Drama Review* 26(2[T94], summer):33–50.

————. 1982b. *From Ritual to Theatre.* New York: Performing Arts Journal Press.

————. 1983. "Body, Brain, and Culture," *Zygon* 18(3, Sept.):221–46.

Williams, F. E. 1940. *The Drama of the Orokolo.* London: Oxford University Press.

Epilogue

15

Making
Experiences,
Authoring Selves

CLIFFORD GEERTZ

R. P. Blackmur, writing, I think, about Henry James and the charge that James's work was so rarefied because he had not lived enough, remarked that no one, artist or otherwise, is ever really short of experience. We all have very much more of the stuff than we know what to do with, and if we fail to put it into some graspable form (not, of course, the case with James in any event) the fault must lie in a lack of means, not of substance. The essays collected in this volume are mainly about people or peoples who quite clearly have such means, or have devised them. It is not that they have had more experience, whatever that could mean, or better. Instead, they have, in Barbara Myerhoff's fine phrase, authored themselves, made themselves someone to whom, in the famous cry of Willy Loman's wife, attention must be paid.

It is at least one of the jobs of the ethnographer (to my mind, the most important) to pay such attention, particularly to the means. We cannot live other people's lives, and it is a piece of bad faith to try. We can but listen to what, in words, in images, in actions, they say about their lives. As Victor Turner, the moving force in all these studies and in so much more in recent anthropology, argued, it is with expressions—representations, objectifications, discourses, performances, whatever—that we traffic: a carnival, a mural, a curing rite, a revitalization movement, a clay figurine, an account of a stay in the woods. Whatever sense we have of how things stand with someone else's inner life, we gain it through their expressions, not through some magical intrusion into their consciousness. It's all a matter of scratching surfaces.

Even this, however, is trickier than it seems. It is not enough,

373

as has recently been more and more suggested, to record streams of directly given cultural materials (chants, myths, dialogues, rites, life histories, designs, terminologies) and then, translating strictly, simply get out of the way so as to let them shine in their own light—an updated version of that most persistent ethnographic will-'o-the-wisp, brute fact. As Renato Rosaldo demonstrates with his maddening (to us) hunting tales which consist of strings of place-names, lists of animals, and vague references to moving about, this sort of text-positivism simply won't do. If we want a story out of this we need to know how, for an Ilongot, a story can be got out of it, or seen to be in it. And so on for what Barbara Babcock calls the "modeled selves" of Puebloan pottery ("we are all in there, in the clay"); for James Fernandez, the "argument of images" (parrot's egg, kralled bull) of African ceremonies; and for Bruce Kapferer, the "continuous present" of Sinhalese curing ritual ("deities and demons . . . coexistent in the . . . flowing motion of music and dance"). The burden of description, saying what it is others are saying, is not so easily shed.

It is here that "experience," the elusive master concept of this collection, one that none of the authors seems altogether happy with and none feels able really to do without, becomes the asses' bridge all must cross. The recent vicissitudes of "experience" in English discourse (or perhaps it is only American)—where individuals no longer learn something or succeed at something but have a learning experience or a success experience, where (as Frederick Turner remarks) "My upbringing tells me one thing but all my experience tells me another" and "Did you read that in a book or was it a real experience?" are taken to be coherent sentences, and where the announcement of some Smiling Jack that he is about to share an experience with you is enough to make you reach for your wallet—make the prospects for honest use of the word seem remote. But it is equally true that without it, or something like it, cultural analyses seem to float several feet above their human ground. If what James Boon, following Alexander Pope at the appropriate distance, calls the Machinery of culture is not to spin on in some frictionless paradise where no one fears or remembers or hopes or imagines, nobody murders or rescues or revolts or consoles, it must engage some sort of felt life, which might as well be called experience. Perpetual signification machines can do no more work than perpetual motion ones; occurrence must break in somewhere.

This perplexity, getting from cultural forms to lived life and back again in such a fashion that neither disappears and both are explicated, at least somewhat, animates all the essays in this volume. Some (Victor Turner, Roger Abrahams, Richard Schechner) approach the issue generally, the majority through one or another special case. Some (Frederick Turner, Phyllis Gorfain) address literary texts; some (Barbara Myerhoff, John Stewart), historical events; some (James Fernandez, Bruce Kapferer), formular dramas. Edward Bruner is worried about ethnographical stories; Renato Rosaldo, indigenous ones. Barbara Babcock ponders a single sort of object crafted by a particular artist; James Boon, the overall structure of a vast and various cultural order. Dewey and Dilthey, Goffman and Schutz, Lévy-Bruhl and Lévi-Strauss, all are invoked; and so is the reptilian brain. But the aim is the same throughout: to discover something about how, to use Victor Turner's capacious phrasing, "the hard-won meanings" that inform "the whole human vital repertoire of thinking, willing, desiring, and feeling" are "said, painted, danced, dramatized, put into circulation."

All these ways of putting experience into circulation (and, for that matter—consider Stewart's tracing of the fluctuating presence of Trinidad's dangerous classes in the carnival and Bruner's of the disappearance of the disappearing Indian in ethnography—taking it out) are well represented by the essays in this volume, which seem almost as though they were constructed in counterpoint to one another. Parades of invisibles in California set off processions of sectarians in Africa. "This is play" theatrical paradoxes in *Hamlet* (acting "mad" and "acting" mad) set off "this is text" sociological ones in Bali ("exceptionally everything can mesh... inherently everything does not"). Autobiographical potteries in Puebloan ceramics set off mechanical gestures in Hindu drama. Murals, campfire tales, steel bands, midnight trances, and Thoreau's hypnotic sand bank: whatever else an anthropology of experience might be, it is clear that it is, like experience as such, abundant, multiform, and a bit out-of-hand. Wherever we are, it is not at the gates of paradigm-land.

The anthropologist's way of putting at least some order into these collections of... shall we call them expresssions? representations? *Darstellungen? signe?* symbols?... has been, of course, to connect them to the life around them—and there are a number of ways of doing that, as illustrated in these pieces, from Boon's or Rosaldo's social poetics to Kapferer's or V. Turner's social phenomenology. But what joins the pieces together is more the one way they do *not* do it; they do *not* match cultural forms, conceived as self-contained systems of beliefs and values, as "conceptual schemes," to social structures, conceived as separately organized patterns of collective behavior, as "institutions." The Durkheimian manner that has been for so long the favored mode of dealing with symbolic materials in anthropology—the "see, it fits!" clanish-thoughts-for-clanish-societies approach to things—is silently but firmly discarded.

In Myerhoff's analysis, for example, those peculiar, intractable, and not unpainful realities—aging, Jewish history, and Southern California—are not set forth as plain texts to which her particular objects of interest, the protest march against "death by invisibility" and the frieze depiction of the passage from home, refer in some isomorphic way, as encoded statements of social facts. Rather, these broader background matters are set forth as part of a somewhat overflowing and not altogether manageable stream of experience stretching back to New York and Poland, of which the narrower, more immediate matters of the march and the frieze are also a part. The "symbolic acts" (are there any other kind?) articulate the "hard-won meanings" of these realities; they make clear to those who enact them, those who witness them, and those who "study" them just what it is to be old and Jewish in a Venice where the canals are boardwalks and the gondolas, bicycles. Myerhoff is concerned with examining those meanings, with tracing out the mutual implications, some of them barely susceptible of discursive statement, between the large and the little, the persisting and the passing, the existent and the felt, that they project. Nothing here of that tired cryptography in which everything stands for something else and always says the same thing: society gets what society needs.

Similarly, Stewart traces the vicissitudes of carnival across time, class, and race in Trinidad, not to show that social conflict is "reflected" in the changes in the symbolic expressions central to the festival, but to show that those changes in symbolism are part of that conflict—and not the least important part at that. Fantasy is not a simple turning of one's back on "reality" but a way, however devious, strange, and explosive, of coming into contact with it; indeed, in part constructing it. The effort of the Trinida-

dian postcolonial elite to take control of this particular bit of collective fantasy, nearly to the point of managing it into a Ministry
of Culture limbo, and more recent moves by the imaginatively dis-
possessed to resist that effort ("The time has come to return carnival to the streets") are directly and literally political, not obliquely
and metaphorically so. These clashes of beauty contests and *danse
macabres* don't mirror another struggle in another place about
something else: they are the thing itself. As Stewart indicates, this
is not unfrightening; but then conflicts in the realm of fancy
rarely are.

In Bruner's confrontation of the stories ethnologists used to
tell about native American culture change in the 1930s and 1940s
with the ones they tell now, it is not some Zeitgeist match between
symbolic and sociological matters that is being set up: vanishing
Indians in depression, resurgent ones in inflation. It is a contrast
between schemes of discourse, schemes by means of which anthropologists, drawing on the more general narrative resources
around them, have formulated what little experience of Indian life
they manage to have obtained. The feathered Indian as exotic
Other, all noble and doomed, fading into an MGM sunset, or the
T-shirted Indian as political victim standing out, angry and in-
domitable, against the hegemony of white society, are, as Bruner
indicates, not mere tropes floating above what is really going on;
they are what is going on at every level from Bureau of Indian
Affairs' policy to the summoning to current use of the Pueblo Revolt. Like murals and carnivals, stories matter. So—and this is
the thing for anthropologists to remember, as well as their readers—do stories about stories.

If, however, the dualism of "culture pattern" and "social
structure" is avoided in these essays as reductive or blinding, two
other resonant terms, "text" and "performance," come into the
center of attention. They are perceived not as independent realities to be fitted together in the name of mechanical or quasi-
mechanical, "such-are-the-facts" explanation; rather, they come as
"seeing-as" elucidations of one another, inseparable moments of
an interpretive dialectic, in principle endless. Whether seeing text
as performance, as F. Turner, Gorfain, Boon, and Babcock largely
do, or performance as text, as Fernandez, Kapferer, Rosaldo, and
Schechner largely do, the empirical passage back and forth between cultural productions—figurines or exorcisms—and personal

experiences—remembrance or solitude—is mainly negotiated in terms of a conceptual passage, no less treacherous, between symbol as action and action as symbol.

The text-as-performance approach is, of course, most clearly seen in the essays by F. Turner on *Walden* and Gorfain on *Hamlet*, for they deal with texts in the most literal sense of the term—elite, canonical, auctorial documents, definitively edited and widely published. Yet neither views their subject as a verbal artifact locked away in a language world. Thoreau, setting out to "carve and paint the very atmosphere and medium through which we look," produced, in Turner's words, "simultaneously a work of self-description and of self-construction." Shakespeare, setting shows within shows to show "that within which passes show," produced, according to Gorfain, "a jest, a gesture, incomplete, a sign about signs." Factive or fictive, a weather report from the Concord woods or an imaginary tragedy with a real melodrama in it, texts are acts; "strategies," in Kenneth Burke's famous slogan, "for encompassing situations."

With Boon and Babcock it is no longer literary productions but materialized images of one sort or another that are the "texts." But the way in which experience is thrust onto the social stage—by the operations of Balinese "semantic Machineries" or the affirmations of Cochiti "speaking objects"—remains the focus of analysis. Boon's Machineries, a cascade of titles, gods, and allegorical geometries, are diverse and abundant; inherently paradoxical, irreducibly plural; ungoverned by any single principle of organization either internal to themselves or brought in, deus ex natura, from outside. Yet "the institutions and performances of Balinese culture"—they give to collective life a collective form. Babcock's (or rather, Helen Cordero's) objects are, in the literal sense anyway, individual creations, but they, too, bring a common sense of life—corn and clay and bread—into the common light of day. An intensely personal text ("It's my grandfather. . . . His mouth is open because he's singing") is a consummately public performance ("[giving] life to the people"); and the one implies the other: "nobody should sing alone."

The reverse movement of the dialectic, from performance toward text (and because it *is* a "seeing-as" dialectic, not a "seeing-through" reduction, that is involved, none of these essays proceeds wholly in one direction or the other), engages the anthropologist in the glossing of acts and the reading of actions. For Fernandez, the doings to be construed are revitalistic rituals; for Kapferer, curing ceremonies; for Schechner, dramaturgical gestures; for Rosaldo, as-I-was-a-huntin' storytellings. Behavioral hermeneutics.

In Fernandez, this movement is perhaps the most explicit: the analysis of African attempts, now extremely widespread, to reinvigorate cultures grown somehow "unsatisfactory"—disjoint, spiritless, obsolete—is conceived to rest on what can only be called a tropology of action. Understanding what "revitalization movements" mean to those who participate in them depends, he argues, on seeing how metaphorical images repetitively enacted in new-made rituals set up chains of "continuous and discontinuous analogies" (man : tree : forest : society) and create unlabeled "superordinate semantic categories" (dweller-talker-parrot-prophet) so as to reconnect the disconnected and restore the faded. "The performance of a sequence of images ["marching to and fro . . . to drumbeats and bugle call"; or "kneeling around a deep hole dug into the sand, at the bottom of which a small trace of ocean water has seeped up"; or "(running) faster and faster in tighter and tighter circles"] revitalizes, in effect and by simple iteration, a universe of [cultural] domains, an acceptable cosmology of participation, a compelling whole." When texts lose their meaning, performances rewrite them; anyway, they try to.

In Kapferer's Sri Lanka the texts have not, so it seems, lost their meaning, at least for the healthy and unpossessed; but it is still performance—"a unity of text and enactment"—that gives them their practical force. In exorcism rituals the reexperiencing of a vital connection to the surrounding society, a connection that the patient, sunk into a solipsistical solitude, has at least temporarily been deprived of, is restored by machinery of Boon-like complexity operating with a Fernandez-like immediacy. It is the movement of such rituals from the "vivid present" subjectivity externalized in music, song and dance, and in an odd way trance, to the "dialogic" intersubjectivity represented in comic drama that cures: patients are rejoined to the common imagination by measured doses of applied art. Schechner's piece, the most speculative in the volume as well as the most free-ranging—a sort of anthropological "My Dinner with André"—seeks a neuro-psychological foundation for the effectiveness of such art and provides an experimental setting, drums and accordions, chanting and deep breathing, in which to examine it. Rosaldo's essay, the most detailed and systematic, seeks to demonstrate how one kind of it—personal narrative—works out in fact, how Philippine hunting stories are made compelling in the recounting of them, how they become "historiable," *lisible*, form into texts. The passage from what is done toward what is meant, like that from what is meant toward what is done, involves above all a capacity to transcend our deep-grained assumption that signs are one thing and experiences another.

It is, after all, the life of signs in society—text-as-performance, performance-as-text—that brings about the contrast both V. Turner and Abrahams, the theorists here (so far as the thing admits of theory), see as critical to "the anthropology of experience": "*mere* experience" as against "*an* experience." "Mere experience," according to Turner, "is simply the passive endurance and acceptance of events. *An* experience, like a rock in a Zen sand garden, stands out from the evenness of passing hours and years and forms what Dilthey called a 'structure of experience.'" Abrahams, invoking John Dewey to the same purpose ("Life is no uniform uninterrupted march or flow. It is a thing of histories, each with its own plots, its own inceptions and movement toward its close . . ."), develops the contrast even further into one between "mere experience," "an experience," and "a typical experience"; between an event, its interpretive replay as we recollect it to ourselves or recount it to others, and its assimilation into the standardized categories that, however we struggle, outline our lives: "the American Experience, the Jewish Experience, the Sixties Experience, even the Growing-Up or Growing-Old Experience."

Experiences, like tales, fetes, potteries, rites, dramas, images, memoirs, ethnographies, and allegorical machineries, are made; and it is such made things that make them. The "anthropology of experience," like the anthropology of anything else, is a study of the uses of artifice and the endlessness of it. The wrenching question, sour and disabused, that Lionel Trilling somewhere quotes an eighteenth-century aesthetician as asking—"How Comes It that we all start out Originals and end up Copies?"—finds in these essays some beginnings of an answer that is surprisingly reassuring: it is the copying that originates.

Notes on Contributors

ROGER D. ABRAHAMS is a folklorist who has written extensively in the areas of Afro-American and Anglo-American traditions and the theory of expressive acts and events. Presently on the faculty of the folklore department at the University of Pennsylvania, he has also taught at Scripps and Pitzer colleges, in California, and at the University of Texas at Austin. Recent books include *Positively Black* and (co-author with John Szwed) *After Africa: Extracts from British Travel Accounts and Journals.*

BARBARA A. BABCOCK is professor of English at the University of Arizona, where she teaches and publishes in folklore, symbolic anthropology, narrative theory, and women's studies. Since 1978 she has worked with Pueblo potters and "potteries," and is the author of *The Pueblo Storyteller* (in press). She is currently writing *Stories Told in Clay: The Art and Experience of Helen Cordero,* of which the essay in this volume is a part.

JAMES A. BOON is professor of anthropology, Asian studies, and comparative literature at Cornell University. His books include *The Anthropological Romance of Bali, 1597–1972* and *Other Tribes, Other Scribes.* He is currently completing a collection of essays on Bali, Indonesian studies, and the ironies of ethnology in general.

EDWARD M. BRUNER is professor of anthropology at the University of Illinois, Urbana-Champaign. He has done field research among native Americans and in Indonesia. He is co-editor of *Art, Ritual, and Society in Indonesia* and most recently has edited *Text, Play, and Story,* proceedings of the 1983 meeting of the American Ethnological Society.

JAMES W. FERNANDEZ is professor of anthropology at Princeton University. He has done work among revitalization movements in Africa and the western Mediterranean. He is the author of *Bwiti: An Ethnography of the Religious Imagination in Africa.*

CLIFFORD GEERTZ is Harold F. Linder Professor of Social Science at the Institute for Advanced Study, Princeton, New Jersey. He has done fieldwork in Indonesia and Morocco and most recently has authored *Local Knowledge: Further Essays in Interpretive Anthropology.*

PHYLLIS GORFAIN, an associate professor of English at Oberlin College, in Ohio, is at work on a book-length study of play and *Hamlet*. She teaches courses in Shakespeare and folklore, and has published articles combining these interests as well as articles on folklore and anthropological topics.

BRUCE KAPFERER, currently professor of anthropology at University College, London, has done research in Zambia, Sri Lanka, and Australia. His major interests are the anthropology of symbolic processes and cultural transformations in former colonial societies. Recent books include *A Celebration of Demons* and *The Power of Ritual*.

BARBARA MYERHOFF was professor of anthropology at the University of Southern California and the author of *Number Our Days*, a book about the elderly Jews of Venice, California. A documentary film based on this work received an Academy Award. She wrote many other books about the experience of ritual, religion, and symbols, including *Peyote Hunt*, and was central to various anthropological films characterized by compassionate objectivity. She died on January 6, 1985.

RENATO ROSALDO is professor of anthropology at Stanford University. He has written primarily on the Ilongots of northern Luzon, Philippines, where he did field research in 1967–69 and 1974. These writings, particularly his book *Ilongot Headhunting, 1883–1974: A Study in Society and History*, were awarded the Harry Benda Prize for Southeast Asian Studies. He is currently preparing a book on theory and discourse in ethnography.

RICHARD SCHECHNER is a performance theorist, theater director, and currently professor in the Department of Performance Studies, Tisch School of the Arts, New York University. His latest theater work is *Prometheus Project;* his latest book, *Between Theater and Anthropology*.

JOHN STEWART is an anthropologist and writer who is affiliated with the English department at Ohio State University. His essay in this volume grew out of several seasons of fieldwork in Trinidad. He has written both anthropological studies and novels, and most recently collected and edited Bessie Jones's *For the Ancestors: Autobiographical Memories*.

FREDERICK TURNER, professor in the School of Arts and Humanities, University of Texas at Dallas, and a former editor of *The Kenyon Review,* has contributed to various anthropological symposia. He is the author of five books of poetry, including *The Garden* and *The New World*, a novel, and several works of literary criticism and aesthetic philosophy. His most recent work, a collection of interdisciplinary essays entitled *National Classicism: Essays on Literature and Science*, will be published soon.

VICTOR TURNER was William R. Kenan, Jr., Professor of Anthropology and Religion at the University of Virginia. He did fieldwork in Zambia, Uganda, Mexico, Ireland, Italy, France, Japan, Brazil, and Israel, and was the author of many books, including the well-known *Ritual Process*. He died on December 18, 1983.

Index